# INTERNAL FACTORS IN
# RUSSIAN FOREIGN POLICY

The Royal Institute of International Affairs is an independent body which promotes the rigorous study of international questions and does not express opinions of its own. The opinions expressed in this publication are the responsibility of the authors.

# Internal Factors in Russian Foreign Policy

NEIL MALCOLM,
ALEX PRAVDA, ROY ALLISON
AND
MARGOT LIGHT

*Published for*
The Royal Institute of International Affairs

*by*

Oxford University Press

This book has been printed digitally and produced in a standard specification
in order to ensure its continuing availability

# OXFORD
UNIVERSITY PRESS

Great Clarendon Street, Oxford OX2 6DP

Oxford University Press is a department of the University of Oxford.
It furthers the University's objective of excellence in research, scholarship,
and education by publishing worldwide in

Oxford New York

Auckland  Cape Town  Dar es Salaam  Hong Kong  Karachi
Kuala Lumpur  Madrid  Melbourne  Mexico City  Nairobi
New Delhi  Shanghai  Taipei  Toronto
With offices in
Argentina  Austria  Brazil  Chile  Czech Republic  France  Greece
Guatemala  Hungary  Italy  Japan  South Korea  Poland  Portugal
Singapore  Switzerland  Thailand  Turkey  Ukraine  Vietnam

Oxford is a registered trade mark of Oxford University Press
in the UK and in certain other countries

Published in the United States
by Oxford University Press Inc., New York

© Royal Institute of International Affairs, 1996

The moral rights of the author have been asserted

Database right Oxford University Press (maker)

Reprinted 2007

ISBN 978-0-19-828011-8

# ACKNOWLEDGEMENTS

In the preparation of a book of this kind, it is impossible to rely simply on printed sources. We have depended to a large degree on face-to-face contacts with officials and specialists, and we wish to thank the large number of people who have given us the benefit of their knowledge and judgement, in interviews conducted in the United Kingdom and in the former Soviet states, and in study groups at the Royal Institute of International Affairs. Some have also been kind enough to make comments on chapter drafts. A large part in the project was played by Peter Rutland, Wesleyan University, Connecticut, who helped, in a series of written contributions, to clarify the economic dimension of Russian politics, and an important contribution was made, especially in the final stages, by Peter Duncan (SSEES, University of London).

In particular we are glad to acknowledge the help that we have received from Russian academics. There are too many to list all by name, but special thanks are due to those who provided written materials—Olga Bychkova, Yury Fyodorov, Boris Grushin, Simon Kordonsky, Andrei Orlov, and Irina Zvyagelskaya—and those who commented on drafts and submitted themselves to interviews—Sergei Blagovolin, Oleg Bykov, Sergei Chugrov, Yury Davydov, Nodari Simoniya, Andrei Zagorsky, and many others. We were also substantially helped during our work on the research project by contributions from scholars in Kiev and Almaty. The ESRC and BASEES (Ford Foundation)-funded seminar series at the LSE on the Foreign Policies of the Successor States to the USSR helped to facilitate contact with colleagues from the CIS.

We must thank, too, our colleagues at Chatham House, in particular Shyama Iyer and Ann Cropper, administrators of the Russian and CIS Programme, and Mary Bone in the Library. Their assistance was generously given and always of the highest quality. We would also like to thank Henry Buglass for preparing the map on p. x.

This book is based on work carried out as part of an RIIA research project investigating internal factors in the foreign policies of the former Soviet states, and supported by the Fritz Thyssen Stiftung.

# CONTENTS

# MAPS, FIGURES, AND TABLES

# THE AUTHORS

ROY ALLISON is Head of the Russia and Eurasia Programme at the Royal Institute of International Affairs, London. He is also Senior Lecturer in Russian International Security Policy at the Centre for Russian and East European Studies, University of Birmingham. He directs a number of research projects at the RIIA on the CIS states and has written or edited five books on Soviet, Russian, and CIS foreign and defence policies. His recent publications include *Military Forces in the Soviet Successor States* (1993) and *Peacekeeping in the Soviet Successor States* (1994).

MARGOT LIGHT is Senior Lecturer in International Relations at the London School of Economics and Political Science. Her research and teaching interests are in international relations theory and Soviet and post-Soviet foreign policy. She is the editor (with A. J. R. Groom) of *Contemporary International Relations: A Guide to Theory* (1994), and of *Troubled Friendships: Moscow's Third World Ventures* (1993).

NEIL MALCOLM is Professor of Russian Politics and Head of the Russian and East European Research Centre, University of Wolverhampton. From 1989 to 1993 he was Head of the Russian and CIS Programme at the RIIA. His research and writing has been in the area of Soviet and post-Soviet foreign policy and foreign policy-making. He is the editor of *Russia and Europe: An End to Confrontation?* (1994).

ALEX PRAVDA is Fellow of St Antony's College and Lecturer in Soviet and East European Politics at Oxford University, and was Head of the Soviet Foreign Policy Programme at the RIIA from 1986 to 1989. He has written extensively on domestic politics and foreign policy in the former Soviet bloc and in the CIS. He is the editor of *The End of the Outer Empire: Soviet–East European Relations in Transition* (1992) and a co-editor of *Developments in Russian and Post-Soviet Politics* (1994).

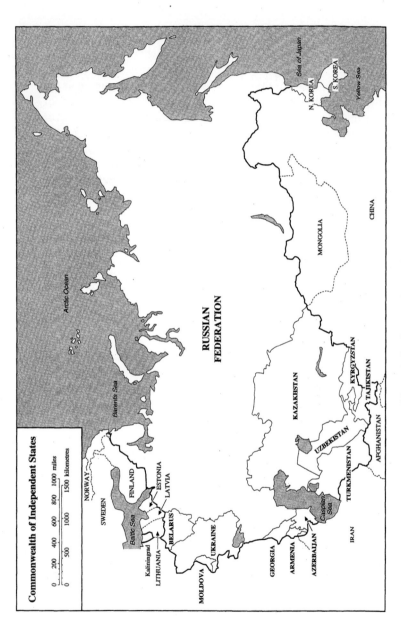

Map of the former Soviet Union

**Commonwealth of Independent States**

0   200   400   600   800   1000 miles

0        500        1000        1500 kilometres

NORWAY

SWEDEN

FINLAND

Baltic Sea

ESTONIA

LATVIA

Kaliningrad

LITHUANIA

BELARUS

UKRAINE

MOLDOVA

GEORGIA

ARMENIA

AZERBAIJAN

Caspian Sea

IRAN

RUSSIAN FEDERATION

KAZAKHSTAN

UZBEKISTAN

TURKMENISTAN

KYRGYZSTAN

TAJIKISTAN

AFGHANISTAN

MONGOLIA

CHINA

Arctic Ocean

Barents Sea

Sea of Japan

N. KOREA

S. KOREA

Yellow Sea

# 1

# Introduction

NEIL MALCOLM AND ALEX PRAVDA

This book is an attempt to analyse the way internal forces are influencing Russian foreign policy in the new, still rapidly evolving post-Soviet environment. It is one contribution to the large enterprise of building up a comprehensive analysis of foreign policy in Russia and the other new states, conceived of as something emerging from a complex process of interaction of domestic and external factors.

We have had to be selective. Michael Brecher's decision-making model pin-points five key domestic factors which, along with external variables, form the operational environment of foreign policy making. It also embraces the attitudes and values of decision-makers, which help to shape the 'psychological environment' in which they work, and which may enhance or diminish the impact of particular objective factors.[1] The five internal factors he selects are military capability, economic capability, political structure, interest groups, and competing élites. In the chapters which follow it is the political level which is dealt with, rather than capabilities, in other words they concentrate on the last three of Brecher's factors.[2] Chapter 2 in particular concentrates on changing élite perceptions. Changes in external aspects of the operational environment are summarized below and in general are woven into the discussion as appropriate.

One aspect of the domestic environment which has recently become more prominent with the growing impact of marketization is the role of economic interests in foreign policy. The transformations under way in the country have helped to encourage much more public lobbying by groups associated with different sectors of the economy, and their impact on foreign policy is considered below, in this chapter and in Chapters 3 and 4. But the rapidity of change, and the size of the topic, mean that it requires a substantial separate investigation, preferably once the pace of change has slackened off, when representative structures and channels of access have become more stable and well-established. A second specialized area of investigation is being created by the increasing political activism of the Russian regions, which in many cases have quite distinct foreign policy interests, and are finding means of promoting them.

The first part of this introductory chapter provides an outline of the main changes in Russia's relations with the outside world since 1991. The second part makes connections with past writing about internal/external links in foreign policy making in the Soviet period, and examines elements of continuity and discontinuity in the factors capable of influencing foreign policy in the period since 1991. It proposes a periodization of Russian foreign policy in the 1990s, and explains some of the terms used in the study.

## The external environment

The pages which follow consider in turn Russia's relations with the wider world, particularly the West, then processes inside the former Soviet area, and finally interactions between these two spheres.

### Global relations

The dismantling in 1987–91 of military-political confrontation between the NATO and the Warsaw Pact states set in train a series of changes in global politics whose consequences are still not clear. In the uncertain post-Cold War environment many of the former Soviet states looked to the West for reassurance. The government of the Russian Federation itself declared early in 1992 that it wished to join NATO in the long term, and it co-operated actively with the Western permanent members of the UN Security Council. Ukraine sought security guarantees from the West as a condition of yielding up the last of its nuclear missiles. Russia, along with the other former Soviet states, became a member of the North Atlantic Co-operation Council (NACC), and in June 1994 announced its intention of participating in the NATO Partnership for Peace. In the same month it signed an ambitious Agreement on Partnership and Co-operation with the European Union. Work was begun to prepare for Russian accession to the Council of Europe.

Yet the 1994 agreements with NATO and the EU were only concluded after prolonged and sometimes difficult negotiation. Both these organizations, not surprisingly, were unwilling to contemplate the prospect of full Russian membership. They did envisage, on the other hand, the eventual entry of most of the states to the west of Russia, excluding only Ukraine, Belarus, and Moldova (and, in the case of NATO, probably, the Baltic states). Moscow saw a danger of being consigned to isolation, or at best second-class citizenship of Europe. Its stated preference was for a radical expansion which would transform the existing Western-Europe-based institutions into pan-European entities, or else for a strengthening of wider bodies such as the Conference on Security and Co-operation in Europe (CSCE). Failing that, it strove to minimize the difference between the way it was treated so far as closeness to the EU and NATO was concerned, and the way Central/Eastern Europe was treated, and to establish new processes of consultation with the Western powers. Russia successfully resisted attempts to settle problems in the former Yugoslavia without its participation.

It would be unrealistic to expect that the decades-long confrontation with the West would evaporate without trace after 1990, particularly as the West was not ready to become engaged in an assistance effort on the scale of a Marshall Plan, and was cautious about incorporating Russia into its own international institutions. The continuing existence of NATO and especially its plans for expansion to the east brought a mistrustful response from Moscow. By the end of 1994, President Yeltsin had warned of the danger of a new 'cold peace', and his foreign minister had announced a halt to participation in the Partnership for Peace. After Russia's armed intervention in Chechnya both the European Union and the Council of Europe suspended progress towards closer relations. Russian diplomatic and trade initiatives with Iraq and Iran provoked tensions with Washington.

Yet the notion of a global political competition has receded into the past. When it comes to matters of military power and political influence Russia's foreign policy horizons seem sometimes to have shrunk to embrace only its nearest neighbours. For all the insistence by Russian leaders that their country be treated with the special respect due to its superpower status, and despite their loud complaints about NATO expansion plans in wider relations the real concerns are economic ones. In this regard Russia and a number of the former Soviet states could be said to have belatedly passed one of the final hurdles of modernization. They now tend to see their priorities in relations with like countries not in terms of the 'high politics' of military security and national survival, but in terms of the 'low politics' of wealth and welfare, as other industrialized states do.[3] This does not necessarily apply so far, as we shall see, in relations *between* some of the former Soviet states.

The attempt to open up the economies of the former Soviet bloc, in contrast to the case of China, has been undertaken in unfavourable conditions: recession in the West, disruptive political conflict and often ill-co-ordinated economic transformations at home. The states concerned are being forced to face up to serious relative economic weakness. By 1994 Russian foreign debt had risen to over $100 billion, and most of the other former Soviet republics were in even worse financial condition.

Large sums of money were allocated in aid by the West, but the overwhelming mass was in the form of loans and credit guarantees. Outright grants and investment capital formed only a small part. Private foreign investment was scanty. Moreover, although Russia was admitted to the IMF in June 1992, and substantial loans were agreed to support a stabilization programme, even greater amounts of capital were reported to have been exported to the West by Russian businessmen and criminals. Over $4 billion worth of technical assistance has been offered to the CIS states, and most of it has been delivered, but it has failed to produce the expected political impact, and is widely considered in Russia to have been used mainly for the benefit of local officials and foreign consulting firms.[4] Discontent over trade issues mounted in 1993 and 1994, with frequent claims in Moscow that Russia was being unfairly excluded from world markets, especially those for military and high-technology products, and that Western firms were dumping consumer goods on the Russian market. Disorder and political uncertainty in the CIS continued, moreover, to inhibit the inflow of foreign private investment.

It is clear that the former Soviet Union has undergone an unsettling change from modified autarky to a situation where internal processes are considerably more penetrated than before by impulses from the international system. Painful conditions of the kind attached to the release of financial assistance (like the conditions attached to political concessions such as acceptance into the Council of Europe) have helped to create and to reinforce links between domestic politics and foreign policy. Overt support from the West for Yeltsin's dissolution of the Russian parliament in September 1993 had a similar effect. Subsequent events demonstrated how internal and external politics could interact in a vicious circle of deterioration of relations. The successes of Zhirinovsky's extreme-right Liberal Democratic Party and of the nationalist-inclined Communist Party of the Russian Federation in the December 1993 elections alarmed the leaders of the Central/East European states and made the West more receptive to their requests for entry to NATO. The prospect of a Western-centred military alliance expanding up to the borders of the former Soviet Union in turn became a powerful element in the case put by supporters of a more nationalist and military-based foreign policy and of welding the CIS into a military bloc.

In a number of respects all the former Soviet states, including Russia, find themselves in a similar position to less-developed countries elsewhere in the world, negotiating from weakness with the Western powers over terms for aid, investment, and technology transfer, and for access to their raw materials, markets, and cheap labour forces.[5] Similar dilemmas confront their governments, as they strive to resolve conflicting pressures for trade liberalization and protectionism, financial stabilization, industrial restructuring, and popular welfare. Economic necessity looms very large. Yet it must constantly be reconciled with the needs of nation-building, fostering national self-respect and building the prestige of the leaders who embody it. Under such pressures it is not surprising that these leaders frequently end up concentrating more and more decision-making in their own hands and in those of their close associates. The democratic principles proclaimed at the foundation of the new state may be eroded, and standards of probity may decline.[6]

In other respects, of course, the states of the region differ from those of the South. The most striking are Russia's continuing position as a military power second only to the United States, its central strategic location, and the influence which it wields, through various channels, throughout the former USSR. Indeed one can talk of a second tier of dependency connected with the ex-colonial relationship of most of the other former Soviet states to the Russian Federation.

## Relations between Russia and the former Soviet states

The breakup of the USSR has left a troublesome legacy in Eurasia. Unlike the old West European empires the Russian/Soviet one was a compact territorial unit. There was a great deal of mingling of populations, and internal (now international) borders in some cases seemed to be deliberately drawn to cut across ethnic boundaries. Some twenty-five million people who describe themselves as Russians live outside the Russian Federation and many non-Russians live inside it. Thus it is not just a matter of post-imperial adjustment: the fact is that many Russians in particular simply do not recognize the new state boundaries as authentic. Whereas a Latvian, say, might perceive the separating of his country from Russia as a process of decolonization, a Russian might see it as the splitting up of a single, 'Russian' nation.[7] Matters are made worse by the fact that areas of Russian settlement in other former Soviet states are typically contiguous to Russia itself (north-eastern Estonia, northern Kazakhstan, eastern Ukraine) and/or in parts of the world perceived by the Russian military as strategically important (the Baltic states, the left bank of the river Dniestr in Moldova, or the Crimea).[8]

Such Russian attitudes tend to blur the distinction between domestic politics and events in what has been labelled the 'near abroad'. There is, moreover, a thick and varied network of contacts between the former Soviet states, in fields like culture, communications, and the economy, which creates a very large 'intermestic' sphere. As in Western Europe, these relations are too extensive to be handled simply by the foreign and defence ministries of the countries concerned, and tend to come under the supervision of other agencies, such as ministries of finance, transport, the economy, and so on. Where the process of disintegration of former Soviet networks will stop, whether it will reverse itself, and for how long, is difficult to say. At present, however, the tendency in most areas seems to be in the direction of a tentative reintegration.

The Commonwealth of Independent States, established at the end of 1991 to replace the USSR, and embracing all of its former members except Georgia and the Baltic states, got off to a poor start.[9] In many states the urge to assert new-found national independence took precedence over economic requirements, which argued for preserving ties, at least in the short term. This was particularly serious in the case of Ukraine. Its politicians described the CIS as a mechanism for bringing about 'a civilized divorce'. They acknowledged the need to retain economic ties, but they resisted attempts to manœuvre their country into a political-security community, and they consistently blocked progress towards setting up CIS-wide supranational bodies. Even in the economic sphere little progress was made towards setting up a proper multilateral frame-work. CIS agreements were often signed only by a nucleus of the membership (Moldova, Azerbaijan, and Turkmenistan frequently joined Ukraine in opting out), and even when agreements were signed they were notorious for not being implemented. The organization did provide a setting for negotiating useful bilateral arrangements, but these were mainly centred on the Russian Federation (in this respect the CIS repeated the 'spokes of a wheel' pattern of the East European CMEA during the Soviet period).

Between 1992 and 1994, however, political and economic changes in Russia and in its neighbours combined to bring about a transformation of the atmosphere in the CIS. In Russia, social, economic, and security issues relating to the 'near abroad' soon rose to the top of the foreign policy agenda, while in the other states economic necessity made itself increasingly felt. By early 1993 the Kremlin had adopted the notion of a Eurasian 'Monroe Doctrine', and by the end of the year the pendulum was swinging back in the direction of accommodation with Moscow, even in Ukraine.[10]

If energetic involvement elsewhere in the CIS at first appeared to occur mainly on the initiative of the Russian armed forces (in Moldova, Georgia, and Tajikistan, for example), in 1993 a more concerted policy became evident. Powerful economic, military, and political pressures were applied to forward Russian interests and to bring CIS governments into line. By the end of the year Azerbaijan had agreed to activate its previously purely formal membership of the Commonwealth, Georgia had agreed to join for the first time, and President Kravchuk of Ukraine had been forced to discuss yielding most of the disputed Black Sea fleet to Moscow in exchange for a cancellation of energy debts and other concessions. By April of 1994 all the states had agreed to full membership of an economic union. 'CIS armed forces' under Russian command were given the task of guarding former Soviet frontiers in Central Asia, and Belarus had signed a treaty of monetary union with Russia. In July deepening economic problems induced voters in Belarus and Ukraine to elect new presidents who had stood on a platform of mending relations with Moscow.

Russia's relations with the other former Soviet states have been more complicated than this brief summary might suggest. There is still a powerful reluctance in Moscow to make material sacrifices for the sake of its CIS partners. The Russian government set stringent conditions, for example, for membership of a rouble zone, tough enough to put off Kazakhstan and Uzbekistan from joining altogether in 1993, and to bog down economic integration talks with Belarus in 1994 and 1995. Whereas in the military sphere it was generally Russia which appeared to be pushing for greater consolidation (with some support from security-dependent states like Armenia and Kazakhstan), against resistance from the others, in the economic sphere the situation was reversed. This pattern was most obvious in the case of Ukraine, where Russia made effective use of economic and demographic levers to constrain Kiev's military and political autonomy. In general little progress was made towards economic union in the Commonwealth.

It is difficult to overstate the intense economic interdependence of the former Soviet states. Soviet planners aspired to organize the economy of the USSR as a single unit: components needed for the manufacture of one product could be shipped to an assembly plant from the four corners of the Union; smaller republics might be left to specialize overwhelmingly in a limited number of sectors. In Uzbekistan, for instance, the cultivation of food crops was deliberately run down in order to concentrate on cotton production. Components from Russia and elsewhere in the Soviet Union were used to assemble advanced jet fighter planes in Georgia. Communications links and commercial ties with the outside world were deliberately left undeveloped.

This dependence was markedly lopsided. The Russian Federation as it emerged at the end of 1991 was much larger and much more self-sufficient than the other countries in the region. It controlled the key communications channels, and the lion's share of energy supplies and raw materials. It could exert immediate pressure on its resource-poor and hard-currency-short neighbours by rationing out exports of oil and gas. The rouble was weak, but it was stronger than the denominations of those CIS states which tried to establish independent currencies.

It is often pointed out that the Russian/Soviet empire differed from, say, the French and British empires in that some peripheral areas were more prosperous or technologically advanced than the metropolis, but the non-Russian states nevertheless found themselves in a kind of post-colonial dependence. This is not just a matter of economics. Independence took most of the new states by surprise. Many can be described as 'quasi-states', prematurely born entities which are primarily juridical in nature, and whose empirical statehood largely remains to be built.[11] In most there has been a marked tendency to concentrate decision-making around the leader and in his entourage. Sovereignty is limited often by sheer absence of administrative capacity.

Another point of resemblance to recently created states elsewhere in the world is the presence in many of the post-Soviet states of élite groups thoroughly socialized in metropolitan values, in some cases more fluent in Russian than in the local language. In a way that was not true for the Soviet-bloc states of Central/Eastern Europe or for the Baltic states, such groups have tended to look to Moscow as a genuine metropolis, a centre of modernity and a point of contact with the world community. In some cases Russia's backing is essential to the political survival of a smaller state's leadership, most explicitly in war-torn Tajikistan and Georgia, and in a less immediate way throughout Central Asia. Leaders look for political support in Moscow, not just from the government but also from military or industrial lobbies with interests in their locality, and from opposition groups.

Russians may still be present in large numbers, often fulfilling key technical roles in the state administration and in industry and communications in the less-developed states. In Ukraine the concentration of Russian speakers in the industrialized eastern regions of the country and in Crimea represents a serious threat to national integrity. A similar situation exists in northern Kazakhstan and in Estonia. These Russian communities, too, have their own backers in Moscow, characteristically among the right-wing and centrist nationalist opposition, and Russian government statements about policy towards the other former Soviet states routinely refer to the need to defend the interests of the expatriates.[12] Apart from the Baltic states, Russian-commanded military units are deployed and Russian military bases are maintained throughout most of the former Soviet Union.

All these factors are of course no guarantee of harmonious relations in the region, or of an untroubled Russian hegemony. On the contrary, they have been and will doubtless continue to be a constant source of argument inside and between the states concerned. The situation is complicated by the fact that the post-Soviet area is now interacting with the outside world in a variety of new patterns.

## 'Near abroad'–'far abroad' interactions

Soon after gaining their independence most of the former Soviet states became involved in discussions with regional co-operation bodies such as those centred on the Baltic Sea and the Black Sea, and with the Economic Co-operation Organization (ECO) in south-central Asia. Estonia, Latvia, and Lithuania forged closer ties with the Nordic countries, while with its neighbours to the west Ukraine explored the possibility of setting up 'Baltic-Black Sea' defence co-operation. Moldova developed relations with Romania, Azerbaijan and the Central Asian states with Turkey, Saudi Arabia, and Iran. War spilled over from Afghanistan into Tajikistan, and economic ties developed between Kazakhstan and China.

Yet it has become clear that, with the partial exception of the Baltic states, scope for manœuvre is limited with respect both to neighbours and to the major Western powers. Nearby countries which have most direct interest in the new states have hesitated to develop strong ties that would significantly bolster the latter's capacity to resist Russian influence. Such hesitation stems partly from concern to avoid friction with Russia, which they recognize as a key actor in preserving regional stability. From 1993 onwards the Russian government raised the stakes, making it increasingly clear that CIS members would have to order their priorities between Moscow-centred economic co-operation and association with other regional groupings.[13] Neighbouring states have tended to see economic engagement as a prudent focus for activity, and to avoid political or military involvement. This has allowed the new states to diversify in trade and investment rather than in strategic alliances.

Strategic access to powers beyond the region, to Western Europe, the United States, and NATO, has also proved to be limited. With a few exceptions the countries concerned do not offer the kind of economic attractions which might provoke closer involvement. The West, too, prefers not to provoke Moscow, and to become entangled in unpredictable conflicts, by adopting too high a profile. This reticence was noticeable in the case of the dispute which broke out in 1994 over exploitation of hydrocarbon resources in and around the Caspian Sea. The Western powers tend to perceive a strong interest in stability, and have advocated nuclear disarmament outside Russia, appropriate economic co-operation in the former Soviet region, a consistent implementation of the principles of sanctity of borders, and careful observance of minority rights.

The West's position tends to provoke resentment among Russians and non-Russians alike. The former are inclined to place little trust in, say, the Council of Europe to protect the civil rights of Russian-speakers in the Baltic states, and are often temperamentally in favour of direct action. Many of them also see no reason why the Russian state should be confined within the borders which it inherited from the old Russian Soviet Federative Socialist Republic. Non-Russians, on the other hand, may perceive their overriding priority as one of resisting Russian expansionism, and blame the West for conniving in Moscow's plans to demilitarize its former dominions, use local Russian-speaking populations to subvert their autonomy, and enmesh them in a new superstate.

When Russian leaders call for the international community to acknowledge Moscow's special role in preserving order throughout the CIS they are in a sense calling for formal recognition of a situation which already exists. The recent history of the former Yugoslavia suggests that the Western powers are scarcely likely to become involved on the ground in areas such as Nagorny Karabakh or Tajikistan. Nevertheless, the issue of recognition and sanctioning of Russia's actions by bodies such as the United Nations and the CSCE (and even by the CIS) is regarded as important, both in Moscow and abroad. Even the desire to have tacit approval by the West of its 'near abroad' activities acts as a constraint on Russia's behaviour. This binds together Russia–West and Russia–CIS affairs around particularly sensitive issues of sovereignty and spheres of influence.

*Internal change and foreign policy*

Any study of international relations, however determinedly it focuses on the international systemic level, has to take into account that states do not behave in a consistently 'rational' way, and that the priorities which shape their policies appear to vary over time. Faced with a similar set of external pressures, different states respond in different ways. Explanations may be sought in terms of the impact of bureaucratic politics and organizational process, the effects of populism and ideology, and so on.[14] But because the domestic factors are most often treated as residual to the main process, they tend to be treated in a relatively cursory way.[15]

In works devoted to analysing domestic factors in foreign policy there is a parallel tendency to fail to indicate clearly the impact of processes in the international environment. There is a danger, for example, of myopically attributing decisive importance for foreign policy to changes in domestic politics (e.g. the increase in influence of a particular group or coalition) when discussing developments which could have been predicted more straightforwardly as an effect of external changes. Examples would be the rise to prominence of 'hawkish' groups following the emergence of a clear-cut threat to national security, or the apparent growing power of a protectionist coalition in response to overwhelming competition in international trade.[16]

This book focuses on the domestic dimension, but seen as part of a comprehensive foreign policy process.[17] It was already clear at the end of the 1980s that the internal transformations set in motion by Gorbachev were likely to have far-reaching repercussions for foreign policy. The first half of the 1990s has been a period of upheaval and transformation in institutions, information channels, and internal political and economic arrangements. The world-view and value system in the light of which policy was formed for half a century have been overturned. New constituencies and lobbies are emerging. A new sphere of external relations has emerged, with the 'near abroad', which is closely intertwined with internal affairs and evokes strong feelings among the Russian population.[18]

At the same time the range of interactions with the international environment has expanded. The importance of the economic and social dimensions has increased sharply compared to the political and military ones. Russia is beginning to experience more keenly the frictions associated with the 'interdependence' which Gorbachev embraced so unreservedly in his New Political Thinking. While its capacity, and its inclination, to exert influence on a global scale have decreased, the outside world, not just the 'near abroad' but also 'the West', looms large in the discourse of internal politics. This underlines the need to locate our analysis of domestic factors in Russian foreign policy firmly in the context of external impulses. The external context will accordingly be referred to regularly in the course of the main chapters.

*Analysing domestic factors*

During the Soviet period a variety of approaches was applied in Western studies of the connections between internal politics and Moscow's foreign policy. One group of authors saw the key factor as inter-agency competition (since all productive enterprises were directly administered by the state, conflicts of interest between sectors emerged largely as bureaucratic struggles). In a much-cited text published in 1972 ('The Soviet Military-Industrial Complex—Does it Exist?'), Vernon Aspaturian highlighted the conflict between those agencies which appeared to have an interest in maintaining a certain level of confrontation with the West—the Communist Party ideological apparatus, the security services, the armed forces and associated producers—and on the other hand those which sought *détente* for the sake mainly of the budgetary redistribution it might allow—the light, consumer goods industries, agriculture, and service bureaucracies.[19]

This analysis was contested from two main stand-points. First, by those who argued that the central apparatus of the Communist Party exercised such tight control over policy, and over policy debate, that the appearance of substantial differences of view was illusory.[20] Second, by those who perceived inconsistency and divisions inside particular institutions. The latter group preferred to talk in terms of 'tendencies' based on differing values and perceptions,[21] or to emphasize intra-agency splits and ambiguities, and the transience of bureaucratic coalitions. Some Soviet defence industrialists, it was pointed out, for example, had a strong interest in keeping open legitimate channels of access to Western technology, parts of the military had an interest in selective arms control, and so on.[22]

By the 1980s Western accounts of the connections between domestic politics and foreign policy in the Soviet Union had become more complex. Writers like Alexander Dallin constructed explanations combining material, 'guns or butter' linkages with mind-set ones, acknowledging the muting effects of Party oversight and discipline, and embracing the role played by regional, generational, functional, organizational, and patronage-network factors. There was still widely recognized to be an underlying 'congruence', however: in rough terms, a preference for domestic liberalizing reform tended to go along with a preference for greater openness to and *rapprochement* with the West—this affected both the political and economic spheres.[23]

We may argue over how applicable these debates are to post-Soviet circumstances. Nevertheless, Soviet-period analysis does offer points of reference against which change can be measured. What is more, the three areas of interest which have been mentioned— the role of the CPSU, contrasting values and perceptions, and competition between sectors—direct our attention to three key dimensions of change in the domestic context of post-Soviet Russian foreign policy: leadership and decision-making, values, and interests. What continuities and discontinuities are evident in these three areas?

## Leadership and decision-making

In this sphere change has at first sight been most radical. The central event has been the disappearance of the Communist Party as it existed in the Soviet period.[24] Before 1991 the Party was at the core of the political system. The Party collated data from more specialized institutions, formulated and publicized new policies and doctrines, controlled the implementation of policy, maintained discipline and morale, and in general held things together. Decisions were taken in the Party Politburo, on the basis of documentation assembled by the Central Committee apparatus.

As Chapter 3 indicates, the Party's role in foreign policy was more limited than in some other areas. Moreover, the system was by no means as smoothly operating and all-embracing as was pretended:

personal networks and powerful institutions exercised some counter-vailing power, and the Party itself was not monolithic. Nevertheless, 'departyization' was bound to have a traumatic effect. The process of change has varied from one former Soviet state to another. In some of the smaller ones the upper levels of the Party machinery were simply restyled as the presidential apparatus, and continued to play a similar role. In Russia it was a new presidential apparatus which aspired to take over the vital functions previously carried out by the Party.

Although this apparatus grew rapidly, absorbing many former Party employees in the process, it lacked the experience, the skills, and the well-established hierarchical internal structure of the old Central Committee bureaucracy. Regular procedures do not seem to have taken root, and many decisions appear to have been taken in a haphazard way.

At the same time, Russian administrative and political culture, and political circumstances, appear to be enforcing a certain continuity. As before, there is no stable distribution of prerogatives among institutions, and strong centralized rule appears to be expected. Some have commented that the President retains much of the arbitrary, meddling management style of the provincial Party secretary which he was earlier in his career. Thus analysts of Russian foreign policy making have still to pay special attention, as in the past, to the personal attitudes and relationships of the top leader and his entourage. On the other hand the weakness of the central authority, and the general political instability, mean that Graham Allison's comment in 1971, that power-struggle considerations dominated Soviet bureaucratic politics, seems also to hold true for the post-Soviet period.[25] The result has been confusion and incoherence in many areas of policy. The responsibilities of institutions have been ill-defined, and their actions have seemed at times beyond the control of the centre. In the military sphere (see Chapter 5) 'departyization' has by no means led to depoliticization—the partisanship of previous decades has persisted, with the difference that it is no longer orchestrated from above.

The role of élite forum previously filled by the Communist Party Central Committee was taken over by new parliaments. The electoral factor has made the Russian parliament sensitive to public opinion on foreign policy matters. Chapter 4 demonstrates how in the new competitive political environment it used foreign policy issues as a weapon in the increasingly bitter struggle with the executive. Partly as a result, its prerogatives in foreign affairs were reduced and eventually sharply curtailed at the end of 1993. Because political parties were weak and there was little interest in and knowledge of matters outside the boundaries of the former Soviet Union, internal Kremlin politics have been even more decisive in foreign policy matters. Nevertheless the democratic element remains an important new factor.

*Values*

The final stages of the collapse of the Soviet regime were accompanied by an upsurge of enthusiasm for Western liberal values in Russia, especially among younger and better-educated sections of the élite. At the same time, as the loosening of central control over the content of the mass media which was begun under Gorbachev advanced even further, and as social inequalities deepened, the attitudes of generations and social groups became more clearly differentiated.[26] Later a mood of nostalgia for the economic security and other certainties provided by the old regime began to spread, reinforcing an upsurge of support for neo-communist and various authoritarian political parties. More striking, however, is the way nationalism emerged as a factor cutting across established political cleavages. In the post-communist period it has been degree of nationalist feeling which has mainly defined allegiances in the Russian foreign policy community, as Chapter 2 shows.

As far as wider public opinion is concerned, it is difficult to judge how serious the impact of nationalist rhetoric has been. In Russia, as in all societies, it appears that everyday preoccupations tend to blot out more distant concerns for most of the population. This is particularly so when economic crisis focuses public attention sharply on material issues. The perceived distance of external matters does vary, of course, between issue areas. While developments in relations with the West are of secondary significance to most people, conflicts within the former Soviet Union attract considerable public attention and concern.

Given the highly volatile domestic political context, opinion on external issues appears to be remarkably consistent, particularly where these relate to developments in the 'near abroad' (see Chapter 4). Even on issues further afield, where the public rely on political and specialist debate, opinion is relatively firm, especially where problems involve principles such as territorial integrity. This is not to say that basic public attitudes are immutable. National pride and emotion, expressed openly by a minority, extend much more widely in latent form and provide ample opportunity for nationalist manipulation.

The policy effects of shifts in public opinion vary considerably by society and by political situation. Even in developed demo- cracies the influence of public opinion on foreign policy is very partial.[27] The former Soviet states provide a peculiar and in some ways a paradoxical context for the operation of public opinion. Regarded in the Soviet period as a product and instrument of pro- paganda, public opinion had no effective established position in the policy process. In the post-Soviet climate, however, politicians are unaccustomed yet committed, at least notionally, to competitive elections. This combination makes them unusually sensitive to shifts in voters' attitudes. Quite apart from affecting electoral outcomes, public opinion stands as a *point d'appui* for government opponents. In this indirect sense it affects the political calculus of a foreign policy which remains centred on the interests of élite groups.

*Interests*

By the early 1990s in Moscow much more of the political struggle was evident to the naked eye than during the Soviet era of crypto- politics. Industrialists created lobbying bodies and backed political parties. Regional leaders bargained openly with the centre. Officials from both civil and military arms of the state expressed their opin- ions about policy remarkably freely. Newspapers printed details of backstage deals being made by political leaders on behalf of client groups.

There were inevitably powerful continuities in economic interests relating to foreign policy. An obvious and frequently cited example is that of the defence-industrial sector. Under Soviet rule the defence industry had enjoyed a whole string of privileges. It had been pro- tected from foreign competition, from sharp fluctuations in military spending, from any pressures a market would have exerted towards reallocating resources to civilian needs. It had been cocooned in a system of special supplies, high wage levels, and welfare services, and its personnel had enjoyed high status and relatively good access to the upper levels of decision-making. All this had been justified by official rhetoric which made the life-or-death struggle with 'Western imperialism' the overriding national priority.

In present-day Russia the defence industry, which is thoroughly intertwined with the high-technology manufacturing sector in general, is a crucial political factor, partly because of what it retains of its previous standing and partly because of its sheer size.[28] The jolting economic set-backs of the 1990s have had a mobilizing effect on it. By the autumn of 1994 official figures showed industrial output down by 44 per cent since January 1990. Defence orders were drastically cut back, valuable traditional arms export markets, like Iraq and Libya, were lost, and research and development capabilities were beginning to wither, as specialists were attracted to jobs abroad.[29]

In broad terms the defence/high-technology sector has a natural community of interest with other important producer groups in a more interventionist economic policy involving more gradual marketization, generous subsidies, and protection from foreign competition, and fostering stability and a single market throughout the CIS area. It can also join efforts with the military to call for higher priority for defence spending, justified by new (and old) threats from abroad and in peripheral regions of Russia. Yet there have been continual and not always successful battles with other producer lobbies over shares in government expenditure. The Ministry of Defence, also hard-pressed, has preferred to spend on manpower rather than on new weapons. Inside the defence/high-technology sector, moreover, there were widely differing priorities. In foreign policy matters a great deal could depend, for example, on whether a particular firm saw realistic prospects of profitable collaboration with Western counterparts.

Other sectoral interests frequently mentioned are the fuel and energy complex, the agrarian lobby, and banking and commercial groups.[30] Lobbies based in these sectors have been active in support of particular foreign policy choices. It seems likely that such pressures play an important part in the calculations of Russian policy makers. As was mentioned above, this situation has come about not just because of internal political changes and the new salience of economic aspects of foreign policy, but also because Western negotiators, especially those representing international financial institutions, make a practice of setting very specific economic policy conditions for assistance.

The Russian government's memorandum to the IMF in September 1994 provides a good demonstration. It undertook to complete price liberalization in the course of 1995, to remove coal subsidies over three years, to implement the bankruptcy provisions which had so far remained virtually a dead letter, to end export duties by 1996, to cut import duties to a maximum of 30 per cent and to an average level of 10 per cent over three years, and to auction access to oil pipelines. Pledges of this kind impinge painfully on a string of actors in the Russian economy, and rebound on reformist politicians. The whole process strengthens connections in the minds of the electorate between pro-Westernism abroad and economic hardship and social disruption at home. In response to demands to protect the struggling economy, politicians are forced to seek out measures which are less obvious to international partners (cheap credits and tax benefits to farmers, for example, rather than higher import tariffs).[31]

Nevertheless, we should beware of overestimating the importance in Russian foreign policy of the kind of economic groupings described here. If the government has been weak and likely to make concessions in individual cases (for example in the area of licences, quotas, and exemptions), those groups seeking to influence it on general matters have tended to be poorly organized and prey to internal divisions. As Chapter 4 demonstrates, attempts to build influential representative organizations have had disappointing results, and the unstable party structure has hindered the development of regular channels of access.[32]

### Leadership strategies

The new attention given to interests should not obscure, then, the continuing importance of broader values and political loyalties, and of leadership factors. In the first place, the contests over the issues listed above were played out as part of a broader political struggle, where 'reformists', 'centrists', and 'conservatives' fought across more familiar terrain. Secondly, times of change and uncertainty, when the policy interests of élite groups are not clear-cut and when the structures of representation are weak, give greater freedom to political leaders to side-step pressures and to get their own way. The Russian President was able to manœuvre between factions, mobilizing some, removing the institutional footholds of others, manipulating information, and employing the multiple techniques available to statesmen intent on maximizing their autonomy in conducting foreign relations.

As in the case of Gorbachev, Yeltsin's strategy depended on the changes in domestic and foreign affairs being mutually supporting, in other words on the operation of what Robert Putnam describes as 'synergistic issue linkage'.[33] Gorbachev's approach was to combine *détente* and internal liberalization in the hope of mobilizing behind his programme the traditionally Westernist liberal-minded intelligentsia.[34] His successor was more ambitious, seeking to call into existence a whole new class with a vested interest in a capitalist market economy. Along with the 'democratic' intelligentsia, and the most prosperous blue-collar workers, they were to form a solid political base for his programme of anti-communism, internal economic liberalization, *rapprochement* with the West, and opening to the world economy. It is clear that Yeltsin had some success with this strategy. With the West's help, key 'swing constituencies' were brought on side: aerospace producers tempted by prospects of international co-operation, officials and managers making the transition to shareholding status through the West-funded State Property Committee, oil and gas enterprises offered access to know-how and slices in new extraction contracts. If nothing else, this helped to divide and to create uncertainty among producer interests, and to lower the temperature of opposition.

But the high expectations of early months were not fulfilled. At first the 'communist' threat to reform was deliberately exaggerated by the government, in order to harness in its support remaining resentments against the old regime, and in order to strengthen its bargaining position at the international negotiating table. Later on, however, the harsh economic and political realities of the global market, and the painful results of internal reforms, appear to have helped to bring about a change of mood among producers, and even in some financial circles, in favour of greater protection, more self-reliance (within CIS boundaries) and more state intervention in the economy. This combined with disappointments in political relations with the West, with problems in the 'near abroad', and with a gradual running down of the momentum of domestic reformism to generate a swing in favour of nationalist and neo-communist parties. Simultaneously Yeltsin's own foreign policy rhetoric and practice began to change. These processes underlie three broad stages in the development of Russian foreign policy since the beginning of 1992.

## Phases of Russian foreign policy

The imprint of pre-existing patterns of thinking and political alignment was bound to be strong in the first period after the collapse of the USSR. There is a natural inertia in perceptions and political alliances, and there are strong structural continuities, as for example in the case of the military sector of the economy. Looking at the general pattern of political cleavages on domestic and international issues in Russia at the beginning of 1992, the overwhelming impression is one of continuity with the late Soviet period, when attitudes to internal Westernizing reform and to relations with the West externally tended to define political allegiances.

The first phase of independent Russian foreign policy was one of more or less unqualified Westernism, and this was consistent with the general tendency, if not the style of implementation, of internal policies. The reformist end of the political spectrum was occupied by the Yeltsin government and its supporters, committed to radical economic reform along liberal lines, as rapid as practicable integration into the world economic system, respect for existing borders and civil rights, and a pro-Western alignment in international affairs.[35] The anti-government coalition of early 1992 drew support from three main élite groups, each internally divided into more moderate ('centrist') and more extreme elements. The first were parts of the military, who demanded more resources and slower withdrawals from abroad, and resisted the breakup of the post-Soviet strategic space. Second came those industrial managers who advocated more caution about marketization and restructuring, a more active arms export policy, maximum preservation of the post-Soviet economic space and protective tariffs around it, less reliance on Western assistance and advice, and in general a more interventionist economic policy. Finally came various neo-communist, nationalist, and statist (*gosudarstvennik*) parties and factions, who argued the necessity of preserving a strong central power in Moscow and of pursuing a more assertive foreign policy, especially in the CIS. The more extreme elements in the opposition, whether 'red' or 'brown', adhered to a *Fundamentalist Nationalism* which rejected important parts of the post-1989–91 international settlement.

From the middle of 1992 a second phase of Russian foreign policy began. This was partly a consequence of the Yeltsin administration being forced to modify its line to take account of the strength of the opposition, which was openly displayed at the Sixth Congress of People's Deputies in April and May. An important part in the change was played, too, by splits in the reformist camp, where domestic and international realities were dissipating the earlier Westernizing euphoria. Some politicians and journalists from this camp ('demo-patriots', 'Eurasianists', or 'national democrats') began to complain that the Foreign Ministry was excessively Westernist and that neglect of the former Soviet region was likely to have damaging consequences. This brought about a shift in the balance of foreign policy thinking on the democratic wing away from *Liberal Westernism* in the direction of a politically less vulnerable *Pragmatic Nationalism*.[36]

During the second half of the year the government, which by now contained former Gazprom director Viktor Chernomyrdin and other ministers drawn from the centrist camp, began to modify its foreign policy rhetoric and its policies. Frequent conflicts over policy inside the administration and with the parliament gave an impression of inconsistency, however. While the Foreign Ministry maintained a resolutely liberal, Westernist stance, the President unexpectedly declared a delay in withdrawing Russian troops from Estonia and Latvia, and suddenly cancelled a visit to Tokyo which would have meant discussions about ceding territory to Japan. It became clear that current targets for restricting the growth of the money supply agreed with the IMF would not be met. Moves by Western companies to invest in oil extraction in Russia were frustrated. The government pushed ahead with arms export deals in the face of Western disapproval.

By the spring of 1993 this uneasy transitional period had come to an end. In its struggle with parliament and the intransigent part of the opposition the leadership was apparently trying to consolidate a broad coalition of reformist and centrist groups, which in foreign policy all appeared to be ready to unite around a distinctly Pragmatic Nationalist programme. A third phase of foreign policy had begun. As we have seen, the government launched a concerted and increasingly determined drive to extend influence in the former Soviet region and to defend Russian interests vigorously in relations with the West. In Moscow the most reformist political leaders and Foreign Ministry spokesmen began cautiously to adopt the 'patriotic' language of their critics. This was not just an effect of political expediency. As Chapter 2 demonstrates, the climate of thinking about foreign policy was changing throughout wide sections of the 'democratic' political élite. The Foreign Policy Conception of the Russian Federation adopted in April reflected a significant shift towards greater readiness to justify the use of force, and towards claiming the right to 'defend' Russians living in the 'near abroad'.[37] Russia succeeded in extending and strengthening its power in the CIS, and bargained hard with the West over intervention in the former Yugoslavia, over the terms of its Co-operation Treaty with the EU, and over the nature of the NATO Partnership for Peace.

Meanwhile, as his struggle for supremacy with the Supreme Soviet moved to a resolution in October, Yeltsin continued to reinforce his relations with industrial and military interests, and his centrist Prime Minister, Viktor Chernomyrdin, acquired greater visibility and authority. This phase continued into 1994 and 1995.

In 1994 there was much talk in Moscow, encouraged by the Yeltsin administration, of civic accord and consensus in Russian politics. The reality, needless to say, was less harmonious. Nevertheless, the atmosphere differed from that of 1992: reformers were less confident and more divided, especially over national issues, while conservatives had begun to accept the irreversibility of some of the changes which had occurred, especially in the economy. Political weakness, highlighted by the need to rely on armed force to remain in power in October 1993 and by the gains made by radical opposition parties in the December elections, encouraged a defensive solidarity in the governing establishment. This made possible some depolarization, and endowed the political 'centre' with a degree of influence quite disproportionate to its poor electoral showing. The same political weakness, and the greater leverage enjoyed since 1993 by the 'power ministers' heading the armed services and security forces, were seen by many commentators as contributing factors in a further hardening of policy at the end of

|  | Domestic policy | Foreign policy |
|---|---|---|
| **Economic sphere** Conservatives | Subsidies, price controls, interventionism, corporatism, stress on established sectors | Protectionism (possibly CIS-wide), export controls, arms exports to traditional clients |

versus

|  | Domestic policy | Foreign policy |
|---|---|---|
| Liberal Reformers (1992) | Rapid monetary stabilization, marketization, and privatization, on liberal model | Co-operation with international financial institutions and aid-givers, low tariffs, world pricing |

and later

|  | Domestic policy | Foreign policy |
|---|---|---|
| Pragmatic Reformers (1994) | Steady continuation of economic reform, with safeguards | Continuing co-operation with IFIs, hard bargaining, arms exports |
| **Political sphere** Conservatives | Strong centralized state power | Preservation of military strength, restoration of union or of 'Greater Russia' |

versus

|  | Domestic policy | Foreign policy |
|---|---|---|
| Liberal Reformers (1992) | Decentralization, federalism, respect for minority and general civil rights, strict constitutionality | Demilitarization, alliance with West, respect for sovereignty of former Soviet states |

and later

|  | Domestic policy | Foreign policy |
|---|---|---|
| Pragmatic Reformers (1994) | Federalism, but with strong centre, reliance on executive power | Conditional co-operation with West, assertion of special rights and responsibilities of RF in former Soviet area |

FIGURE 1.1. Élite policy preference linkages, Russian Federation, early 1992 compared to 1994

1994, when a large-scale armed intervention was undertaken in
the Chechen Republic, in the face of disapproval by the West and
dismay in liberal circles in Moscow. Throughout 1995 international
disagreements over policy in Yugoslavia and NATO's plans for
expansion in Central/Eastern Europe helped to generate an even
more marked nationalist tone in the rhetoric of the Yeltsin administration. This was particularly noticeable in the second half of the
year as the parliamentary election campaign gathered pace.

*The changing map of policy preferences*

If the shifts in the balance of Russian foreign policy in the period
up to the end of 1994 described above are aligned with developments in domestic politics, it is possible to map the evolution of
the broad pattern of linkage between internal and external policy
preferences (see Figure 1.1).

Figure 1.1 is not meant to imply sharp polarization in political
reality, merely to provide a set of clear reference points. By 1994
the diversity of positions among the more reformist and more conservative sections of the political élite was such that the preferences listed above are bound to oversimplify: they are intended
merely to highlight the dominant view or common positions on
each wing.

The chart assumes that the basic reformist–conservative division
remained, in broad terms, similar to the one evident in the late
Soviet period. The main changes affected the reformist side. On
the conservative wing, which was out of power, the imperative
to adapt was weaker. The main development there was a steady
strengthening of nationalist and authoritarian themes, relative to
socialist ones; in foreign policy, reuniting the entire former Soviet
area became a less widely shared goal.

On the reformist wing the most important tendency of change
compared to the beginning of 1992 was a loosening of the tight
association between attachment to (1) out-and-out Westernism in
foreign policy, including recognition of the extensive sovereignty
of 'near abroad' states, (2) radical marketizing reform of the economy, and (3) thorough internal democratization.

If we say that attitudes to Western values and to relations with
the West played a key part in defining political allegiances in the

late Soviet period, we must bear in mind that 'the West' as understood by Russian reformers (and even by some conservatives) was often something rather idealized, closer to a liberal internationalist model of reality than to reality itself. It is not surprising, in retrospect, that Liberal Westernism should have been so rapidly succeeded by a Pragmatic Nationalism which, while not hostile to the West, was markedly cooler, more assertive, and more defensive of Russia's interests.

One of the most striking features of Russian foreign policy thinking on the reformist side, as it emerged in 1992 and 1993, relates to the former Soviet states. Marketizing democrats whose position in regard to Russia's role in the wider world was liberal, tolerant, and pacific were quite likely to support armed intervention and other kinds of energetic interference in the affairs of 'near abroad' states.[38] This was not just a matter of public politics, and the need not to be outflanked by the Fundamentalist Nationalist right, as 'near abroad' issues became more salient during 1992. It appeared to reflect the widespread feeling among Russians, noted above, that events in the former Soviet region are in many ways more a domestic than an international matter, and that different rules apply to Russia's behaviour there. There remained, of course, a great variety of views among reformists about how Russia should exercise its leading role in the CIS, with some envisaging a relatively benign and peaceful dominance, and others seeking to keep financial and security commitments to a bare minimum.

It was to be expected that the link between democratic principles and support for economic liberalization (internal and external) would come under some strain. By 1993 reformists in and near the government were having to come to terms with the unpopularity of their economic policies. To some of them a medium-term strategy of 'market authoritarianism' began to seem more attractive. The constitutional crisis of that year, defiance from regional leaders, the struggles with a conservative parliament, and its forcible dissolution pushed in the same direction. The 'Chinese model' attracts interest in many of the former Soviet states, as their own efforts at reform prove slow to pay off.[39] The drift of opinion among parts of the reformist camp in a nationalist and statist direction was reinforced by the political accommodation which they reached in 1992–3 with those elements of the 'centre' which had adjusted to the idea of private property and the market. However, in the mid-1990s the basic Westernizing–anti-Westernizing pattern of domestic–foreign policy linkages was still largely intact.

The chapters which follow examine the role of internal factors in Russian foreign policy, taking in turn the four areas of foreign policy thinking, foreign policy making, public politics and accountability in foreign policy, and the role of the military in foreign policy. Most of the data are drawn from the period up to the end of 1994. The final chapter reviews the changes which have been identified in the psychological environment of Russian foreign policy, in domestic constituencies, and in the policy process.

## NOTES

[1] M. Brecher, *The Foreign Policy System of Israel: Setting, Images, Process* (London, 1972), 4. See K. Dawisha, *Soviet Foreign Policy Towards Egypt* (London, 1979), 88–90. Brecher's scheme is used here as a convenient way of classifying inputs; its use does not mean that the authors share all aspects of his conception of foreign policy making.

[2] One recent description of the domestic politics of foreign policy lists 'the constellation of political interests in a society, the aggregation of such demands, the debates on issue areas, and the transformation of these processes into foreign policy outputs' (H. Müller and T. Risse-Kappen, 'From the Outside In and From the Inside Out', in D. Skidmore and V. Hudson (eds.), *The Limits of State Autonomy: Societal Groups and Foreign Policy Formulation* (Boulder, Colo., 1993)).

[3] See Edward Morse, 'The Transformation of Foreign Policies: Modernization, Interdependence and Externalization', *World Politics*, 22 (1970), 371–92.

[4] P. Fraser, 'Russia, the CIS and the European Community', in N. Malcolm (ed.), *Russia and Europe: An End to Confrontation?* (London, 1994), 199–203; C. Ranzio-Plath, 'Business Partners', *European Brief*, vol. I, no. vi, 41–2; M. Light, 'Economic and Technical Assistance to the Former Soviet Union', in T. Taylor (ed.), *The Collapse of the Soviet Empire: Managing the Regional Fallout* (London, 1992), 61–5. Western aid commitments to the CIS by 1994 were still well under $100bn. The Marshall Plan provided around $300bn p.a. at 1994 prices, mainly in grants.

[5] This is a common theme among Russian journalists and academic

specialists. See, for example, S. Brillov, 'Naples Summit and Russian Foreign Policy', *Moscow News*, 1994, no. 28; 'Rossiya i yug v mirovom soobshchestve', *Mirovaya ekonomika i mezhdunarodnye otnosheniya*, 1994, no. 5, pp. 69–89.

[6] On the internal political dimension of relations with external aid-providers, investors, and trading partners see P. Burnell, *Economic Nationalism in the Third World* (Brighton, 1986), 72–7; T. Callaghy, 'Toward State Capability and Embedded Liberalism in the Third World: Lessons for Adjustment', in J. Nelson (ed.), *Fragile Coalitions: The Politics of Economic Adjustment* (Oxford, 1989), 116–37; S. Gill and D. Law, *The Global Political Economy* (Baltimore, 1988), pt. 3.

[7] Two separate words in the Russian language denote 'Russian': one by ethnic/linguistic/cultural identity (*russkii*), and the other by association with the Russian state (*rossiiskii*).

[8] For a concise and illuminating treatment of this subject see N. Melvin, *Forging the New Russian Nation* (RIIA Discussion Paper 50; London, 1994).

[9] Georgia joined the CIS in 1993.

[10] Yeltsin's February 1993 speech claiming 'special powers' for Russia in the former regions of the Soviet Union is cited in *BBC Summary of World Broadcasts*, SU/1626, B/1 (2 Mar. 1993).

[11] R. Jackson, *Quasi-States: Sovereignty, International Relations and the Third World* (Cambridge, 1990), 21, 38.

[12] Ethnic Russians (and Russian-speakers) represent 22.1% (32.8%) of the population in Ukraine, 13.2% (31.9%) in Belarus, 37.8% (47.4%) in Kazakhstan, 34% (42.1%) in Latvia, 30.3% (34.8%) in Estonia, 13% (23.1%) in Moldova, and 21.5% (25.6%) in Kyrgyzstan. (Melvin, *Forging the New Russian Nation*, 3. See also pp. 27–48 on the impact on Russian government policy.)

[13] Aleksandr Shokhin pointed out to the Central Asian states that full membership of the Economic Co-operation Organization was incompatible with membership of a more integrated CIS. Pressure was also applied to them by starting discussions with Ukraine and Belarus about setting up a Slavic economic union (S. Shermatova, 'Central Asia Attracted by Turkey, Iran, Pakistan', *Moscow News*, 1993, no. 30).

[14] H. Kissinger, 'Domestic Structure and Foreign Policy', *Daedalus*, vol. xcv, no. ii of the Proceedings of the American Academy of Arts and Sciences (Spring 1966), 503–29; H. Morgenthau, *Politics among Nations: The Struggle for Power and Peace* (New York, 1963), 7; K. Waltz, *Theory of International Politics* (Reading, Mass., 1979), 70.

[15] For a recent discussion see A. Moravcsik, 'Introduction: Integrating International and Domestic Theories of International Bargaining', in P. Evans, H. Jacobson, and R. Putnam (eds.), *Double-Edged Diplomacy:*

*International Bargaining and Domestic Politics* (Berkeley, Calif., 1993), 3–42.

[16] For an explanation of Gorbachev's foreign policy innovations in terms of *external* factors, see D. Deudney and J. Ikenberry, 'The International Sources of Soviet Change', *International Security*, vol. XVI, no. iii (Winter 1991–2), 74–118.

[17] For a painstaking attempt to define appropriate boundaries for the study of foreign policy see J. Rosenau, *Scientific Study of Foreign Policy* (New York, 1971), 78–84. See too C. Hill, 'Introduction', in W. Wallace and W. Paterson (eds.), *Foreign Policy Making in Western Europe* (Farnborough, 1978), 7–30. Examples of models of external-internal interactions in foreign policy can be found in Brecher, *The Foreign Policy System of Israel*, and K. Holsti, *International Politics: A Framework for Analysis*, 6th edn. (London, 1992), 302–6.

[18] A comprehensive initial survey and analysis of the international implications of the new situation is provided in K. Dawisha and B. Parrott, *Russia and the New States of Eurasia: The Politics of Upheaval* (Cambridge, 1994).

[19] *Journal of International Affairs*, 26 (1972), 1–28; see too V. Aspaturian, *Process and Power in Soviet Foreign Policy* (Boston, 1971), esp. 526–43. For a sustained application of a similar approach to a particular case, see J. Valenta, 'The Bureaucratic Politics Paradigm and the Soviet Invasion of Czechoslovakia', *Political Science Quarterly*, 94 (1979), 55–76; J. Valenta, *Soviet Intervention in Czechoslovakia, 1968: Anatomy of a Decision* (London, 1979). Valenta considers Soviet policy making only partly susceptible to a bureaucratic politics analysis. See too, for example, F. Holzman and R. Legvold, 'The Economics and Politics of East–West Relations', in E. Hoffmann and F. Fleron (eds.), *The Conduct of Soviet Foreign Policy* (New York, 1980), 453–8; B. Parrott, *Politics and Technology in the Soviet Union* (London, 1985). Both these works analyse the situation much more subtly than Aspaturian. For a general discussion of methodology in the study of Soviet foreign policy see M. Light, 'Approaches to the Study of Soviet Foreign Policy', *Review of International Studies*, 7 (1981), 127–43.

[20] W. Odom, 'A Dissenting View on the Group Approach to Soviet Politics', *World Politics*, 28 (1976), 542–67; K. Dawisha, 'The Limitations of the Bureaucratic Politics Model: Observations on the Soviet Case', *Studies in Comparative Communism*, 13 (1980), 300–26; J. Lenczowski, *Soviet Perceptions of US Foreign Policy* (London, 1982).

[21] F. Griffiths, 'A Tendency Analysis of Soviet Policy Making', in H. Skilling and F. Griffiths, *Interest Groups in Soviet Politics* (Princeton, NJ, 1971); F. Griffiths, *Images, Politics and Learning in Soviet Behavior Towards the United States* (Ph.D. dissertation, Columbia University, 1972).

[22] D. Simes, *Detente and Conflict: Soviet Foreign Policy 1972–1977* (London, 1977), pt. 3. All these debates are well summarized by Alexander Dallin, 'The Domestic Sources of Soviet Foreign Policy', in S. Bialer (ed.), *The Domestic Context of Soviet Foreign Policy* (Boulder, Colo., 1981), 335–408.

[23] Dallin, 'The Domestic Sources of Soviet Foreign Policy'; J. Snyder, 'The Gorbachev Revolution: A Waning of Soviet Expansionism?', *International Security*, vol. XII, no. iii (1987–8), 93–131; A. Pravda, 'Introduction: Linkages between Soviet Domestic and Foreign Policy under Gorbachev', in Ts. Hasegawa and A. Pravda (eds.), *Perestroika: Soviet Domestic and Foreign Policies* (London, 1990), 1–24. The case *against* the idea of regular linkage patterns in reforming Communist states is made by B. Buzan and G. Segal, 'Introduction: Defining Reform as Openness', in G. Segal (ed.), *Openness and Reform in Communist States* (London, 1993), 1–17.

[24] In some former Soviet states the Communist Party continues to exist under a different name. In Russia the Party has been re-established and claims a large membership. But in both cases its nature and role have been substantially changed: only in some of the smaller states do 'presidential' parties play anything like the part previously played by the CPSU.

[25] G. Allison, *Essence of Decision: Explaining the Cuban Missile Crisis* (Boston, 1971), 182. Cited in Dawisha, *Soviet Foreign Policy Towards Egypt*, 88.

[26] Industrial production and real incomes in Russia fell by 30–40 per cent between 1991 and 1994, and this was *before* any serious economic restructuring, with the inevitable bankruptcies and unemployment, had got under way (*Financial Times*, 27 June 1994, suppl.). In the process the previous hierarchies of status and reward were overturned. The most important victims have been the military, military-industrial employees, the older generation of the intelligentsia, and in general those depending on state incomes and pensions. Some younger representatives of the intelligentsia (and the more enterprising ex-Party officials and industrial managers) have begun to prosper in the private sector of the economy.

[27] B. Cohen, *The Public's Impact on Foreign Policy* (New York, 1973); R. Hinckley, *People, Polls and Policymakers* (Lexington, Va., 1992). For a dissenting view, see M. Nincic, *Democracy and Foreign Policy* (New York, 1992).

[28] Even in the Soviet period, what was known as the military-industrial sector produced a high proportion of civilian goods. For more information see J. Cooper, *The Soviet Defence Industry: Conversion and Reform* (London, 1991) and *The Conversion of the Former Soviet Defence Industry* (London, 1993). In particular regions of Russia, defence/high-technology plants account for an overwhelming share of employment.

[29] Economic statistics are drawn from P. Rutland, 'A Twisted Path toward a Market Economy', *Transition*, 15 Feb. 1995, 12–20.

[30] Iu. Fyodorov, *The Role of Economic Interest Groups and Lobbies in Russian Foreign Policy Decision Making* (RIIA Post-Soviet Business Forum Briefing Paper 5, London, 1995); several of these groups were routinely mentioned in the Russian press. Fyodorov also identifies, in the public sector, the military and security services, the civilian part of the central bureaucracy, and the regional lobby. For an alternative, four-part categorization, based on degree of flexibility and market orientation of firms, see Yevgeny Yasin in *Segodnya*, 12 Jan. 1994.

[31] Leading reformer Anatoly Chubais, addressing farmers on 1 Mar. 1995, acknowledged their problems, and promised them selective state assistance. At the end of the month the liberal Minister of Foreign Economic Relations, Oleg Davydov, argued that this was much preferable to further increases in food import tariffs. *Inside Russia and the CIS*, Mar. 1995, 8–9; Interfax Agency Report, 31 Mar. 1995, cited in *OMRI Daily Digest*, 3 Apr. 1995, pt. 1.

[32] For a general discussion of the role of economic lobbies, see P. Rutland, *Business Elites and Russian Economic Policy* (London, 1993).

[33] For a recent comprehensive review of strategies employed by leaders in this area see R. Putnam, 'Diplomacy and Domestic Politics: the Logic of Two-Level Games', in *International Organization*, 42 (1988), 427–60; also in P. Evans, H. Jacobson, and R. Putnam (eds.), *Double-Edged Diplomacy: International Bargaining and Domestic Politics* (Berkeley, Calif., 1993), 431–68.

[34] Jack Snyder, using Putnam's terminology, argues that Gorbachev's attempt to exploit synergy in relations with Germany failed, partly because of mistrust, partly because of the low level of economic contacts, and partly because of cultural distance ('East–West Bargaining over Germany: The Search for Synergy in a Two-Level Game', in Evans *et al.* (eds.), *Double-Edged Diplomacy*, 104–27).

[35] Even at first there were some deviations from conventional principles of international relations. It was made clear, for example, that respect for Ukraine's borders was conditional on its remaining inside the CIS.

[36] The nature of Russian Liberal Westernism, Pragmatic Nationalism, and Fundamentalist Nationalism in the 1990s is explored in Chapter 2.

[37] *Nezavisimaya gazeta*, 29 Apr. 1993, provided an 'authorized' summary of the final document. An earlier Foreign Ministry draft was published as 'Kontseptsiya vneshnei politiki Rossiiskoi Federatsii', *Diplomaticheskii vestnik*, special issue, Jan. 1993. These documents are analysed in Chapter 2.

[38] See, for example, W. Zimmerman, 'Markets, Democracy and Russian Foreign Policy', *Post-Soviet Affairs*, 10 (1994), 103–25; N. Popov,

'Vneshnyaya politika Rossii (Analiz politikov i ekspertov)', *Mirovaya ekonomika i mezhdunarodnye otnosheniya*, 1994, no. 3, pp. 52–9; no. 4, pp. 5–15.

[39] General Pinochet was regularly referred to in respectful tones by writers from different parts of the Russian political spectrum. For an account of the social and ideological background of the Brazilian 'bureaucratic market authoritarianism' which Pinochet imitated in many respects, see L. Graham, 'Democracy and the Bureaucratic State in Latin America', in H. Wiarda (ed.), *The Continuing Struggle for Democracy in Latin America* (Boulder, Colo., 1980), 255–71; G. Sorensen, 'Brazil', in J. Carlsson and T. Shaw (eds.), *Newly-Industrializing Countries and the Political Economy of South–South Relations* (London, 1980), 107–8.

# 2

# Foreign Policy Thinking

MARGOT LIGHT

## *National identity and the culture of debate*

This chapter examines the evolution of foreign policy views in the Russian Federation after the disintegration of the Soviet Union. It looks at the domestic debates about foreign policy among political élites and at the development of official views, particularly as they were articulated in the official foreign policy 'concept'. We begin, however, in this first section by exploring the problems facing the new Russian leadership in terms of deciding what foreign policy to adopt, how these problems were reflected in the range and nature of the foreign policy debate, and who the political élite was which participated in the debate.

The second section of the chapter turns to the substance of the debate. As we have seen in Chapter 1, it is convenient to divide Russian foreign policy into three phases. The first phase, until May 1992, was distinguished by a consistently pro-Western line in Russian foreign policy. The second phase, from June 1992 to April 1993, was one of increasing disarray in Russian foreign policy, during which Russian foreign policy both towards the West and towards the Commonwealth of Independent States (CIS) gradually became more assertive. The third phase began after April 1993, when there was more consensus and Russian policy was, therefore, more consistent. But the debate about policy was continual, and it covered both the general principles on which participants wished Russian policy to be based and, once consensus had more or less been achieved, the way in which those principles should be implemented in specific responses to external events. For analytical convenience, however, the discussion of the debate will be divided into parts corresponding to the three phases of policy, and each phase will be considered separately. Similarly, it is analytically simpler to

distinguish between discrete groups of views about Russian foreign policy. In fact, there was considerable overlap between groups,
and Russian foreign policy thinking can be seen as a continuum
with extreme pro-Western views at one end of the spectrum and
extreme xenophobic, imperialist views at the other.

Immediately before and after the establishment of an independent Russian state in December 1991, pro-Western views prevailed
in the public discussion of Russian foreign policy, and pro-market
views prevailed in the discussion of domestic policy, opposed only
by those who wanted to reinstate the Soviet Union and its centralized economy. In this chapter we shall refer to those who favoured
a market economy and held pro-Western views as *Liberal Westernizers*. The term *Fundamentalist Nationalist* will be used to describe the people who combined extreme nationalism with antipathy
towards economic reform. By February 1992, however, nationalism
had become quite widespread, and differences of opinion had begun
to appear among the Liberal Westernizers about how to define
Russia's national interests and what policy to pursue to achieve
them.[1] The debate in these early months was characterized by a
division between those who retained strong pro-Western sympathies
and those who proposed a more independent policy *vis-à-vis* the
West and a more integrationist stance towards the other successor
states. We shall call those who held the latter views *Pragmatic
Nationalists*.[2]

As far as domestic politics and economics were concerned,
both Liberal Westernizers and Pragmatic Nationalists believed by
and large that democracy should be consolidated, and that Russia
should have a market economy. The difference between them lay
in whether they thought that Russia should emulate Western
democracies and markets, or whether they believed that distinctive
Russian features would prevail. In other words, the views of the
Pragmatic Nationalists were quite different from the calls for the
reconstitution of the Soviet Union by some Fundamentalist Nationalists, and from the dreams of those communists who wanted to
revive the economic structures of the past.

By the spring of 1993, with the beginning of the third phase of
policy identified in Chapter 1, a rough consensus had begun to
emerge about the principles that should underlie Russian foreign
policy. Difference of detail remained, but there was general agreement about priorities and vital interests. Although domestic political

tension was high and continued to rise until it culminated in the power struggle between President and the Supreme Soviet which ended in violence in October 1993, arguments about Russian foreign policy subsided. The new foreign policy consensus represented a victory of Pragmatic Nationalist views. Yet the fact that the most devoted and influential Liberal Westernizers, the President and the Foreign Minister, modified their views gave the impression that Russian foreign policy had become far more conservative. After the election in December 1993 Western observers frequently claimed that the palpable change in Russian foreign policy thinking was a demonstration of the 'Zhirinovsky effect'. In other words, they believed that domestic pressure from (and fear of) extreme nationalists had forced the Russian government to change tack. It is clear, however, that the new consensus had begun to emerge long before Vladimir Zhirinovsky achieved prominence in the parliamentary elections.[3]

The third and concluding section of the chapter will consider, among other things, whether the new consensus should be interpreted as a realistic retreat from the naïve idealism of the early dominant pro-Western view and a necessary adaptation to circumstances, or whether it demonstrates the power of the nationalists. In other words, it will investigate both why a consensus was reached, and why it was formed around the Pragmatic Nationalist section of the continuum of views.

One reason why the debate about foreign policy was frequently anguished was the difficulty analysts had in deciding what Russia was. Let us turn, therefore, to Russia's identity problems, which constituted the background to discussions about foreign policy.

## The problem of Russia's identity

Many Russians welcomed the proclamation of the sovereignty of the RSFSR in 1990. They were convinced that the Russians had suffered disproportionately under socialism and that their economic well-being had been sacrificed to subsidize the other, less well-developed republics of the Soviet Union.[4] Far fewer of them, however, approved of the dissolution of the Soviet Union. For all their dislike of the central Soviet government, most Russians found it difficult to conceive of Russia without an empire. The problem, in part, was caused by how Russians perceived the identity of their

state. Unlike other empires, the Russian empire and the Russian state
developed simultaneously. One famous pre-revolutionary Russian
historian maintained that

Russia's history, throughout, is the history of a country undergoing colonisation, and having the area of that colonisation and the extension of its
State keep pace with one another. Thus in migration, in colonisation, we
see our history's fundamental factor. With it every other factor in that
history has been more or less bound up.[5]

As a result, the identity of Russia and the idea of Russian statehood have always been closely associated with the existence of an
empire. There has never been a Russian nation-state.[6] The Tsarist
statesman, Sergei Witte, maintained that 'ever since the time of
Peter the Great and Catherine the Great there has been no such
thing as Russia; only a Russian empire.'[7] Moreover, he did not distinguish between Russians, Ukrainians, and Belorussians, including 'Little Russia' (Ukraine) and 'White Russia' (Belorussia) in the
imperial power. For Witte, the colonies of the Russian empire
were areas inhabited predominantly by non-Slavs.

Given this historic association of statehood with empire, it is
not surprising that both democrats and nationalists found it difficult to accept that some areas of the USSR were no longer part of
Russia. A new identity and a new role had to be forged for Russia.[8] Furthermore, it was not just a question of accepting the loss
of the empire, or of forging relationships with the other successor
states to the USSR. There was a dilemma about Russia's role in
the world. From the point of view of geopolitics, for example, the
establishment of new, independent states to the west of Russia
reinvoked an old identity problem: was Russia part of Europe, or
had the loss of empire turned it into an Asian or Eurasian power?
It was certainly geographically further from Europe than it had been
for 300 years. Westernizers, who equated progress and prosperity
with Europe, argued that Russia must be European no matter how
many miles or states separate the country from the rest of the continent. Others, however, claimed a unique Eurasian role for Russia,
bridging Europe and Asia.

There was also the question of status in the international system.
While Russians did not accept responsibility for the policy of the
Soviet Union (or, for that matter, for the conduct of imperial Rus-
sia), they claimed, and were granted, legal inheritance of the Soviet

Union's international treaty obligations, its seat on the Security Council of the United Nations (UN), its diplomatic institutions, nuclear capabilities, and the bulk of its conventional armed forces. As far as the traditional attributes of power are concerned, therefore, Russia inherited the international status of the Soviet Union. On the other hand, Russia's economy was close to collapse, it had taken over the entire Soviet foreign debt and, like the Soviet Union in its last two years of existence, it was a continual supplicant for foreign aid. Moreover, although it occupied a vast expanse, Russia was smaller now than it had been for many centuries (except, perhaps, for a brief period during the Civil War from 1918 to 1920). Unlike the Soviet Union, therefore, it was not a superpower. Indeed, it can be argued that given its present economic predicament and political instability, it cannot even be considered a great power. It was not just politicians who were concerned about Russia's status. Most people distinguished between the Soviet Union and Russia and knew that it was the USSR which had been a superpower. Nevertheless, many of them experienced the loss of superpower status as a national humiliation.[9] The identity problem caused by loss of status was well illustrated by one Russian writer when he explained that 'We are no longer one-sixth of the earth's surface . . . [b]ut we continue to carry within ourselves one-sixth of the globe . . . [i]t is a scale we have become accustomed to.'[10] The problem was to gain international recognition of great-power status while, at the same time, retaining sympathy for Russia's economic plight. The insistence that Russia should be accorded the respect due to a great power became an important theme in the debate about foreign policy.

As far as the identity of Russia was concerned, therefore, Russians had to come to terms with the loss of empire in December 1991, and to clarify the new role and status of their country in the international system. Many intellectuals believed that in defining the principles of Russian foreign policy, the identity of Russia would be established.[11] But the issue of what that identity should be became a contested question which was reflected in the foreign policy debate. While on one level the question of identity is an abstract problem which may seem to have little bearing on policy, in the post-Soviet context it was both closely related to views about Russia's relations with the external world and linked to domestic policy, particularly the question of the applicability of

Western models of democracy and a market economy to Russia. Since the economic reforms launched by Yeltsin's government at the beginning of 1992 (on the recommendation of Western economic advisers) rapidly produced considerable material hardship, economic insecurity soon led to political dissent. As the political situation within the country became more polarized, foreign policy issues inevitably became interwoven into the debates and disagreements about domestic policy. Many of the participants in the debates argued persistently that the government should provide a framework for its foreign policy in the form of a foreign policy doctrine or concept.

It may seem odd that there was so much insistence on an official articulation of the foreign policy principles to which the Russian government intended to adhere. Certainly, given the endless formulations of the Marxism-Leninism of the Brezhnev era and the verboseness of Gorbachev's New Political Thinking, not to mention past difficulties in marrying theory to practice, it is easy to understand why politicians and Foreign Ministry officials might want the latitude to make and execute a foreign policy that has not been formalized and made public in a set of principles and intentions which then have the capacity to serve as constraints or as the source of future embarrassment. In so far as they turned to Western democracies for a model, they might have found the occasional general elaboration of foreign policy aims in the party manifestos and promises that precede an election or, in relation to contentious issues, some specific expressed intentions (for example, membership of the European Community or unilateral disarmament). But there are few Western examples of an articulated set of principles covering all aspects of foreign policy presented by government to parliament for its approval and then formally adopted by government or president.[12] Why did a foreign policy doctrine become such an issue in Russia, and why, despite his reluctance, did the Foreign Minister, Andrei Kozyrev, agree to formulate one?

## The role of foreign policy doctrine and the culture of debate

It can be argued that part of the political culture of the Soviet Union was the adoption, and frequent reference to, programmatic documents about policy. Soviet politicians were not, in the usual sense, accountable either to their electorate or to members of the Communist Party. Yet at Party Congresses the General Secretary of the Party regularly reported on domestic and foreign events and achievements since the preceding Congress and set out a programme for the forthcoming quinquennium. In the period between Congresses, policies were explained in terms of those reports and the resolutions adopted by the Congress, or they were related to the Programme of the Party.[13] The perceived need for a set of foreign policy principles was, therefore, first and foremost the result of habit. But Kozyrev's reluctant acquiescence was probably both acceptance that the habit persisted and recognition that there were functional reasons for an explicit doctrine.

Russia's foreign policy concept fulfils both domestic and foreign aims. It symbolizes sovereignty and demonstrates the extent to which Russia has departed from the foreign policy principles of the Soviet Union. Moreover, it serves to reduce the confusion that arises in the outside world when diametrically opposed views about foreign policy are expressed by political actors. It indicates to foreign governments that policy will be made in the Foreign Ministry and presidential apparatus within guide-lines agreed in the executive and approved by parliament, rather than being subject to the vagaries of domestic political conflict. Presumably, however, it was believed that neither foreign governments nor the domestic public should know all the details of the concept: while the discussion about Russia's foreign policy concept was public, the final version adopted by the President remained a classified document.

The most important domestic function of a foreign policy concept is probably internal to the Foreign Ministry itself. If representatives abroad are either inexperienced or still steeped in the ways of Soviet foreign policy, the explicit statement of foreign policy principles and goals can serve as a guide-line even if it cannot offer detailed instructions to diplomats about how to achieve particular aims.

The discussion and adoption of a general foreign policy line also represents an effort to forge consensus within parliament, and to curb parliamentarians. A minimal agreement about the parameters of external policy may prevent parliament from constantly censuring the Foreign Minister and demanding his recall, thereby undermining his or her authority in the external world (the Supreme

Soviet frequently criticized Kozyrev, raising doubts about his ten-
ure in office). The Foreign Ministry may also have hoped that an
official foreign policy would indicate to inexperienced parliamentarians what the division of foreign policy power must be between
legislative and executive branches of government if foreign policy
is to be effective: even in well-established democracies, parliament
sets the broad parameters of policy, but the interpretation of those
parameters, day-to-day decisions, and the implementation of policy are a matter for the executive. While a foreign policy concept
'gives the political leadership and the people's deputies a comprehensive idea of the aims and means of ... diplomacy in today's
tangled situation',[14] the translation of goals into policies must be
left to the executive.

It is clear, however, that deeper issues were embedded in the
debate about Russia's foreign policy doctrine. As we have seen,
the problem was to define Russia, and to establish its statehood.
As one presidential adviser put it, foreign policy would 'help Russia
become Russia, help shape Russian statehood'.[15] Apart from the
perceived need for foreign policy principles, therefore, the debate
about the concept gave expression to the identity crisis experienced by the intelligentsia.

But arguments about foreign policy principles also fitted into a
Russian political culture that long pre-dated the establishment of
the Soviet Union. The pre-revolutionary Russian intelligentsia were
deeply politically engaged, writing political tracts as well as creative literature, and frequently participating in polemical controversy.
This tradition survived 1917, and in the early years after the October revolution, newspapers and journals were filled with debates
about politics and policy. Even after intra-Party policy disputes
were outlawed in 1921, it was customary to use newspapers and
academic and popular scientific journals to explain Soviet policy
to various categories of citizens. Moreover, notwithstanding the
strict censorship that existed in the Soviet system, policy differences could be detected within these publications, particularly after
the Stalinist era and in relation to foreign policy.[16] At that stage,
however, the political élite which participated in discussion about
policy consisted of a far smaller section of the intelligentsia and differences of opinion were rarely expressed openly. Wider participation in policy debates was encouraged when Mikhail Gorbachev
adopted glasnost as an important aspect of his reform programme,

partly in an attempt to engage the intelligentsia in the process of reform. Gorbachev thus revived and encouraged the culture of robust political debate in Russia. The debate about foreign policy is a continuation of that tradition. Most of its participants, however, are concerned professionally with foreign policy.

## Who are Russia's foreign policy élites?

The participants in the debates which form the subject matter of this chapter include politicians, academic specialists, journalists, and diplomats. Among the politicians, members of the presidential and government administration participated in the debate, as well as those who were outside the administration, or in opposition to it. The parliamentarians who engaged in the debate tended, on the whole, to be members of the Supreme Soviet commissions on foreign policy (the foreign policy programmes of the political parties to which they belonged are dealt with in Chapter 4), and many of them had previously been academic specialists or diplomats or both.[17] The movement of individual specialists between academia and politics and the administration (and, sometimes, back again to academia if their political fortunes changed) was fairly common in the Soviet system and remains a characteristic of the Russian foreign policy élite.[18]

Some of the academics were employed as advisers to President or Foreign Ministry, while others simply aspired to such positions (sometimes opportunistically looking for gaps in the arguments or adopting particular positions in order to establish their credentials). Moreover, because the new bureaucratic structures were inherently unstable (but constantly increasing in size), the foreign policy decision-making system was in flux (see Chapter 3), and policy changed rapidly and often without warning, there was a relatively rapid turnover of advisers. Thus participants were sometimes associated with one part of the administration at a particular stage of the debate, and with another, or speaking independently, as the debate proceeded.[19]

It should also be noted that while many academics doubtless held strong and principled views about the kind of foreign policy that Russia should pursue, there was a certain amount of personal and institutional special pleading. All the institutes of the Russian

Academy of Sciences and their employees suffered very severely from cuts in public expenditure and high and ever-increasing inflation. While individual specialists might hope to supplement their incomes by becoming professional consultants or official advisers, these positions would be in short supply unless the area in which they specialized was seen to be relevant. Similarly, the continued existence of certain institutes depended upon establishing the centrality of the region it studied to Russian policy. It is not surprising, therefore, that many of the academics who advocated a broadening of Russian foreign policy beyond the initial concentration on the West worked at area studies institutes specializing in the Third World or the East.[20]

The desire and need of academics to be engaged in policy-relevant research and writing points to a striking contrast between the foreign policy debate in Russia and published work in the Soviet Union. Although in the Soviet system many academics were commissioned through their institutes to write policy-relevant analyses related to Soviet foreign policy which were privately circulated to the commissioning Party body or ministry, only the most ideologically reliable senior specialists published work on Soviet foreign policy as such. Moreover, there was little room to be creative or independent-minded about Soviet policy. As a result, most *mezhdunarodniki* (as international relations scholars were called) specialized in the foreign policy of foreign countries, and few studied their own foreign policy.[21] Today, however, few people study foreign countries except in relation to their policies towards Russia. The vast majority of academics are engaged in research on Russian foreign policy or the foreign policy of the other former Soviet republics.

Two other characteristics of the participants in the debate about Russian foreign policy should be borne in mind. First, funds for academic institutions have become scarce and career opportunities in the business world have become more attractive. As a result, the academic community has shrunk and there is a dearth of young specialists in particular. Second, functioning diplomats have frequently contributed to the discussion about foreign policy in the Gorbachev period and after in the Soviet Union and in Russia, sometimes publishing views which contradict the policy they have been implementing.[22] This is very unlike the western tradition of civil servants (including diplomats) remaining silent, anonymous, and loyal supporters of government policy.

*Criteria for selection of material*

When the Soviet Union disintegrated, Russia not only took over its diplomatic institutions. It also inherited most of its academic institutes and think-tanks, which were transferred to the Russian Academy of Sciences. Moreover, most of the Soviet academic and popular scientific journals had been published in Moscow and they remained there, becoming Russian publications. Similarly, the Soviet national daily and weekly press simply became Russian, and a number of new newspapers were established. These journals and newspapers provided a forum for contributions to the debate about the direction that Russian domestic and foreign policy should take. Much of the material used in this chapter has been published in these journals and newspapers.

Most of the material was selected for its substantive content, so as to provide a representative sample of the major ideas and the tone of the debate. Attention has primarily been concentrated on the contributions of people who were prominent participants in the foreign policy debate. However, in order to give a fuller picture of the ideas which can be related to a particular group of analysts, material has sometimes been used from lesser-known specialists. Since it *was* a debate rather than the presentation of an ideology, none of the people who are categorized as Liberal Westernizers or Pragmatic Nationalists began with a complete blueprint about the nature of the post-Cold War international system or of Russia's role in that system. In fact, their ideas evolved both in reaction to events, and in the course of exchanging views with one another. This, in part, explains why some analysts who began at one end of the spectrum seemed to move over towards the other end during the debate. In the case of the Fundamentalist Nationalists, those with communist sympathies could turn to the old ideology, while those who were more nationalistically inclined had recourse to earlier Eurasian and geopolitical views. It is easier to detect an entire world-view in their discussions of foreign policy.

As we shall see in the conclusion, it is difficult to be precise about the effect of the debate on policy, and to judge whether Russian foreign policy would have changed in the absence of any arguments about its fundamental principles. It is always difficult to work out the precise relationship between ideas and action, no matter how well-established the country. With regard to Russia it is clear, however, that foreign policy practitioners were as active in discussing foreign policy principles as armchair academics.

## The debate

As far as concrete policy was concerned, it can be argued that for the first few months of its existence as an independent state, Russia's foreign policy was almost entirely reactive. The attention of foreign policy officials was focused, first, on establishing the Commonwealth of Independent States (CIS); second, on trying to please the West, particularly the United States; and third, on taking over those international positions which Russia had inherited from the Soviet Union.

With regard to the 'near abroad', there was great difficulty in redefining what had been domestic politics as foreign policy.[23] The problem was compounded by the fact that there was no specialized knowledge about the former republics of the Soviet Union in the Ministry of Foreign Affairs (MFA) and very little elsewhere (see Chapter 3).[24] As far as Russian policy towards the West was concerned, it was difficult but important to distance Yeltsin's concepts and Russian foreign policy from those of Gorbachev and the Soviet Union. As one journalist expressed it, 'the first half of 1992 saw something of a policy of "discarding the positions of the ex-Soviet Union."'[25] There was also a need to demonstrate Russia's democratic and market credentials and its loyalty to Western policies, since this was perceived to be a *sine qua non* for Western aid. Published discussion of Russian foreign policy was, therefore, in many ways simply a continuation or a repudiation of past debates about Soviet policy and about the New Political Thinking.[26]

### The initial debate

Apart from the President, Foreign Minister Andrei Kozyrev was the most influential proponent of the pro-Western line when the Russian Federation first attained independence. Indeed, the debate about Russian foreign policy began with criticism of his policy. It makes sense, therefore, to begin by looking at his views. At first Kozyrev was very resistant to spelling out a foreign policy programme. Russia's goal, he maintained, was to establish 'friendly and eventually allied relations with the civilised world, including

NATO, the UN and other structures'. This would be a pragmatic process and thought should be given to how it should be carried out, rather than to general principles. Since the means by which Russia's national interests could best be achieved would change over time, any foreign policy concept would be subject to constant modification.[27] Under pressure from opponents and supporters, however, Kozyrev gradually began to talk about the principles underlying Russian foreign policy. Nevertheless, he remained more comfortable discussing concrete policy than elaborating a set of principles which, he believed, were self-evident.

Kozyrev maintained that the New Political Thinking of the Gorbachev years had been a useful antidote to the Messianism of the past, but he was critical of its idealism. Despite his scepticism, however, many of the phrases he used—'the unity of home and foreign policies'; 'parity of security'; 'minimum sufficiency'—came straight from the lexicon of the New Political Thinking. Moreover, just as Eduard Shevardnadze had based his arguments in favour of the New Political Thinking on the domestic economic needs of the Soviet Union, Kozyrev declared that the responsibility of foreign policy was to create conditions in which Russia could prosper, in particular by returning to the international economic system which it had abandoned when the revolution occurred. He maintained that 'foreign policy can be neither a mere onlooker nor an occasional lobbyist in regard to the country's economic interests' and he called, very much as Shevardnadze had done, for the 'economization' of Russian foreign policy. In his view there was a direct link between democracy and a successful market economy. The national interest, therefore, lay in 'transforming Russia into a free, independent state, formalizing democratic institutions, setting up an effective economy, guaranteeing the rights and freedoms of all Russians, making our people's life rich both materially and spiritually'.[28]

According to Kozyrev, the key to Russia's transformation was membership of the club of developed democratic states and the international institutions which they had created. Russian history and geography and its great-power status determined that Russia would occupy a worthy place in these institutions. Other Westernizers agreed that Russian foreign policy ought to be subordinated to the goal of ensuring favourable conditions for a gradual shift from the periphery to the centre of the international economy. They believed that Russia and the West were now partners, rather than adversaries, and that since they shared the same values, they were likely to face similar dangers.[29] Unlike Kozyrev, however, some of them envisaged a potential conflict between Russia's interests as a partner of the West and its role in the former Soviet Union. Co-operation and good relations with the advanced industrialized countries were Russia's first priority, they argued, and any policy which contradicted that aim should be eschewed.

Although most Westernizers recognized the importance of Russia's relations with its immediate neighbours, they warned that accepting the burden of the leading role in the CIS would undermine Russia's position *vis-à-vis* the West. While Kozyrev himself maintained that Russia's interests lay in patiently seeking co-ordination within the CIS, including a common army and an interconnected economy, other pro-Western analysts advised that 'the CIS should be seen as a temporary institution, the main aim of which is to regulate the process of disintegration of the former USSR.'[30] They warned that if Russia did become the dominant state in the CIS, it would willy-nilly inherit the great-power traditions of the Soviet Union which would prevent it from achieving its main task, which was to remain a European nation.[31] Should there be a choice between an Asian and a European orientation, Westernizers had no doubt that Russia should opt for Europe, even if this meant abandoning the CIS. Any illusions about Russia's special role as a bridge between Europe and Asia should be abandoned.[32]

The first doubts among the democrats about the unquestioning Western orientation of Russian foreign policy (which became known as Atlanticism) were voiced by Sergei Stankevich, a presidential adviser. According to Stankevich, 'Atlanticism is drawn to ... becoming part of Europe, entering the world economy as an organic component, joining the [Group of] Seven as an eighth member, putting the emphasis on Germany and the United States as the two dominant factors in the Atlantic Alliance.'[33] Dictated by the need for credits and aid, this policy might seem pragmatic and rational. But Stankevich counselled against relying too much on an Atlantic orientation. Other critics complained that the Russian Foreign Ministry was even more 'Euro-American-centric' than the Soviet Ministry of Foreign Affairs had been under Shevardnadze.[34] For all the good intentions of Kozyrev and his department, they had failed to formulate and identify Russia's national interests and priorities and their policy was essentially reactive. As a result, the domestic public believed that Russian decision makers were making endless unilateral concessions to the West in order to get economic aid and credits. The Foreign Ministry had thus failed to forge a domestic political base for its policy.[35] Moreover, in giving priority to relations with the West, the Foreign Ministry ignored the fact that Russia's relations with the 'near abroad' were the key to achieving its security and its economic and political interests, and thus to its future relations with the West. In terms of Russia's national interests, priority should be given to establishing friendly, or preferably allied, relations with the former Soviet republics.[36]

Stankevich argued that apart from Atlanticism, a second, less well-pronounced trend could be detected among those who were writing about Russian foreign policy: Eurasianism. Since Russia had already been irretrievably Europeanized, the extreme Eurasian views of the nineteenth century were no longer relevant. But Stankevich approved of a modified Eurasianism entailing a balance of Western and Eastern orientations. He pointed out that Russia's geographic separation from Europe meant that it would have to turn to the East. Moreover, it would be many years before Russia could be more than a junior partner of the advanced industrialized states. In the mean time it should develop relations with 'second echelon' states in Latin America, Africa, Europe, and Asia. Warning that abandoning the Messianism of the past should not imply the complete rejection of a sense of mission, Stankevich proposed that Russia should resume its historic role, which he defined as unifying and reconciling Orthodoxy and Islam. It should extend this role by using its position in the UN to promote and support 'a multilateral dialogue of cultures, civilizations, and states'.[37]

While Stankevich envisaged Russia as pacifier, mediator, and unifier in the wider world, a picture reminiscent of the traditional Soviet perception of Russia's role in the empire, the policy he recommended *vis-à-vis* the CIS seemed to contradict this image. Russia should take a firmer stance, he argued, particularly with regard to the political and economic rights of Russians living in the successor states to the USSR. Russian policy in the 'near abroad', including economic and financial relations and the withdrawal of troops, should depend upon the way in which Russian minorities were treated. He also advocated that Russian policy towards CIS members should distinguish between those countries which saw the

CIS as a transitional institution with the primary function of dividing up the spoils of the Union before its final disintegration, and
those which actively chose membership. While it was senseless and
dangerous to make concessions in the hope of keeping the former
in the CIS, as strategic allies the latter should be given preferential
treatment.[38]

Other, less trenchant, critics of immoderate Atlanticism pointed
out that there were bound to be conflicts of interest between Western countries and Russia. They also argued that the advanced industrialized states would use their special relationship with Russia to
prevent it becoming too strong, since the emergence of a powerful
Russian state would not be in the interests of the West. While a
Western orientation should be pursued, therefore, Russia should
not forget the South, with which it had common borders. Morever,
it should retain the political and international positions it had
inherited from the Soviet Union.[39] This would give the Russian
government bargaining power: partnership with the West would
strengthen its position *vis-à-vis* the East and South, whereas partnership with the East and South would give Russia some independence
in its relationship with the West.[40] From an economic point of view,
closer relations with the newly industrialized countries of the Pacific
and the Middle East would be enormously beneficial.[41] Some military specialists, while generally supportive of Russia's pro-Western
policy, worried that Yeltsin's arms proposals were ill-considered
and impossible to put into effect without incurring huge costs and
seriously undermining Russian security.[42]

It is important to stress that these critics were not anti-Western;
they simply argued for a more rational analysis of Russia's national
interests and for a balanced policy. As far as domestic developments were concerned, they were firmly democratic and they supported the construction of a market economy. However worried
they were about the problem of establishing a new Russian identity within what they saw as artificial borders, they did not express
overt nostalgia for the Soviet Union or for the Russian empire.
There *were* critics who mourned 'the decline of the thousand-year-
old Russian statehood and the ultimate breakdown of the USSR', or
who saw the formation of the CIS as a device 'for inflicting a mon-
strous defeat on Russian interests', but they tended to come from
the Fundamentalist Nationalist end of the political continuum.[43]

On the other hand, it is clear that Stankevich's modified

Eurasianism and his view of Russia's mission were not dissimilar in the rhetoric he used to express them from the high-flown phrases of more nationalistically inclined scholars and politicians. Nataliya Narochnitskaya, for example, a Fundamentalist Nationalist who was among the first to use the double-headed eagle of Russia's crest (which has now become a cliché) as a symbol, described Russia's historic mission as that of a 'power maintaining a balance between West European and Oriental civilisations'. Elgiz Pozdnyakov, another scholar with Fundamentalist Nationalist views, maintained that the distinctive character of Russia's geopolitical status was 'an intermediate position between two great world civilisations, Occidental and Oriental . . . a holder of the world balance of forces'. He clearly regretted the passing of the strong centralized state on which this role had rested.[44]

If Stankevich believed in a modified Eurasianism, the Fundamentalist Nationalists whole-heartedly adopted Eurasianism in its original nineteenth- and early twentieth-century form. Some combined it with a close and very literal reading of the early twentieth-century geopolitical theory that had been the theoretical inspiration for Hitler's policy of *lebensraum*. Basing themselves on Sir Halford Mackinder's theories about the superiority of land power over maritime power, they argued that Russia was the 'heartland' which, in alliance with Germany, could conquer the world. They interpreted the new world order as a struggle between Atlanticism and Eurasianism in which Atlanticism (in other words the West) temporarily had gained the upper hand.[45] Behind the idea of a new world order, however, they saw a plot by America to construct a world government.

Conspiracies figured prominently in the writing of Fundamentalist Nationalists; not uncommonly the Western or American plot was portrayed as inspired by Masons and Jews.[46] A belief in the special character of Eurasians, therefore, was accompanied by anti-Westernism and anti-Semitism. Curiously, however, Fundamentalist Nationalists did not, on the whole, proclaim a theory of racial purity. Indeed, one aspect of Eurasianism was its multinationalism, its portrayal of the unique unity of Muslim and Orthodox, of Russian and Eastern.[47] None the less, rejecting any suggestion that there are universal values, they castigated 'mondialism' and called for a return to traditional values. It is clear that the tradition which they had in mind was that of Russian Orthodoxy.[48]

Many Fundamentalist Nationalists believed that the Russian empire should be recreated and that the Russian Federation was 'an offspring of Bolshevik experiments . . . , an unnatural formation'.[49] Russian membership of the IMF was a catastrophe which would lead to America enriching itself at Russia's expense.[50] As far as Russian domestic politics and economics were concerned, Fundamentalist Nationalists interpreted Eurasianism not just in geographic terms but as a 'third way', rejecting economic liberalism, individualism, and democracy in favour of authoritarianism and corporatism.[51]

Much of the Fundamentalist Nationalist writing about international relations was highly mystical. Although the communists cooperated with them in an alliance of national-patriotic forces and were, by and large, in agreement about the causes of the breakup of the Soviet Union, the need to reconstruct a union, and the possibility of an economic alternative to the free market, they eschewed the geopolitical theories and the arcane spirituality of the nationalists.[52] Indeed, their mysticism often made it difficult to imagine that anyone could take Fundamentalist Nationalist theories seriously. As we have seen, however, Pragmatic Nationalists adopted some elements of the theories of the fundamentalists. Moreover, powerful politicians like former Vice-President Rutskoi were sympathetic to some of their ideas.

## The second stage of the debate

In the early months of 1992 the Russian government seemed undecided how to establish the collective defence of the CIS: whether there should be separate Russian and CIS armed forces and, if so, what the relationship should be between them. Under these circumstances it was difficult to formulate a concept of Russian national security separate from the security of the former Soviet Union. The presidential decree in May 1992 which established the armed forces of the Russian Federation thus marked a further stage in the consolidation of Russian sovereignty, and in the separation of Russia from the former Soviet Union. It was followed by a decree, 'On National Security', which established a National Security Council responsible to, and under the chairmanship of, the President.[53] The establishment of the Russian Defence Ministry and the Security Council helped to mobilize Kozyrev's critics. These events, and the response to Stankevich's article, provided the background to the second stage of public discussion about Russian foreign policy.

Many people now called for the formulation and adoption of an official foreign policy concept, and the participants in the debate hoped to influence its contents. The debate thus centred around what Russia's national interests were, and what kind of foreign policy the country should have. As in the first stage, the discussants were primarily concerned with Russia's relations with the West and with the 'near abroad'. The division of opinion became more complex, however, than a simple division into Atlanticists and Eurasians, neither paying much attention to the Fundamentalist Nationalists.

In the course of trying to define Russia's national interests, many commentators who had taken for granted that Western and Russian interests would be identical began to question their own assumptions. Many of them were influenced by the Fundamentalist Nationalists, who became increasingly vocal as domestic political quarrels intensified into open conflict between President and parliament, and between President and Vice-President. It was at this stage, therefore, that the 'modified Eurasians' (as Stankevich called them) began to elaborate a set of ideas about Russian foreign policy which were more pragmatic than those of the Liberal Westernizers, and which they legitimized through moderate, but unmistakably nationalist, views. This is the group which we have called Pragmatic Nationalists. It should be noted that they came, primarily, from among the Liberal Westernizers; in other words, there was a general shift in reformist circles along the spectrum towards more nationalist views.

It is worth repeating, however, that there was considerable overlap in the views of the three 'schools of thought' about domestic and foreign policy. Both Liberal Westernizers and Pragmatic Nationalists stressed the importance of relations with the West, for example, although they differed in the priority and exclusivity they accorded to these relations. Similarly, both Pragmatic and Fundamentalist Nationalists expressed Eurasianist views. The distinction between them with regard to Eurasia lay primarily in how they envisaged implementing their ideas. All three groups also agreed that Russia was responsible for the welfare of Russians in the diaspora. They differed, however, about what the Russian government should do to fulfil its obligations. Moreover, there was some confusion about who was Russian in this context.[54] Some analysts believed that Russia's protection should be restricted to the 25 million Russian nationals who lived in the other fourteen former Soviet republics. Others thought that all Russian-speaking people in the 'near abroad' whose future citizenship and civil rights appeared to be in jeopardy should be defended.[55] All three groups insisted that Russia was, and would continue to be, a great power. They differed, however, on what the implications of great-power status were for Russian foreign policy. It should also be noted that it was not unusual for analysts to change their minds. Indeed, this chapter argues that it was precisely when influential policy makers of Liberal Westernizer persuasion adopted Pragmatic Nationalist views that a broad consensus began to emerge about the principles which should underlie Russian foreign policy. As we shall see, this consensus marked the beginning of the third stage of the debate.

Before we go into the specifics of the different points of view, it is worth pausing for a moment to look at the views of a scholar whose work offers the most direct continuity with the New Political Thinking of the late 1980s. Nikolai Kosolapov stressed the link between Russia's domestic structure and its foreign policy, and recognized the extent to which the structure of the post-Cold War international system would determine Russian foreign policy. Many other participants in the debate about Russian foreign policy had views about Russia's domestic structure but they concentrated their attention on whether a market economy would develop, and whether it would resemble Western market economies or acquire specific Russian features. They also argued about the role of the state: Liberal Westernizers, advised by Western monetarist economists, usually favoured a non-interventionist state. But there was an increasingly widespread belief that one of the peculiar features of Russia was that a market economy would develop only if there was a strong state.[56] Of the analysts who paid attention to domestic structures, few considered the relationship between Russia's foreign policy and its domestic political system.

Kosolapov, on the other hand, maintained that the key variable in Russia's foreign policy would be the relationship between state and society. If, as the statists proposed, the 'state over society' model which had always been characteristic of Russia prevailed, it was likely that Russia would return to its old foreign policy traditions, whether or not it developed a market economy. But if society managed to control the state and make it serve its interests, Russian tradition would be broken. New social and political élites would form, the constitution, political system, and political processes would be different, and the conceptualization of Russia's national interest and the implementation of its foreign policy would reflect these changes. The implication of Kosolapov's analysis was that the primary concern of Russian theorists and policy makers should be the establishment and consolidation of a democratic, liberal domestic political system rather than the construction of an abstract set of foreign policy principles.

Kosolapov also argued that the structure of the international system was an important determinant of foreign policy. The central imperative of Russian foreign policy was not a choice between Atlanticism and Eurasianism, he maintained, but participation in the construction of a democratic international system based on the United Nations and on various regional organizations (including the CIS). Such a system would serve Russian interests because it would compensate for the country's deficit in effective traditional foreign policy instruments and levers. He warned, however, that this did not imply a new brand of international Messianism. Russia could not and should not create the system unilaterally: it should participate but not dictate.[57] Kosolapov represents, perhaps, the clearest example of a Liberal Westernizer: pro-Western, explicitly linking democracy at home with participation both in a liberal, democratic international order and in a freely formed, democratically based regional association of legally equal, sovereign post-Soviet states. Other Liberal Westernizers were less detailed and less clear in their thinking about the connection between domestic politics and foreign policy, and they concentrated more on Russia's predicament and less on the international and subsystemic arrangements in which Russia should participate.

In August 1992 the editors of *Izvestiya* acquired a copy of the recommendations made by the chairman of the Supreme Soviet Committee on International Affairs and Foreign Economic Relations, Yevgeny Ambartsumov, to the Foreign Minister following a closed meeting at which Kozyrev reported to the Committee on the progress which had been made in formulating a foreign policy concept for Russia. An *Izvestiya* journalist published an article criticizing Ambartsumov's recommendations. The quotations he gives from the recommendations serve as a succinct summary of the Pragmatic Nationalist viewpoint, while his case against the Committee's views is an equally concise exposition of the position of the Liberal Westernizers.

Ambartsumov maintained that many people perceived Kozyrev's foreign policy as 'a disorderly retreat and complete capitulation to the West'. Although he recognized that the Russian Federation could not occupy the international role that the Soviet Union had enjoyed and he agreed that Russia should build good relations with the United States and other members of the Group of Seven, he argued that this should not imply abandoning an independent foreign policy. As far as the 'near abroad' was concerned, Ambartsumov insisted that Russia's sphere of vital interests encompassed the entire geopolitical space of the former Soviet Union. He compared Russia's interests in this area to America's Monroe Doctrine and argued that international society should respect Russia's special interests, recognizing its right to be the political and military guarantor of stability throughout the former Soviet Union. Furthermore, the Group of Seven should offer more than simple moral support to Russia in its fulfilment of this role; it should also financially subsidize the rapid reaction forces that would be required to discharge it. He proposed that bilateral agreements with the states of the former Soviet Union and multilateral CIS agreements should include a clause according Russia the role of guarantor, and recognizing its right to defend 'the life and dignity of Russians in the "near abroad" '. Special agreements should be concluded on the status of Russian forces in the countries of the CIS.[58]

The Liberal Westernizer rejection of these views published in *Izvestiya* was uncompromising. Russian foreign policy was based on close identification with the developed democratic countries on questions of human rights and the rejection of aggression. The Monroe Doctrine dated from a different era and, in so far as the United States enjoyed a leading role on the American continent at present, it was based not on force but on America's undeniable social and economic influence. A Monroe Doctrine was inapplicable to the Russian Federation because the price of imposing it on the former republics of the USSR would be war, and armed conflict would bring Russia's democratic development to an end. It was, the journalist continued, preposterous to imagine that international society, which had just begun to construct a genuine collective security system, would subsidize Russia in the function of 'Eurasian gendarme'. Moreover, any attempt to station Russian forces in the 'near abroad' would undermine the difficult first steps that had been taken to establish military co-operation and integration within the CIS. The Russian government should certainly defend the interests of Russians in the 'near abroad', but the instruments it uses should not include military force.[59] Other Liberal Westernizers pointed out that if democratic principles were not used to settle conflicts, 'nationalism would become rife . . . and this would be no normal nationalism, but a distorted and bellicose form of chauvinism.' Russia's real security interests lay not in imposing a Monroe Doctrine, but in 'gradual, careful but certain integration into a security system with the West . . . establishing firm institutional ties with NATO as a whole and with the USA'.[60]

As far as the West was concerned, the Liberal Westernizers and Pragmatic Nationalists thus both agreed that it was important that Russia should maintain good, friendly, and co-operative relations with the advanced industrialized countries. As Kozyrev put it, 'the West is wealthy, we must be friendly with it.'[61] They also recognized that it was important that Russia should establish relations with other countries in the 'far abroad'. The major differences in their views about the West concerned the priority that they felt should be accorded to relations with the major industrialized states as opposed to 'second echelon' states in the far abroad, and whether they believed that Russia should follow the Western lead in responding to international political events, or thought that it should establish its own independent foreign policy line. It was in relation to concrete events that their differences became most obvious: each time the Russian government followed the Western lead, it was subjected to criticism from both Fundamentalist Nationalists and Pragmatic Nationalists. Their response to Russian policy towards the conflict in former Yugoslavia illustrates the problem.

When the war began in Bosnia in 1992, both Yeltsin and Kozyrev believed that the conflict could be settled without recourse to sanctions against Serbia and Montenegro. In part this reflected a strong sense in Moscow that there was a special relationship between Russians and Serbs, as fellow Orthodox Slavs, and that Serbia had been unjustly labelled as the only aggressor in the wars of secession from Yugoslavia. There was, too, a strong echo of New Political Thinking in the policy of the Russian government:

Gorbachev's attitude to regional conflict had been imbued with the idea that negotiated, and essentially political, solutions could be found to bring conflicts within and between states to a peaceful end.[62] Yeltsin and Kozyrev seemed to adopt a similar formula with regard to the conflicts in the former Yugoslavia. By the end of May, however, Kozyrev had to admit that his shuttle diplomacy between Bosnia and Serbia had failed to produce a cease-fire. As a result, Russia supported the United Nations Security Council resolution which imposed economic sanctions against Serbia and Montenegro.

Given that the Fundamentalist Nationalists set great store by the links that bind Slavs and Orthodox believers, it is not surprising that they were highly critical of Russian policy. They published documents which had been leaked to them and which purported to prove that Kozyrev was serving American and not Russian interests. But the Pragmatic Nationalists were almost as vociferously opposed to sanctions as were the Fundamentalist Nationalists. Ambartsumov, for example, accused the Foreign Minister of kowtowing to the United States, while Alexei Arbatov claimed that 'Russia missed an opportunity to gain the initiative in stopping the war, using its historic special relationship with Serbs.'[63] Both Fundamentalist and Pragmatic Nationalists became more comfortable with Russian policy in Yugoslavia when Russia began again to take a more independent line at the end of 1992.

The differences between the views of the Liberal Westernizers and Pragmatic Nationalists were far more substantial at this time with regard to Russian policy in the 'near abroad'. While the Fundamentalist Nationalists wished to restore the unity of the former Soviet Union,[64] by the middle of 1992 both Liberal Westernizers and Pragmatic Nationalists recognized that the independence of the former Soviet republics was a *fait accompli* and that the 'near abroad' represented a vital sphere of Russian foreign policy. There were three separate issues that concerned them in connection with Russia's relations with the 'near abroad'. The first related to the future of the CIS. While both groups believed that it would be best if close, co-operative relations were established within the organization, they disagreed about the efforts and sacrifices that Russia should be prepared to make to bring about economic, political, and military integration. The second issue related to the conflicts on the periphery of the Russian Federation. Both groups believed that Russian security was threatened by these conflicts, and both were concerned that they might spread into the Russian Federation and undermine its fragile integrity. They disagreed, however, about whether and in what way Russia should become involved in bringing them to an end. The third issue concerned Russians who, after the disintegration of the Soviet Union, had become foreigners in independent countries the governments of which seemed unwilling to guarantee their civil rights, irrespective of the stand they had taken with regard to the issues of the sovereignty and independence of the republic. While both groups agreed that Russia should be responsible for the fate of Russians in the diaspora, they disagreed about the implications of this responsibility for Russian foreign policy.

Although regular CIS meetings had taken place since the founding meeting on 21 December 1991 in Almaty, and numerous agreements had been signed, it was rarely the case that all members signed a particular agreement, and many resolutions were simply declarations of intent. Furthermore, as was noted in Chapter 1, few agreements that were reached were implemented. On the one hand, this reflected the fact that some members (for example, Ukraine and Turkmenistan) regarded the CIS as no more than a convenient means of managing the dissolution of the ties that had held the USSR together, while others (for example, Kazakhstan and Kyrgyzstan) saw it as an institution through which new forms of integration would be established. On the other hand, it was also a symptom of Russian indecision about what the CIS should be.

Fyodor Shelov-Kovedyaev, Deputy Foreign Minister in charge of relations in the former Soviet Union, maintained that Russia should actively promote integration within the CIS, and convince other members of the advantages it would bring. He opposed the use of pressure to impose integration, however, arguing that the successful development of Russia's economy would turn it into the 'partner of choice' for other CIS states.[65] Shelov-Kovedyaev's views were at the liberal edge of the Pragmatic Nationalist spectrum. While no government officials went on record as opposing the kind of integration he proposed, their actions (for example, financial measures such as declaring certain denominations of banknotes invalid or withdrawing old banknotes, which created severe difficulties in the republics in which the currency was the rouble) seemed designed to ensure disintegration rather than integration:

in other words, there was considerable disarray within the government itself on the issue of integration. More conservative Pragmatic Nationalists stressed both the interdependence of the CIS states and the dependence of most of them on Russia, which would, they thought, inevitably propel them towards economic integration.

Some Liberal Westernizers were rather optimistic about the future of the CIS, seeing the European Union as the model the Commonwealth might follow. Their theories echoed those of the early European functionalists: co-operation between governments, they thought, might be slow and difficult but horizontal links established between firms in different republics as they co-operated in producing and marketing goods would have spillover effects in due course, which would make functional agreements over a wider range of issues necessary.[66] They seemed to envisage an organic and gradual evolution towards economic integration.

Other Liberal Westernizers took a gloomier view of the prospects for the CIS, arguing that cultural and political diversity within the CIS, and the absence of market or democratic reforms in most of its members, were serious obstacles to integration. Far from Russian reforms acting as an example, the absence of change in the other states would retard the development of the Russian economy. Moreover, integration could harm the Russian economy: since some republics had received far more from the central Soviet budget before the breakup of the USSR than they had contributed to it, the integration of their independent economies with the Russian economy would once again require subsidies from Russia. This would severely handicap Russia's economic recovery.[67] They also believed that there were political costs to greater integration. Given that it was the European republics which were most reluctant to co-operate within the framework of the Commonwealth, the CIS would turn into a 'Russian-Central Asian alliance', which would deflect Russia from its more important interest in developing strong relations with Western Europe.[68] In any case, Russia's dominant position (which did not depend on what government was in power but simply reflected its incomparably greater size) would continue to make other members wary of integration.

Those Liberal Westernizers who were unenthusiastic about the CIS pointed out that bilateral relations between members were developing far faster than multilateral, institutional links, and that few co-ordinating mechanisms had got off the ground. But they also warned that relations within the CIS were, like those in the USSR, vertical rather than horizontal: in other words, bilateral relations between Russia and individual republics predominated over bilateral relations between other republics, and government-to-government relations predominated over links between firms or between non-governmental institutions. Thus Moscow was still acting as the 'centre', and this situation both caused suspicion in the other states and encouraged neo-imperialist chauvinism in Russia. Liberal Westernizers wondered whether Russia required the myth of a Commonwealth to 'moderate the nostalgic memory of the defunct USSR' and whether it did not, in fact, simply fuel disputes rather than providing the conditions for successful integration.[69]

But there were more acute problems within the CIS than the question of integration. Although some analysts pointed out that, seen in historical perspective, the disintegration of the Soviet Union had been remarkably peaceful, commentators of all persuasions were worried about the conflicts on the periphery of the Russian Federation. Not only was Russia's security threatened by these conflicts; many thought that its territorial integrity was in jeopardy. Both Liberal Westernizers and Pragmatic Nationalists thought that the borders of the CIS should be frozen on the principles established by the Helsinki Act, allowing for revision only via peaceful negotiations. Any attempt to change them by force, they maintained, would open a Pandora's box.[70] Sensible though this view was, however, it did not address the problem of what Russia's response should be to situations where secessionist movements had already made a bid for independence, leading to violent conflict.

Liberal Westernizers insisted that Russia should not become entangled in conflicts in the 'near abroad'. They were concerned that the Russian troops still stationed in the 'near abroad' would be drawn involuntarily into local conflicts and seemed unaware of the extent to which Russian military commanders on the ground were, in fact, making their own policy, often interfering in local conflicts (for example, in Transdniestria). They favoured United Nations or CSCE participation in the settlement of the conflicts on the periphery of Russia.[71]

Pragmatic Nationalists also worried about the presence of Russian troops in the 'near abroad', and their voluntary or involuntary influence on local conflicts. But they argued that Russia had no option but to play an active post-imperial role in the former

Soviet Union, containing conflict and protecting minority groups. They wanted the United Nations or the CSCE to approve and support Russia's role as peacekeeper under the auspices of the CIS. Sergei Karaganov, for example, a prominent early exponent of Pragmatic Nationalism, proposed a division of peacekeeping responsibility within the CSCE area: NATO and the European Community should keep the peace in Europe, while Russia would ensure stability within the CIS. He insisted, however, that there should be international control of Russian peacekeeping activities.[72] By March 1993, this had become the policy of the Russian government. In an address to the Civic Union on 28 February, President Yeltsin spoke about Russia's special responsibilities for stability in the 'near abroad', and in March the Russian government proposed to the United Nations that the CIS should be recognized as a regional organization which could deal with local conflict under the auspices of the United Nations.[73]

The problem of conflict in the 'near abroad' was related to the fate of the 25 million Russians who lived outside the Russian Federation. Both Liberal Westernizers and Pragmatic Nationalists widened the definition to include all Russian-speaking people and agreed that the Russian government should protect their welfare. They recognized that a mass exodus of Russian speakers from the 'near abroad' would have catastrophic economic consequences. The task, therefore, was to ensure their civil rights in the 'near abroad' and the problem was how to accomplish this.

Some Liberal Westernizers believed that the rights of the Russian-speaking people in the 'near abroad' should be tackled in the general context of human and minority rights, and by recourse to the guarantees and institutions of the United Nations and the CSCE. There was a real chance, they argued, that 'the problem of the rights of Russians outside Russia can be resolved by civilized means in the framework of the mutual understanding with the West about general human values and the specific features of each country, whether it is Russia, Germany, Yugoslavia or Ukraine.'[74] Pragmatic Nationalists were less optimistic about the efficacy of international norms. They thought that sanctions, including the use of military force as the instrument of last resort, might be necessary. They should be used multilaterally, however, and with the agreement of the United Nations or the CSCE.[75] However, Russia should make it known that if a case arose where international action proved too slow or ineffective, 'it did not exclude unilateral actions—political and economic sanctions and even, as a last resort, direct coercive action.'[74]

Many of the views expressed about Russia's relations with the 'near' and 'far abroad' were intended to influence the content of Russia's foreign policy concept. Let us turn now to the adoption of the concept and its contents.

## The official foreign policy concept

The first attempt by the Foreign Ministry to formulate a foreign policy concept, in February 1992, was sent back to the drawing board by the Supreme Soviet, whose members complained that it was too abstract. A modified version was presented in April, and President Yeltsin assured the Sixth Congress of People's Deputies that work on the concept was proceeding. In response to the many criticisms of his policy and to build up political and academic support, Kozyrev established a consultative body, the Council on Foreign Policy, to advise the Foreign Ministry in July 1992. In November a new draft concept was circulated and an amended version was finally published in January 1993. In the meanwhile a non-governmental organization had been established to discuss Russian foreign and defence policy. Consisting of members of the foreign policy élite who represented a range of different political views, it was called the Council on Foreign and Defence Policy, and in August 1992 it published 'A Strategy for Russia', setting out what it believed should be Russia's foreign policy priorities.[77]

After prolonged discussion of the concept by representatives of the Ministries of Foreign Affairs, Foreign Economic Relations, and Defence, the intelligence services, the Security Council, and the Supreme Soviet Committees on Foreign and Foreign Economic Policy, Defence, and Security, a revised draft was agreed and approved by the Council on Foreign Policy and the Security Council, presented to parliament in February 1993, and confirmed by President Yeltsin in April. A comparison of the draft concept circulated by the Ministry of Foreign Affairs in November 1992 with the version published in January 1993, and of the original and amended Foreign Ministry drafts with the Council on Foreign and Defence Policy's 'Strategy for Russia' illustrates that the Liberal Westernizers

and the Pragmatic Nationalists were concerned with the same problems, although they emphasized different issues. And comparing
the three drafts with the version that was finally adopted indicates
that, by and large, the official concept bore more resemblance to
the views of the Pragmatic Nationalists than to the initial views of
the Liberal Westernizers.

Although the November draft of the Foreign Ministry document was circulated, the January version was published in full,
and the discussion surrounding the document was widely reported,
the final version confirmed by Yeltsin remained classified. It was
described, however, in an article which, according to a member of
the Presidential Council, had been 'authorized' by the President.[78]
Two features of the various drafts of the concept and the report
of the final version are particularly striking: first, throughout the
process more and more attention was accorded to the 'near abroad',
and second, although good relations with the West remained a
high priority for Russian foreign policy, the documents made it
increasingly clear that the 'honeymoon period' of expecting full
compatibility between Russian and Western interests had ended.

According to the preamble of the draft concept published by
the Foreign Ministry, Russia's most important foreign policy tasks
were to bring an end to the military clashes and regulate the conflicts on the periphery of Russia, to prevent them from spreading
onto Russian territory. In the November draft the Russian government was to ensure that individual and minority rights, 'including those of ethnic Russians', were observed; the January version
strengthened and expanded the undertaking by adding to those of
Russians the rights of 'Russian-speaking populations'.[79] The section
on relations with the Baltic states reiterated the demand that the
Russian-speaking population be accorded full civil and social rights.
The heightened concern with the 'near abroad' (or, perhaps, simply
a recognition of geopolitical necessity) was indicated by the fact
that it was listed first in the section of both drafts which set out
the main directions of Russian foreign policy and by the frequency
with which it was mentioned in other sections of the concept.

The Council for Foreign and Defence Policy also declared that
the main danger to Russia's security emanated from its immediate neighbourhood and that the main task, therefore, would be
to regulate conflicts on the territory of the former USSR. As far as
individual and minority rights were concerned, the 'Strategy' stressed

that it was in Russia's interests that the Russians in the 'near abroad' should thrive *as a diaspora*. Russia should, by diplomatic means if possible, insist that Russian-speakers have guaranteed rights 'where they live'. The document went on to suggest various cultural implements of foreign policy which Russia should employ to ensure that these minorities remained Russian-speakers and that the Russian language remained 'the means of communication and of obtaining high-quality education throughout the former USSR'.[80]

According to the Foreign Ministry drafts, Russia should adopt a twofold strategy in its relations with the 'near abroad'. First, there should be the maximum possible degree of integration between the former Soviet republics in all important fields of activity. Since integration should be voluntary, however, the Foreign Ministry accepted that some CIS members would sign up for full integration, while others would agree only to co-operate in fields that suited their interests. The aim, however, should be to retain and develop 'a single economic space on the territory of the former Soviet Union' while moving towards reintegration on the basis of a market economy.[81]

The second aspect of Russia's strategy in the 'near abroad' concerned security. Both Foreign Ministry drafts maintained that Russia and the other republics were jointly responsible for ensuring the security and stability of the entire territory of the former Soviet Union. The January version added, however, that Russia bore the burden of peacekeeping in the CIS. Russia would, therefore, strive to create an effective system of collective security and to retain an integral CIS military infrastructure to safeguard the security of its members.[82] It would also attempt to regulate conflicts by establishing bilateral forms of mediation and peacekeeping, and by creating a multilateral peacemaking mechanism within the new integrative framework of the CIS on the basis of a United Nations or CSCE mandate.

The Foreign Ministry drafts stressed that Russia did not aspire to be the centre of the Commonwealth. On the other hand, there was a limit to the concessions Russia would offer to CIS members. It would defend itself by political and diplomatic means and in accordance with international law against unilateral actions by other CIS states which infringed Russian interests. Although it was generally opposed to the use of force in international politics,

Russia would envisage using it 'in strict accordance with the UN
Charter and other international laws' if its security was threatened
or in response to aggression.

The Council for Foreign and Defence Policy's 'Strategy' also
recommended a policy of 'variable-speed post-imperial integration' within the CIS. The long-term aim should be to create an
organization like the European Community. Efforts should be made
to establish permanent intergovernmental institutions to regulate
relations of various types and to renew the ties which had been
broken when the USSR disintegrated. The 'Strategy' was pess-
imistic about the possibility of establishing a system of collective
security in the former Soviet Union. While it recommended the
internationalization of conflict management in the 'near abroad',
it proposed that Russia should make it known that it would, if
necessary, undertake unilateral sanctions including, in extreme circumstances like the gross infringement of human rights, the use of
force. It recommended, however, that everything possible should
be done to ensure that the use of force was authorized by the international community.[83]

Although co-operation and partnership with the West were
deemed important goals of Russian foreign policy, the Foreign
Ministry drafts stressed the primacy of Russian national interests
and pointed out that it was conceivable that Russian and Western
interests would, in some circumstances, come into conflict. Russia
would co-operate with the West when it suited Russia's interests
and not as a form of 'payment' for aid. Among Western countries,
the United States was given priority. Here too, however, the Foreign Ministry drafts pointed out that the absence of antagonism
did not imply a completely conflict-free relationship.[84]

The Council for Foreign and Defence Policy argued that Russian economic and democratic reform and its policy in the 'near
abroad' would be impossible without co-operation with the developed countries of the 'far abroad'. A Western orientation should
remain Russia's priority. It argued against any tendency in Russia
towards neo-isolationism and advised that a careful balance be
struck between Europe and the United States. As far as Europe
was concerned, Russia's long-term aim should be entry into 'the
European economic and political area'. However, Russian interests were not identical to those of the European Union. Indeed,
the European Union's acquisition of a military dimension was not

in Russia's interests and Russia should, therefore, support the survival of NATO and aim to develop a partnership with it. Although the countries of Central Europe were not high on the list of Russian foreign policy priorities, Russia's interests would be adversely affected if they were to join a security system which excluded Russia.[85]

The continued 'economization' of Russian foreign policy was demonstrated by the inclusion of a section on economic reform in the Foreign Ministry drafts. The task of foreign policy, they stated, was to create a favourable environment in which Russia's economic problems could be resolved. This implied Western participation in the reform process and Russian access to international and regional markets, financial organizations, and scientific and technological projects.[86] The 'Strategy', on the other hand, expressed doubt that the West had the political will or the ability to participate fully in Russia's economic and political renaissance, pointing out that West European energies would be concentrated on the enlargement of the European Union. It recommended that the Russian government should adopt 'a strategy of aggressively asserting Russian economic and business interests abroad', including the export of arms.[87]

Other areas of interest for Russian foreign policy were mentioned in the Foreign Ministry draft concepts. The intention was expressed, for example, to revive economic and other relations with Eastern Europe, an area which was 'historically in the sphere of [Russia's] interests'. Balanced and stable relations would be established with the Asia-Pacific region, where Russia would use its influence to try to prevent the Korean People's Democratic Republic from repudiating the nuclear Non-Proliferation Treaty. Efforts should be made to settle post-war territorial problems, so that Russo-Japanese relations could develop in a direction which would meet their mutual interests. It was also essential that Russia should have intensive and good relations with China, so that other countries could not use the China card against Russia.

Russia's interest in South and West Asia was stated to be a function of the influence this area had on the situation within the CIS. There was a danger, for example, that the Tajik and Afghan conflicts would merge, and that inter-ethnic conflict in the CIS would be affected by the struggle between fundamentalist and secular Islam on the perimeter of the former Soviet Union. There was a similar danger that Middle Eastern conflicts would affect the CIS. Russia would continue to participate actively in the regulation of the Arab–Israeli conflict and to develop bilateral relations with Israel. At the same time, Russia should replace the Soviet friendship and co-operation treaties in the Middle East with more suitable agreements, being careful not to lose the political and economic advantages the treaties had afforded the USSR.[88] In the rest of the world (Latin America, Africa) Russia should similarly build on the positions established by the USSR and, at the same time, expand beyond this into co-operation with countries which had been ignored by the Soviet Union.

The 'Strategy' paid less attention to Russia's interests beyond the developed industrialized world. It argued, however, that the difficulties of penetrating Western markets would dictate a diversification of Russian policy and recommended that political and economic relations should be developed with politically and economically important Asian countries like Saudi Arabia, India, Egypt, the United Arab Emirates, Israel, and Iran. The authors of the 'Strategy' also warned that the change in the Russo–Chinese balance of power required careful attention to relations with China, which were as important to Russia as relations with Europe and America.[89]

Both the Foreign Ministry draft concepts and the 'Strategy' argued that although Cold War confrontation had ended, military threats would continue to exist. Thus force would continue to play a significant role in international relations. The Foreign Ministry drafts maintained that Russia should retain sufficient arms for defence and to deter potential threats but it did not specify the quantity or quality of forces required to fulfil these functions. The authors of the 'Strategy' devoted more attention to defence policy. In order to deter aggression, prevent the escalation of crises, and defend the country from internal unrest and external threats, they recommended creating a professional army with mobile rapid reaction forces on constant alert which could also be used for peacekeeping purposes.[90]

It can be seen that despite differences in emphasis, the Foreign Ministry concept and the 'Strategy for Russia' were based on similar perceptions of Russia's national interests. Where they differed quite markedly was in the way that they envisaged Russia's future domestic structure and their view of Russia's status in the world.

The assumption throughout the Foreign Ministry drafts was that Russia was already, and would continue to be, a democratic state, modelled on the Western industrial democracies. Indeed, the function of foreign policy was to ensure the conditions in which democratic development could prosper. It also assumed that the best economic system for Russia would be a market economy. The 'Strategy', on the other hand, expressed a preference for both democracy and the market, but pointed out that Russia was more likely to become a moderately authoritarian state with a mixed economy. Economic underdevelopment, the authors argued, would prevent early membership of the community of advanced industrialized states with effective democratic institutions. Moreover, the vested interests of the new ruling classes would make them oppose the complete openness of Russia's political institutions and economy.[91] Paradoxically (or perhaps in keeping with its general optimism about Russia's future), the Foreign Ministry's concepts insisted that Russia enjoyed great-power status. The authors of the 'Strategy', by contrast, argued that Russia had become a medium power and warned that its geostrategic ambitions should not exceed its limited capabilities.[92]

According to an article on the official concept, both the Foreign Ministry drafts and the 'Strategy for Russia' contributed to the version that was finally adopted in April 1993. In form it seemed to consist of the outline of the January Foreign Ministry draft, with the addition of sections on economic security, and on military security and defence policy. The Foreign Ministry's view that Russia was a great power seemed to have prevailed. This status gave Russia responsibility for the post-Cold War world order and for the maintenance of stability in the former Soviet Union, and formed the basis of its foreign policy concept.

The final version of the concept identified the potential threats to Russia's vital national interests as actions aimed at destroying the integrity of the country or the integration of the CIS, the violation of human rights and freedoms, the violent conflicts in contiguous states, and any steps which might be taken to weaken or destroy Russia's international positions. Nuclear proliferation remained a danger and the possibility existed that strategic stability would be undermined if other countries violated international arms-limitation agreements. Military security was a complex problem because of the disintegration of the Soviet Union. Considerable impatience was expressed in the report of the concept about the delay in sorting out the control and management of the strategic weapons of the former USSR, the destruction of the integrity of the Soviet defence system, and the undefined status of Russian troops stationed in the 'near abroad'.[93]

Russia also faced certain economic threats according to the final version of the concept. There was a danger, for example, that the progressive opening-up of the economy to the outside world would undermine Russia's economic self-sufficiency and its technological and industrial capacity. The report implied that other countries' attempts to restrict Russia's access to foreign markets and to advanced technology exacerbated the danger that Russia would remain a source of raw material and energy for the world economy. In the section on economic security, measures were listed which would create favourable conditions for Russia's foreign economic activity. These included retaining and developing economic links within the former Soviet Union, getting trade barriers against Russia lifted, and preventing unfair business practices by foreign firms directed against Russian enterprises and organizations. The state should support Russian industrial exports.

With regard to the 'near abroad', Russia would strive for the maximum possible degree of integration with those states that wished to co-operate. Russia's responsibility for ensuring the stability and security of the territory of the former Soviet Union demanded the development of an effective system of collective security, co-operation in strengthening the external borders of the CIS, and the retention of a military infrastructure sufficient to safeguard the security of its members. Particular emphasis was placed on the need for a peacekeeping mechanism which could operate on the basis of a United Nations or CSCE mandate.

Assuming that the article analysing the concept dealt with topics in the order in which they were covered in the final version, Eastern Europe was given precedence over Western Europe, and Russian policy towards Western Europe was listed before the relationship with the United States. As far as Eastern Europe was concerned, the official concept appeared to have adopted the Foreign Ministry formulation, referring to it as an area 'historically in Russia's sphere of interest'. Russia's policy in Yugoslavia was demonstrated by its participation in the United Nations and CSCE efforts to regulate the conflict. According to the report, the concept stressed that Russia started from the position that all the direct participants bore responsibility for the conflict.

Western Europe was the key to Russia's entry to the European political and economic space and the concept argued that Russia's interests would be seriously damaged if it were excluded from the integration of Europe. Like the Foreign Ministry drafts, the final version of the concept listed the areas in which Russia and the United States could co-operate but pointed to the possibility that their interests might not coincide. It also specified that the discrimination which limited Russian access to American high technology should be removed. With regard to Japan, the search would continue for a solution to the territorial problem which did not harm Russia's interests.

If the published report on Russia's official foreign concept was an accurate reflection of the document that President Yeltsin signed, the tone of the final version differed from that of either the Foreign Ministry drafts or the 'Strategy'. Where the latter two were matter of fact and, in the case of the Foreign Ministry drafts, occasionally rather idealistic, the final version appeared to be less convinced that Russia's external environment was benign and more assertive about Russia's future role. The resentment expressed at attempts to squeeze Russia out of foreign markets, to limit its access to state-of-the-art technology, and to undermine its position in the international arms market implied an underlying suspicion of Western intentions towards Russia. Moreover, the concern lest Russia be relegated to the position of energy and raw materials supplier to the international economy it aspired to join suggested doubt that openness would necessarily bring about the kind of economic development that would enable Russia to occupy its rightful place in the international hierarchy along with the members of the Group of Seven. In other words, although there was no open hostility or belligerence towards the outside world in the report, the assumptions in the final version of the official foreign policy concept of the Russian Federation appeared to be far removed from the initial presumptions about Russian foreign policy shared by the Foreign Minister and the Liberal Westernizers.

According to one newspaper report the final version of the official concept was produced by Yuri Skokov, Secretary of the Security Council. The form that it took was explained, according to this commentator, by the struggle for influence between the Inter-Agency

Foreign Policy Commission of the Security Council, which Skokov chaired, and the Foreign Ministry. Although the Foreign Ministry lost the battle, as Chapter 3 makes clear, the concept was Skokov's final victory: a week after Yeltsin endorsed it, the Secretary of the Security Council was forced to resign. As we shall see, however, the balance of thinking about Russian foreign policy had shifted to such an extent by then that the concept fairly reflected a widely agreed view of Russia's role in the world.

## The third phase of the debate

Although the adoption of the official foreign policy concept marked the beginning of a period of greater consensus, this does not mean that the Fundamentalist Nationalists had reconciled themselves to the disintegration of the USSR or that they approved of Russia's foreign policy. On the contrary, the conflict between the 'Red-Brown coalition' and the government reached crisis proportions between March and October 1993, turning into a confrontation between the Supreme Soviet and the executive which culminated in the suspension of parliament in September and the bombardment of the White House in October. Although the conflict primarily concerned domestic issues, the irreconcilable opposition continued its criticism of Russian foreign policy, referring to Yeltsin and his government as 'destroyers of Russia' and arguing, like the Pragmatic Nationalists, that both Gorbachev and Yeltsin had made huge but useless concessions to the West in their futile attempts to have Russia admitted to the Group of Seven.

Convinced that Russia had sufficient natural resources and economic and intellectual potential to regain substantial economic autarky, the Fundamentalist Nationalists opposed any further integration into the international economy. They maintained that it was only when Yeltsin set the tanks on the Russian White House that Western leaders put their hands in their pockets to assist Russia and even then they offered far less money than Russia needed and imposed humiliatingly harsh conditions.[94] Incensed by Western support for Yeltsin's actions in October 1993, they argued that military co-operation between Russia and the United States was designed to give the latter access to Russia's natural resources and to its scientific and industrial achievements in the military field. The agreement to hold combined exercises in peacekeeping was 'one more proof that the Yeltsin leadership, content that Russia should be a third-rank power dependent on its American "partner", has betrayed Russia's national interests'. They also continued criticizing the Russian government for supporting United Nations policy in Bosnia, arguing that Kozyrev gave in too easily to Western views.[95]

Some Fundamentalist Nationalists argued that the purpose of Western aid was to weaken Russia and to prevent it playing a special role in the 'near abroad'. Pointing to the growing tendencies towards integration in the former Soviet Union, they predicted that the time would soon come when it would be both fashionable and politically advantageous to call for the re-establishment of a unitary state.[96]

The growing atmosphere of consensus also did not mean that differences of opinion about Russian foreign policy ceased entirely between other groups of the political élite. In a survey of foreign policy views conducted in June and July 1993, for example, slightly more than half of the respondents (all of whom were participants in the foreign policy process, whether as practitioners, legislators, or commentators) could still be classified as Westernizers according to their convictions. Analysts found, however, that in reply to specific questions the distinction between Westernizers and Pragmatic Nationalists tended to disappear. An overwhelming 96 per cent of respondents were in favour of the continuation of economic reform, for example, but 60 per cent of them felt that the reforms should be more gradual than the current government programme. This implied that market reform was supported by both Liberal Westernizers and Pragmatic Nationalists but that many self-styled Westernizers had become critical of the shock-therapy programmes advised by Western economists. More significantly, 63 per cent of all respondents were in favour of a unique, Russian model of development, while only 33 per cent believed that the 'tried and tested' general model of economic development was suitable for Russia. In other words, some Liberal Westernizers had shifted towards a Pragmatic Nationalist view about the specificity of Russia.

As far as Russian foreign policy was concerned, 68 per cent of the sample listed good relations with the West as an important foreign policy goal and only one individual respondent named the United States as Russia's main enemy. More than 50 per cent of respondents listed the retention of great-power status as a very important foreign policy goal. With regard to the CIS, 70 per cent

of the respondents (including, therefore, many Liberal Westernizers) expressed a preference for it turning into a unified state (con-
federal, federal, or union), while only 33 per cent thought that
this outcome was likely. 54 per cent believed that it was more
probable that the CIS would develop on the basis of independent
states.[97]

According to the foreign policy expert Alexei Arbatov, writing
in mid-1994, the distinction between Liberal Westernizers and
Pragmatic Nationalists had virtually disappeared by the end of
1993. Throughout the year a new assertion of Russia's particular
national interests and its mission in the world had gained prominence in discussions about foreign policy. As a result, Russia's
interests began to be defined not only as different from, but also
as opposed to, those of the advanced democratic countries. Ideas
about universal interests which had been carried forward from the
New Political Thinking into the values of the Liberal Westernizers
began to be rejected and anti-Western views became more acceptable in society as a whole. More importantly, the 'near abroad'
began to figure far more prominently both in theoretical discussion and in concrete policy. A broad consensus had been reached
about Russia's national security: the goal was to remain a great
power and the area in which this status was to be demonstrated
was the 'near abroad'.[98]

Arbatov himself was a moderate Pragmatic Nationalist. He
believed that a combination of factors—the deterioration in the economy and growing dissatisfaction with the results of the reforms,
the political struggle between the legislature and the executive, increasing pressure from nationalist forces, the promotion of a new,
inexperienced foreign policy élite into positions of influence—had
caused a regrouping of forces in relation to foreign policy. Liberal
Westernizers, including their leader, Andrei Kozyrev, had moved
over to join the Pragmatic Nationalists, while the views of some
Pragmatic Nationalists had grown closer to those of the Fundamentalist Nationalists.[99] Within the Foreign Ministry, he argued, most
professional diplomats had moved even further towards Pragmatic
Nationalist positions than had Kozyrev. And while leading officials
in the Ministry of Defence tended to be more hardline than the
Foreign Ministry, their views were far more moderate than those
of the majority of commanders in the field, who were outright
Radical Nationalists. Arbatov maintained that the new military

doctrine approved by President Yeltsin in November 1993 provided evidence of this shift in views. It legalized the use of military force in domestic conflicts, and took a more aggressive position with regard to the use of force in relations with the former Soviet states. He warned that the new military doctrine marked the end both of Russian military reform and of the withdrawal of Russian armed forces from the post-Soviet space. What is also significant about the military doctrine is that it was subject to far less published debate and discussion than the foreign policy concept.[100]

Clearly alarmed by the change in Russian foreign policy, particularly in relations with the 'near abroad', where he detected a new determination that Russia should have a dominant role, Arbatov warned that the results of the new policy would be catastrophic. He called for the withdrawal of Russian troops from the 'near abroad', arguing that the use of diplomatic and economic levers, and an active role in mediating (rather than meddling in) conflicts, would be a far more rational way to attain Russia's foreign policy goals. If intervention was necessary in the last resort, it should only be undertaken on the basis of multilateral decisions and actions. Although he was also critical of many aspects of Russian policy in the 'far abroad', he attributed some of the blame to the West. He called for the West to show greater sensitivity to Russia's national interests, pointing to Russia's marginalization in international decisions about Yugoslavia, and to the problems that the Conventional Forces in Europe (CFE) provisions created for Moscow's new security predicament. He also maintained that Russian hawks would derive great political benefit from the expansion of NATO eastwards.[101]

Arbatov was not the only Pragmatic Nationalist who had become concerned about the turn Russian foreign policy seemed to have taken. In May 1994 the Council for Foreign and Defence Policy published a second 'Strategy for Russia', which 'aimed to influence some key long-term elements of Russian policy, particularly relations with the countries of the former USSR, and to caution against some dangerous tendencies which have become noticeable in Russian policy'. The authors pointed to the proclivity of officials to adopt 'a great-power rhetoric', which might be intended for internal consumption, but which fuelled suspicion that Russia had embarked upon a policy of 'imperial revenge' in both the 'near abroad' and the 'far abroad'.[102]

Arguing that many in the West were afraid of Russian expansion and keen to limit Russia's international influence, the authors of the second 'Strategy for Russia' warned that relations with the West could deteriorate, causing a third Cold War. Russia's most important interests in the 'far abroad' were to retain and develop a stable and realistic partnership with the countries of the northern hemisphere, from the United States and Canada through to Japan. Any unnecessary deterioration of relations should be avoided, but at the same time Russia's own interests should not be undermined. If Russia was to prevent isolation and a return to military confrontation in Europe, a proper European security system would need to be constructed in which Russia played a full part. This required the retention in Europe of the belt of semi-demilitarized states which had been formed after the end of the Cold War. Whereas Central and East European membership of the European Union would not infringe its national interests, Russia should not permit the expansion of NATO eastwards.[103]

In analysing the situation in the 'near abroad', the authors of the second 'Strategy for Russia' pointed to the prevalence of weak, unviable states with deteriorating economies whose governments were increasingly in favour of integration with Russia. This was occurring at a time when nationalist tendencies within Russia were gathering strength, making it more likely that Russia would be drawn into conflicts on its periphery. Even if the purpose of intervention was to stabilize the situation in the 'near abroad', it would have the reverse effect, with the added danger that the territorial integrity of the Russian Federation would be undermined. According to the second 'Strategy for Russia', the problem was that Russia could not separate itself completely from the CIS. Moreover, the trend towards integration seemed inexorable. Russia should seek to ensure, therefore, that the form that integration took suited its national interests. In other words, Russia should not, as in the past, become 'an economic colony of the states which it unites around itself'.[104]

The second 'Strategy for Russia' proposed a policy of 'leadership without control'.[105] This implied integration through creating the political, military, and other conditions necessary for economic co-operation and mutual economic penetration, rather than on the basis of territorial or political union. While it would be costly in terms of political effort as well as economics to create a system of friendly states which were economically open to Russia, the gain would be Russian access to the natural, economic, and human resources of its neighbours. In concrete terms, Russia should insist that all barriers to the movement of goods and to the participation of foreign (i.e. Russian) capital in CIS privatization be removed; it should offer to exchange the debts owed to it by CIS countries for industrial and other assets; and it should create an effective bilateral accounting system without attempting full financial union. It should also embark on a gradual process of creating a military and political union and on a policy giving all citizens of the former USSR the right to dual citizenship and protection against discrimination.

This policy should be implemented through strengthening the CIS, but on a firm basis of bilateral relations. It was also important that Russia should tailor its policies individually to each former Soviet state: with regard to the Baltic states, for example, Russia should aim to establish good-neighbour relations which were based on civilized solutions to the problems of ethnic minorities and which took Russian security interests into account. While every effort should be made to prevent the collapse of neighbouring countries, Russia should avoid becoming the guarantor of any particular regime. The authors of the second 'Strategy for Russia' warned that 'the concept of Russia's special responsibility should not lead to the expansion of Russia's participation in regulating conflicts.' Although intervention could not be ruled out entirely, 'the less direct intervention by Russia the better.' As far as human rights were concerned, Russian policy should be directed towards the defence of the rights of all national minorities, and Moscow itself should become a symbol of guaranteed minority rights. There should also be an independent policy directed towards ensuring the rights and interests of Russians abroad and an active cultural policy designed to ensure that the Russian language retained currency in the 'near abroad'.[106]

Both Arbatov and the authors of the second 'Strategy for Russia' expressed particular alarm lest Russia's assertion of a special responsibility to ensure the stability of the post-Soviet space should draw its army into an increasing number of intractable conflicts. As we have seen, the campaign to win international recognition of the right to act as chief peacekeeper in the area began in earnest during the second phase of the debate, and the issue was prominent in the official foreign policy concept. It could be argued, however, that domestic debates about peacekeeping and the desire for international approval were no more than attempts to legitimize something that was already taking place: Russian troops had been involved in peacekeeping since the summer of 1992.[107]

Part of the difficulty in obtaining an international imprimatur for Russian peacekeeping activities (not to mention financial assistance to support Russian or CIS operations) arose from the suspicion in the West and within the former Soviet Union that peacekeeping was simply a cover for the re-establishment of the Russian empire. There were frequent allegations, hotly denied by officials, that Russia first interfered on one side of a conflict and then, having exacerbated it, reappeared as peacekeeper.[108] There was a further problem in the use by Russians of the term 'peacekeeping' to cover peacekeeping, peacemaking, and peace enforcement activities, and the regular involvement of interested parties in peacekeeping/enforcing operations within the former Soviet Union. Russian officials appeared not to understand that there was a distinction between the terms, and between the activities each term entailed, and they were unwilling to accept that there were important principles and practices at stake.[109]

Accusations of imperialist behaviour and the unconcealed reluctance of the international community to approve Russia's peacekeeping efforts made officials ever more insistent about Russia's rights and duties in the 'near abroad'. Moreover, Kozyrev was at pains to point out that there was little sign of anyone replacing Russia in the fulfilment of peacekeeping tasks. He argued that 'instead of inflaming fears of Russian neo-imperialism, it is time to embark seriously on sharing this burden with Russia, particularly through the creation of a voluntary fund to assist peacekeeping operations on the territory of the former Soviet Union.'[110] As time went on there was more and more impatience about international objections to Russia's conduct. In a speech to a meeting of the Foreign Ministry Council on Foreign Policy in 1994, for example, Kozyrev complained that at a recent CSCE meeting it had been proposed that the criteria for determining the legitimacy of Russian peacekeeping should be worked out. 'What for?' he asked. 'Why should we do that when our actions are 150 per cent legitimate?' He went on to argue that Russia's peacekeeping activity rested on the rules of international law, Russia's responsibility as a permanent member of the UN Security Council, and on appeals from sovereign states and participants in the conflict.[111]

The irritable responses of Russian commentators to Western criticisms of their peacekeeping operations are, to some extent, understandable. As Kozyrev pointed out, there was little evidence that the UN or any other organization would undertake the task. Even if agreement could be reached at a political level about international intervention to resolve the conflicts in the former Soviet Union, it was unlikely that the UN would be able to muster the necessary forces. Indeed, for all the dire warnings that Russian military actions in the 'near abroad' were neo-imperialist, the West seemed undecided whether or not its interests were served by Russia's military intervention and, if its interests *were* served, 'what criteria should be used to establish a boundary between stabilizing intervention and intervention for neo-imperialist purposes.'[112]

Despite Kozyrev's reproaches about the lack of international efforts to resolve the disputes on the periphery of the Russian Federation, however, external participation in peacekeeping operations on CIS territory seemed increasingly unattractive to Russian commentators. It is perhaps not surprising that any idea of the United States becoming involved in the former Soviet Union was vetoed.[113] But the view that the post-Soviet space was, by right, Russia's sphere of influence gained increasing salience. Kozyrev warned that any plans 'to create a sphere of influence in the post-Soviet space and to exclude Russia are as hopeless as they are dangerous. No country . . . can take upon itself that special role which belongs to Russia in ensuring stability in this enormous region. We recognize this responsibility and must cope with it.'[114] In President Yeltsin's annual address to the Federal Assembly in February 1994, he made it clear that Moscow wanted a free hand in peacekeeping operations in the CIS.[115]

As far as peacekeeping was concerned, therefore, and more generally in relation to the 'near abroad', the tone and content of Russian foreign policy thinking was distinctively more assertive from the second half of 1993 than it had been before the official concept was adopted. Moreover, there were fewer critical voices from within the foreign policy élite. The Liberal Westernizers and Pragmatic Nationalists seemed to agree that the 'near abroad' was Russia's sphere of influence, and that keeping the peace in the area was Russia's burden. Even those who warned of the dangers of intervention could see no alternative to Russia's increasing involvement and they tended to concentrate on ways in which the costs could be minimized and the benefits maximized.

Western apprehension that the new centripetal tendencies in the CIS were the outcome of Russian pressure affected Russian attitudes towards the West. There was a strong feeling in some quarters that the West really wanted to prevent Russia from regaining great-power status.[116] Increasingly, more assertive views about Russia's relations with the 'far abroad' could be detected which were not necessarily anti-Western but which certainly had a 'Russia first' flavour. This was particularly noticeable in the discussions about the possible expansion of NATO eastward.

The question of Russian membership of the Partnership for Peace (PFP) provoked a lively debate when the programme was first mooted, in which most Liberal Westernizers favoured membership, and most Pragmatic Nationalists were more hesitant.[117] Analysts of all political persuasions, however, opposed the enlargement of NATO to include the countries of Central and Eastern Europe. The first argument most of them made was that the expansion of NATO would provoke a nationalist backlash within Russia and strengthen the political influence of Fundamentalist Nationalists. Whether or not the expansion was directed against Russia, they pointed out, there was a paradox: if NATO were to expand eastwards so that it bordered Russia, it would almost certainly be perceived as an anti-Russian alliance. The result would be that 'those forces which the West would like least to see in the Kremlin would advance to centre stage and might even come to power.'[118] In other words, one analyst warned, the expansion of NATO might result in the policy of democracy and partnership with the West being defeated by those who favoured authoritarianism and anti-Western isolation. Another maintained that the psychological and political consequences of expansion would be very unpleasant. The Russian military élite would react negatively and its influence on policy would increase.[119]

There was also genuine concern that Russian security would be undermined if the eastern border of NATO moved closer to Russia's new western border. Even if there was no immediate danger of an attack on Russia by NATO, Russia would be isolated and separated from Europe by a cordon sanitaire stretching from the Baltic to the Black Sea.[120] Sooner or later it was bound to form its own military bloc to counteract NATO and there would be a return to confrontation in Europe. Russian analysts asked the obvious question: who was the enemy against whom the enlarged alliance would be directed? They discounted explanations based on the democratizing or modernizing influence that NATO would have on its new members, or the idea that membership of NATO would help the East-Central European countries deal with their own territorial and ethnic disputes.[121] Echoing Khrushchev, who once pungently pointed out that NATO was not a sports organization, Kozyrev scoffed at the insistence of some East European leaders that they wanted to join NATO because of its 'civilizing' effect. 'NATO', he said, 'is not some kind of cultural, educational organization, but a military-strategic union.'[122]

Russian analysts thus took for granted what was obvious, but rarely admitted by NATO politicians: any plan to expand NATO into Eastern Europe while at the same time excluding Russian membership implied that Russia was viewed as a potential aggressor. The plan to enlarge NATO was, therefore, interpreted as a new version of the containment policy that had underpinned Western policy during the Cold War. And as Kozyrev bluntly put it: 'The enlargement of NATO without Russian participation does not suit us.'[123] Despite Kozyrev's unequivocal statement, there was some doubt whether the Foreign Ministry was responding adamantly enough to NATO. The President's security aide complained, for example, that Moscow was sending contradictory and confusing signals. He warned that whatever possibilities Foreign Ministry officials were discussing with their Western counterparts, 'the final say rests with the President.'[124]

It should be noted that the Russian response to the idea of an expanded NATO which excluded the Russian Federation was perfectly natural and did not necessarily imply, as many Western commentators assumed, that a new hard-line policy prevailed in Russia. Expansion eastward could not be perceived in any other way except as a threat to Russian security and an attempt to isolate the country and keep it outside Europe. Indeed, one has only to think of Soviet security fears in the 1930s, and to compare the borders of the USSR then to those of Russia today, to understand why the foreign policy élite responded so vehemently. Nor was the response particular to Russia; a similar reaction might be expected from any country which was faced with a defence alliance which

included all surrounding countries and from which it was excluded.
What was significant about the response was not so much the objections that were raised about the expansion of NATO, as the evidence it offered that there was now little to distinguish the views
of the previous Liberal Westernizers from those of the Pragmatic
Nationalists.

Although Western leaders announced that Russia would not be
allowed to veto NATO membership, Russian apprehension played
into the doubts some NATO members felt about the wisdom of
enlargement. The decision was postponed (only to be revived with
increased vigour when Russia launched its brutal attack against
separatist Chechnya) and the PFP was designed as a temporizing
measure. The PFP was offered to the Russian Federation and other
former Soviet states as well as to East-Central Europe and, as we
have seen, at first it was warmly, although not universally, welcomed. However, negotiations over Moscow's membership of the
PFP soon became a lever in the deteriorating relations between
Russia and the West. The membership negotiations also served to
demonstrate an increasingly insistent demand by Russian officials
that the West should recognize that Russia is a great power.

Participants in the foreign policy debate had frequently raised
the issue of Russia's great-power status. In the past, however,
it had often been posed by Liberal Westernizers as a question
rather than asserted, and even when the statement was reiterated
by those at the more nationalist edge of the Pragmatic Nationalist
group, it frequently sounded like self-reassurance. In relation to
the terms of accession to the PFP, however, the demand for special
treatment which would demonstrate that Russia was not only a
great power, but was recognized as such by the rest of the world,
became something of an *idée fixe*. Russian officials insisted that
Russia could not join the PFP on the same terms as the countries
of the 'near abroad' and East-Central Europe. Its special status as
a great power should be recognized in the terms of accession. It
could not be expected to be on the level of Luxemburg and it was
inconceivable that 'in the taking of decisions, Iceland's vote could
outweigh Russia's simply because it is a full member of NATO'.[125]
Although it was assumed in the West that the military were particularly opposed to the PFP, according to one Russian analyst,
the military took a more moderate stance with regard to the PFP
than did politicians.[126]

'Great-power rhetoric' was more common among politicians

and officials than among academics, and it is clear from the second 'Strategy for Russia' that it embarrassed many academic analysts. Indeed, in the wake of the attack on Grozny, one academic blamed the revival of plans to expand NATO equally on the attack and on innumerable mistakes which 'were sufficient to persuade many of the growth of negative tendencies in Russian foreign policy'. High on the list of mistakes he put 'verbal declarations on every conceivable occasion of the special "great-power" role of our country'.[127] Despite their disapproval of the rhetoric, however, academic commentators were as opposed to NATO expansion as were practitioners. And they too believed that the 'near abroad' represented Russia's historical and natural sphere of interest. In relation to policy toward both the larger external world and the 'near abroad', therefore, a consensus of opinion was evident, even if there were differences in detail.

The attack on Chechnya revived the tendency to criticize government policy and reopened the debate about domestic and foreign policy. Kozyrev, however, was not among the government's critics. At a CSCE meeting in Stockholm in December 1992 Kozyrev had made a speech which shocked his fellow diplomats: he denounced Western interference in the Baltic states and United Nations sanctions against Serbia, claimed that CSCE norms did not apply to the former Soviet Union, and declared the 'near abroad' as Russia's sphere of interest, where it would feel free to protect its interests by all available means. Less than an hour later he claimed that his speech had been a device to alert the international community to the consequences of the 'forces of reaction' taking control of Russia. In the preface to the book that he published in 1995 he argued that his trick had served its purpose: the West had been alerted and the forces of reaction had been repelled.[128] What he did not point out, however, was how closely his own current thinking resembled many of the things he had warned against in 1992. The debate about Russian foreign policy may well revive, but neither the present President nor the former and present Foreign Ministers (Kozyrev resigned in January 1996) are likely champions of Liberal Westernizer views.

## The domestic and external causes of change

Whether or not the debate about Russian foreign policy revives as a result of the repugnance aroused in most of the political élite by the attempt to force Chechnya to remain in the Russian Federation, it is clear that the parameters of the debate will be very different from those that existed at the beginning of 1992. It is unlikely that uncritical and unquestioning pro-Western views will again prevail among the Russian political élite, and inattention to the 'near abroad' is equally implausible. In order to explain this, we need to examine why, when a consensus was reached about Russian foreign policy, it was the Pragmatic Nationalists who appeared to win the day.

The domestic and external factors which contributed to a general disillusion with the West and a more assertive policy towards the 'near abroad' were closely interconnected. The domestic factors stemmed in part from the effects of economic reform. No matter how successful economists judged the reforms to be, they caused an enormous amount of hardship to very many people. Economic insecurity, the uncertainty caused by rapid change, and fear that the absence of law and order would produce chaos fostered a pervasive sense of national humiliation which led not only to nostalgia for the certainties of the past and a surge of nationalism, but also to a search for scapegoats. And since the Russian government received economic advice from Western economists, adopted policies which were approved by the IMF, and supplicated the Group of Seven for assistance, the West was perceived by many as the cause of Russia's economic woes. This was the basic ingredient of the credo of Fundamentalist Nationalists, of course, but resentment of the West became a widespread popular phenomenon.

The political élite understood that the Russian economy had been in catastrophic decline when the reforms were launched, and it was far too sophisticated to see the West as the culprit. But it was not immune to nationalism or unaffected by the wave of anti-Westernism (even if only because some of its members hoped to be elected or re-elected to parliament). It is not surprising, therefore, that it became less optimistic about Russia's relations with the West and generally more nationalistic. In other words, the entire spectrum of foreign policy thinking tended to shift sideways towards the more nationalist end of the continuum.

The second domestic factor which contributed to the change in foreign policy thinking arose from the disintegration of the Soviet Union. Few people (whether in Russia or in the other republics) had really comprehended in advance what the implications were of the sovereignty and independence of individual republics. Early euphoria about putative economic advantages gave way to post-traumatic shock when it was discovered how very difficult it was to separate the Russian economy from the rest, how vulnerable Russia was to events in other republics, and the extent to which Russia's central role in the former Soviet Union had been taken for granted. Since Russians believed that they had subsidized many of the other republics of the Soviet Union, they resented the attitudes of the newly-independent states to Russia and they became more assertive about Russia's past burdens and present rights, as well as about the rights and dignity of Russian-speaking peoples who lived in the 'near abroad'.[129]

The intense power struggle which dominated Russian politics between December 1992 and October 1993 both reflected these domestic factors and affected foreign policy thinking. The effect, however, was unusual. Political conflict usually leads to a polarization of views, and one might have expected that the middle of the spectrum (in other words, the ideas of the Pragmatic Nationalists) would fall away, leaving a struggle between Liberal Westernizers and Fundamentalist Nationalists. Indeed, with regard to domestic politics, the results of the December 1993 elections seemed to indicate that this had occurred: at one extreme of the political spectrum, Nationalists, Communists, and Agrarians won a large number of seats, and at the other end, Russia's Choice did relatively well, while the Civic Union, which represented the centre, was completely routed.[130] As far as foreign policy thinking was concerned, however, it was the extreme Westernizer end of the spectrum which fell away, leaving only Pragmatic Nationalists (among whom former Liberal Westernizers held slightly more moderate views than the rest) and Fundamentalist Nationalists.

Some Russian analysts also argue that the early pro-Western euphoria was caused by the fact that the Liberal Westernizers who held positions of power and influence immediately after the disintegration of the Soviet Union were political novices who had no previous foreign policy experience. As they became more seasoned, they abandoned their naïve utopian ideas in favour of realism and adopted a more robust stance towards Russia's relations with the outside world. This enabled the traditional foreign policy élite (diplomats, intelligence officers, senior academics, and journalists), which had 'suffered from and was bereaved by the breakup of the

Soviet Union' in much the same way that nationalists and Communists were affected (although their policy preferences were different), to recover some of their previous influence.[131]

The debate about foreign policy was based in part on the search for a Russian identity. But much of it was also a response to events in the outside world. In other words, the search for a Russian identity took place within an external environment that proved less sympathetic than Liberal Westernizers had expected, and the results of their early pro-Western policies were disappointing. Apart from the domestic reasons, therefore, there were external factors which influenced the shift in foreign policy thinking. Some of these have been mentioned in Chapter 1, and we will concentrate here on those factors which made the political élite more assertive in its thinking about Russian foreign policy.

It was anticipated, for example, that the West would provide substantial financial assistance to underwrite Russia's economic reform. Bilateral aid was parsimonious and tended to be tied to the commercial interests of the donor, however, and the negotiations for multilateral aid proved complex and long-winded. The conditions attached to loans seemed unreasonably stringent and the means by which they were established unnecessarily intrusive. Moreover, assistance rarely came in the form of grants, and loans, even on favourable terms, made Russia's already massive debt burden even heavier. Some of the staunchest Liberal Westernizers began to wonder whether the West really intended to sponsor Russia's economic recovery. As one analyst put it, 'from a practical point of view, the USA and the West have not yet thrown their authority or the material means they have . . . into assisting Russia's revival.'[132]

Liberal Westernizers' doubts increased when it turned out that the much-vaunted free market did not necessarily mean that Russia would have free access to the few markets where its goods enjoyed comparative advantage. The European Union's external trade barriers, anti-dumping measures levelled against Russian aluminium producers, American objections to Russia's projected sale of cryogenic rocket engines and associated know-how to India, and to Russian penetration of the Asian arms market, irked Russians. In the middle of 1993, as Chapter 3 relates, Russia gave in to American pressure and, to the chagrin of the Indian government, modified the rocket deal. By 1994, however, the Russian government was convinced that Western strictures on Russian arms sales were based less on international security interests than on commercial criteria. It is significant that intense American pressure did not make the Russians withdraw from a deal to sell nuclear reactors for civilian use to Iran in 1995.[133]

Disillusion was also caused by the difficulties the Russian government experienced in joining international organizations. Although it was understandable that the Group of Seven would not expand into the Group of Eight until the Russian economy recovered sufficiently, Russians resented having to supplicate to participate in its political discussions. They were incensed by what they saw as the double standards of organizations like the Council of Europe, which accepted Estonia as a member with indecent haste despite its dubious civil rights standards, yet refused Russia's first application in July 1992, and delayed subsequent consideration of Russian membership (the decision was postponed when the attack was launched on Chechnya). An economic agreement with the European Union took so long to negotiate that it too fell temporarily victim to the wish to exert pressure over Chechnya.[134] These delays and difficulties contributed to the perception that Western politicians patronized Russians and treated them as if Russia had been vanquished in the Cold War. The deputy editor of the relatively pro-Western *Moskovskie novosti* complained, for example, that the USA felt that because it had given Russia some economic aid, it could 'tell Russia what deals it could conclude with India or Iran, how to behave itself in the Middle East or in its disputes with the Baltic Republics'.[135]

There was also a strong sense in Moscow that the West did not understand, or refused to take seriously, Russia's security interests. This was demonstrated by the planned eastward extension of NATO, the refusal to consider Russia's proposals to turn the CSCE into an effective security organization, the failure to appreciate why the CFE provisions no longer reflected Russia's urgent defence requirements and, perhaps most importantly, by the lack of sympathy shown by the West to the threats to Russian security posed by the conflicts in the 'near abroad'. In short, Western policy toward the Russian Federation was, in many respects, inadequate and this affected the debate on Russian foreign policy.

With regard to the 'near abroad', two things in particular made analysts increasingly aware that it would have to be regarded as an area of Russia's vital interest. The first was the perception that the borders of the Russian Federation were permeable, and that conflict on its periphery could spread into the country. This was true in a very concrete sense: there were no physical borders or border posts between the republics when the Soviet Union disintegrated. There are still no borders separating Central Asia from Russia. When Russians argue that the Russian border has to be defended in Tajikistan, they mean this literally. There is no other physical border between Russia and Afghanistan. At first, the perception of vulnerability was particularly strong in relation to the external borders of the southern republics. Recently the border between the former Soviet Union and Eastern and Central Europe has become an equally sensitive issue. Moreover, despite the formation of National Guards and armies, and their 'nationalization' of the military equipment located in the other republics, it rapidly became clear that most of the governments were incapable of dealing with the domestic conflicts and civil wars which plagued the newly-independent states. Russia seemed to have little choice in the matter of defence and peacekeeping in the CIS and this affected the foreign policy debate.[136]

The second problem in relation to the 'near abroad' that influenced Russian foreign policy thinking was economic interdependence. As soon as Russia embarked upon economic reform the quandary became evident. As long as the republics were tied together economically, and particularly if they used the same currency, Russian economic reform would depend on the other republics adopting similar programmes in the same order and at roughly the same pace. Excluding those who did not reform their economies from the rouble zone helped a little. But it did not deal with problems like the energy dependence on Russia of the other republics, and the debts they incurred as a result. Nor did it make it easy to devise a workable economic programme for the CIS. Many members of the political élite began to view the 'near abroad' as an inescapable economic and military burden and to think about ways to ensure that Russia gained from the relationship. This affected their view of how independent the 'near abroad' could be. Thus both domestic and external factors contributed to the fact that many Liberal Westernizers shifted towards Pragmatic Nationalist opinions. It is not surprising, therefore, that the consensus reached in the third phase of the debate reflected those views particularly strongly.

We need briefly to consider what the effect of the foreign policy debate was on policy. Was Russian policy based on the ideas which were expressed during the debate, and is it now based on the officially adopted concept, if one sees that as the outcome of the debate? Or, on the contrary, was the debate simply a running commentary on events or an interpretation of actions? The relationship between ideas and action has always been a vexed question, both generally and with specific regard to the Soviet Union, where ideology was actively articulated but where it was frequently difficult to relate specific actions to particular elements of doctrine. In the case of the Soviet Union, it was clear that whatever the relationship was between ideology and policy, it was far less direct than Soviet theorists suggested. As far as Russia is concerned, the period which we have examined was a transitional stage when there was an active search for Russia's identity and new policies were being tried out. Moreover, many of the people who participated in the debate were foreign policy practitioners, who were talking about and making policy, or at least advising about policy, simultaneously. The debate, and also the continual barrage of criticism to which the Foreign Ministry was subjected, affected the political atmosphere in which policy was made and encouraged the adoption of a more assertive stance. As Chapter 3 demonstrates, the relationship between the foreign policy debates and Russian foreign policy behaviour was, therefore, very close during the period we have covered.[137]

There is one final important point to make about the change in Russian foreign policy thinking. Pragmatic Nationalism represents the standard view one might expect the foreign policy élite to hold in any country. While the rhetoric employed by Russian officials is sometimes excessive, and the brutality with which the army has attempted to reclaim Chechnya is horrifying, the robust identification and defence of the national interest is normal, in the sense of being in accord with political realist practice. From this standpoint, the initial views of the Liberal Westernizers were an aberration, or at least naïve and utopian. It was unrealistic to expect a complete coincidence of Russian and Western national interests, or that the West would always sympathize with the way Russia perceived its interests. It was naïve to believe that the establishment of a market economy would somehow and instantly turn Russia into an advanced industrialized Western state. It was utopian to think that the end of the Cold War would transform the international system into an arena of peaceful co-operation. But it was not just the Russian Liberal Westernizers who were unrealistic in their expectations: Western governments were also rather naïve. The prevailing Pragmatic Nationalism in Russia caused disquiet in the West and considerable alarm in Eastern and Central Europe, leading many to fear that it represented a capitulation to extreme nationalist views and was a symptom of the growing power of the Fundamentalist Nationalists. As one Russian analyst pointed out, however, 'the current adjustments remain squarely within the framework of a realistic partnership with the West . . . a non-Western Russia does not mean an anti-Western one.'[138] Both Russian and Western politicians will need to be pragmatic realists if a partnership is to survive.

## NOTES

[1] In February 1992 the Foreign Ministry held a conference on Russian foreign policy in which 800 people from various walks of life participated. Some of the conference papers were published in the March 1992 edition of *Diplomaticheskii vestnik*, pp. 29–46, and were reprinted in *International Affairs* (Moscow), 1992, no. 4–5, pp. 81–104. It was already clear from these papers that some of Yeltsin's academic supporters believed that Russian foreign policy should be less unquestioningly pro-Western.

[2] While most analysts are in rough agreement about the criteria to be used for distinguishing between views about Russian foreign policy, they use a variety of terms to define different groups of views. Vladimir Lukin ('Our Security Predicament', *Foreign Policy*, Fall 1992, 57–75) talks about 'ideologized democratic internationalism', Russian chauvinism and those who have 'an enlightened understanding of Russia's national interest'. Vera Tolz ('Russia: Westernizers Continue to Challenge National Patriots', *RFE/RL Research Report*, 11 Dec. 1992, 1–9) refers to Westernizers, isolationists, and imperialists/unionists. Alexei Arbatov calls them pro-western, moderate liberal, centrist and moderate conservative, and neocommunist-nationalist ('Russia's Foreign Policy Alternatives', *International Security*, 18, 5–43). Renée de Nevers, on the other hand, divides them into 'internationalist, centrist post-imperialists, neocommunists and

agrarians, and extreme nationalists' (*Russia's Strategic Renovation*, Adelphi Paper 289; London, 1994). While Westernizers certainly believe that Russia should be an active member of the international system, the term 'internationalist' should not be confused with its usage in the pre-Gorbachev period, when it meant someone who believed in international revolution. See also the fivefold division of schools of thought in K. Dawisha and B. Parrott, *Russia and the New States of Eurasia* (Cambridge, 1994), 199–202.

[3] N. Malcolm, 'The New Russian Foreign Policy', *The World Today*, 50 (1994), 28–31.

[4] S. White, *After Gorbachev* (Cambridge, 1993), 170–1.

[5] V. O. Kluchevsky, *A History of Russia*, tr. C. J. Hogarth, 5 vols. (London, 1931; 1st pub. 1904–21), v. 209.

[6] Nor is there one now, of course, since the Russian Federation is a multinational state.

[7] Cited in S. Maksudov and W. Taubman, 'Russian-Soviet Nationality Policy and Foreign Policy: A Historical Overview of the Linkage Between them', in M. Mandelbaum (ed.), *The Rise of Nations in the Soviet Union: American Foreign Policy and the Disintegration of the USSR* (New York, 1991), 26.

[8] For an advance warning about the identity problems that Russians would experience if the USSR disintegrated, see V. Razuvaev, 'Budushchee Evropy svyazano c Rossiei', *Mezhdunarodnaya zhizn'*, 1991, no. 11, pp. 39–47. On the absence of the tradition of Russian statehood, see T. Yarygina and G. Marchenko, 'Regional'nye protsessy v byvshem SSSR i novoi Rossii', *Svobodnaya mysl'*, 1992, no. 14, pp. 17–28, who see this as one of the main reasons why disintegration threatens the Russian Federation itself.

[9] V. Tolz, 'The Burden of the Imperial Legacy', *RFE/RL Research Report*, 14 May 1993, 43.

[10] S. Razgonov, cited in I. Bremmer and R. Taras (eds.), *Nations and Politics in the Soviet Successor States* (Cambridge, 1993), 68.

[11] See, for example, S. Stankevich, *Nezavisimaya gazeta*, 28 Mar. 1992; N. Narochnitskaya, 'Russia's National Interest', *International Affairs* (Moscow), 1992, no. 4–5, p. 105; K. Eggert, *Izvestiya*, 7 Aug. 1992. For an opposing view—that there had to be a clear idea of what Russia was before a foreign policy concept could be formulated—see E. Pozdnyakov, 'We Must Rebuild what We have Destroyed with our Own Hands', *International Affairs* (Moscow), 1992, no. 4–5, pp. 129–36.

[12] Foreign Minister Andrei Kozyrev, who was at first very reluctant to specify and articulate Russia's national interests, pointed out to those who urged an explicit formulation of Russian foreign policy that other countries' diplomats found the idea of a foreign policy concept extremely

90    *Margot Light*

strange. See his speech at the conference on Russian foreign policy held at the Ministry of Foreign Affairs in February 1992, in *Diplomaticheskii vestnik*, 1992, no. 6, p. 33, and his interview in *Nezavisimaya gazeta*, 1 Apr. 1992. His opponents, however, disagreed. A member of the Supreme Soviet Committee on Defence and Security insisted, for example, that Russians 'need a foreign policy ideology . . . all Western powers have one' (Ye. Kozhokin, in 'What Foreign Policy Russia should Pursue', *International Affairs* (Moscow), 1993, no. 2, p. 12).

¹³ The Programme of the Communist Party of the Soviet Union (CPSU) was adopted in 1961 and revised regularly. Although to all intents and purposes a new programme was adopted in 1986, it was still called the Revised Programme of the CPSU.

¹⁴ B. Pyadyshev, in 'Russia's Foreign Policy: Agenda for 1993', *International Affairs* (Moscow), 1993, no. 3, p. 31.

¹⁵ S. Stankevich, in 'A Transformed Russia in a New World', *International Affairs* (Moscow), 1992, no. 4–5, p. 98.

¹⁶ For detailed examinations of these policy differences, see, for example, N. Malcolm, *Soviet Political Scientists and American Politics* (London, 1984); M. Light, *The Soviet Theory of International Relations* (Brighton, 1988).

¹⁷ To give just two prominent examples, Yevgeny Ambartsumov, Chairman of the International Affairs and Foreign Economic Relations Commission of the Supreme Soviet from 1992, was an academic who worked at the Institute of the Economy of the World Socialist System until 1991. His predecessor, Vladimir Lukin, had alternated between the diplomatic service and academia, working at the Institute of the USA and Canada from 1968 to 1987, and then working in the Foreign Ministry. In 1989 he was elected to the Congress of People's Deputies of the RSFSR and became chairman of the RSFSR Supreme Soviet Committee on Foreign Affairs and Foreign Economic Relations. He was appointed Russian Ambassador in Washington in 1992. In 1993, however, he returned to political life as co-chairman of the political party which was known as Yabloko (an acronym of the first letters of the three leaders, Yavlinsky, Boldyrev, and Lukin) and he became chairman of the Foreign Policy Commission of the first Duma.

¹⁸ Alexander Yakovlev, for example, was Deputy Head of the Central Committee Propaganda Department when he fell out with Brezhnev in 1973 and was 'exiled' to be Soviet Ambassador to Canada. When he was recalled in 1983, he became Director of the Institute of World Economy and International Relations before being promoted by Gorbachev in 1986 to the position of Central Committee secretary responsible for ideology, propaganda, and culture.

¹⁹ Sergei Stankevich, another former academic (from the Institute

of General History), was probably the most important participant to change from being a presidential adviser to speaking as an independent commentator.

[20] Two prominent examples of such academics are A. Vasil'ev, director of the Institute of Africa and Asia, and S. Goncharov of the Institute of Oriental Studies. For a vivid illustration of specialists defending their areas of expertise, see the discussion 'Russia's National Interests' in *International Affairs* (Moscow), 1992, no. 8, pp. 134–43.

[21] This probably explains why the most radical writing and views in the early glasnost period emanated from the Institute of the Economy of the World Socialist System (which is now called the Institute of International Political and Economic Studies), where academics were studying the socialist countries and were in no doubt about the depth of the crises of their economic and political systems.

[22] Mikhail Gorbachev and Eduard Shevardnadze promoted diplomats and party officials who shared their new political thinking. Many of the ideas of New Thinking were transmitted via articles they wrote. See, for example, V. F. Petrovsky, 'Sovetskaya kontseptsiya vseobshchei bezopasnosti', *Mirovaya ekonomika i mezhdunarodnye otnosheniya*, 1986, no. 6, pp. 3–13; A. Dobrynin, 'Za bez'yadernyi mir, navstrechu XXI veku', *Kommunist*, 1986, no. 9, pp. 18–31.

[23] The term 'near abroad' began to be used by Russian analysts soon after the disintegration of the USSR. It is usually used to refer to the republics which had constituted the USSR. The rest of the world is called 'the far abroad'.

[24] In February 1992 Vladimir Lukin, then chairman of the Committee on International Affairs of the Supreme Soviet, pointed to the lack of experts on the other republics, and complained that Russian embassies had not yet been established in all the republics. See 'A Transformed Russia', 93. Kozyrev did not visit any 'near abroad' countries until April 1992. In reply to criticism that the MFA was only concerned with the West, however, Kozyrev claimed that it spent more time on the CIS than on anything else and maintained that 80 per cent of his time was devoted to CIS matters. See *Nezavisimaya gazeta*, 1 Apr. 1992, and J. Lough, 'Defining Russia's Relations with Neighbouring States', *RFE/RL Research Report*, 14 May 1993, 53–60.

[25] A. Pushkov, 'Russia's Foreign Policy: Agenda for 1993', *International Affairs* (Moscow), 1993, no. 3, p. 22.

[26] A. Kortunov, 'The Soviet Legacy and Current Foreign Policy Discussions in Russia', paper presented to the Russian Littoral Project Conference, Washington, DC, May 1993.

[27] 'A Transformed Russia', 85–91, quotes on pp. 86 and 87.

[28] 'A Transformed Russia', 90, 86.

[29] A. Rahr, ' "Atlanticists" versus "Eurasians" in Russian Foreign Policy', *RFE/RL Research Report*, 29 May 1992, 17–22.

[30] A. Zagorsky *et al.*, *Posle Raspada SSSR: Rossiya v novom mire* (Moscow, 1992), p. 11.

[31] A. Zagorsky, in *Moskovskie novosti*, 1 Mar. 1992.

[32] Zagorsky *et al.*, *Posle Raspada SSSR*, 17, 23.

[33] S. Stankevich, in 'A Transformed Russia', 98–101, quote on p. 99.

[34] S. Goncharov, *Izvestiya*, 25 Feb. 1992.

[35] A. Arbatov, 'Russia's Foreign Policy Alternatives', 5–43. The failure to forge domestic support for policy was also evident with regard to domestic economic reform: very little effort was made to explain either domestic or foreign policy to the public.

[36] S. Rogov, in *Nezavisimaya gazeta*, 6 Mar. 1992.

[37] S. Stankevich, in *Nezavisimaya gazeta*, 28 Mar. 1992. Stankevich's article provoked considerable debate about where Russia's foreign policy interests lie. Most commentators seemed to accept the idea of a particular Russian 'mission', even if they disagreed about what it was. One critic, however, wryly pointed out that most nationalities were convinced of the uniqueness of their countries and worried about preserving their national cultures. However, when it came to international co-operation, they unquestioningly accepted the conventional rules of the game. See K. Viktorov, in *Nezavisimaya gazeta*, 5 Jun. 1992.

[38] *Nezavisimaya gazeta*, 28 Mar. 1992.

[39] A. Pushkov, in *Moskovskie novosti*, 1 Mar. 1992.

[40] S. Goncharov, *Izvestiya*, 25 Feb. 1992.

[41] A. Vasil'ev, *Izvestiya*, 19 Mar. 1992.

[42] See, for example, V. Belous, in *Nezavisimaya gazeta*, 28 Feb. 1992.

[43] The phrases cited come from N. Narochnitskaya, in 'Russia's National Interests', 105, 109. Narochnitskaya worked at the Institute of World Economy and International Relations and was also chair of the international commission of the Constitutional Democratic Party.

[44] Ibid. 110; E. Pozdnyakov, 'We Must Rebuild', 132.

[45] A. Dugin, in *Den'*, 1992, nos. 4–7.

[46] 'Ideologiya mirovogo pravitel'stva', *Elementy*, 1992, no. 2, pp. 1–2; V. Petrov, 'Pravda ob Amerike', *Nash sovremennik*, 1992, no. 2, pp. 171–3.

[47] 'Yevraziiskoye soprotivleniye', *Den'*, 1992, no. 2.

[48] D. Kalaich, in *Den'*, 1992, no. 24.

[49] S. Baburin, in *Nezavisimaya gazeta*, 9 Jan. 1992, cited in I. Torbakov, 'The "Statists" and the Ideology of Russian Imperial Nationalism', *RFE/RL Report*, 11 Dec. 1992, 10–16. The author of one article published in 1992 refers to Russia throughout as 'the USSR', adding in a footnote that the formation of the CIS on the ruins of the USSR is unconstitutional.

See A. Chichkin, 'Islamskii vopros', *Molodaya gvardiya*, 1992, no. 3–4, pp. 99–107. Some Fundamentalist Nationalists, however, notably 'village writers' like Valentin Rasputin and Vasily Belov, did not want the Soviet Union re-established.

[50] V. Yurovitsky, *Den'*, 1992, no. 24.

[51] I. Torbakov, 'The "Statists"', 10–16.

[52] See, for example, the round table in which the leader of the Russian Communist Party, Gennady Zyuganov, participated (*Den'*, 1992, no. 22).

[53] The law was published in *Rossiiskaya gazeta*, 6 May 1992.

[54] As A. Kortunov ('Konfliktnyi potentsial "blizhnego" zarubezh'ya i adekvatnaya strategiya Rossii', *Diplomaticheskii vestnik*, 1992, no. 21–2, p. 41) pointed out, since the Russian Federation was itself multinational, citizenship was based on the principle of territory, so that all the people who lived in the RSFSR automatically became citizens of the Russian Federation. But the right to defend Russians in the 'near abroad' required granting them Russian citizenship by virtue of their ethnicity. See also A. D. Bogaturov, M. M. Kozhokin, and K. V. Pleshakov, 'Vneshnyaya politika Rossii', *SShA: Ekonomika, politika, ideologiya*, 1992, no. 10, pp. 27–41.

[55] Russian was the lingua franca of the Soviet Union. It was natural, therefore, that non-nationals living in other republics tended to speak Russian. Thus Belorussians or Ukrainians living in Uzbekistan, say, were likely to be Russian-speakers (whatever nationality was accorded to them in their passports), and they were unlikely to know much Uzbek. The Jews of the Soviet Union were usually Russian native speakers. Russian native speakers were affected by two related features of the immediate indigenization which occurred in all the republics after the Soviet Union disintegrated: all the republics adopted the indigenous language as the official language, which disadvantaged Russian speakers; and most republics adopted explicit or implicit policies of positive discrimination in employment which favoured indigenous people.

[56] Those who thought that Russia required a strong state were known as *gosudarstvenniki* or statists.

[57] N. Kosolapov, 'Vneshnyaya politika Rossii: Problemy stanovleniya i politikoformiruyushchie faktory', *Mirovaya ekonomika i mezhdunarodnye otnosheniya*, 1993, no. 2, pp. 5–20. Kosolapov also developed interesting and original theories about the nature of security in the post-Cold War world. See N. Kosolapov, 'Natsional'naya bezopasnost' v menyayushchemsya mire', *Mirovaya ekonomika i mezhdunarodnye otnosheniya*, 1992, no. 10, pp. 5–19; 'Mezhdunarodnaya bezopasnost' i global'nyi politicheskii protsess', *Mirovaya ekonomika i mezhdunarodnye otnosheniya*, 1992, no. 11, pp. 5–18; and 'Sila, nasiliye, bezopasnost': sovremennaya dialektika vzaimosvyazei', *Mirovaya ekonomika i mezhdunarodnye otnosheniya*, 1993, no. 11, pp. 45–58. His theoretical work during this

period was highly original and it was rooted in democratic ideals. He was thus probably the most direct heir to the traditions of New Political Thinking (a tradition which he probably had a hand in building as Alexander Yakovlev's aide during perestroika).

[58] K. Eggert, in *Izvestiya*, 7 Aug. 1992.

[59] Ibid.

[60] S. Chugrov, 'Rossiya mezhdu Vostokom i Zapadom?', *Mirovaya ekonomika i mezhdunarodnye otnosheniya*, 1992, no. 7, p. 81; S. Blagovolin, 'O vneshnei i voennoi politike Rossii', *Svobodnaya mysl'*, 1992, no. 18, pp. 8–9.

[61] Vladimir Orlov's interview with Kozyrev, *Moskovskie novosti*, 14 Jul. 1992.

[62] On the natural sympathy for fellow Slavs, see Kozyrev's article in *Izvestiya*, 8 Jun. 1992. As far as New Political Thinking about conflict is concerned, Kozyrev's attempts to negotiate a cease-fire in the Bosnian war were not dissimilar to the mission Yevgeny Primakov undertook for Gorbachev to the Gulf before Operation Desert Storm was launched and again before the ground attack began in 1991. See M. Light, 'Soviet Policy in the Third World', *International Affairs*, 67 (1991), 263–80.

[63] For the Fundamentalist Nationalist position, see, for example, *Den'*, 1992, nos. 23 and 30. Ambartsumov's arguments are in *Izvestiya*, 27 Jun. 1992, while Arbatov's reference to a special relationship can be found in 'Russia's Foreign Policy Alternatives', 32. See also S. Crow, 'Ambartsumov's Influence on Russian Foreign Policy', *RFE/RL Research Report*, 17 May 1993, 36–41.

[64] See, for example, the report by V. Bragin on the founding congress of the National Salvation Front, *Izvestiya*, 27 Oct. 1992.

[65] F. Shelov-Kovedyaev, 'Strategy and Tactics of Russian Foreign Policy', cited in J. Lough, 'Defining Russia's Relations with Neighbouring States', *RFE/RL Research Report*, 14 May 1993, 53–60.

[66] T. T. Timofeev, 'O vozmozhnykh variantakh dal'neishego razvitiya SNG', *Polis*, 1993, no. 1, pp. 37–43.

[67] M. A. Khrustalev, 'Evolyutsiya SNG i vneshnepoliticheskaya strategiya Rossii', *Diplomatichesky vestnik*, 1992, no. 21–2, pp. 39–40.

[68] A. Zagorsky, 'Russia and Europe', *International Affairs* (Moscow), 1993, no. 1, pp. 43–51.

[69] A. Zagorsky, 'The Commonwealth', *International Affairs* (Moscow), 1993, no. 2, pp. 45–53, at p. 53. For Moscow as the centre of the CIS, see Khrustalev, 'Evolyutsiya,' 39–40.

[70] A. V. Kortunov, 'Konfliktnyi', 41–3; A. Arbatov, 'Imperiya ili velikaya derzhava', *Novoye vremya*, 1992, no. 50, pp. 20–3.

[71] The brochure published by the Moscow State Institute of International Relations' Centre for International Research (*Sodruzhestvo nezavisimykh gosudarstv: Protsessy i perspektivy*, Moscow, 1992), for example,

maintained that Russia had 'remained in the role of an outside peace-keeper or a passive participant and has avoided direct involvement in conflict' (p. 20). It also warned that the order to Russian forces to shoot if they were attacked (this was the policy for peacekeeping forces agreed by the CIS in July 1992) carried the danger that extremist forces in other republics or what they called the 'party of war' in Russia would provoke conflict with Russia. It made no reference to conflict situations in which Russian commanders had already become involved. For the Liberal Westernizers' response to the idea of CSCE involvement in the settlement of CIS conflicts, see the interview with Kozyrev in *Rossiiskaya gazeta*, 25 Jul. 1992.

[72] S. Karaganov, 'Problemy zashchity interesov rossiisko–orientiro-vannogo naseleniya v "blizhnem" zarubezhye', *Diplomaticheskii vestnik*, 1992, no. 21–2, pp. 44–5. See also Arbatov, 'Russia's Foreign Policy Alternatives', 27–8.

[73] The development of Russian government policy with regard to peace-keeping is chronicled in S. Crow, 'Russia Seeks Leadership in Regional Peacekeeping', *RFE/RL Research Report*, 9 Apr. 1993, 28–32.

[74] Bogaturov et al., 'Vneshnyaya politika Rossii', 37.

[75] Arbatov, 'Russia's Foreign Policy Alternatives', 27; Karaganov, 'Problemy', 45.

[76] 'Strategiya dlya Rossii', *Nezavisimaya gazeta*, 19 Aug. 1992.

[77] The evolution of Russia's foreign policy concept is traced in K. Komachi, 'Concept-Building in Russian Diplomacy: The struggle for Identity: From "Economization" to "Eurasianization"', unpub. paper written at the Center for International Affairs, Harvard University, 1994. See also A. Pushkov's interview with A. Migranyan and D. Ryurikov in *Moskovskie novosti*, 20 Jul. 1993. The full version of the Foreign Ministry draft appeared in a special issue of the Foreign Ministry journal, 'Kontseptsiya vneshnei politiki Rossiiskoi Federatsii', *Diplomaticheskii vestnik*, Spetsial'nyi vypusk (Jan. 1993). A three-page summary was published as 'Russia's Foreign Policy Concept', *International Affairs* (Moscow), 1993, no. 1, pp. 14–16. The names of 30 of the 37 members (politicians, academics, military personnel, diplomats, and entrepreneurs who represent various political persuasions, excluding communist and extreme nationalist) of the Council for Foreign and Defence Policy are given in S. Crow, 'Competing Blueprints for Russian Foreign Policy', *RFE/RL Research Report*, 18 Dec. 1992, 46–7. Both Kozyrev and Stankevich were members but neither participated in drafting the report.

[78] For an example of the discussion surrounding the document, see 'What Foreign Policy', 8–21. The official version that was finally adopted is described in V. Chernov, 'Natsional'nye interesy Rossii i ugrozy dlya ee bezopasnosti', *Nezavisimaya gazeta*, 29 Apr. 1993.

[79] 'Kontseptsiya', 3.

[80] 'Strategiya dlya Rossii', p. 5, paras. 1.4.1, 2.3.9, 2.3.12, 2.3.13.

[81] 'Kontseptsiya', 10.

[82] Less than two weeks before the final concept was adopted by President Yeltsin, however, defence ministers dissolved the joint CIS military command. See Allison, 'Military Forces in the Soviet Successor States', Adelphi Paper 280; London, 1993, p. 12 and ch. 5.

[83] 'Strategiya dlya Rossii', p. 5, paras. 2.3.4, 2.3.5, 2.3.7, 2.3.15, 2.3.16.

[84] 'Kontseptsiya', 5.

[85] 'Strategiya dlya Rossii', p. 5, paras. 2.2.3, 2.2.4, 2.2.6, 2.2.7.

[86] 'Kontseptsiya', 9–11.

[87] 'Strategiya dlya Rossii', p. 5, paras. 1.3.3, 2.2.8, 2.2.11.

[88] 'Kontseptsiya', 19–20.

[89] 'Strategiya dlya Rossii', p. 5, paras. 2.2.8, 2.2.10.

[90] 'Kontseptsiya', 8; 'Strategiya dlya Rossii', p. 5, paras. 2.4.1, 2.4.3, 2.4.5.

[91] For examples of the Foreign Ministry's democratic and market assumptions, see 'Kontseptsiya', 3, 5. The gloomier prognosis of the Council for Foreign and Defence Policy is reflected in 'Strategiya dlya Rossii', p. 4, paras. 1.2.2, 1.2.3.

[92] See, for example, 'Kontseptsiya', 5, 9; 'Strategiya dlya Rossii', pp. 4–5, paras. 1.2.1, 1.2.4, 1.2.5, 2.2.9. The Strategy and the Foreign Ministry concept are compared in H. Adomeit, 'Great to be Russian?', *International Affairs*, 71 (1995), 35–68.

[93] Chernov, 'Natsional'nye interesy Rossii'.

[94] M. Lobanov, 'Komy ugrozhaet novaya Rossiya?', *Molodaya gvardiya*, 1994, no. 4, pp. 79–87, at p. 81; G. Zyuganov, in *Sovetskaya Rossiya*, 22 Sept. 1994; V. Bol'shakov, in *Pravda*, 28 May 1994.

[95] 'TsK VKPB o strategicheskom partnerstve mezhdu SSha, NATO i Rossiei', *Bol'shevik*, 1994, no. 14, pp. 2–3; Ye. Popov, *Sovetskaya Rossiya*, 2 Aug. 1994. Russian National Unity maintained that the attack on the White House was co-ordinated by two high-ranking members of the CIA and a unit of NATO's rapid reaction forces. See its publication *Russkii poryadok*, no. 9–1 (12–13), Dec. 1993–Jan. 1994, p. 2. On his release from prison, Rutskoi also maintained that the current regime was in the service of Western and international financial interests. See his speech in *Zavtra*, Jun. 1994.

[96] S. Kara-Murza, *Sovetskaya Rossiya*, 2 Jul. 1994; V. Alksnis, *Sovetskaya Rossiya*, 9 Aug. 1994.

[97] N. Popov, 'Vneshnyaya politika Rossii (Analiz politikov i ekspertov)', *Mirovaya ekonomika i mezhdunarodnye otnosheniya*, 1994, no. 3, pp. 52–9; no. 4, pp. 5–15.

[98] A. Arbatov, 'Russian National Interests', in R. Blackwill and S. Karaganov (eds.), *Damage Limitation or Crisis? Russia and the Outside*

*World* (Washington, DC, 1994), 55–76. A. Pushkov argued that it was not so much that Liberal Westernizers changed their mind, however, as that Pragmatic Nationalists gained predominant influence in the foreign policy decision-making structures. See A. Pushkov, 'Letter from Eurasia: Russia and America: The Honeymoon's Over', *Foreign Policy*, no. 93, Winter 1993–4, 76–90.

[99] Arbatov had originally divided Russian thinking about foreign policy into pro-Western, Moderate Liberal, Centrist Moderate Conservative, and Neo-Communist Nationalist ('Russia's Foreign Policy Alternatives') and he classified himself as a Moderate Liberal. He believed that pro-Westerners and Moderate Liberals had now adopted the views of the Moderate Conservatives, while some Centrist Moderate Conservatives had become Radical Nationalists.

[100] A. Arbatov, 'Rossiya: natsional'naya bezopasnost' v 90-e gody', *Mirovaya ekonomika i mezhdunarodnye otnosheniya*, 1994, no. 7, pp. 5–15. An account of the main guide-lines of the new Russian military doctrine can be found in *Izvestiya*, 18 Nov. 1993. Its adoption and concepts are discussed in Chapter 5.

[101] Arbatov, 'Russian National Interests'.

[102] 'Strategiya dlya Rossii (2): Tesizy Soveta po vneshnei i oboronnoi politike', *Nezavisimaya gazeta*, 27 May 1994; the quotes are from the introduction and para. 1.1. Arbatov is prominent among the many specialists whose work the authors of the Strategy used in preparing their theses.

[103] Ibid. para. 4.

[104] Ibid.; passage quoted from para. 3.5.

[105] Ibid. para. 3.7.

[106] Ibid.; quotes from para. 3.10.5. Part of the second 'Strategy for Russia' was devoted to criticizing the ineffectiveness and inefficiency of Russian foreign policy decision-making and suggestions for how it might be improved. See Chapter 3.

[107] For a detailed analysis of Russia's peacekeeping operations, see Allison, *Peacekeeping in the Soviet Successor States* (Chaillot Papers 18, Paris, 1994).

[108] A. Chereshnya, 'Big Brother as an Equal', *New Times*, 1993, no. 17, pp. 12–13. Kozyrev seemed later to admit that the Russian military in Abkhazia had been involved in the politics of the conflict. See A. Kozyrev, *Preobrazhenie* (Moscow, 1995), 113. The role played by the military in various conflicts in the former Soviet Union is discussed in Chapter 5.

[109] See, for example, Kozyrev's article in *Nezavisimaya gazeta*, 13 Oct. 1993, particularly his statement that 'there is no need to scorn non-traditional methods like the participation of contingents from the conflicting sides themselves and from the neighbouring state-mediator in the

operation . . . This model should not be ignored, but used in other regions in the interests of the UN, which is overburdened with peacekeeping operations.' In UN terminology peacemaking consists of diplomatic activity designed to achieve a negotiated peaceful settlement of a conflict, while peacekeeping is a military presence designed to implement arrangements related to the control of conflict. To be fair, it is not just in Russia that there is confusion about the terms; in relation to Bosnia, in particular, popular criticism of the UN role has frequently been based on mistaken ideas about the terms under which humanitarian intervention is undertaken.

[110] Kozyrev's speech at Chatham House, published in *Segodnya*, 4 Nov. 1993. See also A. Pushkov, *Moskovskie novosti*, 1994, no. 11. It should be noted that efforts *have* been made to agree guide-lines on CSCE monitoring of Russian peacekeeping activities. Russia has been reluctant, however, to give the CSCE (from 1995, OSCE) automatic right of access to the political negotiations which accompany peacekeeping activities. See 'Peacekeeping in the Commonwealth of Independent States', *Background Brief*, FCO (London, 1995).

[111] 'Interesy Rossii v SNG', *Mezhdunarodnaya zhizn'*, 1994, no. 9, pp. 13–35, at p. 18. See also V. Kuznechevsky's report on the decision to send troops to Abkhazia in *Rossiiskaya gazeta*, 18 Jun. 1994.

[112] N. Kosolapov, 'Novaya Rossiya i strategiya zapada', *Mirovaya ekonomika i mezhdunarodnye otnosheniya*, 1994, no. 2, p. 14.

[113] Statement by Russian Foreign Ministry spokesman Mikhail Demurin in *RFE/RL News Brief*, 16–20 Aug. 1993, cited in Allison, *Peacekeeping in the Soviet Successor States*, 36.

[114] Kozyrev, *Preobrazhenie*, 115.

[115] See S. Chugrov, 'NATO Expansion and the Chechen Link', *European Brief*, vol. II, no. vi (Mar.–Apr. 1995), 5–6.

[116] See, for example, A. Poleshchuk, *Nezavisimaya gazeta*, 22 Sept. 1994, on the report by the Foreign Intelligence Service 'Rossiya-SNG: nuzhdaetsya li v korrektirovke pozitsiya Zapada?'

[117] I. Lagunina ('Pochemu ne ustraivaet partnerstvo?', *Novoe vremya*, 1994, no. 14, pp. 28–9) gives a lively summary of the arguments for and against Russian membership of the PFP. The arguments of the Liberal Westernizers are well represented by A. Konovalov and S. Oznobishchev, *Segodnya*, 26 Mar. 1994. See also the article by V. Litovkin in *Izvestiya*, 24 May 1994. For the doubts of the Pragmatic Nationalists, see A. Pushkov's interview with Vladimir Lukin in *Moskovskie novosti*, 1994, no. 16, and the article by S. Stankevich and V. Kalashnikov in *Segodnya*, 8 Apr. 1994. Note, however, that not all Pragmatic Nationalists were opposed to membership; Sergei Karaganov (*Izvestiya*, 24 Feb. 1994), for example, was convinced that Russia would gain from joining the programme.

[118] Kosolapov, 'Novaya Rossiya', 14.

[119] A. Pushkov, *Moskovskie novosti*, 1993, no. 39; S. Karaganov, *Moskovskie novosti*, 1993, no. 38, and *Izvestiya*, 24 Feb. 1994.

[120] When it was announced that after attending the Victory Day commemoration in Moscow, President Clinton would visit Kiev in May 1995, *Izvestiya* (30 Mar. 1995) saw this as evidence of an American determination to establish a double buffer zone separating Russia from Europe. The first would contain the East-Central European states which joined NATO, while the second would contain the Baltic republics and Ukraine.

[121] S. Karaganov, *Moskovskie novosti*, 1993, no. 38; S. Pavlov, 'Rossiya i evropeiskaya bezopasnost', *Novoye vremya*, 1994, no. 10, pp. 24–5; A. Pushkov, *Moskovskie novosti*, 1993, no. 39.

[122] Kozyrev, *Preobrazhenie*, 200.

[123] See P. Podlesny, *Segodnya*, 29 Apr. 1994 for the conclusion that the purpose of expanding NATO was to contain Russia. Kozyrev's objection is in *Preobrazhenie*, 199. An excellent, detailed account of the course of events which led to the plan to enlarge NATO and the adoption of the PFP instead is given in V. Cherbyakov, 'Rasshireniye NATO i izmeneniye balansa sil v Yevrope', *Svobodnaya mysl'*, 1994, no. 6, pp. 27–47.

[124] Interview with Y. Baturin in *Moscow News*, 1995, no. 22.

[125] For the Luxemburg example, see General Volkogonov's remark to Steven Erlanger, *The New York Times*, 23 May 1994. The example of Duma deputy Vyacheslav Nikonov's objection to Iceland outvoting Russia is cited in M. Pavlova-Sil'vanskaya, 'Vverkh-vniz', *Novoye vremya*, 1994, no. 17, pp. 4–6.

[126] A. Pushkov, reported in S. Erlanger, *The New York Times*, 23 May 1994. On the matter of NATO expansion, however, it was the Minister of Defence, Pavel Grachev, who warned the US Secretary of Defence, William Perry, that Russia might suspend its fulfilment of the CFE treaty if NATO was expanded. See *OMRI Daily Digest*, 4 Apr. 1995, part 1.

[127] S. Oznobishchev, *Segodnya*, 3 Feb. 1995.

[128] A. Kozyrev, *Preobrazhenie*, 5–8.

[129] This is not to argue that the disintegration of the USSR was universally welcomed. But almost all those who supported independence believed that it would bring economic benefit. It is almost certainly accurate to say that Russia subsidized many of the other republics. But the Russians who reiterate this fact rarely consider the non-material gains that imperial centres derive from their empires.

[130] For analyses of the results of the elections, see R. Sakwa, 'The Russian Elections of December 1993', *Europe-Asia Studies*, 47 (1994), 195–227, and S. Chugrov, *Russia between East and West* (New York, forthcoming).

[131] S. Karaganov, 'Russia's Elites', in Blackwill and Karaganov (eds.),

*Damage Limitation or Crisis?*, 43. See also Arbatov, 'Rossiya', 10–11 and, for the growing influence of Pragmatic Nationalists (he called them 'statist democrats'), A. Pushkov, 'Letter from Eurasia', 78–9.

[132] N. Kosolapov, 'Kakaya Rossiya nuzhna Zapadu?', *Mirovaya ekonomika i mezhdunarodnye otnosheniya*, 1994, no. 2, p. 9. A. Pushkov ('Letter from Eurasia') argued that part of the problem was that Gaidar's government and the democratic media oversold the magnitude and value of the anticipated aid. On the volume of aid, see I. Maksimichev, 'Russia and Western Europe', in Blackwill and Karaganov (eds.), *Damage Limitation or Crisis?*, 174–5.

[133] See Chapter 3, and also *The Economist*, 17 Jul. 1993 for Russia's search for new arms markets; *Financial Times*, 24 Mar. 1995, for the refusal to call off the sale of nuclear reactors to Iran. V. Kremenyuk, *Nezavisimaya gazeta*, 24 May 1994, expresses a typical Russian reaction to Western interference in Russia's foreign trade.

[134] The postponement of the decision on Russian membership of the Council of Europe is explained by Daniel Tarschys, its Secretary-General, in *The International Herald Tribune*, 11 Feb. 1995. Russia was finally admitted to the Council in February 1996. Oleg Davydov, Russian Minister for Foreign Economic Relations, accused the EU of using protectionist measures against Russia claiming that Chechnya was simply an excuse for postponing the trade agreement. See *Financial Times*, 18 Mar. 1995.

[135] A. Pushkov, *Moskovskie novosti*, 1994, no. 17. V. Kremenyuk (*Nezavisimaya gazeta*, 24 May 1994) also complained of many occasions on which the West had been arrogant in its relations with Russia. A journalist pointed out to American Deputy Secretary of State, Strobe Talbott, that the Russians were tired of being treated 'like schoolchildren in front of a strict teacher'. See *Literaturnaya gazeta*, 1994, no. 18–19.

[136] It is worth noting that for all the rhetoric about defending Russian-speaking people in the 'near abroad', this has so far not been necessary. Even in relation to the conflict between Moldova and Transdniestria, Russia's attitude cannot be explained entirely in terms of defending Russians: ethnic Moldovans form 40% of the population of Transdniestria, while Russians and Ukrainians together form 54%. But many Russians live in the rest of Moldova. It must also be said that there was absolutely no sign of the Russian army protecting the Russians who live in Chechnya. They were not evacuated before the attack and they have not received any special treatment in the areas which are now under Russian control.

[137] The correlation between the recommendations in the Council for Foreign and Defence Policy's second 'Strategy for Russia' and current Russian foreign policy is extremely close (far closer than the correlation with the official concept). Its strictures on great-power rhetoric have not, however, had much effect.

[138] A. Pushkov, *Wall Street Journal*, 5 Apr. 1994.

# 3

# Foreign Policy Making

## NEIL MALCOLM

In most countries foreign policy questions are handled among a relatively small circle of officials in the executive arm of government. Access to information about foreign policy making is not easy, and the process tends to be relatively insulated from domestic politics.[1] The Soviet system was one of the most secretive of all. However, since the collapse of the Communist order considerably more information has become available about how foreign policy is made in Moscow. What is more, the confusion and conflict of Russian political life mean that the boundary between domestic politics and the foreign policy process has become much more penetrable. The political struggle is likely to have an impact even on the innermost decision-making circles greater than it would in a more stable and routinized setting.

The first main section of this chapter describes the network of foreign policy institutions which was constructed in Russia after the passing of Soviet power, and the second analyses the political context and the political consequences of their interactions with each other during the period to 1995. These two sections are preceded by a brief discussion of the Soviet legacy in foreign policy making. The new Russian state, after all, inherited not only a set of institutions and several thousand trained personnel from its Soviet predecessor, but also a distinctive culture and style in policy making.

## The Soviet legacy in Russian foreign policy making

One of the defining characteristics of the Soviet system of rule was the supreme position of the Communist Party, enshrined in ideology and in law, and largely observed in practice. Most strikingly this was evident in the control of flows of information. The state bureaucracies possessed great reserves of expertise, and in some cases enjoyed great authority, but only (with the exception of the KGB) in a well-defined, specialized area. Even senior civilian officials were deprived of access to the kind of basic information needed to argue a case on arms control issues, for example.[2] It was only in the apparatus of the Party Central Committee and its Secretariat that the information was collated, and only there that an overall view could be formed. A relatively high proportion of decisions could not be taken at any level lower than in the Party Politburo, which formed the 'cabinet' of the system. The Party was responsible, too, for developing the ideological framework and justification for policy, and for supervising policy implementation.[3]

The other side of the coin of restrictions on information was that particular agencies were even more likely than in other states to remain imprisoned within a specialist perspective and focused on their own particular interests. As in other areas of Soviet life, the Party's omnipresent controlling and leading role was matched by what were frequently complained of in Party documents as 'localism' and 'departmentalism' in the bodies that it sought to control.[4]

More broadly, secrecy and the impossibility of free-ranging discussion meant that there could exist nothing resembling an 'informed public'. The enforcement of a detailed Party line on foreign policy issues left no room for open debate, or for the emergence of the kind of broad élite foreign policy consensus which is considered to be normal in more open societies. During the Brezhnev years a large network of foreign affairs research institutes was established in the Soviet Academy of Sciences. Foreign affairs journals were published and conferences were held. But discussion was strictly confined and substantial disagreements could only be expressed in oblique terms.

To excise the Communist Party from such a system, as happened in the autumn of 1991, would at first glance appear to condemn it to disabling internal conflict. Since 1991, George Kennan's prophecy has been frequently cited:

The membership at large has been exercised only in the practices of iron discipline and obedience and not in the arts of compromise and accommodation. If disunity were ever to seize and paralyze the Party, the chaos and weakness of Russian society would be revealed in forms beyond description . . . Soviet Russia might be changed overnight from one of the strongest to one of the weakest and most pitiable of national societies.[5]

Yet Kennan was writing in 1947. Four decades later the Party leadership ruled in a less straightforward way. The General Secretary, it was argued by some, was forced to rely on the support of coalitions drawn from different parts of the party-state oligarchy. The Politburo had won, and retained, decision-making supremacy, but, if we are to believe one Soviet foreign policy expert writing in 1984, it had changed its character during the Brezhnev years:

The Politburo was transformed from a group of personal associates and aides to the dictator, as it was under Stalin and to a lesser extent under Khrushchev, into a kind of supreme legislative committee of the Soviet élite, representing all the principal power groups—the central party apparatus, local party cadres, economic management, the military, the KGB, the foreign policy establishment and the military-industrial complex.[6]

Thus policy was shaped in part by a process of compromise and accommodation among interested representatives. The weight of their views would vary according to the issue, and also, to a degree, according to their personal standing. There was no stable distribution of roles between the main bureaucracies.[7] In foreign policy, as in defence matters, the Party apparatus seems not to have enjoyed the same dominance it exercised over the ministries responsible for internal affairs. Western experts found it difficult to agree, for example, about the size of the general information-gathering and supervisory powers wielded by the Central Committee's International Department, which also had the specialized task of maintaining liaison with non-bloc Communist Parties.[8] Its general role was probably steadily undermined from 1973 onwards by the presence in the Politburo of the Ministers of Foreign Affairs and Defence, and of the head of the KGB. When he became General Secretary in 1985 Mikhail Gorbachev was keen to enhance the standing of the International Department, according to one of its senior officials, so that the Foreign Minister should understand that 'his monopoly was coming to an end'.[9]

What this illustrates, of course, is the ability of a determined Party leader and Secretariat, leaning on Politburo solidarity and authority, to rein back special interests if they began to appear overweening. It should be noted that the Soviet regime, like its imperial predecessor, set great store by the military instrument in policy. Between 1953 and 1985 Soviet leaders at certain times tended to defer to the military out of political weakness and at other times appeared simply to find the military definition of reality the most congenial one.[10] Care was always taken, however, to limit the scope for military influence: Brezhnev's Minister of Defence, Ustinov, came from a civilian, albeit defence-industrial, background, and the Defence Council appears to have been dominated by civilian officials.[11]

In general, then, despite the apparently increasing collective aspects of Politburo rule, the Soviet policy making system was designed to operate with a strong centre, with deep role specialization of institutions and individuals, and with very little participation by the public. When central control was slackened, at times of transition or uncertainty at the top level, bureaucratic conflicts frequently bubbled up onto the surface, and policy coherence suffered.[12]

This kind of disarray was particularly evident in the final part of Gorbachev's period in power. Apparently understanding that extreme centralization, specialization, and lack of free debate in foreign policy matters in fact weakened the top leadership's ability to make good decisions, he had broken the military monopoly on discussion of security issues, sanctioning the setting-up of arms control departments inside the Foreign Ministry and the Party apparatus. He appointed a generalist as Foreign Minister. He permitted much more wide-ranging discussion, not just in the specialized journals but even in the general newspaper press, touching on the most central parts of foreign policy doctrine.[13]

At the same time Gorbachev strove to preserve and exploit the authority, information sources, analytical capacity, and controlling powers of the Party apparatus. Even after the instituting of a presidential system, the Central Committee departments continued to fulfil important functions in foreign policy. But by 1990–1 these levers of power no longer had the same effectiveness. Reforms had weakened the authority of the Party, and their outcome had weakened the authority of its leader. Thus relations with the Western alliance, and with Eastern Europe, were complicated by an ever more apparent lack of co-ordination between the positions of agencies such as the Foreign Ministry, the Party International Department, the Ministry of Defence, and the KGB.[14]

At the end of 1991 Boris Yeltsin and his government inherited a system of state institutions accustomed to working under strong leadership and central control and within the guidelines of doctrines justified by an elaborate state ideology. The attributes which in other societies substituted for strict centralization, namely more or less stable, sometimes legally reinforced procedures, prerogatives, and responsibilities, and underlying consensus on the broad lines of policy among officialdom and a wider, well-informed élite, had had little opportunity to develop during the relatively short period of reform and freer debate ushered in by glasnost and democratization. Indeed the tensions of 1990–1 had deepened disagreements in the élite, and had sparked a renewal of bureaucratic conflicts, particularly in the foreign policy area. The politically active public in general were ill-informed about international matters and likely to be vulnerable to appeals to support simple, extreme solutions. Things were made worse by the rapid turnover in the political élite which occurred in Moscow in 1990–2,[15] and the general sense of loss of ideological bearings. In such circumstances the final elimination of Party control and attempts to reconstruct the whole foreign policy making system were likely to provoke serious confusion and damaging inter-agency conflict.

Complications were introduced by changes in the external environment. As a result of the departure made under Shevardnadze from the traditional Russian priority for military-security concerns the Cold War had been ended, but the country had ceded its superpower status, and had been forced to retreat behind its sixteenth-century boundaries. There was a widespread feeling of national humiliation. The role of military agencies in foreign policy making and the place of military means in policy were bound to be a vexed issue. New Political Thinking had helped to raise unrealistic hopes concerning a new partnership with the West, and the assistance the West might be prepared to provide. The disappointment of these hopes was to provide another source of tension inside the Russian government.

There were now fourteen former Soviet states among Russia's neighbours, a new 'abroad'. Relations with these states were bound to be particularly intense and complicated, because of close economic ties, because of inflamed security concerns on both sides, and because of the millions of Russian-speakers living outside the Russian Federation. The Foreign Ministry in Moscow inherited no departments able to deal with these newly foreign countries, and specialist knowledge about them was hard to find.

As for the new states, they were struggling to build their own foreign policy machinery at a moment when difficult, fundamental decisions had to be made, especially about relations with Russia. Ukraine, Kazakhstan, and Belarus had possessed their own 'foreign ministries' during the Soviet period, but these were small bodies, around fifty-strong in the case of the two larger states. Some staff were transferred from the Soviet Foreign Ministry to Kiev, and some to Almaty, but this could do little to alleviate a severe shortage of skill and experience. In the Ukrainian case domestic political influences, in particular the power of nationalist sentiment, were especially important. They were able to make relations with Russia uncomfortable and at times confrontational in 1992 and 1993, which in turn put further strains on Russian foreign policy making.

In such a situation any one or a combination of three outcomes were conceivable for the Russian foreign policy making system: worsening disorder, imposition of strong leadership as had occurred in the past, or development of a workable *modus vivendi* among the main bureaucratic players. Clearly, a lot would depend on the domestic political context, and that will be discussed later in the chapter. We shall begin by outlining the institutional structure as it grew up in the first years of post-communist rule.

## Russian foreign policy institutions

During the first three years after the collapse of the Soviet Union, there was a whole series of substantial changes in the Russian foreign policy system. In the early months the Russian Foreign Ministry and like-thinking officials in the President's staff dominated affairs: the military and security apparatus and its political allies were still in disarray in the aftermath of the August 1991 coup attempt, and until May 1992 there were no separate Russian armed forces. In May 1992 the Security Council was endowed with substantial foreign policy responsibilities. Simultaneously Russia's parliamentary assemblies (the Supreme Soviet and the larger Congress of People's Deputies) began to assert a more active role. The second half of 1992 was a period of acute struggle between the Foreign Ministry and these other bodies, centring on the demarcation of duties and powers and on policy itself. In 1993 wider political battles impinged more and more. In particular the role of the Security Council was twice redefined, and, at the end of the year, constitutional change deprived the legislative arm of some of its power. Yet this was a period during which a broader consensus on policy among the main institutions began to emerge. By the end of 1994 an atmosphere of greater stability in the distribution of roles seemed to have established itself. The principal agencies concerned are listed in Figure 3.1.

## The President

The Soviet-era constitution which was in force for the first two years of independence gave great formal powers to the legislature, powers which with the passing of communist rule it occasionally tried to put into practice. Parliament was given the right to lay down the main lines of foreign policy, while the President and the government were responsible for implementing it. In the constitution adopted at the end of 1993, by contrast, the President 'directs the foreign policy of the Russian Federation', within the framework set by the constitution and laws of the country (Articles 80 and 86). He no longer needs parliament's approval of ministerial appointments, or of the composition of the Security Council (Article 83), although it retains some less important rights in the foreign policy area (see below).

In practice, Russian foreign policy was essentially 'presidential' from the start. The new constitution merely made it more difficult for the legislature to mount challenges to the President's role, and to cause disruption. Inside the executive arm, the President has played the key role, despite the powers conferred by the constitution on the Prime Minister, who is supposed to determine 'the main lines of activity of the government and organize its work' (Article 113).

It is an aspect of continuity with Soviet tradition that the Russian Prime Minister and his 'government' (in the narrower sense) are concerned primarily with internal and economic affairs. The President has kept hold of the overall political and security roles of the Politburo and General Secretary of the CPSU, and this includes most of the non-economic side of foreign policy.[16] Thus

*Neil Malcolm*

*Presidential Apparatus*

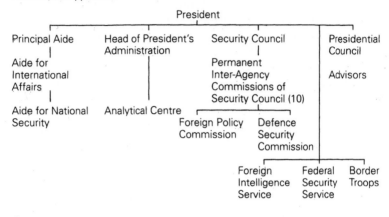

President

| Principal Aide | Head of President's Administration | Security Council | Presidential Council |
|---|---|---|---|
| Aide for International Affairs | | Permanent Inter-Agency Commissions of Security Council (10) | Advisors |
| Aide for National Security | Analytical Centre | Foreign Policy Commission    Defence Security Commission | |

Foreign Intelligence Service    Federal Security Service    Border Troops

*Government*

Prime Minister

| *Ministry of Foreign Affairs | Ministry for Cooperation with CIS States | Ministry of Foreign Economic Relations | *Ministry of Defence |
|---|---|---|---|

and Joint Coordinating Committees

* Ministers reporting directly to the President

*Legislature*

State Duma Committees:

| Committee for International Affairs | Committee for Defence | Committee for Security | Committee for CIS Affairs and Links with Compatriots | Committee for Geopolitical Questions |
|---|---|---|---|---|

Subcommittees

Federation Council Committees:

| Committee for International Affairs | Committee for Security and Defence | Committee for CIS Affairs |
|---|---|---|

*Sources*: 'Key Officials in the Russian Federation: Executive Branch', and 'Key Officials in the Russian Federation: Legislative Branch', both in *RFE/RL Research Report*, 4 Mar. 1994, pp. 9–17 and 18–20 respectively.

FIGURE 3.1. Russian foreign policy decision making—principal institutions, mid-1995

the Director of the Federal Security Service (FSS), the Director of the Foreign Intelligence Service (FIS), and the Commander-in-Chief of the Border Troops are all described as members of the President's Staff. Moreover the Minister of Defence and the Foreign Minister, who are members of the government, also report directly to the President, and are members of the President's Security Council. This has created, in the words of one Russian commentator, a wing of the Russian government which is 'to all intents and purposes directly under the President'.[17]

Although it has been repeatedly predicted that the Security Council will emerge as a 'new Politburo' and its apparatus as a new 'Central Committee', it appears that the President prefers to maintain multiple channels of information and advocacy. He works closely with his aides, who provide him with a daily summary and analysis of reports from the intelligence agencies, the General Staff, the diplomatic service, parliament, and the media.[18] There is provision for a presidential 'adviser' on foreign affairs.[19] Several foreign policy experts sit on the Presidential Council (a specialist advisory body). Materials from the Council and its working groups, as well as the output of the presidential Analytical Centre, are channelled to the President through the aides and the Head of his Administration.[20] There is also a presidential Expert-Analytical Council chaired by the Head of Administration, and composed of several members of the Presidential Council, a number of aides, the head of the Analytical Centre, and some independent specialists.[21]

More importantly, Yeltsin allows generous direct access by key ministers. According to one authoritative report, the heads of the FSS and the FIS, the Foreign Minister, and the Minister of Defence 'see the President on an almost daily basis'.[22] A strong impression emerges of a chief executive who is determined to keep his hands on the levers of power, and to intervene actively in the policy process, choosing who to listen to and who to ignore (this is certainly the testimony of his senior aide).[23] Which parts of this network the President decides to favour have varied sharply from time to time, giving rise to bitter complaints from those who find themselves excluded.[24]

In an interview given in 1993 Dmitry Ryurikov, the President's aide for international affairs, stated a view of the Security Council's role that is conceivably not too distant from Yeltsin's:

To my mind, it is hardly advisable to have a structure which would
possibly be below the President but above the government, and lay down
the strategic and tactical aspects of the activities of ministries and other
government departments. These prerogatives belong and must belong to
the President.[25]

Like political leaders in other bureaucratized great powers, Yeltsin
is obliged to fight to retain some power of personal decision.[26]
But each solution carries inescapable costs. Refusing to accept the
emergence of an intervening super-ministry means, for example,
that the President and his close aides are faced with huge tasks of
information-handling, co-ordination, and supervision, tasks which
it is sometimes suggested may be beyond their capabilities. The
danger of arbitrary and ill-founded decisions being taken is increased. In May 1994 the report of an autonomous commission
of experts and officials concluded:

The President has so far paid insufficient attention to foreign-policy and
security issues . . . ; he clearly does not have the bureaucratic capability
to supervise effectively, even in a broad sense, the formation and implementation of a coherent foreign-policy strategy.[27]

The question of the effectiveness of Russia's foreign policy machine
will be discussed at the end of this chapter. In the meanwhile it
should be said that in such a system a great deal must depend on
personnel factors, on the professionalism of the President's entourage and on his relationships with other members of the government.
Communications with the Foreign Ministry, for example, were
undoubtedly assisted by Yeltsin's appointment as his aide for international affairs of Dmitry Ryurikov, an expert on international
law, and a former professional diplomat who was head of the
Soviet Foreign Ministry's Middle East Department. Diplomats and
ex-diplomats have also occupied key positions in the Security
Council.[28] Yet the system as a whole was far from harmonious in
its operation.

## The Security Council

The Security Council was designed as a consultative body which
would make recommendations and proposals, and 'prepare decisions
for the President of the Russian Federation' on security matters,

which he would implement by decree.[29] It has a broad remit, covering internal as well as external security, and this is reflected in the responsibilities of its permanent Inter-Agency Commissions (see Fig. 3.2). In 1994 the Council also acquired a consultative Academic Council.[30]

The membership, scope of activities, and influentiality of the Council have all changed several times since 1992 (see Figure 3.2).[31] When it was first established, a distinction was made between permanent, voting members (the Secretary, the Vice-President, the Prime Minister, and the First Deputy Chairman of the Supreme Soviet) and others.[32] In the middle of 1994 a Deputy Secretary of the Council, Valery Manilov, stated that resolutions were not adopted by majority vote, but by consensus, implying erosion of the earlier two-tier structure, and other reports confirmed that impression.[33] However, in January 1995 it was announced that the group of 'permanent members' had been enlarged, and now would include the President, the Prime Minister, the Secretary, and the two Speakers. The effect was to correct any impression that Yeltsin was submitting himself to collegial authority or to undue influence on the part of the 'power ministers'. The latter, it was emphasized, lacked a formal vote, and the inner core of the Security Council could meet in their absence.[34]

In May 1993 the President had acted with similar decisiveness to remove an overmighty Secretary of the Council, Yury Skokov, and to downgrade the importance of the institution (see below). The Secretary appointed in September 1993, Oleg Lobov, was widely considered to have been selected for the post mainly because of his loyalty to the President, and the Security Council grew in importance under his management.[35] It is described as the duty of the Secretary to co-ordinate the Council's work and to manage its staff, to prepare agendas and other documents for its sessions, including draft decisions, to monitor implementation of decisions, to maintain co-ordination with legislative and executive bodies, and in addition to keep the President informed on internal and external security problems. He is assisted by a Secretariat, an Information and Analysis Department, and a Department for Co-ordination and Interaction, which prepares materials for Council sessions. There are three Deputy Secretaries.[36]

The Security Council has been described at different times as a forum for senior government officials, an apparatus for gathering

```
                                    President
                                        |
                                    Secretary of the
                                    Security Council
                                        |
                                    Security Council
                                    (13 other members)
      ┌─────────────────────────────────┴──────────────────┐
Inter-Agency Commissions                 Apparatus of the        Academic
      |                                   Security Council        Council
Foreign Policy                  ┌─────────────────┴──────────────────┐
      |                    Department of      Department of       Secretariat
Defence Security           Information and    Co-ordination
      |                    Analysis           and Interaction
Regions                                       (preparation of
      |                                       Security Council
Social Security                               sessions)
      |
Information Security
      |
Science and Technology in the Defence Industry
      |
Ecological Security
      |
Economic Security
      |
Health Protection
      |
Fight against Crime
```

Permanent members: The President (B. Yeltsin), Security Council Secretary
(O. Lobov), Prime Minister (V. Chernomyrdin), Speakers of State Duma
(I. Rybkin)* and Federation Council (V. Shumeiko)*

   * The Speakers were given full membership in January 1995

Other members: Deputy Prime Minister and Nationalities Minister (S.
Shakhrai), Foreign Minister (A. Kozyrev), Defence Minister (A. Grachev),
Interior Minister (V. Erin), Director of the FSS (S. Stepashin), Director of the
FIS (Ye. Primakov), Commander-in-Chief of Border Troops (A. Nikolaev),
Justice Minister (Yu. Kalmykov), Minister for Civil Defence and Emergencies
(S. Shoigu), Nationalities Minister (N. Yegorov)

FIGURE 3.2. Structure and membership of the Russian Security
Council, mid-1995

data and preparing decisions, and a political actor in its own right. What part does it play in practice in the making of Russian foreign policy? It is striking that the contingent of staff allocated to the Council in June 1992 was just eighty-strong. By the summer of 1994 the figure had increased only slightly, to just over one hundred.[37] The intention was plainly that the new body would operate principally by focusing and co-ordinating the activities of other parts of the executive.

Much of its work appears to be carried out by the temporary and permanent Security Council Inter-Agency Commissions, on which other departments are normally represented at deputy minister level. One of its own officials described these Commissions as 'the basic working organs' of the Council, and the forum where 'the interests and positions of ministries and agencies are harmonized'.[38] It is the Commissions which have the task of drawing up drafts for many of the Council's resolutions. However, the Commissions appear to meet infrequently, and they are characteristically headed by a representative of the ministry most closely concerned. In the first part of 1994 the Foreign Policy Commission was chaired first by Ednan Agaev, the head of the Foreign Ministry Analysis and Forecasting Administration, and subsequently by First Deputy Minister Anatoly Adamishin. As well as 'preparing draft decisions on the basic direction of Russian foreign policy' for the President, the tasks defined for it when it was set up at the end of 1992 included research, policy-planning and co-ordination, and reviewing proposals on military-political issues and foreign economic relations.[39]

The second point to be made is that, as the titles of its Inter-Agency Commissions indicate, the Council has had very wide responsibilities: it does not have the resources to analyse, plan, co-ordinate and supervise all the areas concerned except on a selective, episodic basis. Reports of its meetings refer to resolutions and programmes of action being adopted on subjects such as subsidizing key parts of the defence industry, fighting organized crime, preventing food contamination, and investigating the fall of the rouble in October 1994.[40] In interviews in May and June 1994 Deputy Secretary Manilov provided a long list of questions which his organization had either recently discussed, or planned to deal with. They included such topics as inequalities between rich and poor, slowing the brain drain, and preserving the country's scientific and technological base.[41] In February 1994 the Security Council managed the selection process for 250 senior posts in the new Federal Counter-Intelligence Service.[42]

The Security Council has tried to sustain work on long-term, strategic tasks. In 1992–3, for example, it was its Inter-Agency Foreign Policy Commission that organized the final stages of discussion and preparation of the new Russian foreign policy 'concept'.[43] Later in 1993 it was to the Council that Defence Minister Grachev brought his draft of a new military doctrine, and in July 1994 a Commission was set up in the Council to compile a 'national security concept'.[44] Yet, when discussing the activity of the Security Council in foreign affairs, its own officials have acknowledged that it is under pressure to fulfil a fire-fighting role, reacting to crises and conflicts around Russia's borders.[45] Matters such as unrest in the Caucasus, political tension in Crimea, disputes over the Black Sea Fleet, and the fighting in Tajikistan have taken up much of the Council's time.

At times the predominant function of the Security Council has seemed to be one of providing an arena for departmental competition and self-promotion. On 26 July 1993, for example, its members met to discuss the situation in Tajikistan. Its deliberations were reported briefly at the time, but the nature of the proceedings was revealed quite clearly in the presidential decree which was issued on the following day. This document noted the threat posed to Russia's vital interests by the deterioration of conditions on the border with Afghanistan, aggravated by 'irresponsibility', 'unpreparedness', and 'uncoordinated actions' by different agencies. In order to ensure coherence in policy, it announced the dismissal of the Commander of Border Troops and the appointment of the Foreign Minister as the President's Special Representative for Tajikistan, with the task of co-ordinating the efforts of different ministries and working out agreed recommendations for the Security Council. The latter were to be presented in one month's time, taking into account the views of the Ministries of Security, Foreign Affairs, and Defence, the Interior Ministry, and the Foreign Intelligence Service.[46]

The first meeting of the 'Inter-Agency Working Group' on Tajikistan duly took place on 17 August, and it met repeatedly during the subsequent year. However, this body, which co-ordinated policy in the area in a more sustained way, was not part of the

Security Council system: it was a government co-ordinating committee chaired by the Deputy Foreign Minister and convened on Smolensk Square.[47] The outcome answered to Foreign Ministry preferences, with the strong emphasis given to diplomatic solutions and the granting of the main co-ordinating role to Kozyrev, although in practice it did not seriously reduce the dominant role of the Defence Ministry on the ground in Tajikistan.[48]

The programme for stepping up the struggle against crime announced in May 1994 was described as the first one that the Council apparatus had devised itself: previous policy documents had all originated in separate government departments.[49] In August 1994 the Commander of the Border Troops stated in an interview: 'When the question of Russia's state border was examined in the Security Council, the border guards drew the Council members' attention to sensitive areas . . . The President, the Prime Minister and Council members supported the border troops' proposal about the need to devise a Russian Federation state border policy, based on recognition of diversity of borders.'[50] The Security Council as such did not appear able to exercise a veto. In the case of the new military doctrine drafted by the Ministry of Defence, misgivings in the Council were simply overridden by Presidential decision.[51]

Thus the work of the Security Council was hampered not just by the political upheavals and organizational disruption that are described in the next section of this chapter, but by limitations on its capacity (which were no doubt also political in origin). Nevertheless, since the summer of 1994 its officials have spoken with more confidence about the Council's role, and it has enjoyed greater prominence in decision-making. In discussing its work it is helpful to distinguish between the Security Council as apparatus, and the Security Council as a gathering of the President and his ministers.

The Council's apparatus has the advantage of access to all foreign-policy-relevant information, including top-level intelligence data. At its head is the Secretary, who is responsible for setting the decision-making agenda 'in consultation with ministers'. Before meetings, information and analytical documents are circulated to the ministries concerned, along with draft decisions. In most cases general agreement is reached on a decision before the session convenes. In cases of emergency the Secretary may go directly to the President with reports and alternative policy recommendations which his apparatus has prepared. The Security Council also has specific responsibilities and powers for monitoring implementation of decisions taken as a result of its work, and it appears to have become more effective in this area of activity.[52]

Officials of the Security Council have been ready to speak openly about their work to the press, and to explain their policy priorities. Deputy Secretary Manilov has been particularly active in fostering an impression of the importance of the Council. In April 1994 he declared that it intended 'to play a special role in the further establishment of Russia's political links with the United States and the countries of Western Europe'. He described its part in preparing a Russian response to the NATO Partnership for Peace proposals as follows:

In view of its strategic importance, the resolution of this issue is not the concern of individual agencies, in my opinion. The Partnership for Peace programme—the substantive part, not the declaratory, framework part—will be discussed in the Russian Security Council, which will direct the appropriate organizations to formulate a thoroughly researched Russian position, a position that will not damage Russia's national interests. And after that procedure, the Russian President will make a decision in the form of a decree or a Security Council protocol approved by him.[53]

The Defence Minister confirmed that 'a group of Russian specialists' was compiling a document for discussion at the Security Council outlining ideas for Russia's response to NATO. The Council's decisions would form the basis for his position during the visit to Brussels planned for 24 May.[54]

Plenary sessions of the Security Council enjoy a great deal of publicity, compared to similar events in other countries. They are regularly reported in the press, and the opening minutes are frequently shown on television. Clearly it is intended to strengthen the impression that the President takes important decisions only after thorough consultation and deliberation, and that his ministers are subject to collective discipline. The sense is created that the nation is benefiting from vigorous leadership, and that the chief executive is putting his stamp on all important decisions.[55]

No doubt the Council does play an important role in formulating an agreed view on key foreign policy problems and in deciding on ways of solving them. It is less probable that, as one of its Deputy Secretaries claimed in October 1994, its decisions are taken 'in a total absence of departmentalism, opportunism, and subjectivity'.[56] There is no reason why it alone should be immune from the destabilizing effects of the political battles which traverse the Russian administration. Whether as forum or as apparatus the Security Council can serve a variety of political purposes, at the behest of a variety of actors. The following assessment was made in a Council for Foreign and Defence Policy document released in May 1994:

The apparatus of the Security Council has in the last six months acquired a greater co-ordinating potential. But in practice it cannot exercise it. As before, the key role in defining policy is played by the relevant departments, which despite all the differences between them are united in one thing—in their refusal to be subordinated to anyone.[57]

One well-known Russian journalist commented: 'The president believes that the Security Council is first of all Lobov, "his own man". But it is a gathering of the most varied politicians: hard-bitten, efficient, and calculating, having their own interests and aims.'[58] And in any case the President, as we have seen, has no obligation, and feels no obligation, to respect Security Council decisions.[59]

As we shall see below, how important the Security Council happens to be at a given time—and by the end of 1994 it appeared to have become particularly prominent—depends first of all on the state of the political game, and in particular on the power position of its Secretary, at present Oleg Lobov, and his allies. Participants in the process testify that there are several centres of power in Russian foreign policy making. Decisions depend on the influence which each of them can exert on the President at any given time.[60] The following pages examine the role of the most important agencies outside the presidential apparatus.

## The Foreign Ministry

Before the setting-up of the Security Council's Inter-Agency Foreign Policy Commission, the Foreign Ministry was the only agency with formal responsibility for overseeing international policy. 'The Russian Foreign Ministry,' read a decree of 3 November 1992, 'will be entrusted with the function of co-ordinating and monitoring work by other Russian ministries, committees, and departments to ensure a unified political line by the Russian Federation in relations with foreign states.'[61] When the Inter-Agency Commission was established shortly afterwards, Foreign Minister Kozyrev's press spokesman refused to see this as a challenge: 'It is not a question of a hierarchical but rather a horizontal structure . . . Nobody questions the coordinating role of the Foreign Ministry in the foreign policy sphere.'[62]

Behind the scenes, as we shall see, things were less calm, and a fierce interdepartmental struggle was under way. However, thanks to the administrative resources at his command and his closeness to the President, Kozyrev seems to have been successful in retaining a dominating position in Russian foreign policy making. As was noted earlier, former diplomats have occupied important posts in the parts of the President's apparatus concerned with foreign policy. Even at times of change and inconsistency in the content of Russian policy, and despite the criticisms of the Foreign Ministry which emerged from the President's office from time to time, it was rare in the period 1992 to 1995 to see any serious divergence between substantial public statements by Yeltsin and Kozyrev on international matters, especially on those concerning East–West relations.[63]

Since the end of 1991 a continual process of reorganization and adaptation to international and domestic change has been under way in the Russian Foreign Ministry. These adjustments have had to be made at a time of strict spending constraints.

The Ministry inherited from its Soviet predecessor a body of highly skilled and experienced staff. However, poor pay and the attractions of employment in the new private sector have created serious problems in retaining and recruiting employees. By the middle of 1993 the number of staff in Moscow had shrunk by almost a thousand, to around 3,000, of whom 60 per cent were described as diplomats. The number employed abroad had dropped from 9,500 to 7,500, including approximately 2,500 diplomats. A year later the corps of diplomats deployed abroad had shrunk to 1,800. Staff resignations were running at around 500 a year (twenty times the rate in the 1960s and 1970s), leaving hundreds of posts unfilled. In August 1995 Ministry press spokesman Grigory Karasin spoke of a crisis in his agency brought about by the outflow of employees caused by 'catastrophically low salaries'.

The Russian diplomatic service is still comparable in size to that of other large European states, and the closing down of some distant embassies has no doubt had a negligible impact, but there are worries about quality. A meeting of the Foreign Ministry Collegium in 1994 was devoted to discussing the 'alarming situation' which had arisen in the recruitment field. It discussed proposals for incentive systems for younger staff and appealed to the government for help. It has been difficult to persuade staff to take up posts in the former Soviet states and in other less popular areas, while specialists working on the advanced industrialized countries are the most likely to leave the service. When matters came to a head over the future of the Kurile Islands, in 1992, it is reported that the Ministry's Far Eastern Department could find only one Japanese specialist to join the *ad hoc* section dealing with the issue.[64]

It was inevitable that problems would be caused by the way in which the relatively inexperienced, reformist leadership of the small Russian Republic Foreign Ministry of 1991 was put in charge of the old Soviet Ministry. In April 1992 Andrei Kozyrev declared that 60 per cent of his subordinates were either 'cynical or demoralized'.[65] However, the Minister pushed ahead energetically with structural and personnel changes and imposing a Liberal Westernizing political line.

An extra tier—'department' (*departament*)—was added, above the existing 'administration' (*upravlenie*) and 'section' (*otdel*) levels. The Analysis and Forecasting Administration was rejuvenated and strengthened.[66] New departments were set up to deal with economic relations, scientific co-operation, and other areas previously outside the Ministry's sphere. A Department for the CIS Countries was established in March 1992, but the decree setting up embassies in the capitals of the 'near abroad' was issued only in September, and the whole operation was scantily funded.[67] The Department had an Administration for CIS Affairs (multilateral), and an Administration for the CIS Countries (for bilateral relations). Staff complained that they bore at least half of the burden of the Ministry's work, while receiving considerably less than their share of resources. Diplomats could often only be persuaded to serve in CIS capitals if they were promised a more attractive posting to follow. Although a number of Arabists transferred to work on Central Asian affairs, there was a painful shortage of specialist knowledge on the former Soviet states in general.[68]

Russia's more active policy in the CIS from 1993 was accompanied by institutional changes in Moscow. In November of that year a session of the Foreign Ministry Collegium launched a wholesale reorganization, in the course of which responsibility for bilateral relations with the CIS states was distributed to the well-established departments dealing with states beyond the borders of the former USSR. The intention was evidently to redirect talent and expertise towards urgent 'near-abroad' problems. Moreover the department responsible for multilateral CIS affairs was to be 'strengthened by the transfer of specialists on disarmament issues and on international relations'.[69] The resulting internal structure of the Ministry is shown in Figure 3.3.

Like other Russian ministries, and its counterpart in the Soviet era, the Ministry of Foreign Affairs possesses a Collegium, a consultative group which in April 1994 contained eleven deputy ministers, nine department heads, the Minister's Executive Secretary, and his Adviser. Reported meetings of the Collegium appear to have been devoted mainly to internal administrative matters.[70] The Executive Secretariat acts as the private office of the Minister, and manages the work of the Ministry. There is a consultative Co-ordination and Analysis Group inside the Secretariat, staffed mainly by senior diplomats, and there is a separate Group of Advisers. Deputy Ministers are assigned responsibilities corresponding to those of one or a group of the specialized geographical or administrative departments, and regular reports in the media of their meetings and statements mean that they have a much higher public profile than their counterparts in most other governments.

The Russian Foreign Ministry participates in numerous consultative and co-ordinating bodies inside and outside the government. Kozyrev's initiative in promoting the formation of an Inter-Agency Commission on Tajikistan under his First Deputy's chairmanship has already been described. Several other bodies of this kind have been created, typically bringing together a dozen or more deputy ministers from different departments (some contain over forty members), and meeting several times a year. There are Inter-Agency Commissions on Russian Federation Participation in UN Agencies, on UNIDO Affairs, on Russian Federation Participation in Peacekeeping Activities, on Military-Technological Co-operation with Foreign Countries, on Defence of Russia's Border Interests, and so on.[71]

As early as October 1991 the first Russian Foreign Ministry

round-table meeting was held with private businesses, with the aim of 'determining their interests in the sphere of foreign policy'. One outcome was the establishing in February 1992 of the Foreign Policy Foundation, 'a non-government body dedicated to harmonizing the interests of Russian public and private bodies in the sphere of foreign policy'. The Foundation was supported by a string of media, commercial, financial, and industrial enterprises. The practice of regular consultations with economic interests continues, for example through the holding of conferences on topical issues of foreign economic policy such as technology export controls.[72]

Several times a year, meetings of the Council on Foreign Policy bring together senior officials (usually including the Minister) with specialists from research institutes and businesspeople. In the late 1980s foreign policy experts from the Academy of Sciences enjoyed a period of enhanced influence on policy, as Gorbachev and Shevardnadze sought assistance in their effort to displace traditional Soviet foreign policy thinking. In the 1990s politics has become more open, many experts have become politicians or journalists, and their special role appears to have diminished. Nevertheless there is a small group of a dozen or so highly visible specialists, some of whom are members of the Presidential Council, some of whom are invited regularly to the Council on Foreign Policy, and some of whom help in the drafting of speeches and policy documents.[73]

In March 1994, a meeting was held at the Foreign Ministry with 'representatives of the public' to discuss the situation of Russian-speakers outside Russia.[74] Intensive work is done in the parliament to promote policies, facilitate legislation and ratification, answer questions, and provide briefings. In 1992 the Minister and his deputies appeared 84 times in the Supreme Soviet and its committees.[75]

At the end of October 1991 the Soviet Ministry of Foreign Trade was combined with the Ministry of Foreign Affairs to form a new Ministry of External Relations, but in February 1992 a separate Ministry of Foreign Economic Relations was established. The Ministry was given the task of supervising the remnants of the Soviet system of monopoly Foreign Trade Organizations, which continued to operate alongside private trading firms. The Ministry plays the main part in export-promotion activities, setting tariffs and import controls, and negotiating international trade agreements,

Minister

First Deputy Minister, 9 Deputy Ministers

Collegium (around 20: Deputy Ministers and Department Heads, Adviser)

Executive Secretariat

Co-ordination and Analysis Group

Group of Advisers

Ambassadors at Large with special responsibility for conflict resolution

Department for CIS Affairs

Analysis and Planning

Multilateral Affairs

Conflictology

Department for Liaison with Subjects of the Federation, Parliament, and Political and Public Organizations

First European Dept. (Albania, Belgium, France, Italy, Luxemburg, Netherlands, Portugal, Spain, Yugoslavia)

Second European Dept. (Baltic states, Denmark, Finland, Norway, Sweden, UK and Ireland)

Third European Dept. (Austria, Belarus, Czech Republic, Germany, Hungary, Poland, Slovakia, Switzerland)

Department for Security and Co-operation in Europe

Department for North America

Department for Central and South America

Department for North Africa and the Near East

Department for Africa

First Asian Dept. (China, Hong Kong, Kazakhstan, Korea, Kyrgyzstan, Mongolia, Taiwan)

Second Asian Dept. (ASEAN states, Australia, Cambodia, Japan, Laos, Myanmar, New Zealand, Vietnam)

Third Asian Dept. (Afghanistan, Bangladesh, India, Iran, Pakistan, Sri Lanka, Tajikistan, Turkmenistan, Uzbekistan)

Fourth Asian Dept. (Armenia, Azerbaijan, Georgia, Turkey)

Department for International Organizations and Global Problems

Department for Disarmament and Monitoring of Military Technologies

Department for Non-Proliferation, Arms Transfers, and Conversion

Department for International Humanitarian and Cultural Co-operation

Department for International Scientific and Technological Co-operation

Department for Information Technology

Department for Regional Co-operation and Economic Problems

Department for International Economic Relations

Also **Legal Department, Historical Department, Personnel Department, Protocol Department, Information and Press Department, Consular Service**

FIGURE 3.3. Internal structure of the Russian Ministry of Foreign Affairs, mid-1995

such as the Partnership and Co-operation Agreement signed with
the European Union in the summer of 1994.[76]

## Security and defence agencies

Military and security agencies have become increasingly important in Russian foreign policy making. The Soviet Communist Party
had always paid special attention to the task of keeping the military under political control, and the end of communism, combined
with the weakening of civilian authority, provided new leeway
for the Russian Ministry of Defence and the officer corps. It was
soon clear that in the new era the long-standing partisanship of the
armed forces was by no means coming to an end. It was simply
taking on a less manageable form.

The stalemate at the upper levels of civil power during Yeltsin's
struggle with the Supreme Soviet in 1992 and 1993, and Yeltsin's
reliance on force and on the loyalty of the 'power ministries' to
win his constitutional battle, offered special political opportunities
to the military and the security agencies. Security concerns moved
higher up the foreign policy agenda, too, as conflicts continued to
flare up around the periphery of the former Soviet Union, and the
climate of opinion on foreign policy began to reflect a preoccupation with redefining 'national interests' and asserting them more
vigorously.

Changes in the balance of military and civilian influence on
policy are described in the second half of this chapter, and in
Chapter 5 there is a comprehensive analysis of military factors in
Russian foreign policy. The Ministry of Defence, the Foreign Intelligence Service, and the Federal Security Service, like the Foreign
Ministry, enjoy direct access to the President as well as regular
representation in the Security Council. The first two secretaries of
the Security Council, a leading military industrialist and the former
CIS Commander-in-Chief, could be expected to be receptive to the
armed forces' point of view, and in general the balance of representation in the Council favours military and security departments.

In the former Soviet area, agencies concerned with security
matters have tended to communicate directly with their counterparts in neighbouring states, and to act with a freedom they would
not enjoy in the wider world. By October 1994 the then Federal
Counter-Intelligence Service had signed co-operation agreements

with the corresponding ministries of all the CIS states except Turkmenistan and Azerbaijan.[77] Russian border troops guard a large part of the frontiers of the former Soviet Union.[78] Throughout this region the Ministry of Defence has at times appeared to usurp diplomatic functions, bringing protests from the Foreign Ministry, or to make decisions without due consultation with civilian agencies. In October 1992, for example, after representations by the Ministry of Defence and others the President announced an immediate halt to Russian troop withdrawals from Lithuania, without the Foreign Ministry being informed.[79] Foreign Ministry preferences appear to have been ignored, too, during the early stages of the peace keeping intervention in Tajikistan.[80]

Local commanders in trouble spots such as Moldova and Abkhazia have often appeared to be taking far-reaching decisions on their own initiative, in defiance of Moscow's declared policy (see Chapter 5). From time to time certain generals express extreme views to the press on the most sensitive political issues. The fact that they can carry on doing so with impunity suggests that they have powerful protectors, and/or an intimidating level of support among their fellow officers. This introduces an additional factor into the decision-making equation, one which is bound to weigh against civilian views. Current plans to reinforce military co-operation with other CIS states are likely to entrench the influence of the armed forces in the region. In the words of one Russian commentator, whereas the dinner suit has tended to dominate Russia's wider foreign policy, the camouflage jacket has been more in evidence in the 'near abroad'.[81]

Since 1991 the former Soviet KGB has been broken up, step by step, into several smaller entities. Those most engaged in international affairs are the Foreign Intelligence Service, the Federal Security Service (Federal Counter-Intelligence Service from December 1993 to April 1995, previously Ministry of Security), and the Federal Border Guards Service.[82] Fragmentation and upheaval served initially, as doubtless they were intended, to reduce the political weight of the intelligence services, but the agencies concerned do not appear to have suffered a disabling loss of confidence. The commander of the Border Guards, General Andrei Nikolaev, has become a well-known public figure, and has written that 'the relative shares of the army and the special services in guaranteeing national security have changed dramatically' in favour of the latter.[83] He and the other chiefs of the 'special services' are ready to participate in public policy debate in a way unusual in most other countries.

During 1993 and 1994, for example, the FIS issued a number of 'open reports' on important and politically sensitive international issues. The first, on nuclear weapons proliferation, was followed by an analysis of the consequences of NATO expansion in Eastern Europe. The second of these documents was launched amid great publicity and with assurances about its widespread endorsement by the Russian defence establishment.[84] In September 1994 the agency's head, Yevgeny Primakov, gave a press conference to launch a report analysing Western attitudes to CIS integration. He commented that while President Yeltsin had not read the document in full he had 'naturally enough been informed about this analysis', and the problems it raised would undoubtedly surface in his forthcoming talks in London and Washington. Yeltsin's decree of 14 September 1995, 'On Approving the Russian Federation's Strategic Course in Relations with CIS Member States', echoed a number of themes from the FIS report.[85]

*Economic relations: the role of the Prime Minister and his government*

According to the constitution, the Russian Prime Minister has the task of planning and co-ordinating government activity, including the areas of defence and foreign policy, in accordance with legislation and presidential decrees. As we have seen, however, these two areas have tended to be reserved to the presidential structures and the 'presidential ministries' (defence, foreign affairs, security agencies). The Prime Minister and the government nevertheless have an important part to play in foreign relations, especially in the economic and social sphere and in the former Soviet area, where economic issues are relatively more salient. The Foreign Ministry Statute of March 1995 states that control of its activities shall be exercised 'by the President and the government of the Russian Federation along the respective lines of their authority'.[86]

Relations between the CIS states, until recently part of a single, highly integrated USSR, are complex and multidimensional. As in the European Union, they imply constant interaction between a far wider range of ministries than those traditionally involved in foreign affairs; an important network of ties exists, too, at the regional level. The Russian government contains a State Committee for Economic Co-operation with Member States of the CIS, which was given Ministry status in January 1994. It is not, however, a 'super-ministry' capable of managing the whole sphere of activity its name refers to, and matters are organized through a complicated process of interministerial co-ordination.[87]

A stimulus to organizational development was given by the September 1993 CIS summit meeting, which agreed to establish an Economic Union. In December the Russian government issued instructions to over 30 of its agencies to draw up plans for implementing the 29 separate decisions reached in September and to draft the 10 intergovernmental agreements associated with them. The programme embraced matters as diverse as setting up a CIS court of human rights, copyright regulation, peacekeeping, technological co-operation, trade in agricultural machinery, fighting organized crime, harmonizing price and taxation legislation, and establishing a payments union. Joint co-ordinating and monitoring responsibility was given to the State Committee for CIS Co-operation and the Foreign Ministry.[88]

However empty many of the plans for CIS integration have turned out to be, this does not take away from the importance of the network of ties at ministerial and middle level linking Russia with the former Soviet states in spheres such as those mentioned above, ties which are rooted in decades of history and are perpetuated in many cases by practical necessity as well as by routine. They are formalized in bilateral agreements between Moscow and the CIS capitals, typically negotiated by ministries of finance, economics, and foreign economic relations. Certain of these agreements contain clauses referring to future harmonization of positions in talks with 'external' agencies, such as the IMF and the World Bank.[89]

In economic relations with other parts of the world a bigger part is played by the Ministry for Foreign Economic Relations, the Deputy Prime Minister in charge of external economic affairs, and the Prime Minister himself. The Russian Prime Minister, Viktor Chernomyrdin, came to deputize for the country's leader on trips abroad and for receiving visitors, as was done during the last decades of the Soviet era. In May 1994 Chernomyrdin travelled to Poland and China, in June to the United States to attend a session of the Gore-Chernomyrdin Commission, which was examining projects for collaboration on energy, space, and nuclear power engineering projects, and in July to Saudia Arabia and the Gulf. Subsequently he visited London, Prague, Bratislava, Sofia, and Bucharest.[90] Chernomyrdin, who was a permanent member of the Security Council from his appointment, cautiously marked out his own, centrist position on a number of foreign policy issues.

## The legislature

The Russian parliament's role in foreign policy making is discussed in detail in Chapter 4. Under the constitution adopted at the end of 1993 its lower house, the State Duma, and the Council of the Federation (sometimes referred to as the 'Senate') have the power to ratify and denounce international treaties (Art. 106 (g)), and ambassadors are nominated by the President 'in consultation with appropriate committees' of the parliament (Art. 83 (m)). Neither of these prerogatives affords deputies much leverage over policy.[91] As for their power of legislation, it is less effective because of the extensive use of executive decrees, and the President's rights of veto.[92] In May 1994 the Duma voted in favour of a law obliging the government to lift trade sanctions on Yugoslavia unilaterally, but Russian commentators interpreted the action as a political gesture which would have few practical consequences. Parliament's leaders themselves are ready to acknowledge the limited extent of its influence on foreign policy.[93] The Duma has five committees which deal with international matters (the Committee for International Affairs, the Committee for CIS Affairs and Links with Compatriots, the Committee for Defence, and the Committee for Geopolitical Questions), and the Council of the Federation has three (see Figure 3.1).

Now that the balance of power has been adjusted in its favour the executive arm seems to have developed a less confrontational relationship with parliament in the foreign policy sphere. This was particularly noticeable in the early months of 1994; the legislature subsequently rediscovered some of its assertiveness. Parliamentary delegations, such as the one which visited Washington in March 1994, tend to provide support to official diplomacy, rather than disrupting it as in the past. Parliamentary opinion is treated with respect by members of the administration, at least in public.[94]

The interaction of legislature and executive in foreign policy matters, like the interaction of different executive agencies, has been overwhelmingly dominated by movements in the overall political context. The political system is still at a formative stage. The part played by different institutions has been dependent much less on constitutional provisions and on any informal but stable division of prerogatives than it has on shifts of power and allegiance among the individuals and groups participating in a fierce and at times violent political struggle. The institutional and procedural framework conditions this struggle, but this framework is itself regarded as provisional and is continually contested. This means that the account given above can provide only a partial understanding of how Russian foreign policy is made. What is still needed is an explanation of how underlying political forces and the changing agenda of debate have shaped the relations between institutions and their role in the policy process.

## The politics of Russian foreign policy making

Between 1991 and 1994 the political context in which Russian foreign policy was made altered in a variety of ways. There were changes in the external environment, changes in élite perceptions, changes in the balance of internal political pressures, and changes in the institutional structure.

The implications of the ending of the Cold War and the opening up of Russia to the world economy set a long agenda of new problems for policy makers in Moscow. However, it was the breakup of the Soviet Union in December 1991 which turned out to have the most far-reaching impact. It touched on the personal lives of millions of Russians, and it disrupted economic and military networks. It made more acute the basic questions which were being posed about Russia's identity and role in the world, about what its 'national interests' were and what was the best way of promoting them.

One upshot of the external changes was to encourage the ferment of ideas among the foreign policy élite, analysed in Chapter 2, which ended in an decisive shift in the balance of perceptions away from unqualified Liberal Westernism. The main target of criticism was the idea promoted in Gorbachev and Shevardnadze's New Political Thinking that the old East–West confrontation could be replaced by a partnership of equals. This idea had already been badly dented by the working out of the new European settlement in 1990 and 1991, which left Russia in a much weaker strategic position, but the reform impetus was still strong enough to propel the radical liberalizing and Westernizing strategy of early 1992. In the period which followed, Western reluctance and set-backs in internal political and economic reform emerged as serious obstacles to full-scale Russian membership in the European-Atlantic club. Simultaneously, problems in the former Soviet area became more pressing. An immediate strategy emphasizing 'Eurasian' perspectives and more assertiveness *vis-à-vis* the West gained in attractiveness.

This tendency was powered not just by rational calculation, but also by emotion, in particular by feelings of humiliation and exclusion. As Chapter 4 demonstrates, nationalist sentiment does not seem to have dominated wider public opinion in 1992–4, but it was increasingly widespread at all levels in the political and policy making world. By the end of that period a nationalist tone had begun to colour the rhetoric even of the most Western-oriented officials and politicians. No doubt tactical considerations played a part, but there was also genuine disappointment among those who had originally championed the idea of partnership with the West.[95]

The domestic political environment pushed in the same direction. Opposition parties were eager to seize on vulnerable aspects of government policy—'giving away' territory to Japan, 'selling off' the nation's natural resource birthright, 'betraying' compatriots in the 'near abroad', and so on. After the defeat of its common enemy, the CPSU, it was to be expected that the democratic movement itself should split into rival factions competing for power. Several of the latter latched onto unpopular aspects of Westernization, and tried to harness resentments provoked by the breakup of the Soviet Union.

While the government was able to rely on broad support for its foreign policies from most of the banking and commercial sector, it came under pressure from producer interests complaining about the fragmentation of the former Soviet economic space, about the loss of arms export markets in countries like Iraq and Libya, and about the damaging effects inside Russia of over-ambitious economic liberalization and stabilization policies promoted by Western aid-givers and advisers. Fundamental doubts were raised about the whole opening-up strategy. Western assistance had been relatively

limited in size and disappointing in its effects. Foreign investment
and the inflow of advanced technology had been minimal. Russian
exports were making little headway in world markets, and attempts
were being made, it was claimed, to shut them out of markets
where they posed a danger to established suppliers.

All these forces were resolved in an institutional framework
which was still in the first stages of development. The general flux
and constitutional uncertainties, combined with the Soviet heritage of politicized bureaucracies, created an uneasy foreign policy
making environment. Different political tendencies and economic
interests found representation not only in the new parties and pressure groups but also in different parts of the administration and
in the government itself.

One survey of opinion among the foreign policy élite carried out
in 1993 attempted to relate political views to institutional affiliation. It concluded that 'Westernizers' were mainly to be found
'in foreign policy institutions, including the Foreign Ministry, the
academic community and the press, among politicians supporting Yeltsin, and among members of the Supreme Soviet Foreign
Affairs Committee'. 'Slavophiles' tended to be drawn from opponents of the President, other members of the Supreme Soviet, and
officials from other government departments (i.e. the Ministry of
Defence, the Foreign Intelligence Service, and the Council of Ministers apparatus).[96]

These correlations were of course only approximate: there was
no monolithic view among those who worked in particular departments. However, they draw attention to the main lines of battle
in the interdepartmental struggles over foreign policy in 1992 and
the early part of 1993. Subsequently the picture became less clear-
cut: Pragmatic Nationalism began to dominate in reformist circles,
wider agreement was reached over policy, and the pattern of inter-
agency conflict turned out to be less predictable. The account of
the politics of Russian foreign policy making given below revolves
around two important turning points, in early summer 1992 and
in spring 1993. The latter each coincide with the beginning of
new phases in Russian foreign policy as described in Chapter 1. It
was in early summer 1992 that internal opposition to Foreign
Ministry Westernism first began to be effectively mobilized. This
marked the start of a period of confusion in policy making and
unevenness in policy. By spring 1993 a compromise appears to

have been reached between the main foreign policy institutions, based on Pragmatic Nationalist thinking, which laid the basis for a degree of inter-agency co-operation and stability of policy.

## Challenges to the Foreign Ministry

From the passing of Soviet rule until the early summer of 1992 the Foreign Ministry enjoyed unprecedented dominance in foreign policy making. Party supervision had been removed, its traditional rivals in the form of the military and the security services were in disarray after the 1991 coup attempt and the break up of the USSR. Under the patronage of Gennady Burbulis, State Secretary and close adviser to Yeltsin, Andrei Kozyrev was granted general powers of oversight and co-ordination in foreign affairs, and was able to forward an uncompromising pro-Western line aimed at integrating Russia into what he called 'the democratic Northern Hemisphere'.[97]

The setting-up of the Security Council in May 1992 coincided with the end of Yeltsin's honeymoon period as President of an independent Russia. It also marked the beginning of a new phase of turbulence in Russian foreign policy. To many reformist politicians there seemed an ominous coincidence between the concessions made by Yeltsin to centrists at the recent Sixth Congress of People's Deputies and the emergence of Yury Skokov, a conservative-minded defence industrialist, as Security Council Secretary. Among the other three voting members of the Council was Vice-President Aleksandr Rutskoi, who publicly questioned the legitimacy of the new post-Soviet borders, and its wider membership included senior members of the defence/security establishment who also found Kozyrev's foreign policy uncongenial. Gennady Burbulis, the most highly placed protector of the liberals in the government, was not included. An adviser to President Yeltsin later commented that the Security Council under Yury Skokov 'was used more as a weapon in the internal political struggle than as a staff office for working out Russian policy'. Indeed, throughout its short history the Security Council has been an important focus for political manipulation, both in its role as a meeting place for senior officials and (later) in its information-gathering and analytical role.[98]

It was not long before the opposition to Kozyrev began to test its strength. Echoing the anxieties expressed by 'Eurasianist' foreign policy intellectuals (see Chapter 2), members of the Security Council criticized the Foreign Minister for neglecting Russia's relations with the other former Soviet states, and called for his resignation. Although Kozyrev survived, his deputy, Fyodor Shelov-Kovedyaev, was forced out. While Yeltsin did not yield to demands in the Council that a separate Ministry be set up to deal with 'near-abroad' matters, he nevertheless declared that the Foreign Ministry had 'proved unprepared to deal with the CIS countries'.[99] An embarrassingly public demonstration of the disruptive power of the institutions and tendencies represented in the Security Council occurred in September 1992, when a long-prepared visit by Yeltsin to Japan was cancelled at the last minute.[100]

The most serious rival to the Foreign Ministry in the second half of 1992, however, appears to have been the newly formed Ministry of Defence. Its Soviet predecessor had been accustomed to wide powers in foreign affairs, and more importantly had had the satisfaction of carrying out policies which harmonized with its world-view. The new generation of senior defence officials appeared determined to recapture influence and to reassert traditional values associated with national greatness. Soon after his appointment as Minister, Pavel Grachev put on the mantle of defender of the millions of Russians living outside the Russian Federation, and declared his readiness to fight 'for the honour and dignity of the Russian population'.[101]

The armed forces soon became involved in conflicts on the southern periphery of the former USSR, in ways that cut unceremoniously across the cautious diplomacy of the Foreign Ministry. The contradictions which this created are described in Chapter 5. In Moldovan Transdnestria and Georgian Abkhazia, for example, they appeared to give open support to the separatist side in civil wars. Vice-President General Rutskoi, who had close connections with the military, acted as a highly placed and vocal spokesman for those who questioned the new post-Soviet borders. Kozyrev reacted with fury: 'The party of war, the party of neo-bolshevism, is rearing its head in our country. Wholesale transfers of arms are taking place in the Transcaucasus and Moldova . . . Under what agreement is this effected, I would like to ask . . . ? Why are the military deciding the most important political issues?'[102]

With the Ministries of Defence and Security, by one account, simply 'refusing to co-operate with the Foreign Ministry under the current minister', the scene was set for a period of damaging confusion and incoherence in Russian foreign policy.[103] As Emil Pain, a member of the Presidential Council, was to put it in 1993:

> The real policy of Russia in the near abroad until recent times emerged from a fierce struggle between two political blocs—moderate reformers led by Yeltsin, and national-imperial forces, who had gained a stable major- ity in the supreme legislative bodies at the beginning of 1992 and were also represented in certain parts of the executive (in the office of the Vice- President and partly in the army).[104]

Parliamentary resolutions designed for domestic political impact, for example those proclaiming Russia's right to sovereignty over Crimea or the Kurile Islands, or pan-Slavic solidarity with the em- battled Serbs, had large disruptive side-effects in international rela- tions. This was particularly serious when the executive appeared split. In September 1992, for example, the effect of a cease-fire agree- ment signed by Yeltsin, Shevardnadze, and secessionist Abkhazian politicians was damagingly undermined by a Supreme Soviet vote which appeared to invite a renewal of hostilities by the rebels.[105] Resolutions on the Black Sea Fleet and on the status of Crimea and Sebastopol helped to inflame Ukrainian nationalist feeling.

In the midst of these contradictions, Yeltsin appeared frequently to be aggravating the lack of co-ordination, endorsing independent Ministry of Defence initiatives, for example in the Baltic states, and launching some of his own, while blaming the Foreign Ministry for lack of consultation. The feeling seemed widespread that only substantial organizational change could remedy things. *Krasnaya zvezda*, the army newspaper, declared at the end of 1992: 'We do not have a procedure for inter-agency consultation prior to the taking of foreign policy decisions. That is, *prior to*, and not *after* the decisions have been made.' Even a department head in the Foreign Ministry was prepared to acknowledge that his agency 'lacked the necessary powers to overcome interdepartmental conflicts'.[106]

At first sight the Inter-Agency Foreign Policy Commission of the Security Council, which was set up on 16 December, was destined to restore order, but the same tensions which made such an agency appear necessary helped to ensure that it never lived up to the hopes which were placed in it. In the turmoil of Russian politics in 1992 and 1993 it was inconceivable that a politician like Kozyrev would accept arbitration by a body chaired by Yury Skokov, who in his eyes was using the Security Council in an openly political way, striving, as he later expressed it, to resurrect Party-style controls and to stifle policy 'in a suffocating embrace'.[107] The President, too, was in no hurry to set up a super-ministry which would diminish his powers of final decision. The Foreign Policy Commission accordingly turned out to have a limited role. It had a small staff (only ten strong at first), and by June 1993 it had only met once in full session, to approve the new foreign policy concept.[108]

## From conflict to 'consensus'

By the summer of 1993 a third phase in foreign policy was under way. The alignment of forces in the Russian foreign policy establishment had changed fundamentally, in a way which removed a large share of the previous confusion and inconsistency, but organizational change had little to do with it. Several other factors seem to have combined to favour a more co-operative atmosphere. Liberal Westernism was becoming discredited among large parts of the reformist camp. In politics, the President and his reformist supporters were moving to consolidate a broader-based 'left-centre' coalition capable of resisting the more and more intransigent opposition based in the Supreme Soviet. In the upper levels of power, Yeltsin strove to construct a unified anti-parliamentary front, selecting Viktor Chernomyrdin as a Prime Minister who would both remain loyal and appeal to a broad base of support, and disowning his Vice-President. Kozyrev modified the Foreign Ministry line to incorporate Pragmatic Nationalist preferences for a more active policy in the former Soviet area and a tougher line *vis-à-vis* the West. The seal was put on a new, albeit imperfect consensus when in April 1993 all the participants endorsed the new compromise foreign policy concept.[109] Just as the outbreak of hostilities in the summer of 1992 claimed a victim with the departure of Shelov-Kovedyaev as Deputy Foreign Minister in charge of CIS affairs, so the coming of greater harmony was marked soon after by the departure of Kunadze, liberal Deputy Foreign Minister responsible for relations with Japan, to head the Russian embassy in Seoul.

It would be difficult to find a more striking demonstration of the fluidity of institutional structures in Russian policy making than the events which followed. Skokov had guided the new

Foreign Policy Commission through its first major task, laying down strategic guide-lines for Russia's new foreign policy. He had even managed to have inserted in the concept a passage declaring that foreign policy should be 'supervised by the President relying upon the Security Council'. Days later, however, the apparently all-powerful Secretary had been sacked for showing insufficient solidarity with Yeltsin in the struggle against the opposition, and the Council itself slid into a six-month period of neglect and isolation.[110] Former CIS Commander-in-Chief Yevgeny Shaposhnikov was appointed as Secretary but resigned after only two months, complaining that he was being required to demonstrate 'political loyalty and a minimum of activity'. The function of the Security Council, in his judgement, had become one simply of 'organizing conferences between Boris Yeltsin and the heads of specific departments'. In early drafts of the new constitution the Council was not even mentioned.[111] Finally, in September 1993 the Council was put under the control of one of Yeltsin's closest associates, Oleg Lobov, and appeared to begin to play a more important but less foreign-policy-focused and less politicized role.[112]

What did prove durable was the emergence of a much smoother relationship between the Foreign Ministry and its previous critics in the military and the legislature. By January 1993 Kozyrev was describing Pavel Grachev as 'a man of flexible intellect, a man able to listen to interlocutors'. Yevgeny Ambartsumov, who chaired the Supreme Soviet Foreign Affairs Committee, had already begun to acknowledge that Russian foreign policy in the former Yugoslavia had become 'more adequate': 'Serious positive moves have been noticed in the actions of the Russian Foreign Ministry.' The peacemaking process appears to have been helped along by persistent bridge-building on the part of Kozyrev and his colleagues.[113]

Conflicts between the executive and the legislature over international issues persisted and indeed intensified during the summer of 1993, creating an impression of serious disarray over policy in the Balkans, towards Ukraine, and in the Caucasus. But the Supreme Soviet was disunited in its opposition, and there was less disunity in the executive. While the Foreign Ministry continued to defend the sanctity of existing post-Soviet borders and to warn against the danger of provoking a nationalist reaction in states such as Ukraine, it had after all accepted the priority of establishing the 'near abroad' as a sphere of predominant Russian influence.[114] In the course of 1993, as Moscow moved to assert its power in the region, political, economic, and military levers appeared to be used in an effective, concerted way. Foreign Ministry spokesmen characteristically adopted a 'softer' tone than the military, but this difference could often be interpreted as part of a natural division of labour.[115]

Developments in relations between the main foreign policy institutions in 1993 have to be seen in the context of the kind of developments in thinking about key international issues among the Russian political and specialist élite which are described in Chapter 2. It would be a gross oversimplification to give the impression that all that happened was a matter of political manœuvring on the part of Yeltsin and the Foreign Ministry. Inside the Ministry and among the President's advisers a wide range of views was represented, and the balance of opinion was constantly changing in response, among other things, to changes in the international environment.

The broader climate of thinking was affected by the activities of journalists and academic specialists. The degree of influence that they exerted is hard to be certain of, but the strengthening of Pragmatic Nationalist thinking occured simultaneously in the academic, journalistic, and policy spheres. A part in bringing these spheres together was played by new public associations such as the Council on Foreign and Defence Policy. In *Nezavisimaya gazeta* in August 1992 the Council announced itself as 'a non-government organization containing 37 members, including politicians, entrepreneurs, members of the armed forces, diplomats, and scholars'. It described as one of its main tasks 'to collaborate in working out strategic conceptions of the development of the country, especially in the foreign policy and defence spheres'.

The Council's founding manifesto, 'A Strategy for Russia', articulated a pragmatic nationalist set of priorities in terms which could be endorsed by a membership ranging from the Chief of the General Staff and leading industrial lobbyists, through senior civil servants from the security and diplomatic services, to bankers, reformist politicians, and liberal intellectuals.[116] It also rehearsed a number of the ideas contained in the official foreign policy concept adopted the following April, and conceivably played a catalytic role in the overall process of realignment. Bearing in mind the provisional character of political loyalties and groupings in

Russian society in the 1990s, we should be careful not to over-
rate the importance of entities such as the Council on Foreign
and Defence Policy as institutions. What was important was the
impressive list of signatures from individuals in different walks of
public life which appeared below its public statements, and what
that implied about the emergence of some kind of common view
about foreign policy among the ruling establishment.

## The effects of political weakness

By 1994 the high-voltage political tensions around foreign affairs
had lessened. Policy itself continued to evolve in a more assertive
direction. At a Foreign Ministry conference in January, Kozyrev
entrenched the new position by declaring in the course of a discussion of Russian military deployments in the CIS: 'We should
not depart from regions which have been Russian spheres of influence for centuries. And we should not be afraid of saying these
words.' After the armed suppression of parliamentary resistance in
October 1993 Yeltsin was overtly dependent on the military and
the security services for keeping his hold on power. The extreme
nationalist Liberal Democratic Party of Vladimir Zhirinovsky had
become the second largest faction in the Duma, and enjoyed widespread support among the officer corps. At the end of 1993 the
Security Council had given the go-ahead to a string of new high-
technology weapons-development projects; there was talk of Yury
Skokov returning to the government as a First Deputy Prime Minister.[117] The feeling became widespread in the Moscow foreign
policy community that the government was deferring over-much
to the preferences of the 'power ministers'. In a second 'Strategy
for Russia' document published in May the CFDP found it necessary to warn against excessive influence of nationalist views on
policy.[118]

   In domestic politics Yeltsin was pursuing a line of reconciliation,
persuading both houses of parliament and most of the political
parties to sign an Agreement on Civic Accord. Despite the large
Fundamentalist Nationalist presence there, the leading officials
of the new parliament took a determinedly co-operative line. The
speaker of the Council of the Federation, Vladimir Shumeiko, declared that his views on international matters coincided '98 per
cent' with those of the Foreign Minister. Vladimir Lukin, who had

returned to his earlier post as head of the lower house's foreign affairs committee, called for deputies and officials to co-operate in developing a concerted foreign policy: 'A consensus is taking shape . . . , which makes me very happy because foreign policy should be at minimum based on a broad consensus . . . Why were we able to play a serious role in Yugoslavia? Because of consensus.' Despite continued dissent from opposition legislators, Deputy Foreign Minister Vitaly Churkin voiced his welcome for 'the democratic consensus' which had emerged between President and parliament on foreign policy—'a very remarkable phenomenon, . . . unlike in the past'.[119] On 17 November President Yeltsin chaired a meeting of the leaders of the two chambers of the legislature, down to the level of committee chairmen. The Duma Speaker Ivan Rybkin reported that 'virtually all participants agreed that great-power patriotism and extricating the country from the present crisis are ideas everybody is ready to work for.'[120]

This mood of national accord on foreign policy was bought at a price, of course. Whereas at the outset Yeltsin and Kozyrev had the confidence to forward a clearly defined pro-Western line, however much ammunition this gave to their political opponents, by 1994 domestic political weakness seems to have contributed not just to a sense of abandonment of principle, but to a lack of clarity in policy.[121] It was even argued that the legacy of domestic conflict made Kozyrev's task an impossible one. As one commentator wrote at the end of the year, 'he has finally lost support among Russian liberals, without scoring any points among his enemies, who do not and never will trust him.' There were increasing signs of disarray inside the reformist camp over foreign policy. A number of senior figures in the Foreign Ministry were unexpectedly posted abroad, and reports began to emerge of frictions between Kozyrev and the President's foreign policy aide Dmitry Ryurikov. It was said that Ryurikov, in common with a number of officials in the Foreign Ministry itself, disagreed with the supposed excessive attention being given by Kozyrev to relations with the United States, and advocated a more multipolar perspective, emphasizing relations with states in Europe and Asia.[122]

The Yeltsin administration was so dependent for support on sympathetic industrial and commercial circles that it found it difficult to refuse requests for special treatment in the area of foreign trade. Because sectoral lobbying organizations tended to be weak or non-existent, and because central government itself was disorganized, concessions tended to be made on an irregular, individual basis, and generated an atmosphere of cynicism. As one observer expressed it, 'Gaidar's avowed policy of foreign trade liberalization soon turned into a Swiss cheese, riddled through with exemptions and special favours.'[123]

The Minister of Foreign Economic Relations, Sergei Glaz'ev, initially a strong supporter of Gaidar's reform programme, had emerged as a critic of its damaging effects, and as an advocate of more interventionist economic policies. During 1993 he instigated a review of trade exemptions, as a result of which over a hundred organizations were deprived of tariff and other privileges. He proposed the competitive sale of export quotas to replace the existing system of 'distributing' them, and began to investigate the murky area of arms exports, where different government agencies were fighting for rights of oversight and regulation. On 21 August Glaz'ev threatened to resign, complaining that since he began his attempts 'to tighten control over the observance of legislation in foreign economic activity' he had been openly persecuted by powerful figures in the government, including Vladimir Shumeiko, and false accusations of corruption had been made against his colleagues in the Ministry. Glaz'ev's final resignation came a month later, in protest at Yeltsin's decision to dissolve the Supreme Soviet.[124]

Political weakness also affected the leadership of the Ministry of Defence, where persistent accusations of corruption, and the unpopularity of General Grachev and his associates, made them more and more dependent on the President.[125] The kind of civilian-military dissonances in policy characteristic of 1992 were now much rarer and less strident. A unified front was preserved even on difficult issues such as Russia's approach to the NATO Partnership for Peace.[126] On occasion the President appeared to be taking a more 'patriotic' line than his Defence Minister, as when he announced the postponement of joint Russian–United States military exercises in the Urals, 'guided by a spirit of accord and constructive dialogue, . . . taking an understanding view of the doubts expressed in the State Duma'. This provoked the liberal Chairman of the Duma Defence Committee to protest publicly against what he described as an absence of leadership in the executive branch.[127]

Thus the politics of foreign policy in Moscow resembled less the period between 1987 and 1992, when strong leadership was used to force through radical changes, and more the preceding decades, when domestic support was ensured at the cost of a degree of vagueness and contradictoriness in policy. In discussions of policy making, newspaper reports tended to emphasize not so much the clash of polarized world views as a shadowy game of economic lobbying and factional intrigue. At the level of rhetoric a quasi-imperial tone emerged: there began a tedious repetition of statements about the might of the Russian state and the respect which was due to it inside and outside the nation's boundaries. Three episodes involving conflicting political and economic interests in Russian policy will serve to illustrate how the politics of foreign policy evolved between the early and mid-1990s.

### Political and economic priorities in foreign policy

In January 1991 the Soviet government agency responsible for the space industry, Glavkosmos, signed a contract with the Indian Space Research Organization to supply it with cryogenic rocket engines and associated technological know-how, beating off competition from rival French and American contractors. After the demise of the Soviet Union Russia agreed to take over the agreement. In April 1992 the United States declared that the deliveries would contravene the Missile Technology Control Regime, and threatened to impose corresponding sanctions on Moscow and Delhi. The Russian Foreign Ministry appeared to agree that the deal should be reviewed, and promoted the idea that an international committee of experts should consider the international legal situation. However, at the Sixth Congress of People's Deputies representatives of the space industry protested that any backing down would involve substantial losses, unemployment, and damage to Russia's reputation as a reliable exporter to one of its most well-established partners. Glavkosmos denounced Washington's move as 'a typical case of trade war'.

By the first half of 1993 the eventual outcome of the dispute was still unpredictable. On a visit to Delhi in January President Yeltsin had assured the Indian Prime Minister that Russia would stick to the 1991 agreement. In talks about the matter in Washington in May the Russian delegation, which was led by Deputy

Prime Minister in charge of Foreign Economic Relations Aleksandr
Shokhin, took a hard line: it was reportedly because of failure to
reach agreement on the rocket engine deal that Prime Minister
Chernomyrdin called off a visit to the United States planned for
the end of June. However, at the G7 meeting in Tokyo in July
Yeltsin was said to have reached an agreement with President
Clinton which satisfied Washington. Shokhin was replaced as chief
negotiator by Yury Koptev, head of the new Russian Space Agency,
which was soon to sign agreements with NASA on co-operation
in launching satellites and in implementing the Freedom Space
Station project.

During July the outlines of a compromise were revealed. Russia
would be permitted to supply India with the rocket hardware but
not with the know-how. Moscow also agreed to keep the United
States informed of its space exports to CIS and Third World states
and accept certain restrictions on them. In return the threat of
sanctions on Russia was removed, a shadow was lifted from plans
to remove the COCOM restrictions on exports to the former Soviet
states, and fears of a delay in Russia's admission to GATT were
dispelled. Supporters of the compromise pointed out that the RSA's
access to global markets in co-operation with American firms was
worth potentially much more than the $350 million to be paid by
Delhi, and that in any case the Indian deal was merely being
modified, not abandoned.

This did little to console supporters of the original agreement,
who were particularly angered by a report that it was a Foreign
Ministry official who had sent the first notification, to the Indian
embassy in Moscow, that it could not be fulfilled. Aleksandr
Shokhin and the government Committee for the Defence Sector
protested about the decision. Deputy Minister of Defence Kokoshin
attested that the rockets concerned could have no military application. Glavkosmos and Ministry of Foreign Economic Relations
employees stated to the press that the President had been 'misin-
formed' by the Foreign Ministry and the RSA about what was at
stake. Commentators accused Kozyrev and his colleagues of acting
arbitrarily, and proposed that the Security Council be given greater
powers of co-ordination. As we have seen, there was little chance
of this happening in mid-1993, and the Foreign Ministry's advice
still weighed most heavily where relations with Washington were
concerned. At this time the advice which came from Smolensk

Square was still coloured by confidence in a future based on co-operative partnership with the West.[128]

The second case concerned 'near-abroad' matters. Shortly after the breakup of the USSR a meeting was held at the Russian Ministry of Fuel and Energy in Moscow, where agreement was reached between Russia, Azerbaijan, Kazakhstan, and Turkmenistan on each state's share of the oil and gas fields around the Caspian Sea shelf. On 23 October 1993 a Russian-Azerbaijani intergovernmental agreement was signed which specified a 10-per-cent share for the Russian state-owned oil concern Lukoil in a large oil extraction project near Baku supported by a consortium of Western oil companies led by BP. In July 1994 Lukoil representatives, accompanied by a senior official from the Russian Fuel and Energy Ministry, held a press conference to announce the imminent signing of an agreement to confirm the 'deal of the century'.

Shortly before this, however, it was revealed that the Russian Foreign Ministry had delivered a note to the British government announcing that, since the Caspian Sea was an object of joint use by the littoral states, any unilateral action by one of them aimed at exploiting its resources would be 'devoid of a legal basis'. In subsequent months the Foreign Ministry reiterated its objections. The initial reaction of the Ministry of Fuel and Energy was one of frustration. Its head, Yury Shafranik, announced that he would take the initiative of setting up a co-ordinating council of the Caspian Sea states to approve all energy-extraction projects in the area. On 20 September 1994 the oil contract was signed in Baku. Although a Deputy Minister of Fuel and Energy attended the signing ceremony, the Foreign Ministry issued a statement declaring that Russia would not recognize the agreement, 'with all the ensuing consequences'. A Ministry spokesman commented to the press, 'We do not agree with the Azerbaijani side's attempt to carve up the Caspian Sea.' Finally, in November, after talks between Yeltsin and the President of Azerbaijan, Kozyrev announced that his department was not against the deal 'in principle', and that once the legal status of the Caspian Sea had been defined satisfactorily the contract would no doubt be implemented.

It was clear that political considerations once again lay behind the Foreign Ministry's actions. This time the intention was apparently to put pressure on Baku, and in particular to induce it to agree to channel the export of the oil through Russia, and not along

either of two alternative, more southerly routes, through Iràn or
(more likely) Turkey. Such an outcome would offer Moscow an
additional lever on Azerbaijan and reinforce the southern boundary
of its sphere of influence, and would set a precedent for the large
oil and gas exports expected from Kazakhstan.

Initially the Russian press speculated that the main motivation
for the affair was to strike a blow against the 'oil and gas lobby'
and the Prime Minister, Viktor Chernomyrdin. Certainly there
was ample public evidence of friction and disarray. One Russian
newspaper wrote of 'a scandalous lack of co-operation' between
the Foreign Ministry and the Ministry of Fuel and Energy.[129] Yet
the oil and gas industry also stood to benefit materially if Azerbaijan
could be pressured into choosing the northern pipeline route, and
it is arguable that the Foreign Ministry was not acting against that
industry's long-term interests.[130] What was important about this
case was first, that it confirmed the continuing overriding priority
of long-term political goals (articulated by the Ministry of Foreign
Affairs) relative to shorter-term economic ones, and secondly, that
it underlined the reordering of foreign policy priorities in the Russian leadership to the detriment of partnership with the West and
in favour of safeguarding security and reinforcing control in the
CIS region.[131]

In the case of trade with Iraq and Iran the Russian Foreign
Ministry acted even more assertively. Here it possibly estimated
that Russia could resist pressure from Washington, demonstrate
its continuing great-power capability, and at the same time gain
economic advantages. In October 1994 Kozyrev chose a moment
at the height of an international crisis provoked by redeployment
of Iraqi troops towards the Kuwait border to visit Baghdad and to
call for a lifting of United Nations sanctions on Iraq. This turned
out to be a mistake. The Western powers rejected the proposal
with indignation, and the prospect of realizing Russia's frozen
assets in Iraq seemed if anything even more distant. Moreover, an
extended tour to the Gulf states in November led by Viktor
Chernomyrdin failed to placate Iraq's neighbours and produced
very few of the expected trade contracts.[132]

With regard to Tehran, Kozyrev argued that since a new international weapons-technology export regime had not yet been
established to replace NATO's COCOM, and that since (more
importantly) Russia had not been invited to participate in designing

such a regime, it could see no reason, despite the United States' displeasure, to stop its sales of fighters and fighter bombers to the country. The $1 billion contract to build four light-water nuclear reactors in Iran signed by Moscow in early 1995 not only brought welcome export earnings, and bought support in the arguments over Caspian oil, but also provided yet another opportunity to demonstrate to the United States that Russia was still an actor to be reckoned with and taken seriously.[133] As with the Baku oil contract, there were strong arguments both for and against the government's policy in terms of maximizing export income, preserving jobs, and guaranteeing Russia's future as a high-technology producer. It seems probable, looking back at the 1992–3 arguments over the deal with India, and taking overall changes in Russian policy into account, that broader political calculations were decisive.[134]

### A further concentrating of power?

In such a political context the relative weight of the security and intelligence agencies was bound to increase. When FIS Director Primakov launched his agency's report about the implications of NATO expansion in November 1993, he noted that, although it was widely supported throughout the administration, it had received an ambivalent response from the Foreign Ministry. 'Tactical interdepartmental differences naturally exist,' he commented, adding, 'I do not know of any agency which could object in principle to our report. And that includes the Ministry of Foreign Affairs.'[135] The FIS's next report, in September 1994, about CIS integration, was billed to contain 'disturbing facts' about the West's attitude. 'Whenever there is a negative, or at the best reserved, attitude to Russia's peacekeeping actions,' its authors remarked, 'the question arises: "Aren't certain circles interested in preserving conflict situations along Russia's perimeter border, and probably transferring them into a slow-going phase?"' They went on to argue that the military preparations of other great powers strengthened the case for establishing a common CIS defence space.[136] A similar note was struck by the director of the Federal Counter-Intelligence Service (now the FSS) during a visit to the agency by Yeltsin in June, when he commented on the reluctance of 'many people' in the West to allow Russia to re-establish itself as a political and economic competitor.[137]

By the end of the year the Yeltsin administration had committed itself to a forceful resolution of the Chechen crisis. Fears were aroused in liberal circles in Moscow of a possible sharp turn to authoritarianism in government, and to extreme nationalism in foreign policy. The tension was increased when members of the FCS leaked an internal document which accused hundreds of Western research institutes of undertaking subversive action in Russia, in order 'to help realize United States foreign policy, aimed at keeping Russia in check'. One countermeasure which was proposed was to restrict foreign travel by Russian academics.[138] Subsequently an official FCS statement announced that the widening intelligence and subversive activitites of foreign special services presented a serious threat to Russia's national security.[139]

The events of December 1994 fed liberal suspicions of the 'power ministries', but the most frequent target of criticism was the presidential apparatus. Because of the centralized style of policy making, the balance of power between different factions in Yeltsin's entourage had been a long-standing preoccupation of his reformist supporters. Attention initially focused on the role of three men who had been subordinates of Yeltsin during his time as Secretary of the Sverdlovsk Communist Party organization—Yury Petrov, in 1991 and 1992 the Head of the President's Administration, Viktor Ilyushin, his principal aide, and Oleg Lobov, a Deputy Prime Minister from 1991 and from October 1993 Secretary of the Security Council. Long-standing apprehensions about the authoritarian potential of the Security Council were renewed.

As early as October 1991 the pro-reformist *Moscow News* denounced what it called 'the vicious practice by which the President's decisions on major operational-political matters are prepared in a factional, unpublicized manner in a narrow circle of persons linked by their *nomenklatura* past and their incompetence in the field under examination.'[140] As it turned out, this was an exaggerated view. Yeltsin made a practice of maintaining a rough balance in his administration between figures such as Ilyushin and Skokov, on the one hand, and Burbulis and Gaidar on the other. When Sergei Filatov replaced Petrov as Chief of Staff, he was able to act as an advocate at the top for liberal-tending consultative parts of the apparatus such as the Presidential Council and the Analytical Centre. Foreign policy aide Dmitry Ryurikov and National Security aide Yury Baturin were liberal officials of the younger generation.[141]

However, there were fears that if Yeltsin's vigour or health declined he might be taken hostage by one particular faction in his apparatus, and these fears intensified towards the end of 1994. During 1995 there were persistent reports that the 'Sverdlovsk group', allied with the head of the presidential security service Aleksandr Korzhakov and with the military and security chiefs, were dominating decision making and cutting the President off from more liberal members of his staff. After the assault on Grozny many of the latter were desperate enough to air their grievances to the press, complaining that an information blockade was being imposed on the President, and that their advice was no longer being sought. Ex-Prime Minister Yegor Gaidar declared that Yeltsin's closest aides 'agree with everything he says and only pass on information that will not disturb him. However, in this way the servants are secretly taking over the regime.'[142]

## Conclusion

It is equally possible to apply to foreign policy making in Russia the words used by President Yeltsin in February 1994 when he publicly criticized the processes of decision-making which led to the Chechnya crisis, and to say that it 'reflects as in a drop of water all the problems of Russian statehood'.[143] As a part of the Russian state, the foreign policy machine contributes to its strengthening or weakening. What is more, the conditions of foreign policy making are affected by the degree of effectiveness and health of the state as a whole. What is the diagnosis?

In view of the political conflicts, ideological upheavals, and institutional turmoil which accompanied the setting up of the new Russian foreign policy system, it may be helpful to begin by looking for evidence in it of the 'consensus, community, legitimacy and organization' which, it has been suggested, are the key characteristics of a stable civic polity.[144]

There has undoubtedly been a shift in the direction of a policy consensus among the main foreign policy institutions in the period since early 1992, and this represents an important step forward. At that time polarization of perceptions and preferences was so extreme that it is doubtful if the categories of bureaucratic politics could be applied: rather than 'pulling and hauling' it was a matter of unilateral actions and attempts to undermine the whole policy system.[145] This change reflects a wider stabilization in Russian politics. It is now less common, for example, to come across comments about the risk of civil war.

Yet there is another side to the coin. As was suggested above, a variety of factors contributed to the decline in conflict and the greater co-operation among the main foreign policy agencies in 1993. One of them was undoubtedly a genuine discarding of unrealistic expectations of an extreme pro-Western or extreme nationalist/restorationist kind. This helped to strengthen the centre and to expand the influence of Pragmatic Nationalist thinking in various quarters of the government. A second important factor, however, was the urgent need for the executive to consolidate its forces and extend its base of support in order to protect itself against domestic political threats. The expediency which in part drove the main players to declare their attachment to it meant that consensus often turned out to be more apparent than real, and that confusion and ambiguity persisted, albeit with less dramatic effects.

Often the apparent unanimity of senior officials was not echoed at the middle levels, and policy when implemented failed to match top-level declarations. A lot of the uncertainty still arose from sheer lack of co-ordination. Different ministries persisted in following their own agendas, especially in 'near-abroad' matters. In negotiations, when the other side had prepared a unified position in advance, Moscow could find itself at a serious disadvantage.[146]

Compared to the late 1980s, then, foreign policy lacked consistency and a hard edge. As well as being useful in domestic politics, a degree of blurring could be convenient, of course, and it could even be deliberately accentuated: a combination of 'diplomatic' methods and military/economic coercion was remarkably effective in forwarding Moscow's goals in the CIS without unduly alarming the West. In the end, however, it tended to cause mistrust and irritation. As one Russian specialist put it: 'The foreign public, as well as our own, has no time, as at a tennis match, to turn its head to follow the players.'[147]

By 1994 reformism in Russian politics was on the ebb. Yeltsin and his associates no doubt perceived their best strategy as being one of compromise and coalition-building, designed to salvage as much as possible of what had been achieved and to ward off an extreme backlash. What is more, after the revolutionary upheavals and the stress of the preceding years it was not surprising that the Russian political élite should value an imperfect reconciliation over absolute clarity in policy. Yeltsin made a point of appearing to defer to parliamentary opinion.[148] Towards the end of 1994 attempts were made to bring representatives of more political parties into the government. Nationalist themes in foreign policy rhetoric were used, with a degree of success, to build a sense of community and legitimacy. But this was not accompanied by any moves to greater transparency, regularization, and institutionalization in policy making. The new constitution, and Yeltsin's style of implementing it, concentrated even more of the process in the President's ever-growing bureaucracy.

The head of the executive arm was signing approximately a hundred decrees a month, many of them ill-prepared and contradicting each other, some subsequently countermanded and more simply unimplemented by the government.[149] It was commented that the system had retained the centralization of the Soviet period but had lost the organizational capacity to make it work properly. In international affairs embarrassment succeeded embarrassment, as when Yeltsin's office announced without consultation with the Foreign Ministry, in April 1994, that Russia intended to maintain a military base in Latvia. This was subsequently dismissed as 'a technical error', but serious damage was done to relations with the Baltic states. Damage was also caused closer to home. Later in the year, when the President returned from talks in Washington in which arms export control and disarmament issues played an important part, a Ministry of Defence official revealed seething discontent in his department about lack of consultation:

Surely never before has a package of military questions for talks at such a level been prepared by the President's team and the Foreign Ministry in such haste and with such a level of secrecy. The military issues relating to the visit were not discussed either by the Presidential Council, the Security Council, the relevant committees of the two chambers of parliament, or the Defence Ministry Collegium. Even Pavel Grachev did not know until shortly before the summit that he would be flying to Washington.[150]

It was not a question of a shortage of institutions. The necessary consultative, deliberative, and collegial institutions had all been in place for several years. But they were burdened with the Soviet legacy of centralism and bureaucratic parochialism, aggravated by what has been described as the 'Byzantine' style of rule preferred by the President.[151] Although the tensions in Russian politics had become less disabling than in 1992 and 1993, they were still strong enough to reinforce Yeltsin's preference for working as far as possible with a small circle of trusted associates, in his staff and among a few members of the government. This tendency was not unique to Russia, of course, but in this case it appears to have been taken to an extreme, and with damaging effects.[152]

The history of the Security Council shows how the body best placed to introduce more harmony and effectiveness to foreign and security policy was unable to carry out its task. It failed to do so in its first phase, under Skokov, because other departments, and apparently later Yeltsin, came to see it as a political threat. In its second phase, under Shaposhnikov, it was deliberately kept on ice. In its third phase, under Lobov, it was put in the hands of a man selected more for his trustworthiness than his expertise, and it was still only allowed selective control of policy. In addition it refused to consult adequately with other agencies. As a result it generated bad decisions which lacked support from key groups in the administration. Deputy Defence Minister Boris Gromov admitted in January 1995, after the invasion of the Chechen Republic, that he and the entire Collegium of the Ministry of Defence had been shut out of the preparations for the action.[153]

Quite apart from the loss of effectiveness in policy, well demonstrated in the domestic but security-related case of the Chechen war, absence of 'organization' and the consequent blunders had a damaging effect on the legitimacy not just of Yeltsin's administration but of the whole post-Soviet order. This loss of legitimacy had immediate effects in the foreign policy field. It sapped morale, and weakened the authority of the leadership even more. Decisions remained unimplemented, cases of blatant corruption and insubordination went unpunished. It undermined, too, the confidence of foreign partners, and reduced their willingness to make agreements. In the longer term it threatened a descent into chaos, followed by the kind of 'strong' government which might seek a new basis of legitimacy in extreme nationalism or aggressive behaviour abroad.

Thus the story of foreign policy making in the first three years of the new Russian state is in one respect an encouraging one, in so far as the immediate legacy of the Soviet period was absorbed without excessive damage, and the extreme political tensions of the initial phase of transition were successfully overcome. To a large extent this is to be explained by the political skills of the main players, who, finding themselves in a position of weakness, deployed co-operation and compromise to ensure their own survival. There was also a degree of institutional development and 'settling down' of the new structure. Subsequently, however, as the political base of the Yeltsin administration narrowed even further, there were growing signs of reactiveness and drift. As before, foreign policy remained a hostage to domestic political struggles.

## NOTES

[1] W. Wallace, *Foreign Policy and the Political Process* (Oxford, 1971), 10.

[2] D. Simes, 'The Politics of Defence in the Soviet Union: Brezhnev's Era', in J. Valenta and W. Potter (eds.), *Soviet Decisionmaking for National Security* (London, 1984), 78–9.

[3] A. Ulam, 'Anatomy of Policymaking', *The Washington Quarterly*, vol. VI, no. ii (1983), 72–3; J. Hough, *Soviet Leadership in Transition* (Washington, DC, 1980), 109–10; R. Kitrinos, 'The CPSU Central Committee's International Department', *Problems of Communism*, vol. XXXIII, no. v (1984), 47–65; M. Kramer, 'The Role of the CPSU International Department in Soviet Foreign Relations and National Security Policy', *Soviet Studies*, 42 (1990), 429–46; J. Hough, 'Soviet Policymaking towards Foreign Communists', *Studies in Comparative Communism*, 15 (1982), 166–83.

[4] Soviet 'departmentalism' was related to, although naturally different from, the 'bureaucratic parochialism' described in the USA's foreign policy establishment by writers such as Graham Allison ('Conceptual Models and the Cuban Missile Crisis', *American Political Science Review*, 63 (1969), 700). On Soviet 'departmentalism' see J. Valenta, *Soviet Intervention in Czechoslovakia, 1968: Anatomy of a Decision* (London, 1979), 34; T. Gustafson, *Reform in Soviet Politics: Lessons of Recent Policies on Land and Water* (Cambridge, 1981), 93–4; Simes, 'The Politics of Defence in the Soviet Union', 76–81.

[5] X, 'The Sources of Soviet Conduct', *Foreign Affairs*, July 1947, 580.

[6] Simes, 'The Politics of Defence in the Soviet Union', 76.

[7] A. Brown, 'The Foreign Policy-Making Process', in C. Keeble (ed.),

*The Soviet State: The Domestic Roots of Foreign Policy* (Aldershot, 1985), 191–216.

[8] See the contributions referred to in note 2 above, especially Kitrinos; also L. Schapiro, 'The International Department of the CPSU: Key to Soviet Policy', *The International Journal*, 32 (1976–7), 41–55.

[9] A. Chernyaev, *Shest' let s Gorbachevym* (Moscow, 1994), 37.

[10] See Simes's argument that 'bureaucratic politics Soviet-style provides a considerable structural and psychological edge to the military-industrial complex', and his remarks concerning 'the unusual reliance on and fascination with force which for centuries was a pivotal element in Russian political culture' ('The Politics of Defence in the Soviet Union', 82). See also C. Linden, *Khrushchev and the Soviet Leadership* (Baltimore, 1990); G. Breslauer, *Khrushchev and Brezhnev as Leaders* (London, 1982); H. Gelman, *The Brezhnev Politburo and the Decline of Detente* (London, 1983).

[11] M. Mackintosh, 'The Military Role in Soviet Decision-Making', in Keeble (ed.), *The Soviet State*, 173–90. According to Chernyaev, the decision to invade Afghanistan in 1979 was pushed through by Gromyko and Ustinov, despite resistance from the General Staff (*Shest' let s Gorbachevym*, 38).

[12] Franklyn Holzman and R. Legvold argued that 'centralization, differentiation and less participation' were the distinguishing characteristics of the Soviet policy making system ('The Economics and Politics of East–West Relations', in E. Hoffman and F. Fleron (eds.), *The Conduct of Soviet Foreign Policy* (New York, 1980), 455).

[13] A. Pravda, 'The Politics of Foreign Policy', in S. White, A. Pravda, and Z. Gitelman (eds.), *Developments in Soviet and Post-Soviet Politics* (London, 1992), 259–60; M. Kramer, 'The CPSU International Department', 433–8.

[14] H. Adomeit, 'The Atlantic Alliance in Soviet and Russian Perspectives', and A. Pravda, 'Relations with Central- and South-Eastern Europe', both in N. Malcolm (ed.), *Russia and Europe: an End to Confrontation?* (London, 1993), pp. 31–58 and 123–50, respectively. Sensitive issues were preserving a special relationship with the ex-Warsaw Pact states and defining equipment covered by the Conventional Forces in Europe arms agreement. According to one report, 'Relations between two of the primary contestants —the Ministries of Defence and Foreign Affairs—had become so bad that at many high-level meetings representatives of the two institutions would not even address each other' (J. Checkel, 'Russian Foreign Policy: Back to the Future?', *RFE/RL Research Report*, 16 Oct. 1992, 22).

[15] A. Arbatov, 'Rossiya: natsional'naya bezopasnost' v 90-ye gody', *Mirovaya ekonomika i mezhdunarodnye otnosheniya*, 1994, no. 7, pp. 10–11.

[16] The main exception is the (new) sphere of economic and social

relations with the CIS states, where the government (in the narrower sense) plays a big part. See later in this chapter.

[17] *Nezavisimaya gazeta*, 2 Feb. 1994. For the structure of the executive apparatus in 1994, see 'Key Officials in the Russian Federation: Executive Branch', *RFE/RL Research Report*, 4 Mar. 1994, 11; *Nezavisimaya gazeta*, 11 Jan. 1994, 1. The Border Troops Commander is also a member of the government; the Minister of the Interior also reports directly to Yeltsin. More information about the memberhip of the Security Council is given later in this chapter.

[18] Interview with Yury Baturin, National Security Aide, *Izvestiya*, 6 Jan. 1995. Baturin appears to have been concerned mainly with internal security issues, and to have been excluded from many important policy discussions by powerful security chiefs.

[19] The position was occupied in Jan. 1992 by the senior diplomat, Yuly Vorontsov. However, he subsequently spent most of his time on duty in the United States, and the post seems to have been effectively vacant (*Diplomaticheskii vestnik*, 1992, no. 6, p. 16; *Moscow News*, 1992, no. 32, p. 14; *Rossiiskie vesti*, 13 Aug. 1992).

[20] The structure of the President's staff is frequently modified (*Izvestiya*, 5 Jan. 1995; Yu. Fyodorov, 'Foreign Policy Making in the RF and Local Conflicts in the CIS', in H.-G. Ehrhart, A. Kreikemeyer, and A. Zagorski (eds.), *Crisis Management in the CIS: Whither Russia?* (Baden-Baden, 1995), 119–22). Parts of this chapter are based also on consultations with Russian specialists.

[21] O. Latsis, in *Izvestiya*, 6 Jan. 1995.

[22] V. Vyzhutovich in *Moscow News*, 1994, no. 28, p. 6. The article is based on an interview with the President's chief aide, Viktor Ilyushin, who, the author implies, is responsible for obstructing the information flow to the President. Vyzhutovich does not question Ilyushin's claim about free access by key ministers, however. The Minister of Defence referred during the 'Itogi' television programme (NTV) on 6 Nov. 1994 to his daily 10.00 a.m. briefing sessions with the President (*RFE/RL Daily Report* (electronic mail edn.), 8 Nov. 1994). See also interviews with Ilyushin in *Moscow News*, 1993, no. 39, and *Nezavisimaya gazeta*, 10 Feb. 1994.

[23] Viktor Ilyushin in *Moscow News*, 1993, no. 39, p. 3; *Nezavisimaya gazeta*, 10 Feb. 1994.

[24] Mikhail Malei, Yeltsin's adviser on conversion of the defence industry, complained in 1993 that he had tried in vain for three months to see the President (*Komsomolskaya pravda*, 17 Sept. 1993). See also the next section of this chapter.

[25] *Moscow News*, 1993, no. 25, p. 3. He goes on to mention the bad precedent of the CPSU Central Committee. Fresh in Yeltsin's mind must have been the memory of how Gorbachev was treated by his Central Committee staff in the run-up to the 1991 coup attempt.

²⁶ See H. Kissinger, 'Domestic Structure and Foreign Policy', *Daedalus*, vol. xcv, no. ii of the Proceedings of the American Academy of Arts and Sciences (Spring 1966), 503–29.

²⁷ 'Strategiya dlya Rossii (2): Tezisy Soveta po vneshnei i oboronnoi politike', *Nezavisimaya gazeta*, 27 May 1994. The activity of the Council on Foreign and Defence Policy, which was responsible for the report, will be discussed later in this chapter. See also Fyodorov, 'Foreign Policy Making in the RF', 117–22.

²⁸ *Izvestiya* (18 Dec. 1993, 3) described him as (Foreign Minister) 'Kozyrev's man'. A biographical note on Ryurikov appears in *Moscow News*, 1993, no. 31, p. 6. His Foreign Ministry sympathies are apparent in the interview article, cited in note 25, from *Moscow News* (p. 3). See later in this chapter for references to later frictions with Kozyrev, and for information about participation in the Security Council and its committees. A National Security Aide was appointed for the first time in Jan. 1994. The person concerned, Yury Baturin, seems to be a more independent figure: he had been a presidential adviser on legal issues and had played a large part in reorganizing the Ministry of Security in 1993 (*Nezavisimaya gazeta*, 11 Jan. 1994).

²⁹ Law on Security of 5 May 1992 (*Rossiiskaya gazeta*, 6 May 1992). A detailed account of the setting-up of the Security Council is given in E. Jones and J. Brusstar, 'Moscow's Emerging Security Decisionmaking System: The Role of the Security Council', *Journal of Slavic Military Studies*, 6 (1993), 345–74. See too S. Crow, *The Making of Foreign Policy in Russia under Yeltsin* (Munich, 1993), 13–37; R. Sakwa, *Russian Politics and Society* (London, 1993), 152–3.

³⁰ Information about the structure and membership of the Council is drawn from interviews with its Deputy Secretary Valery Manilov in *Moskovskie novosti*, 1994, no. 23, p. A6, and *Krasnaya zvezda*, 29 Oct. 1994.

³¹ These changes, and their political context, are discussed in the next section of the chapter.

³² *Rossiiskaya gazeta*, 6 May 1992.

³³ *Moscow News*, 1994, no. 23, p. 2. A prominent member of the Russian Duma stated at the end of 1994: 'We know, for example, that the votes of the Security Council members were divided nearly in half when deciding the question of bringing military pressure to bear on Chechnya' (*Moscow News*, 1994, no. 49, p. 2). A similar impression of *de facto* voting rights for all members was given by former Justice Minister Kalmykov on 'Vesti', Russian TV Network, 9 Dec. 1994, cited in *RFE/RL Daily Report* (electronic mail edn.), 13 Dec. 1994.

³⁴ *Nezavisimaya gazeta*, 11 Jan. 1995; *The Guardian*, 11 Jan. 1995. The Council's Charter makes explicit provision for separate meetings

of the 'permanent' membership (*Vedomosti Rossiiskoi Federatsii*, 1992, no. 24, pp. 1662–9). Yeltsin's action was taken at a time when his authority over the military was being publicly doubted, during the invasion of the Chechen Republic.

[35] Biographical details of Yury Skokov can be found in Crow, *The Making of Foreign Policy*, 83; of Oleg Lobov in *Moscow News*, 1993, no. 39, p. 3. There is an extended interview with Lobov, in *Moscow News*, 1994, no. 29, p. 6.

[36] Jones and Brusstar, 'Moscow's Emerging Security Decisionmaking System', 361–5; Crow, *The Making of Foreign Policy*, 13–18. The first Deputy Secretary was a former diplomat, Yury Nazarkin. By Mar. 1994 he was no longer Deputy Secretary, but continued to head the Council's Directorate of Strategic Security (now disbanded) (*Nezavisimaya gazeta*, 18 Mar. 1994). The three Deputy Secretaries in 1994 were Lt.-Gen. Valery Manilov (formerly an information officer in the Soviet Defence Ministry, and later press secretary of Yevgeny Shaposhnikov in his role as C-in-C of the CIS forces), Vladimir Rubanov (formerly on the staff of Vadim Bakatin, Gorbachev's last KGB head), and Aleksandr Troshin (names from 'Key Officials in the Russian Federation: Executive Branch', 9). Biographical information about Manilov is provided in *Moskovskie novosti*, 1994, no. 23, p. A6, and *Krasnaya zvezda*, 29 Oct. 1994.

[37] Manilov, interviewed in *Krasnaya zvezda*, 28 Jun. 1994.

[38] Ibid.

[39] *Nezavisimaya gazeta*, 29 Jan. 1993; *Rossiiskaya gazeta*, 3 Feb. 1993; Crow, *The Making of Foreign Policy*, 23–4; V. Yasmann, 'Security Services Reorganized', *RFE/RL Research Report*, 11 Feb. 1994, 10; 'Andrei Kozyrev's Trojan Horse', *Inside Russia and the CIS* (European Press Agency Bulletin), Mar. 1994, 1; Manilov in *Krasnaya zvezda*, 28 Jun. 1994; Fyodorov, 'Foreign Policy Making in the RF', 6; on Anatoly Adamishin's post, *Moscow News*, 1994, no. 19, p. 4. When it was set up in 1992, the Foreign Policy Commission was a more heavyweight body, bringing together the heads of the Foreign Ministry, the Ministries of Defence, the Interior, Justice, Foreign Economic Relations, the Foreign Intelligence Service, and others.

[40] *Nezavisimaya gazeta*, 18 Feb. 1994; Radio Rossiya, 10 Mar. 1994, 14.00 GMT, reported in *BBC Summary of World Broadcasts*, SU/1945 (14 Mar. 1994), B/3 (SC Working Conference on War on Crime); *Izvestiya*, 11 Mar. 1994 (SC report on food contamination prepared by an SC Commission on Protecting the Health of the Population, and by its Commission on Ecological Security); *Izvestiya*, 26 May 1994 (publication of Federal Programme for Stepping up the Struggle against Crime: 'This voluminous programme was prepared in the inner recesses of the Security Council with the help of specialists from a wide variety of government

156        *Neil Malcolm*

departments as well as from research units and public organizations');
*Moscow News*, 1994, no. 42, p. 2 (SC role in investigating causes of
currency crisis).
    [41] 'Vesti', Russian TV Network, 5 May 1994, 16.00 GMT, reported
in *Foreign Broadcast Information Service* (hereafter *FBIS*), SOV-94-088
(6 May 1994), p. 20; *Moscow News*, 1994, no. 23, p. 2.
    [42] *Nezavisimaya gazeta*, 2 Feb. 1994; *Izvestiya*, 3 Feb. 1994. In the lat-
ter, FCS head Nikolai Golushko revealed that the work of the various intelligence organs and law-enforcement agencies would be co-ordinated by
the new SC Commission on Public Safety. In 1992 Security Council Secretary Yury Skokov had played an important part in selecting the leadership
of the new Russian Ministry of Defence (*Moscow News*, 1992, no. 43,
p. 2). In April, in an article entitled 'What does the Security Council do?',
an *Izvestiya* journalist concluded that since the appointment of Oleg
Lobov as Secretary, it had tended to concentrate primarily on economic
matters (*Izvestiya*, 2 Apr. 1994: 'The Security Council has its own council
of economists and its own commission on privatization'; it had recently
given 3.8bn roubles to a group of economic institutes to work out a 'concept of economic security'). On 2 Feb. 1994, however, *Nezavisimaya gazeta*
had noted the removal from the Security Council of the Ministers of Economics, Health, Finance, and the Environment, appointed as recently as
20 Oct. 1993, implying a closer focus on political/security issues.
    [43] 'Press-Tsentr', *Diplomaticheskii vestnik*, 1993, no. 7–8, pp. 67–8;
*Nezavisimaya gazeta*, 29 Apr. 1993. The starting-point was a Foreign
Ministry draft. For a discussion of the political significance of the process
see Chapter 2, and the next section of this chapter.
    [44] *Segodnya*, 9 Oct. 1993; *Moscow News*, 1994, no. 48, p. 3. By the
autumn of 1994 the Council was also working on a new Law on National
Security (*Krasnaya zvezda*, 29 Oct. 1994).
    [45] See, for example, Manilov in *Moscow News*, 1994, no. 23, p. 2. He
argues that 'even when examining "hot" spots, [the staff] try to approach
the issues in a solid way.' Jones and Brusstar, in 'Moscow's Emerging
Security Decisionmaking System', 367, commented on the first months of
the Council's work: 'The Security Council has been reacting to events
after the fact, instead of anticipating them.'
    [46] 'Ukaz Prezidenta Rossiiskoi Federatsii', *Diplomaticheskii vestnik*,
1993, no. 17–18, pp. 3–4; 'Press-Tsentr', *Diplomaticheskii vestnik*, 1993,
no. 15–16, p. 59. The Defence Ministry's role in 'peacekeeping' is discussed in Chapter 5.
    [47] 'Rossiya–Tadzhikistan', *Diplomaticheskii vestnik*, 1993, no. 17–18,
p. 54. The Commission was set up by the Council of Ministers (the government) on 13 Aug.
    [48] 'Ukaz Prezidenta Rossiiskoi Federatsii', 'Press-Tsentr', *Diplomati-*

*cheskii vestnik*, 1993, no. 15–16, p. 59. On the powers of the Defence Ministry in Tajikistan, see Chapter 5.

[49] *Izvestiya*, 26 May 1994. In *Segodnya*, 15 Jun. 1994, Deputy Secretary Vladimir Rubanov announced that the Council and presidential staff would also take charge of implementing the programme.

[50] *Rossiiskaya gazeta*, 26 Aug. 1994. A Security Council meeting on border security was held in May 1994 (Interfax Agency Report, 18.05 GMT, 5 May 1994, cited in *FBIS*, SOV-94-088 (6 May 1994), p. 4.)

[51] *Segodnya*, 9 Oct. 1993, reports that the Council accepted the Ministry of Defence draft without amendments. Oral reports stated that the Minister simply ignored objections in the Council and published the doctrine in its existing form, with backing from Yeltsin. In March 1994 Security Council staff complained to the press that if Yeltsin's advisors had not ignored their recommendations about the handling of an amnesty for those involved in the 1991 coup attempt and the conflicts of October 1993, much of the damage to his authority could have been averted (*Moskovskie novosti*, 1994, no. 23, p. A6; *Krasnaya zvezda*, 28 Jun. 1994, 29 Oct. 1994; Jones and Brusstar, 'Moscow's Emerging Security Decisionmaking System', 354; interviews with Russian specialists).

[53] *Nezavisimaya gazeta*, 5 Apr. 1994. The first passage quoted is from 'Vesti', p. 20. Yury Nazarkin, then head of the Strategic Security Department of the SC, appeared before the Duma Defence Committee in March 1994 to give an authoritative account of the administration's attitude to the Partnership for Peace plan (*Nezavisimaya gazeta*, 18 Mar. 1994).

[54] ITAR-TASS Agency Report, 11.24 GMT, 6 May 1994, cited in *FBIS*, SOV-94-088 (6 May 1994), p. 4; ITAR-TASS Agency Report, 18.09 GMT, 12 May 1994, cited in *FBIS*, SOV-94-093 (13 May 1994), p. 7. In June Manilov spoke in detail to *Moscow News* about his recommendations for policy on the Crimea (no. 23, p. A6).

[55] Manilov described Yeltsin as a vigorous chairman of SC sessions in *Krasnaya zvezda*, 29 Oct. 1994.

[56] *Krasnaya zvezda*, 29 Oct. 1994.

[57] 'Strategiya dlya Rossii (2)', para. 1.15.2.

[58] Valery Vyzhutovich, *Moscow News*, 1994, no. 52, p. 4.

[59] As *Nezavisimaya gazeta* commented on 11 Jan. 1995: 'The President takes his decisions alone, taking into account or not taking into account as he sees fit the recommendations of the Security Council and the personal opinions of its members.' Even Deputy SC Secretary Manilov acknowledged at the end of 1994 that Russian policy was still 'characterized by impulsiveness and inconsistency' (*Moscow News*, 1994, no. 48, p. 3).

[60] See the interview given by former Deputy Foreign Minister Shelov-Kovedyaev in *Segodnya*, 31 Aug. 1993; Fyodorov, 'Foreign Policy Making in the RF', 119.

[61] *Rossiiskaya gazeta*, 18 Nov. 1992. 'I would not like to talk about a "monopoly" here,' commented one deputy minister earlier in the same year, '. . . because the President, of course, has his own advisers and so on, but we are the agency responsible both for working out the general foreign policy line and for planning concrete foreign policy actions' (*Diplomaticheskii vestnik*, 1992, no. 2–3, p. 44.) The agency's overall co-ordinating and monitoring powers were confirmed in the presidential decree of 14 Mar. 1995 on the 'Statute' of the Ministry of Foreign Affairs (*Politica Weekly Press Summary*, vol. ii, no. 14 (8–14 Apr. 1995)).

[62] 'Press-Tsentr', *Diplomaticheskii vestnik*, 1993, no. 1–2, p. 67. In June 1993 a supporter of strengthening the Security Council protested that in the absence of a co-ordinating centre 'it appears as if the Foreign Ministry and the Minister of Foreign Affairs receive a monopoly on moulding foreign policy and influence on the President' (Andranik Migranyan, in *Moscow News*, 1993, no. 25, p. 3).

[63] On Kozyrev's ability to determine the 'presidential' foreign policy, see *Moscow News*, 1994, no. 50, p. 5. This is not to say that Yeltsin has chosen to prevent other parts of the foreign policy machine from acting in ways which contradict these statements.

[64] 'V tsentral'nom apparate MID RF potrebovalos' peregruppirovka kadrov', *Diplomaticheskii vestnik*, 1993, no. 11–12, p. 39; 'Disappearing Diplomats', *Inside Russia and the CIS* (European Press Agency Bulletin), 1984, no. 8, p. 7; 'V Kollegii MID RF', *Diplomaticheskii vestnik*, 1994, no. 13–14, p. 53 (meeting on 15 Jun. 1994); 'Predmet osobogo vnimaniya', *Diplomaticheskii vestnik*, 1994, no. 1–2, pp. 59–60. The departure of German specialists from the Ministry was declared to have led to a loss of momentum in Russian–German relations in 1992 (*Izvestiya*, 18 Mar. 1992). See too Checkel, 'Russian Foreign Policy', 24; *Segodnya*, 5 Aug. 1995.

[65] *Nezavisimaya gazeta*, 1 Apr. 1992. See too Kurochkin in *Rossiiskaya gazeta*, 27 Mar. 1992.

[66] The average age of ministers and deputy ministers dropped to 46 in 1992. Four of the seven deputy ministers had post-graduate degrees (Checkel, 'Russian Foreign Policy: Back to the Future?', 25). The radical journalist from *Novoe vremya*, Galina Sidorova, was put in charge of Kozyrev's Information Service (S. Crow, 'Personnel Changes in the Russian Foreign Ministry', *RFE/RL Research Report*, 17 Apr. 1992; *Izvestiya*, 1 Apr. 1992), and later became advisor to the Minister.

[67] Checkel, 'Russian Foreign Policy', 24.

[68] Parts of this chapter rely on information obtained in interviews with Russian and British officials, in Moscow and London. Kozyrev stated in 1992 that 80% of his time was taken up by relations with former Soviet states (*Nezavisimaya gazeta*, 1 Apr. 1992). See too 'V tsentral'nom', 39–40.

[69] 'V Kollegii MID RF', 54. The structural changes are described in 'V Kollegii MID RF', 58–9. The Administration for Analysis and Forecasting, headed by Ednan Agaev, was originally located in the Department of International Organizations and Global Problems. At the end of 1993 two separate analysis groups were set up, in the Executive Secretariat and in the CIS Department.

[70] The Collegium met on 6 July 1993 to discuss the work of the consular service; on 12 Nov. 1993 to discuss restructuring to improve work with the CIS states; on 15 Jun. 1994 to discuss personnel problems (*Diplomaticheskii vestnik*, 1993, no. 13–14, p. 53; 1993, no. 15–16, p. 35; 1994, no. 23–4, p. 54).

[71] See reports in *Diplomaticheskii vestnik*, 1993, no. 1–2, pp. 44–5; no. 19–20, p. 56; 1994, no. 1–2, p. 8; no. 3–4, pp. 69, 71; no. 13–14, p. 6. The UNIDO body was described as a 'council'. The commission on military technology was chaired by Deputy Prime Minister Soskovets; the one on peacekeeping jointly by Deputy Defence and Foreign Ministers; the remainder of those mentioned by Foreign Ministry officials.

[72] V. Biryukov, 'MID i ekonomicheskie preobrazovaniya Rossii', *Diplomaticheskii vestnik*, 1992, no. 19–20, pp. 36–40; 'Fondu vneshnei politiki Rossii—rovno god', *Diplomaticheskii vestnik*, 1993, no. 5–6, pp. 57–9. The Foundation's public activity has been devoted mainly to organizing a series of conferences on topical international issues. The Foreign Ministry itself has held a number of international official/academic conferences, some with the help of the Foundation.

[73] The first meeting of the Council was held on 2 Jul. 1992. Topics have included the position of Russians outside Russia, relations with CIS states, inward investment, relations with Eastern Europe, NATO, and the CSCE, and CIS economic integration ('Zasedanie Soveta po vneshnei politiki Rossii', *Diplomaticheskii vestnik*, 1992, no. 15–16, p. 62; this and reports in subsequent issues normally list those invited). Aleksei Arbatov 'worked in the team which wrote the President's UN address' in September 1994; he was accompanied at an experts' press conference in New York by Andrei Kortunov and Sergei Rogov (*Segodnya*, 28 Sept. 1994). Sergei Karaganov and Andranik Migranyan are able to take advantage of membership of the Presidential Council, although this is no guarantee of access to the inner circles of power.

[74] *Diplomaticheskii vestnik*, 1994, no. 7–8, p. 56.

[75] V. A. Savel'ev, 'Parlamentskaya diplomatiya', *Diplomaticheskii vestnik*, 1993, no. 9–10, pp. 53–5; more briefly in *Nezavisimaya gazeta*, 5 Mar. 1993.

[76] From mid-1992 the MFER's activities in the field of inward investment were limited as a result of the establishing of the Russian Agency for International Co-operation and Development, headed by Deputy

Prime Minister in charge of Foreign Economic Relations Aleksandr Shokhin (P. Stavrakis, 'Government Bureaucracies: Transition or Disintegration?', *RFE/RL Research Report*, 14 May 1993, p. 28; *Moscow News*, 1994, no. 27, p. 9). Some parts of the MFER were hived off to form the basis of commercial organizations, such as the arms exporter Rosvooruzhenie.

[77] Interfax Agency Report, 16.34 GMT, 20 Oct. 1994, cited in *FBIS*, SOV-94-204 (21 Oct. 1994), p. 14.

[78] A. Nikolaev in *Rossiiskie vesti*, 30 Dec. 1994.

[79] Crow, *The Making of Foreign Policy*, 53–4.

[80] The move to set up an Inter-Agency Commission on Tajikistan (see above) was an attempt to rectify this. In 1994 its chairman, First Deputy Foreign Minister Adamishin, was reported as complaining that Russian military personnel in Tajikistan 'frequently overstep their functions'. See Arkady Dubnov in *Izvestiya*, 10 Mar. 1994.

[81] Dmitry Furman in *Moscow News*, 1993, no. 37, p. 7. How far officials in Moscow have connived in local military initiatives is unclear. The President of Georgia, Eduard Shevardnadze, accused the Russian Defence Ministry of creating 'its own military state' in Abkhazia by arming local rebels against his government (ITAR-TASS Agency Report, 5 Oct. 1992; Crow, *The Making of Foreign Policy*, 47–54). Yeltsin's Apr. 1994 decree authorizing negotiations for permanent bases throughout the CIS helped to strengthen the view that a unified military space could be maintained (J. Lepingwell, 'The Russian Military and Security Policy in the Near Abroad', *Survival*, vol. xxxvi, no. iii (1994), 71–4; M. Shashenkov, 'Russian Peacekeeping in the Near Abroad', *Survival*, vol. xxxvi, no. iii (1994), 51–6). See also Chapter 5.

[82] V. Yasmann, 'The Role of the Security Services in the October Uprising', *RFE/RL Research Report*, 5 Nov. 1993, 12–18; V. Yasmann, 'Security Services Reorganized', *RFE/RL Research Report*, 11 Feb. 1994, 7–14. After his appointment as head of the new FCS, Sergei Stepashin claimed that his agency had 'as before, a very good level of co-operation with the FIS. We are developing a general strategy.' He also referred to a joint meeting being planned with the President and his National Security Aide by the FCIS, the FIS, the General Staff Main Intelligence Administration, the Border Troops, and other bodies to reach agreement on further co-operation, 'in order to create, if you like, a kind of prototype intelligence community' (Russian TV, Ostankino Channel, 18.00 GMT, 5 Mar. 1994, reprinted in *BBC Summary of World Broadcasts*, SU/1939 (5 Mar. 1994), B/6).

[83] *Rossiiskie vesti*, 30 Dec. 1994. Nikolaev commented that over 2,000 former army and navy officers were by that time serving under his command.

[84] *Nezavisimaya gazeta*, 26 Nov. 1993 (introduction and part of the text of the second report).

[85] ITAR-TASS Agency Reports on 21 Sept. 1994, cited in *BBC Summary of World Broadcasts*, SU/2108 (23 Sept. 1994), B/11–15. See also Primakov's introduction to a history of Russian foreign intelligence, containing his forthright assessment of current external threats (*Trud*, 15 Oct. 1994). The content and political impact of these reports are discussed in the next section of this chapter. *Moscow News* (1995, no. 37, p. 1) described the decree as 'in many ways a sequel' to the FIS report.

[86] The Statute is published in *Politica Weekly Press Summary*, vol. ii, no. 14 (8–14 Apr. 1995). See para. 14. On Chernomyrdin's key role in relations with Ukraine, see for example *Nezavisimaya gazeta*, 8 Oct. 1994.

[87] The change in status was reported by Interfax, 19 May 1994; cited in *RFE/RL Daily Report* (electronic mail edn.), 20 May 1994. It was originally intended that it would be headed by Aleksandr Shokhin, then Deputy Prime Minister in charge of External Economic Relations. Many of the staff previously worked in the Soviet Statistical Committee and State Planning Committee.

[88] 'Postanovlenie Soveta ministrov—Pravitel'stva Rossiiskoi Federatsii', *Diplomaticheskii vestnik*, 1994, no. 5–6, pp. 10–15. The document was signed by Prime Minister Viktor Chernomyrdin.

[89] For reports of the talks with Ukraine see UNIAR Agency Report, 24 Aug. 1994, cited in *FBIS*, SOV-94-164 (24 Aug. 1994); UNIAN Agency Report, 29 Sept. 1994, cited in *FBIS*, SOV-94-190 (30 Sept. 1994).

[90] Interfax Agency Report, 3 May 1994, cited in *FBIS*, SOV-94-085 (3 May 1994), p. 7.

[91] There is a large backlog of unratified treaties. The extent and significance of parliament's ratification rights were still unclear at the end of 1994 (V. Gustov in *Nezavisimaya gazeta*, 25 May 1994; V. Trofimov in *Nezavisimaya gazeta*, 30 Sept. 1994).

[92] At the beginning of 1994 the Foreign Ministry sent the new legislature a list of 105 international treaties and agreements, most of which had presumably been awaiting ratification for some time, as well as a long menu of necessary legislation touching on the most basic aspects of foreign relations ('Press-Tsentr', *Diplomaticheskii vestnik*, 1994, no. 5–6, pp. 65–6). A presidential veto can be overridden only by a two-thirds majority in both houses of parliament (Art. 107.3).

[93] See Vladimir Lukin in *Segodnya*, 1 Apr. 1994. The Yugoslavia bill is discussed in *Segodnya*, 30 Apr. and 14 May 1994; Ekho Moskvy Radio, 15.00 GMT, 13 May 1994, cited in *FBIS*, SOV-94-094 (16 May 1994). In the same month the Duma Budget Committee's Sub-Committee on Currency Regulation drafted a bill restricting the size of foreign borrowing by the government (*Segodnya*, 5 May 1994).

[94] See later in this chapter.

[95] S. Crow, 'Why has Russian Foreign Policy Changed?', *RFE/RL Research Report*, 6 May 1994; see too H. Adomeit, 'Great to be Russia? Russia as a "Great Power" in World Affairs: Images and Reality', *International Affairs*, 71 (1995), 35–68. For a survey of Russian foreign policy élite opinion in mid-1993, see N. Popov, 'Vneshnyaya politika Rossii (Analiz politikov i ekspertov)', *Mirovaya ekonomika i mezhdunarodnye otnosheniya*, 1994, no. 3, pp. 52–9; no. 4, pp. 5–15.

[96] Popov, 'Vneshnyaya politika Rossii', 53, 58.

[97] *Nezavisimaya gazeta*, 1 Apr. 1992. Burbulis was responsible for 'operative leadership of the activity of the Foreign Ministry' (*Diplomaticheskii vestnik*, 1992, no. 6, p. 16). On Burbulis and his role, see *Moskovskie novosti*, 1992, no. 51–2; *Rossiiskaya gazeta*, 17 Jan., 29 May, and 24 Aug. 1992; Checkel, 'Russian Foreign Policy', 19–20.

[98] Fyodor Shelov-Kovedyaev dated the beginning of Burbulis's political decline from the moment of his non-inclusion in the Security Council (*Segodnya*, 31 Aug. 1993). The quotation is from Emil Pain, *Izvestiya*, 29 Sept. 1993. For evidence of liberal concern at the time about the powers of the new Security Council, see Crow, *The Making of Foreign Policy in Russia*, 13–32; R. Sakwa, *Russian Politics and Society*, 52–3.

[99] *Rossiiskaya gazeta*, 6 May, 1 Aug., and 8 Aug. 1992; *Nezavisimaya gazeta*, 10 Jul., 31 Jul., and 15 Oct. 1992; Jones and Brusstar, 'Moscow's Emerging Security Council', 353.

[100] Kozyrev blamed the decision on 'the failure of our government to get a hold on the apparat' (*Moskovskie novosti*, 1992, no. 38; cited in Crow, *The Making of Russian Foreign Policy*, 25–6).

[101] *Izvestiya*, 5 Jun. 1992; ITAR-TASS Agency (in Russian), 29 Jun. 1992.

[102] *Izvestiya*, 30 Jun. 1992. On this conflict, see Crow, *The Making of Russian Foreign Policy*, 47–57.

[103] *Nezavisimaya gazeta*, 31 Jul. 1992; Crow, *The Making of Russian Foreign Policy*, 72.

[104] *Izvestiya*, 29 Sept. 1993. See too Shelov-Kovedyaev in *Segodnya*, 31 Aug. 1993. For a similar judgement from a nationalist perspective, see Andranik Migranyan in *Nezavisimaya gazeta*, 12 Jan. 1994.

[105] See Pain's account in *Izvestiya*, 29 Sept. 1993. On the legislature's activities at this time see Crow, *The Making of Russian Foreign Policy*, 38–46.

[106] *Krasnaya zvezda*, 23 Dec. 1992; Interfax Agency Report, 18 Dec. 1992, cited by K. Dawisha and B. Parrott, *Russia and the New States of Eurasia: The Politics of Upheaval* (Cambridge, 1994), 204. In Oct. 1992 Yeltsin made a visit to the Foreign Ministry and criticized its employees for poor discipline, for the poor quality of the data and analysis they

supplied, and for not consulting adequately with other departments (*Russkii vestnik*, 29 Oct. 1992).

[107] A. Rahr, 'Yeltsin's New Team', *RFE/RL Research Report*, 28 May 1993; Crow, *The Making of Russian Foreign Policy*, 32–3, 37. For typical liberal accounts of the Security Council see V. Orlov in *Moscow News*, 1993, no. 7; or E. Pain in *Izvestiya*, 29 Sept. 1993.

[108] Interviews with Russian officials and specialists; V. Orlov in *Moscow News*, 1993, no. 20, p. 9; A. Rahr, 'Yeltsin and New Elections', *RFE/RL Research Report*, 22 Aug. 1993, 4. See the second section of this chapter ('Russian foreign policy institutions') for the views of Yeltsin's foreign policy aide on restricting the Security Council's role ('Andrei Kozyrev's Trojan Horse', *Inside Russia and the CIS*, 1994, no. 3, p. 1).

[109] See Chapter 2. A summary of the concept, which was never published in full, appeared in *Nezavisimaya gazeta*, 29 Apr. 1993. The Deputy Head of the Strategic Security Department which at that time existed in the Security Council gave an interview about the contents of the concept in *Rossiiskaya gazeta*, 29 Apr. 1993. An earlier Foreign Ministry draft is in *Diplomaticheskii vestnik*, special issue, Jan. 1993. V. Orlov analysed the compromises behind the final version in *Moscow News*, 1993, no. 20, p. 9: there is some hardening of policy compared to the Foreign Ministry version. For example, 'protecting' Russians in the former Soviet states becomes a major priority.

[110] Skokov had been given the highest number of votes by parliamentarians as a candidate for Prime Minister, he had shown less than total loyalty to Yeltsin, and his powers were said to be resented by the 'power ministers'. See *Rossiiskie vesti*, 12 May 1993; *Segodnya*, 12 May 1993; *Moscow News*, 1993, no. 20, p. 9; *Nezavisimaya gazeta*, 12 Aug. 1993. The presidential decree endorsing the foreign policy concept placed responsibility for general co-ordination of policy on the Security Council Inter-Agency Foreign Policy Commission. The Foreign Ministry was given responsibility for operational co-ordination and monitoring of day-to-day foreign policy work (*Pravda*, 30 Apr. 1993).

[111] *Nezavisimaya gazeta*, 12 Aug. 1993; *Segodnya*, 13 Aug. 1993. In an interview in *Izvestiya*, 12 Aug. 1993, Shaposhnikov commented that Yeltsin had not received him since 30 Jun.

[112] See the second section of this chapter. Lobov, a civil engineer by profession, and a supporter of Yeltsin since his days as Party Secretary in Sverdlovsk, had little expertise in foreign policy matters. Among the new senior officials in the Security Council, Valery Manilov, from Shaposhnikov's staff, and Vladimir Rubanov, from the Security Ministry, appeared to be centrist, pragmatic nationalist figures. On Rubanov, see *Rossiiskie vesti*, 12 Aug. 1993; for examples of Manilov's views, see Interfax Agency Report, 18.05 GMT, 5 May 1994, cited in

*FBIS*, SOV-94-088 (6 May 1994), p. 4; *Moscow News*, 1994, no. 23, p. 2.

[113] Russian Television Service, 'Utro', 6 Jan. 1993; *Trud*, 3 Sept. 1992; Interfax Agency Report, 26 Jan. 1993. First two cited in Crow, *The Making of Russian Foreign Policy*, 45–6, 56–7. See too V. A. Savel'ev, 'Parlamentskaya diplomatiya', *Diplomaticheskii vestnik*, 1993, no. 9–10, pp. 53–5; Kozyrev's speech to the parliament reported in *Diplomaticheskii vestnik*, 1993, no. 5–6, pp. 39–42; 'Parliament and the Foreign Ministry: A Rapprochement', *Moscow News*, 1993, no. 9, p. 9. The first joint meeting of the collegiums of the Foreign and Defence Ministries was held on 6 May 1993, to discuss peacekeeping.

[114] See the complaints by Deputy Foreign Minister Vitaly Churkin and by presidential adviser Emil Pain in *Diplomaticheskii vestnik*, 1993, no. 3–4, p. 67; *Izvestiya*, 29 Sept. 1993. In May 1993 the Foreign Ministry official responsible for liaison with the legislature insisted that more characteristic was a search by both sides for compromises and mutually acceptable solutions (Savel'ev, 'Parlamentskaya diplomatiya', 54–5).

[115] N. Malcolm, 'The New Russian Foreign Policy', *The World Today*, 50 (1994), 28–32; A. Lynch, 'After Empire: Russia and its Western Neighbours', *RFE/RL Research Report*, 25 Mar. 1994, 10–17; Crow, 'Why has Russian Foreign Policy Changed?'

[116] *Nezavisimaya gazeta*, 19 Aug. 1992. The membership is listed in *Nezavisimaya gazeta*, 27 May 1994. The Council is run by Sergei Karaganov, Deputy Director of the Russian Academy of Sciences Institute of Europe.

[117] D. L'vov in *Russkii vestnik*, 20 Jan. 1994.

[118] *Nezavisimaya gazeta*, 27 May 1994. Kozyrev's statement is cited in *Nezavismimaya gazeta*, 19 Jan. 1994. For a fuller discussion of Russian security policy in the former Soviet area as it developed in 1993 and 1994, see Lepingwell, 'The Russian Military'.

[119] *Moscow News*, 1994, no. 13, p. 4; no. 16, p. 4; *Segodnya*, 26 Feb. 1994. Anatoly Adamishin, then First Deputy Foreign Minister and Chair of the SC Inter-Agency Foreign Policy Commission, declared in May 1994 that 'on a whole number of fundamental foreign policy issues there is a groundwork for more or less broad national accord in Russia' (*Moscow News*, 1994, no. 19, p. 4).

[120] Interfax Agency Report, cited in *RFE/RL Research Institute Daily Report* (electronic mail edn.), 18 Nov. 1994. A former adviser of Mikhail Gorbachev commented that parliament's role in foreign policy debate was more and more coming to resemble that of 'a doctoral discussant' (A. Grachev, *Moscow News*, 1994, no. 51, p. 7).

[121] A. Grachev, 'Russia's Foreign Policy is a Tale of Sound and Fury', *Moscow News*, 1994, no. 51, p. 7.

[122] *Izvestiya*, 27 Sept. 1994; *Moskovskie novosti*, 1995, no. 53. On Kozyrev's problems, see Aleksei Pushkov in *Moscow News*, 1994, no. 50, p. 5. It should be said that Kozyrev's change of line did win him praise among Pragmatic Nationalists. The political journalist Stanislav Kondrashov remarked in *Izvestiya* (2 Jul. 1994): 'By abandoning the voluntary status of pupil and beginning to speak its mind in recent months, Russia seems to be finding its place among the world's leading powers. This is a considerable accomplishment for our foreign policy.' It was also warmly welcomed in the military newspaper *Krasnaya zvezda* (20 Jan. 1994). On reshuffles in the Foreign Ministry see K. Eggert in *Izvestiya*, 6 Jan. 1994.

[123] P. Rutland, 'The Economic Foundations of Foreign Policy in the States of the Former Soviet Union' (mimeo, 1993), 25.

[124] *Nezavisimaya gazeta*, 24 Aug. 1993; *Izvestiya*, 24 Aug. and 26 Aug. 1993; *Segodnya*, 12 May and 24 Aug. 1993. Glaz'ev was Deputy Minister until Dec. 1992, when he succeeded Pyotr Aven. Glaz'ev was also accused of collusion with Rutskoi and the parliamentary opposition.

[125] 'The Generals are Protesting—in Silence', *Komsomolskaya pravda*, 4 Oct. 1994.

[126] For statements by Grachev on the Partnership for Peace, see *Segodnya*, 15 Feb. 1994; *Pravda*, 27 May 1994. Harmony was also preserved in disputes with Latvia and Ukraine. See *Izvestiya*, 2 Feb. 1994; *Segodnya*, 26 Apr. 1994. Differences of emphasis persisted, of course, in some areas, for example over strategy in Tajikistan. See the second section of this chapter.

[127] *Segodnya*, 28 Apr. 1994; *Obshchaya gazeta*, 6–12 May 1994. The exercises were strongly backed by Grachev, and opposed in the Security Council, where Valery Manilov insisted on the need to pay attention to 'moral and economic factors' (Interfax Agency Report, 18.05 GMT, 5 May 1994, cited in *FBIS*, SOV-94-088 (6 May 1994), p. 4; *Kommersant-Daily*, 5 May 1994).

[128] *Moscow News*, 1992, no. 18, p. 6; no. 20, pp. 2, 13; 1993, no. 31, pp. 1, 4; no. 34, pp. 1, 7; *Izvestiya*, 20 Jul. and 21 Jul. 1993; *Pravda*, 20 Jul. 1993; *Segodnya*, 10 Aug. 1993; *Rossiiskie vesti*, 4 Jan. 1994.

[129] Razuvaev, in *Segodnya*, 21 Oct. 1994.

[130] One newspaper commented that the Foreign Ministry 'in this instance is conveying the view of part of Russia's oil and gas circles' (*Segodnya*, 22 Sept. 1994).

[131] *Financial Times*, 31 May and 9 Nov. 1994; *Izvestiya*, 22 Sept. and 29 Sept. 1994; *Moscow News*, 1994, no. 39, pp. 1, 5; no. 42, p. 4; *Segodnya*, 22 Sept., 21 Oct., and 22 Nov. 1994; Interfax Agency Report, 14.54 GMT, 27 Sept. 1994; ITAR-TASS Report, 12.00 GMT, 27 Sept. 1994, both cited in *FBIS*, SOV-94-188 (28 Sept. 1994). At the time the Russian state had an 80% shareholding in Lukoil.

[132] *Izvestiya*, 9 Aug. 1994; *Guardian*, 15 Oct. 1994; *Moscow News*, 1994, no. 42, p. 5; no. 47, p. 1; no. 48, p. 5; no. 50, p. 5.

[133] *OMRI Daily Digest* (electronic mail edn.), 3 Apr. 1995, pt. 1; *Segodnya*, 12 Aug. 1994. It was reported in Sept. 1994 that Russia had concluded $3bn in contracts for arms exports in general in the first half of 1994 (total contracts for 1993 were $1.5bn to $2bn) (*Izvestiya*, 22 Sept. 1993). During Yeltsin's visit to Washington in Sept. 1994 it was announced that Russia would be joining the body to replace COCOM (the Co-ordinating Committee on Multilateral Export Controls). Indeed at the moment when it was announced that COCOM was to be abolished, in Nov. 1993, it was stated that Russia would be invited to participate in the work of its successor (*Nezavisimaya gazeta*, 18 Nov. 1993).

[134] Moscow sought to appear co-operative in discussions on these matters with the United States. In Washington in Sept. 1994, for example, Yeltsin assured President Clinton that Russia would cease weapons deliveries to Iran 'as soon as the commitments assumed by the former USSR are fulfilled'. The American side, however, set little store by such reassurances (*Izvestiya*, 1 Oct. 1994).

[135] *Nezavisimaya gazeta*, 26 Nov. 1993. See also the previous section of this chapter. Kozyrev had consistently opposed the eastward expansion of NATO, even when Yeltsin appeared to take a softer line, but there were no doubt differences of view in his ministry about the best way for Russia to respond.

[136] ITAR-TASS Agency Report, 09.46 GMT, 21 Sept. 1994; Interfax Agency Report, 10.44 GMT, 21 Sept. 1994; both cited in *BBC Summary of World Broadcasts*, SU/2108 (23 Sept. 1994), B/11–14.

[137] Yeltsin's own speech referred to the threat from abroad to Russia's natural resources and high-technology potential (*Nezavisimaya gazeta*, 26 May and 27 May 1994).

[138] *Nezavisimaya gazeta*, 10 Jan. 1995.

[139] Interfax Agency Report, 31 Mar. 1995, cited in *OMRI Daily Digest* (electronic mail), 3 Apr. 1995, pt. 1.

[140] Stepan Kiselyov, 'How to Capture the "White House", without using Tanks, Paratroopers or Special Forces (a Coup from Within)', *Moscow News*, 1991, no. 39, pp. 8–9.

[141] See Ilyushin's dismissive comments about quarrelsome 'self-styled democrats' in his interview in *Nezavisimaya gazeta*, 10 Feb. 1994; also the portrait by Valery Vyzhutovich in *Moscow News*, 1994, no. 28, p. 6 (contains information on Filatov's links with the Analytical Centre). See too ITAR-TASS Agency Report, 13.57 GMT, 24 Aug. 1994, cited in *FBIS*, SOV-94-165 (25 Aug. 1994) for a sample of the views of the head of the Analytical Centre, Mark Urnov. On Ryurikov see *Moscow News*, 1993, no. 25, p. 9; no. 31, p. 6; *Izvestiya*, 18 Dec. 1993 and 27

Sept. 1994. On Baturin, see *Nezavisimaya gazeta*, 11 Jan. 1994 (on his appointment) and 6 Jan. 1995. On the influx of radical democrats to the presidential *apparat* after Filatov's appointment, see *Nezavisimaya gazeta*, 6 Mar. 1993.

[142] Gaidar interview with ARD (German radio station), cited by DPA, 31 Jan. 1995, reproduced in *OMRI Daily Digest* (electronic mail), 1 Feb. 1995. See too *Guardian*, 5 Oct. 1994; *Izvestiya*, 5 Jan. 1995 (Otto Latsis, member of the Presidential Council) and 6 Jan. 1995 (interview with Yury Baturin); the testimony of ex-minister Boris Fyodorov, repeated in *The Times*, 11 Mar. 1995, Magazine Section, p. 13; *Nezavisimaya gazeta*, 22 Apr. 1995; L. Radzikhovsky in *Ogonek*, 1995, no. 33, pp. 14–17 (on Filatov's decline). *Segodnya*, 20 Dec. 1994, repeated recent statements by Presidential Council members Georgy Satarov, Leonid Smiryagin, and Emil Pain to the effect that 'no-one had been asking for or listening to their advice for months'. See also *The Times*, 29 Dec. 1994.

[143] *Izvestiya*, 17 Feb. 1995.

[144] S. Huntington, *Political Order in Changing Societies* (New Haven, Conn., 1968), 1.

[145] See G. Allison and M. Halperin, 'Bureaucratic Politics: A Paradigm and some Policy Implications', in R. Tanter and R. Ullman (eds.), *Theory and Policy in International Relations* (Princeton, NJ, 1972), 56: 'Beneath the differences that fuel bureaucratic politics is a foundation of shared assumptions about basic values and facts. These . . . are reflected in various attitudes and images which are taken for granted by most players.'

[146] Shelov-Kovedyaev in *Segodnya*, 31 Aug. 1993.

[147] Andrei Grachev in *Moscow News*, 1994, no. 51, p. 7.

[148] See Chapter 4.

[149] *Guardian*, 5 Oct. 1994.

[150] *Komsomolskaya pravda*, 4 Oct. 1994. Russia had negotiated temporary continued use in Latvia of a radar station only. The Russian Foreign Ministry claimed that they first found out about the statement from the Latvian side (*Segodnya*, 8 Apr. 1994). Another *faux pas* was made in Yeltsin's speech at the UN in Sept. about opportunities for foreign investment in Russia, when he apparently unwittingly chose as examples projects which had been dogged by controversy and hold-ups (*Segodnya*, 28 Sept. 1994).

[151] *Inside Russia and the CIS*, 1995, no. 1, p. 1. For an authoritative opinion on the continuing disabling effects of political rivalries in security policy matters, see Sergei Shakhrai's interview reported by ITAR-TASS, 10.18 GMT, 5 Jan. 1995, cited in *FBIS*, SOV-95-003 (5 Jan. 1995), pp. 9–10.

[152] See the trenchant criticisms in the CFDP's second report, 'Strategiya dlya Rossii (2)', paras. 1.14, 1.15. It is doubtful to what extent the

bureaucratic politics paradigm can be usefully applied even to the post-1992 setting, if we accept Graham Allison's definition—'bargaining along regularized channels among players positioned hierarchically within the government'—since it was difficult to speak with confidence of regularized channels or respected hierarchies ('Conceptual Models and the Cuban Missile Crisis', *American Political Science Review*, 63 (1969), 707).

[153] *Moscow News*, 1995, no. 2, p. 3. Gromov complained of a general trend to centralize decision-making in the Ministry among a smaller number of officials.

# 4

# The Public Politics of Foreign Policy

ALEX PRAVDA

Bringing foreign policy into the domain of public debate and effective parliamentary control constitutes one of the most challenging tasks for any state seeking to become a democracy. Andrei Kozyrev stressed the importance for Russia of fostering a role for public discussion and parliamentary scrutiny that would secure a balance between professional executive management of foreign policy and democratic oversight.[1]

The climate of political struggle which has complicated professional management (see Chapter 3) has also vitiated attempts to create a system of democratic control. Russian democratic institutions remain fragile, the processes and habits necessary for their proper operation embryonic. This chapter is concerned with the ways in which this difficult and unstable environment conditioned the public political dimensions of the foreign policy process in the period 1992 to 1995. We shall examine how questions of external policy figured in three arenas: political parties and lobbies; public opinion; and parliament. Central to our interests are patterns of connection between developments in these domestic arenas and foreign policy. In the first two arenas, assessing these linkages largely involves mapping the configuration of stances adopted by domestic actors on international issues. It also means trying to gauge the import of such stances for the foreign policy process. In the third arena, where we are dealing with parliamentary efforts to affect policy directly, the focus is more squarely on assessing whether and how such attempts have impinged on the course of Russian foreign policy in the CIS and further afield. Here, as in the other arenas, there are significant differences between the ways in which public politics bear on policy in the 'near' and 'far abroad'.

The overall bearing which public politics have had on foreign policy has largely been one of conditioning and indirect influence, since the executive, however fragmented, has retained control over decisions on external issues (see Chapter 3). Political party stances contributed to the general debate on foreign policy (see Chapter 2) and set out policy criticisms and alternatives before the electorate. Voters' preferences coloured the political mood and the policy environment in which executive decisions on foreign policy were shaped. Those decisions were further influenced by the specific lobbying of parties and corporate groups. Some lobbying was done through parliament, which itself provided an important forum for scrutiny and vigorous criticism of government foreign policy. Together with the general climate of opinion which it affected and reflected, parliamentary activity helped catalyse the evolution of executive thinking and action in the direction of more assertive external policies.

## Political parties and lobbies

The Russian political landscape is inhabited by a large and ever-changing population of political parties. Generally small and ill-organized, these parties or proto-parties are 'stepchildren', to use Dahl's expression, of a political structure in the flux of systemic transformation. During the years under examination the parties themselves were often in flux, splitting and re-forming in alliances and blocs to reflect relations between key political figures around whom most of the organizations revolved. As leaders often shifted policy ground in response to changing political power opportunities, party policy platforms often lacked consistency, coherence, and precision. This applied in particular to the international elements of party programmes, which were typically very general, dealing with issues in a broad-brush fashion and elaborating few specific foreign policy proposals, let alone coherent alternative strategies.

This lack of coherence and focus reflected at least three factors: lack of expertise, conviction politics, and political expediency. Specialists on foreign affairs were few in number and concentrated in the centrist parties. Shortage of expertise reinforced a strong tendency towards making sweeping statements based on fundamental beliefs and values rather than substantive analysis. The prevailing climate of conviction politics, frequently verging on the ideological, affected the stances on foreign (as on domestic) policies of all parties, and especially those at the ends of the political spectrum. Both radical reformers and their conservative opponents derived many of their stances on foreign policy from basic values and orientations. For reformers, Western development was often the embodiment of the modern and progressive. For the conservative opposition parties, nationalist and patriotic values were particularly vital to their self-identity as truly 'Russian' parties. While such embedded values often made for overly general stances, they also strengthened these parties' interest in foreign policy issues.

Political expediency had a similar dual effect: it reduced the quality of party utterances on foreign policy as well as keeping international issues relatively high on the agenda. Moves on international issues were frequently made in order to score easy domestic political points: the government and reformers were vulnerable to attack and detractors could make effective points without having to offer viable policy alternatives, something less easy to do in the economic area. Point-scoring sometimes gave party lines on foreign policy a piecemeal and *ad hoc* quality. At the same time, the relative ease of scoring points made international questions politically attractive and gave them greater prominence in what was typically an agenda dominated by domestic problems.

During the period under review, there were well over a hundred parties and movements, perhaps a third of which could be regarded as significant and only a dozen or so as politically important.[2] While focusing on the major parliamentary parties, we give some consideration to organizations which did not return deputies but made influential contributions to public discussion on foreign policy.

Viewed in domestic policy terms, the most important parties and blocs active in the period under review may be divided into three broad categories: radical reformers, conservative oppositionists, and centrists. Radical reformers were associated with a programme of liberal democracy and rapid marketization, and for most of the period remained close to the government. Radical conservatives opposed the government and reformers on communist and non-communist platforms of a strongly statist kind. Centrists favoured moderate and more state-managed change on political and economic fronts. They were the most differentiated group, including both moderate reformers and moderate conservatives.[3] These categories

remained valid throughout the period. The organizational composition of each category changed with the rise, decline, and regrouping of parties and blocs. The political balance between the
categories also altered, from mid-1993, as radical reform parties
fragmented and the government gravitated towards more centrist
positions.

Viewed in foreign policy terms, the stances of the major parties
and blocs can be grouped under the headings used in this volume:
Liberal Westernism, Fundamentalist Nationalism, and Pragmatic
Nationalism. Broadly speaking, there was a close correspondence
between these foreign policy groupings and the main party categories. Party positions on domestic and international issues were
fairly congruent, with radical reformers espousing Liberal Westernism, radical conservatives propounding Fundamentalist Nationalism,
and centrists taking a Pragmatic Nationalist line. It is worth noting that this pattern of congruence was not common to all states
in the early years of post-Soviet transformation. Much hinged on
the international position of the state. In Ukraine, for instance,
Fundamentalist Nationalism was associated with radical political
and economic reform, since nationalists advocated *rapprochement*
with the industrially developed West in order to secure independence from Russia.

In Russia the association between nationalism and conservatism
on the one hand and reformism and Westernism on the other was
strong, though far from absolute and uniform. Its strength varied
with areas of external policy and with location in the political spectrum. Domestic divisions tallied more closely with different positions on 'far-abroad' policy than they did with stances on issues
involving the 'near abroad.' The degree of fit between domestic
and foreign policy stances was greatest at the two ends of the political spectrum, where ideological conviction and political partisanship were strongest. In between the two ends the coupling between
domestic and international positions was looser. On the domestic
front, the centre included parties which aligned more closely with
reform and others which inclined towards the conservatives. On international issues, centrist parties were more tightly clustered around
Pragmatic Nationalist views. Over the course of these three years,
the boundaries between parties initially committed to reformist/
Westernist and centrist/Pragmatic Nationalist stances became more
politically blurred as radical reformists became more moderate and

increasingly nationalist. The following survey of party stances on international questions seeks to sketch basic positions and bring out the relationships between them.[4]

## Radical reformists and Liberal Westernism

The parties which fell into this category in 1992–3 included mainly those associated with the umbrella-movement Democratic Russia and, from 1993, with its effective successor, Russia's Choice. These were parties sympathetic to the government programme and until late 1994 generally supportive of its policies. Many of the most reformist members of the government belonged to these parties' ranks, notably for our purposes the Foreign Minister, Andrei Kozyrev.

Central to the foreign policy thinking of these parties was a general orientation favouring openness to the outside world in general and to the developed West in particular. They saw no external military threat to Russia and regarded the industrial democracies of the West as its natural partners and allies. In the Democratic Russia programme of late 1992, there was overwhelming preoccupation with the West, and Asian Pacific countries were mentioned almost as an afterthought.[5] The stress on co-operation with the West and the international community was closely linked with these parties' commitment to rapid democratic and market reform at home. The case for a pro-Western strategy corresponding to Russian national interests was put first and foremost in terms of direct domestic benefits. Russian interests, simply put, lay in close relations with the richest countries. Western aid and assistance were seen as essential to Russian development and sometimes depicted as almost a panacea for its problems.

Panacea-like terms were also used in justifying alignment with the developed countries on the international diplomatic front. This was not only seen as serving Russian national interests; it was also portrayed as the key to resolving problems of world instability.[6] Helping to maintain stability through co-operation was seen by the radical reformers as Russia's main international imperative.[7] This meant actively collaborating with the UN; it also involved backing US action, where this had widespread international endorsement, in major conflicts, whether in the Middle East or south-eastern Europe. Representatives of all the radical reformist parties in one late 1992 survey expressed support for Russian participation in UN sanctions against Serbia. In similarly internationalist vein, they all approved of US action against Iraq in early 1993; some went as far as favouring active support. Such active siding with the West, against what opposition conservatives regarded as Russia's traditional allies, sometimes reflected domestic political partisanship as much as principled internationalism. The democratic reform parties, for most of the period under review, strongly supported the Kozyrev line and found little fault with his running of foreign policy. Even the handling of the Kurile Islands issue was not seen as a failure.[8] The one criticism they levelled at the Foreign Minister, and it became more telling after mid-1993, was that laudable foreign policy aims were not always pursued in a consistently civilized fashion.

Using civilized means, in accord with international norms, was an issue of particular importance in the context of the 'near abroad'. Here these parties generally favoured a relatively liberal and tolerant line towards Russia's neighbours, respecting them as sovereign states. In late 1992, they came out for negotiation over the Transdnestr region and for dividing rather than claiming the Black Sea Fleet. In part, the softer political approach to 'near-abroad' problems should be seen as a reaction against the tough stance taken by their conservative opponents.[9] Having avoided identification with 'patriotic' excesses, the radical reform parties realized in the course of 1993 that they had to show greater concern for safeguarding Russian interests in relations with the former republics. Still, in autumn 1993 Russia's Choice programme had little to say about 'near-abroad' policy beyond a general commitment to defend the rights of Russians living beyond its borders.[10] The impact of the election, and the generally more assertive line on the 'near abroad' it catalysed, prompted the democrats to strengthen and broaden their commitment. Speaking as leader of the Democratic Choice of Russia party established in mid-1994, Yegor Gaidar highlighted the primacy of defending not just Russians but all Russian-speaking peoples throughout the former Soviet Union.[11] Radical reformists retained a distinctively liberal position on the means by which such defence of Russian minority rights was to be achieved. Gaidar and others broke with Kozyrev over his endorsement of forceful intervention in the 'inner-abroad' republic of Chechnya in late 1994.

*Radical conservatives and Fundamentalist Nationalism*

Like the radical reformers, their radical conservative opponents were driven both by emotional and ideological commitment and political partisanship. The general thrust of their very different international stance reflected suspicion of the West, regret at the loss of superpower status, and a desire to see Russia as a great power dominating the former Soviet space and acting independently on the world stage; these were the themes of their self-styled patriotism. On more specific foreign policy questions, the radical conservative line was typically shaped by the partisan interests of the opposition parties to attack and counter government policies. The imperative to oppose radical reform and liberal Westernism gave the rather disparate parties in this category a common cause.

Differences on domestic issues between the communist and non-communist parties of what was often known as the Red-Brown coalition were balanced to some extent by broad agreement on a Fundamentalist Nationalist foreign policy platform. Even here, however, there were important contrasts between Zhirinovsky's motley Liberal Democratic Party of Russia, itself divided on most issues, and the more cohesive neo-communists, represented from 1993 mainly by Zyuganov's Communist Party of the Russian Federation.

The international agenda of the radical conservatives centred on an emotional Fundamentalist Nationalist core, which figured early on as an important basis of identity for the Red-Brown coalition that emerged as the opposition to Yeltsin and the reformers soon after the establishment of the Russian Federation. In February 1992 over seventy communist and nationalist parties and organizations, including Aksyuchits's Christian Democratic Movement, Baburin's Russian Popular Union, and the Union of Cossacks, formed the Russian People's Assembly. This umbrella group represented a variety of views on social and economic issues, all critical of radical reform yet far from united on alternatives. The parties making up the movement found it easier to mobilize around 'patriotic' criticism of national humiliation and betrayal. The Assembly upbraided the government for failing to protect Russians isolated by the dismemberment of the old Greater Russia (USSR) and for neglecting the importance of policy in the 'near abroad'. Where 'far-abroad' policy was concerned, the conference attacked Yeltsin for betraying Russia and focused on claimed readiness to

give territory away to Japan.[12] The Kuriles, together with the
Crimea and the Baltic, provided the new Red-Brown alliance with
policy ammunition for its power-political salvos against the President and government. Within this and similar umbrella opposition fronts, such as the Council of People's Democratic Forces of
Russia,[13] the more extreme nationalist and near-fascist elements—
notably those surrounding the ex-KGB general Sterligov—set some
of the key policy themes which were later developed, in slightly
more moderate tones, by mainline Red and Brown parties.

The mainline movements and parties generally subordinated
international issues to domestic constitutional and social and
economic questions. In 1993 the Communist Party of the Russian
Federation gave little prominence to foreign policy issues. Its most
important electoral ally, the Reddish Agrarian Party, had nothing
to say directly on international affairs. Only Zhirinovsky placed
foreign policy high on his national agenda and only the Liberal
Democratic Party developed Fundamentalist Nationalist points into
a central plank of its platform.[14] While many of his foreign policy
statements were extreme and seemed outlandish, they were often
deliberately wild. However incoherent, Zhirinovsky's remarks frequently echoed popular sentiments, particularly on the need for
Russia to act as a great power in the international arena.

The starting point of opposition Fundamentalist Nationalism
was indignation about the disintegration of the USSR and the loss
of superpower status. These parties posed as the self-styled champions of national dignity and defenders of Russian security, contrasting their loyalist position with Yeltsin's and the radical reformers'
betrayal of Russia.[15] Oppositionist nationalists even condemned
the President and his Foreign Minister as 'agents of influence' of
the US Special Services, introducing radical reforms in order to
destroy Russian strength and open the country up to Western
exploitation.[16] Couched in more restrained terms, the general line
of argument warning against Western penetration was made by
Aleksandr Rutskoi (Vice-President until 1993), who began as a
centrist critic but rapidly distanced himself from Yeltsin, ending up
as a highly nationalist co-leader (with Khasbulatov) of the opposition in the autumn 1993 showdown with the President.[17] It was
in response to these kinds of arguments and personal attacks that
Kozyrev regularly warned the West against the threat to peaceful

relations posed by the opposition 'party of war', who wished to see Russia deal with its security problems in forceful fashion.

Nationalist oppositionists saw Russia operating in an international climate made dangerous not just by internal instability, but by the readiness of old enemies to take economic advantage of weakness. They were the first to point in stark terms to the dangers of Russia being transformed into a 'raw materials appendage' of the West and being enslaved as a colony,[18] a claim reiterated by the communists in their 1993 electoral programme. In the January 1995 version, the party, by then the largest and most formidable organized political movement in Russia, called for an end to all kinds of 'Westernism and Americanism'.[19] It was the extreme nationalist opposition which first warned in alarmist terms against the dangers of naïve acceptance of aid and advocated protectionism.[20] The communists in 1995 advocated the establishment of a state foreign trade monopoly for the export of all strategically significant goods.[21]

As far as security and political dangers were concerned, the radical conservatives cautioned against rapid disarmament agreements, notably START-2, and warned against membership of Partnership for Peace. They launched early attacks against what they viewed as Russian kowtowing to the US in Yugoslavia and the Middle East. They protested against what they depicted as American attempts to use force to assert their hegemony in conflict zones. Radical conservatives openly advocated Russian support for traditional allies, such as Serbia and Iraq. Zhirinovsky and other extreme nationalist leaders visited Belgrade and Baghdad and championed active aid to what they saw as unjustly beleaguered states. All opposition parties and groups argued for Russia to use its position in the UN Security Council to counter sanctions.

More generally, they criticized what they saw as a misguided obsession with the US and Japan, and advocated a wider network of alliances, centring on Germany, India, and China.[22] All espoused the Fundamentalist Nationalist line that Russia was a Eurasian state and therefore had to operate bi-continental strategies.[23] Beyond recommending strategic diversification and arguing for a far more assertive international stance, conservative opposition leaders, such as Zyuganov, apart from espousing the fashionable rediscovery of geopolitics, put forward few positive ideas on the 'far-abroad' front.

In typical fashion, the 1995 Communist Party programme intoned about the need to strengthen 'the international authority of Russian power' and 'annul all agreements that offend against the interests and pride of Russia'.[24]

On the 'near abroad', Fundamentalist Nationalist argument was more coherent. However, it revealed more clearly differences between the Red and Brown components of the opposition. Communists felt the strongest regret at the passing of the Soviet Union. Other radical conservatives, while criticizing the breakup, sometimes pointed to the burdens which the USSR imposed on Russia, and advocated a return to tsarist arrangements. The Liberal Democratic Party supported neither a resurrected Soviet Union nor the new CIS. Zhirinovsky championed a powerful new Russian state within old Soviet borders, divided into tsarist-like provinces rather than ethnically based republics.[25] When they referred to the CIS, most opposition parties favoured a Slav union with the possible addition of Kazakhstan. The nature of this union remained far from clear. On the one hand, all paid lip-service to its voluntary nature and rejected the principle of Russian military intervention. On the other hand, they favoured forceful methods to ensure compliance. Nationalists supported the idea of Cossacks, who were largely aligned with the opposition camp until 1994, once again acting as the defenders of Russia's borders. Zhirinovsky recommended tough economic measures to force the former republics to return to the fold.[26]

Similar ambiguities and differences within radical conservative ranks arose when these parties discussed the 'near-abroad' question to which they gave highest priority: the protection of Russian minorities. There is no doubt that the nationalists were the first to insist on the importance of the issue in Russia's foreign policy agenda. They led the way in pointing to threats against Russian minorities and territory, from external powers as well as from the ruling majorities of the new states, conjuring up a picture of near encirclement of Russia by the 'near abroad'. Extreme nationalists called in mid-1992 for drastic action against Romanian 'threats' against the Transdnestria enclave.[27] The strongest attacks were reserved for the Baltic states, with Kazakhstan coming under heavy fire, mainly from Zhirinovsky. Here as elsewhere, the nationalist opposition parties pioneered particular lines of argument. The charges of apartheid levelled by extreme nationalists against the

Estonians in late 1992 had found their way into official speeches by early 1994.[28]

While formally rejecting the use of force to ensure Russian rights, all opposition parties criticized the government for taking a 'soft' attitude on the defence of Russians and Russian values. Fundamental to the nationalist case on both 'near' and 'far abroad' was the identification of Russian national interest with something they called Russian, and at times more broadly Slav, traditions and values. These embraced a multitude of ideas. They included the notion that Russia was an essentially Eurasian rather than Western nation and state; hence the alien and threatening nature of Western economic, political, and cultural models. Islam was equally seen by many as a threat to Russian/Slav identity and, by some of the neo-fascist elements, to the Slav 'gene pool'.[29] Others saw the power of Islam as a good reason for Russia to maintain good relations with the South. For Zhirinovsky, the best solution to this problem was for Russia to 'surge' to the South and secure the extended borders to which Moscow had historically aspired.[30]

The actual components of the Russian idea the Fundamentalist Nationalists championed are difficult to pin down; their very elusiveness was a strength in widening appeal. In essence they seemed to amount to maintenance of Russia as a large multi-ethnic imperial state, with a world spiritual mission.[31] The nationalists saw it as their patriotic mission to attack 'soft' 'near-' and 'far-abroad' policies and fight to maintain the integrity of the Russian state and its dominance within the former Soviet area.

*Centrists and Pragmatic Nationalism*

Centrists were concerned to ensure that radical conservatives did not manage to appropriate patriotism and use it to legitimize Fundamentalist Nationalism. They were anxious that radical reformers' extreme Westernism should not damage Russian interests and discredit the idea of a more open and co-operative policy towards the West, which most centrists considered important in itself and for the further economic and political development of Russia. It is because they sought to balance the two polar-group agendas that they were often labelled 'demo-patriots'. Centrist parties often played the role of a loyal rather than implacable opposition, criticizing rather than either fully supporting or whole-heartedly rejecting the government line. This role and the considerable foreign affairs expertise within the centrist group enabled these parties to develop a Pragmatic Nationalist approach, based on a Realist analysis of national interest. It was the most considered, and arguably the most influential, contribution to the party-political debate on Russian foreign policy.

The centrists were more differentiated than the other groups and their boundaries more difficult to define. We include in this group the various Social Democratic organizations, the Democratic Party of Russia, Renewal, and the People's Party of Free Russia, all core members of the umbrella Civic Union which dominated the centre of the political spectrum until early 1993. Most of the Civic Union's members were critical of both the reformist domestic agenda and the Liberal Westernist orientation. Some, such as the People's Party of Free Russia long associated with Rutskoi, came close to radical conservative attitudes by mid-1993. After the autumn clashes the most policy-active parties at the centre, Yabloko and the Party of Russian Unity and Accord, were closer on both domestic and international fronts to a government which had moved towards more centrist positions.

One of the main early points made by the centrists was that the government's 'naïve' pro-Westernism involved the loss of an independent Russian foreign policy. The thrust of their Pragmatic Nationalist argument was that Moscow had to elaborate a more balanced strategy based on Russian geostrategic interests.[32] The balance they wanted to see struck was between developing cooperation with the international community and ensuring that this served rather than submerged Russian national interests as a Eurasian Great Power.

While sharing some Fundamentalist Nationalist perspectives about the Eurasian nature and interests of Russia, centrists were far more favourably inclined to the West and to collaboration with the international community. This position corresponded to the rather straddling stance taken on this question by most of the élite, according to one early 1993 poll.[33] The general Pragmatic Nationalist approach advocated was one which Yabloko labelled 'sensible egoism'. Being sensible meant diversifying relations, paying equal attention to all major powers as well as developing partnership with the leading Western states.[34] It also involved dealing with all states highly pragmatically, avoiding naïvety about others' motives and Russia's own long-term interests.

According to these Pragmatic Nationalist views, the West, while not hostile to Russia, had regard to its own interests when seeking political co-operation or extending assistance. Aid was seen neither as the threat conjured up by Fundamentalists nor as the panacea depicted by Liberal Westernizers. Rather, aid and assistance had a part to play, but unless carefully managed, they might reinforce the distortion of Russian economic development. What centrists had mainly in mind, and here they articulated conservative opposition views in more moderate terms, was that Western assistance and trade could well help to advance the 'Kuwaitization' of Russia, turning the country essentially into an exporter of raw materials. It was in the economic sphere that centrists put their strongest case for developing relations with the West on an equal basis, serving Russian national interests.[35] Some centrist groups, like Travkin's Democratic Party of Russia, concentrated heavily on economic issues and argued that national interests required trade policies which focused more on Russia's traditional partners, in Eastern Europe, Asia, and the CIS rather than on the US.[36] All centrists urged the government to promote its hard-currency-earning exports even at the risk of incurring the displeasure of Western competitors. This argument was applied in particular to arms exports, where the Pragmatic Nationalist line enjoyed widespread élite support, even among Westernizers.[37]

Pragmatic Nationalist criticism of dependence and advocacy of greater self-reliance applied as much to political as to economic relations with the West. Centrist feelings towards the West ranged from wary amicability (Lukin, Ambartsumov) to suspicion (Travkin). Only some regarded the West as a residual threat; most were prepared to improve security and political relations as long as this was done with care. Centrist arguments in early 1993 for amending the START-2 treaty before ratifying the accord were a case in point. Such wary pragmatism also emerged in attitudes towards co-operation with the West and the UN in regional conflicts. Opinions differed within the centrist group. At the tougher nationalist end of this spectrum, the Democratic Party of Russia condemned US action in the Gulf and came out in support of the Serbs. Most centrists were critical of US and NATO actions but not overtly pro-Iraqi or pro-Serb. As a whole, they followed a line somewhat to the nationalist side, without generally espousing extremist causes. Centrists typically thought of their position in terms of 'enlightened patriotism'.[38] The 'patriotic' element led them to condemn signs of concessions on territorial issues, such as the Kurile Islands. The 'enlightened' aspect prevented them from taking a Fundamentalist view of all negotiations as equivalent to national betrayal.

If centrists' criticism of 'far-abroad' policies may have helped to toughen the government's stance, their advocacy of a more robust line towards immediate neighbours contributed, more than any other group, to injecting an increasingly assertive tone into the policy climate. In summer–autumn 1992 the Civic Union called for more energetic government pursuit of a confederative Slav-centred CIS and more vigorous defence of Russian minority rights. The Union programme asserted the need for Moscow to use all legal means, including sanctions, against states which discriminated against Russian minorities.[39] This stress on legal and political, rather than military, means was characteristic of the Pragmatic Nationalist perspective on policy in the 'near abroad'.[40] Advocacy of such tempered assertiveness seems to have had an impact: the centrist line presaged shifts in official policy. By late 1993 the government and all political parties had defence of Russian minorities at the top of their 'near-abroad', and indeed overall foreign policy, agendas. Characteristically it was Yabloko, the most foreign-policy-oriented centrist party, which offered the fullest and most cogent policy menu for the CIS in its electoral platform. It recommended a gradualist strategy of economic integration and firm legalized military means for stabilizing conflict areas. Singling out defence of the Russian population as the most important priority, Yabloko advocated agreements with the other states on minority rights and the elaboration of Russian laws on refugees.[41] Such relatively sensible and balanced recommendations on the 'near abroad' may have contributed to the strengthening of Pragmatic Nationalist elements in government policy.

### Parties, economic groups, and lobbies

Centrist domestic policies and Pragmatic Nationalist preferences on both 'near' and 'far abroad' gained policy weight after mid-1993 and particularly following the December elections.[42] The election results, notably the remarkably high Liberal Democratic Party

vote, heightened the Kremlin's awareness of the need to build consensus around more centrist policies at home and abroad.
The case for centrism was reinforced by the preferences of major
economic groups. The disappointing electoral performance of the
radical reformers, followed by internal conflicts, led some financial
backers to withdraw their support. Oleg Boiko, a key patron of
Russia's Choice, broke with the party in early 1995. Claiming to
speak for a number of major business groups, Boiko even called
for the postponement of the parliamentary elections, due in December 1995, in order to allow the political situation to stabilize.[43]
Aware of the political costs of postponing the elections, the Kremlin
sought in early 1995 to stabilize and increase its hold over the
fragile post-Chechnya environment by establishing two centre
parties closely linked to the executive. In April 1995 the Prime
Minister, Viktor Chernomyrdin, announced the establishment of a
new centre-right party, Our Home is Russia, which made 'pragmatism' its credo and, in catch-all fashion, highlighted the need
for 'stability and development, democracy and patriotism, confidence and order'.[44] (The formation of a complementary centre-left
party, headed by the speaker of the Duma, Ivan Rybkin, encoun-
tered organizational difficulties.) Clearly a party of the governing
establishment, Our Home is Russia was so widely associated
with Chernomyrdin's old bailiwick, the gas industry, that it became known colloquially as Nash Dom Gazprom (Our Home
is Gazprom).

The gas industry, and more generally the energy sector, was the
most prominent of the range of business groups which from 1993
became increasingly involved in the politics of domestic and foreign policy. The key economic role of the energy sector in Russian
exports—oil and gas account for the bulk of foreign exchange
earnings[45]—gave it an enormous stake in and considerable influence over external economic policy. The large oil corporations
were closely associated with government, and Gazprom had direct
access to Chernomyrdin and other officials who had come with
him from the gas industry. This combination of economic weight
and political access gave the energy sector first place among economic lobbies.

The traditional holder of this position in the Soviet period,
the defence industry, was severely weakened by large cuts in production as well as in domestic and foreign markets. In an effort to

counter such losses, sector leaders formed a League for the Support of the Defence Industry and worked with umbrella industrial lobbying organizations such as the Federation of Russian Commodity Producers, headed by Yury Skokov. Defence industry interests were represented in the Duma in the New Regional Policy faction. They enjoyed considerable influence among the regional administrators who dominated the Federation Council, the speaker of which, Vladimir Shumeiko, was himself a former defence industrialist.

The new entrepreneurs, especially those in the banking sector, primarily wielded financial rather than social and political assets. Unlike the energy or defence industry lobbies, they were unable to bring to bear the political weight of labour and regional élite support. The larger commercial banks, however, were closely associated with major industrial corporations (for instance, Imperial Bank and Gazprom) and some formed part of financial industrial groups, business conglomerates often aligned with particular political groups.

Given the extensive economic and political resources of the main economic groups, one might have expected them to have exercised a major influence on those aspects of external policy in which they had a direct interest. In some areas, the efforts of major sectoral lobbies appeared to have paid dividends, as in the case of defence industry advocacy of an active arms exports strategy. The shift in government policy from initially playing down the priority of exporting arms to promoting sales may, however, only partly have reflected lobbying by the depleted military-industrial complex. In other cases where tension arose between diplomatic and economic advantage, as over the sale of cryogenic rocket-engine technology to India or over developing Caspian Sea oil reserves, political priorities could play a decisive role (see Chapter 3).

Such cases caution against exaggerating the policy impact of economic groups and lobbies. Their considerable potential to influence external policy was conditioned by the diversity of their objectives as well as by the vagaries of lobbying in an institutionally fragmented and factionalized political environment. Both sets of factors meant that in strategic external policy terms economic groups punched below their potential weight.

Let us first consider the nature and cohesion of economic-group policy interests. There are very few general areas of foreign policy

on which major economic groups held strong and sl
ferences. One exception was economic relations withii
Fostering stability and a single market in the CIS are
a process of economic integration was a preference com
the key groups. The traditional-sector groups had powertul vested
interests in trying to ensure that relations across former republican
borders are compatible with the continuation of long-established
economic ties. Organizations such as the Russian Union of Industrialists and Entrepreneurs therefore co-operated with their counterparts in other former republics and lobbied for strong bilateral
and multilateral economic links.[46] Similar objectives were furthered
through developments on the ground, including moves by components of old Soviet industrial structures, located outside the
Russian Federation, to new Russian-based corporations, such as
Gazprom.[47]

While transnational links were clearly strongest in the traditional sectors, they also proved attractive to new corporate groups
in the financial sector. Russian bankers, for instance, were keen to
promote CIS ties which would allow them to expand their operations into Belarus or Ukraine. Russian banks form a key element
in the financial-industrial groups, which have many transnational
interests in the CIS area.[48] The fact that Moscow from 1993 made
the kind of moves towards CIS integration advocated by key economic corporate groups does not necessarily mean that their lobbying played a decisive role in shaping 'near-abroad' policy. It is
arguable that economic-group views and interests coincided with
those of government officials. However, it is far from coincidental
that many government leaders, notably Chernomyrdin, were informed by economic corporate priorities and placed these high on
their 'near-abroad' policy agenda.

Issues relating to the 'far abroad' shed more light on how divers-
ities of interest conditioned group influence on government preferences, which in many instances differed from corporate priorities.
On critical questions of external economic policy, notably degrees
of protection from international competition, group interests differed between sectors and sometimes even within them. These
interests depended largely on market position, as indeed they do
in capitalist economies.

The defence industries, and indeed many traditional producers,
shared a natural interest in a more interventionist economic policy

involving gradual marketization, generous subsidies, and protection from foreign competitors. Oil and gas producers, on the
other hand, opposed subsidies given to manufacturers in the form
of cheap energy and have a strong interest in free access to world
markets. Differences in market position within the energy sector,
as within others, made for internally diverse or even conflicting
preferences, sometimes favouring elements of both liberalization
and protectionism.[49] Commercial banks, for instance, were divided
over the issue of foreign access to the Russian market. In 1993,
most seemed to favour placing considerable restrictions on foreign
banks, at least for a few years. These protectionists argued that
they had neither the capital nor the expertise to compete effectively with their international rivals on a level playing-field. A
large minority of bankers, on the other hand, including some linked
to large industrial clients, were more confident and opposed tough
constraints on foreigners, especially as these might lead to recip-
rocal measures against Russian banks operating abroad.[50] Such
divisions weakened the case made by the Association of Russian
Bankers for restrictions and contributed to the failure in late 1992
to introduce protectionist legislation. Success a year later in getting a presidential decree, imposing some restrictions on foreign
banks for a limited period, probably had much to do with changed
political circumstances. But lack of solidarity among bankers might
help to explain the limited nature of the protection provided in the
decree and subsequent banking legislation.[51] More generally, diversity of interests and the pursuit of narrow objectives in the form
of specific tariffs or quotas meant that economic lobbies rarely
pressed for coherent policies. Indeed, the particularistic nature of
demands helped to encourage government in its piecemeal approach to policy making.

Particularism of interest reflected and compounded problems of
organizational fragmentation. Lobbying as a co-ordinated and institutionalized political activity remained poorly developed throughout the period under review. The smaller and weaker economic
interests, organized in sectoral associations, were typically ill-
equipped for effective lobbying activity. The largest and most
powerful corporate groups had little incentive to help raise levels
of organization, as they enjoyed privileged access to the executive.
Access to government ministries often followed neo-Soviet lines.
Lobbying the Kremlin in these years was even more personalized

than in the days of the Communist Party, which at least had provided a firm organizational hierarchy. The absence of such an overarching hierarchy brought both gains and losses for lobbyists. On the plus side, it made it easier for individuals to get favours, such as subsidies, licences, or exemptions from quotas, on a personal basis. Such deals between individuals and networks fostered and were greatly eased by rampant corruption, more monetized and conspicuous than in Soviet times. For economic groups wishing to affect government strategy over a longer period, this kind of policy making environment had definite drawbacks. Unclear jurisdiction and bureaucratic infighting produced inconsistent or even contradictory ministerial moves on issues where large corporate interests are at stake (see Chapter 3). Banking legislation and Caspian Sea oil are both cases in point. The highly personalized politics of the Kremlin made lobbyists dependent on the favour of presidential gatekeepers and thus vulnerable to the capricious nature of the Yeltsin court. Lobby causes could become hostages to political struggles, as indeed happened in the tussle over oil export quotas in late 1994.[52]

Political parties may increasingly provide channels through which economic lobbies can exercise more reliable longer-term influence over external policy. From 1992 onwards, various economic groups made efforts to promote their interests by forming political parties and movements. Konstantin Borovoi, a leading financier, established the Economic Freedom Party in May 1992 to further the priorities of new entrepreneurs, but it failed to make a significant impact.[53] More important were the centrist party vehicles established by traditional industrial-sector groups to promote their preferences for gradual reform at home and Pragmatic Nationalism abroad. The All-Russian Renewal Union, headed by Arkady Volsky, represented industrial interests in the Civic Union which exercised considerable influence until spring 1993. Volsky was also involved in the establishment in spring 1995 of the United Industrial Party.[54] Grigory Yavlinsky and the entrepreneur Konstantin Zatulin together formed Entrepreneurs for a New Russia in spring 1993, even though they later joined different reform-inclined centrist parties (Yavlinsky was a co-founder of Yabloko; Zatulin moved to the Party of Russian Unity and Accord), both of which exercised considerable policy influence in the Duma.

On occasion, party connections provided particular corporate groups with useful opportunities to exert leverage on specific external policies. There is a good deal of circumstantial evidence that pressure via Russia's Choice helped produce the presidential decree of November 1993 restricting the operation of foreign banks in Russia. Shortly before this decree appeared, key bankers reportedly persuaded Gaidar of the merits of the protectionist case by threatening to boycott his party.[55] The impressive performance of the Agrarian Party in defending the economically conservative interests of its traditionalist rural constituency, notably in the 1994 budgetary struggles, may encourage other economic lobbies to try to strengthen party links.

There is little or no effective regulation of party funding and scarce information about external sources of financial support. Traditional-sector groups have made substantial contributions to radical conservative organizations; we have already noted their involvement in centrist parties. Newer corporate interests have spread investments across a portfolio of radical reformist and centrist parties to maximize influence.[56] Such influence is likely to grow as parties require more funds for organization and publicity. More parties will find it easier to accommodate the policy requests which accompany donations, as their platforms become more pragmatic along the lines of Our Home is Russia. The expanding centrist band of the Russian party spectrum provides a favourable setting for the corporatization of policy.

As well as using their financial resources to buy better representation in parties and parliament, economic groups may well strengthen their position *vis-à-vis* the executive, particularly if the government accepts schemes for close co-operation such as that proposed by leading banks in spring 1995 to make available loans to help finance the budget deficit.[57] The combination of growing executive and party-political dependence on corporate funding looks set to increase the role and influence of economic groups and lobbies in external policy.

## Public opinion

It is a commonplace that mass views on international affairs are often ill-defined and play a very indirect role in shaping foreign policy, even in highly developed democracies.[58] In the Russian context, both the definition of opinion on international issues and its policy role are still in their infancy. The Russian public, exposed to full and varied information on international affairs only since the late perestroika years, have recently had to make their way through a mass of frequently confusing material. Nor are they accustomed to opinion polls except as officially sponsored investigations, largely organized to mould rather than reflect views. When making use of poll data, we have borne in mind the relative novelty of sophisticated opinion surveys in Russia, for respondents and pollsters alike.[59] Most of the survey data used in this chapter come from the regular surveys conducted by the All-Russian Centre for the Study of Public Opinion, the largest, most experienced, and arguably the most professional of the polling organizations in the country.[60] Even though these are among the most reliable data available on international issues, they are better treated as indicating patterns of orientation rather than reflecting precisely the views of the Russian population on foreign policy questions.

The extent to which such views are taken into account by Russian leaders is also affected by the novelty of public opinion in the life of the country. In the Soviet period, public opinion was typically something politicians shaped, rather than an independent phenomenon to which they responded. In a context of embryonic democratization, including multi-party elections, political élites are understandably more sensitive than their predecessors to voters' opinions.[61] New to the whole process of competitive elections which yield unpredictable results (like those of December 1993), political leaders, aware of the fragility of their position, might well be wary of shifts in mass views. This is not to claim in any sense that in these years the Yeltsin administration was deflected from decisions by public opposition. The outcry of protest against the Chechnya intervention had little apparent impact on government action. However, the leadership may reasonably have expected a generally favourable public response to intervention, given the poor reputation of the Chechens among the Russian population. Public opinion certainly figured in policy calculation and deliberation on some controversial international questions. In the course of arguments on the Kurile Islands issue in mid-1992, for instance, both sides made extensive use of public opinion.[62] Public sensitivity to the issue of Russian minorities in the former republics throughout the CIS was used by the opposition to highlight this as a top-priority item on Moscow's international agenda.

External policy issues typically do not figure very highly in public attention except at times of war. In a climate of high domestic political tension and economic collapse, one would expect international questions to be at the back rather than the forefront of people's minds. While external issues were not at the centre of public interest in Russia in the years under review, they occupied quite a prominent position, often on a par with all but the most pressing economic problems. Problems in the 'near abroad' had a sufficiently 'intimate' impact on the public to place them high on the popular agenda.[63] Armed conflict in the north Caucasus and, to a lesser extent, the Transdnestr region, figured in Russian minds in late 1992 almost as prominently as the rapid fall in production. Concern about the conflicts in the 'near abroad' was concentrated not simply among the politically marginal, the elderly and low-income groups in smaller cities who most regretted the passing of the USSR and supported the communist and nationalist opposition. Anxiety was spread across key groups from the politicians' point of view: the younger generation and the well-educated specialists who supported Yeltsin and his government.[64]

By late 1993 the external policy attention of some of these groups had shifted from conflict in the 'near abroad' to more abstract and distant issues, relating to the international standing of the new Russia. With strife in the south rumbling but not spilling over into general conflict, those worried about this aspect of external developments declined by two-thirds and the issue fell from third to eleventh place in the rank order of perceived problems.[65] Concern about the closely related issue of weakening ties within the CIS also diminished. Declining unease about conflicts and tensions in the 'near abroad' meant that these questions were overtaken as issues of public concern by the loss of Russia's prestige as a Great Power. Nearly one in three singled this out as the most worrying development and double that number wanted to see Russia's status restored, albeit by economic rather than military means. The slight growth in such concern over the course of 1994 year might be seen as the result of those nostalgic for the USSR shifting their grievances to a larger international context. For the most part, those distressed by the international decline of Russia were from the older generation, who tended to support a statist economy and opposition parties. But they also included the higher-educated and substantial numbers of supporters of reformist groups. Russia's international standing seems to be an issue of wide and growing appeal across the social and political spectrum.

It is difficult, of course, to generalize about popular interest in international affairs on the basis of poll questions focusing on a limited number of issues over a broad spectrum of developments. There is no doubt that Russia follows the universal rule that people are less interested in and familiar with developments abroad than with domestic issues. Surveys repeatedly showed that many simply did not have any opinion on international questions, particularly if these related to specific 'far-abroad' issues.[66]

All the same, on some aspects of 'near-abroad' problems there seems to have been less public uncertainty than on some central issues of economic and political reform. In an early 1994 poll, for instance, one in four respondents failed to give a definite answer to questions about their position on political and economic reforms, while only one in seventeen fell into this category when addressing issues about relations with the former republics.[67] This may be because domestic-reform issues simply seemed too complex, while questions on relations with the former republics appeared to be more straightforward.

On issues relating to the 'near abroad' and matters of territorial integrity, Russian public opinion seemed not just well defined but remarkably steady. The volatility of events surrounding the CIS in 1992–3, for instance, was not mirrored in public perceptions of current and future developments in the Commonwealth, which varied only slightly. On CIS matters, then, the public seemed to have had firm and fairly constant underlying beliefs and views.

### Images of security

Apart from suggesting a remarkable degree of constancy on foreign issues close to home, survey results from 1992–4 give some indication of how popular perceptions of Russia's international position and relations corresponded to Liberal Westernizer, Pragmatic Nationalist, and Fundamentalist Nationalist views. Very few Russians appeared to see the security climate in terms of either neo-Cold War confrontation or the kind of new encirclement of a weak Russia conjured up by Fundamentalist Nationalists. In the early months of Russia's independence a large number (over a third in one poll of Muscovites) believed that the country had no enemies. And though the proportion of such 'romantic' optimists declined somewhat in the course of the next two years, only a few members of the public could name specific enemies. Élite opinion, according to one mid-1993 survey, ran along broadly similar lines.[68] Even the US, the traditional *bête noire* of the extreme nationalists, carried little conviction as an enemy among the general public.[69] All but a small minority of Russians seemed untroubled by any traditional Western military threat. However, a larger number, perhaps a fifth, thought Russia friendless and were apprehensive about a diffuse threat which might involve aggression at some future date.[70]

If Russians perceived a threat, they located it closer to home, within the former Soviet Union. Very few took an alarmist view of the new states and fewer still shared extreme nationalist views of the Muslims and the Caucasians as the new enemy; the Estonians and Latvians attracted far more hostility, as indeed they did from the élites. The Ukrainians, regardless of the highly antagonistic picture painted by some Russian nationalists, were seen over-whelmingly as partners and friends.[71] What alarmed many Russians and qualified as a major threat to security were conflicts around their new borders. Armed clashes in the south were seen by some-thing between a fifth and a third of Russians (the proportion decreased over time) as intensifying and threatening to spill over into the Russian Federation. Concerns about the fragility of the Federation underlay much of the apprehension about conflicts around its borders. Even if such anxiety declined markedly after 1992, the threat from instability within the former Soviet area, particularly the Caucasus, loomed far larger than any external threat. In this sense, the public shared the fears of the Pragmatic rather than those of the Fundamentalist Nationalists.

## The 'far abroad'

Views of relations with the West reveal a finer differentiation in popular opinion on foreign policy issues. Overall attitudes displayed an uneasy combination of a wish to be well-disposed and uncer-tainty about the consequences of a closer relationship. The early months, in particular, saw public reaction against old stereotypes of hostility and positive response to new official ones of Western goodwill. Liberal Westernizer sentiments seemed to be shared by at least two-fifths of the public, especially younger better-educated men, who took a positive view of Western culture and intentions towards Russia (a third were critical and the remaining quarter were unsure).[72] Reflecting in spring 1994 on over two years of post-Soviet relations with the West, nearly one in two thought that *rapprochement* had done Russia more good than harm. The very young and those with higher education were particularly positive. Only a fifth of respondents, especially the older on lower incomes, thought that Russia had lost out from closer ties.[73]

Where greater uncertainty entered the picture was on the diplomatic and economic implications for Russia of building closer relations. Toeing the international community line in crises did not seem to arouse as much concern among the public as it did in élite political debate. In general terms a large majority of the Russian public wanted to see the restoration of Great-Power status.[74] Even larger numbers consistently opposed territorial concessions to the Japanese.[75] Yet few seemed to feel strongly about co-operation with the West. While nationalist and centrist critics inveighed against kowtowing to the West over the Middle East or Yugoslavia, the average Russian seemed indifferent. On issues of supporting UN sanctions against Serbia, around a quarter of the public took Liberal Westernizer positions; a fifth or so, mainly older respondents, adopted a Fundamentalist Nationalist stand. Iraq evoked less sympathy, although most took the official and centrist line in being critical of the Western use of force.[76]

Doubts about the West also emerged strongly in assessments of the dangers of domestic and external reform bringing economic dependency. A majority of Russians in early 1994 thought that economic reforms would make the country dependent on the West and nearly all were alarmed at the prospect. The extent of popular anxiety over the question of dependency and exploitation broadly paralleled that among the élites.[77] Economic dependency figured increasingly in public concern across the board, so much so that by late 1994 a majority favoured rejecting aid if that helped secure economic independence.[78]

Responses to less loaded questions suggest that on practical matters of aid, trade, and investment most Russians took a pragmatic approach. Even when counterposed to economic independence, foreign investment was rejected by no more than one in three respondents.[79] The majority approved of financial and technical assistance. Only a minority (around a third in one 1993 poll as compared with perhaps a quarter of the political élite) considered all forms of aid unnecessary and undesirable.[80] Where trade was concerned, Western states emerged in a more favourable light than members of the CIS. The absolute level of trust, however, was fairly low and left both the US and Japan with a negative balance; only Western Europe came out slightly on the positive side.[81] While investment was generally welcomed, foreign ownership was understandably a more difficult issue and one which evoked a generally negative attitude. Where large factories were concerned, opposition was strong, with four out of five ill-disposed and only a handful taking a positive view.[82] In this particular instance, the Russian public took a Fundamentalist Nationalist stance. The strength of popular feeling varied markedly, though, with the kind of property at stake. On foreign ownership of small enterprises and retail outlets, opinion was split fairly evenly (42 per cent for and 50 per cent against).[83] On the question of foreign ownership in general, then, the position adopted by the Russian public was closer to the Pragmatic than to the Fundamentalist Nationalist approach.

For the most part, Russians took a measured, Pragmatic Nationalist view of the West, generally favourable on the political front and wary on the economic. The public seemed relatively unconcerned about Russia taking too passive a diplomatic line on the world stage, less so than members of the élite arguing the Pragmatic Nationalist case. Members of the public, not surprisingly, also tended to be less informed and more generous than the critical élite in assessing the government's foreign policy performance. A quarter seemed to think quite highly of it, a third were critical, while a plurality (two-fifths or so) gave it middling marks.[84] Such a mixed stance located public opinion here as on other issues in the Pragmatic Nationalist band of the spectrum.

## The CIS

Tracing the divisions of opinion on the 'near abroad' in this period is more difficult simply because they were far less starkly defined than views on the wider world. The tendency towards consensus was greater, differentiation along social and political lines less pronounced. Public consensus paralleled, and to some extent reflected, broader agreement among the élites on 'near-' than on 'far-abroad' questions. The emotional significance and familiarity of CIS issues made it less easy to see them in black-and-white terms. Deeply-held general beliefs here meant that there were remarkably few who had nothing to say and fewer still who delivered simple evaluations or judgements. The public often took the cautious middle ground on CIS questions. Still, it is possible roughly to map popular views according to our Liberal Westernizer, Pragmatic Nationalist, and Fundamentalist Nationalist categories.

Liberalism in this context essentially amounted to support for regarding the former republics as sovereign states and treating them according to accepted international norms. About a fifth of the public—men and those with high incomes in particular— favoured a 'live and let live' attitude towards the 'near abroad' rather than any closer co-operation.[85] Twice that number took a 'liberal' view when asked to choose between CIS members being a zone of Russian special interest or simply existing as independent states.[86] Identifying such views as falling within the Liberal Westernizer grouping is of course open to question, as a small minority of proponents of 'live and let live' perhaps interpreted this option in terms of ridding Russia of responsibility for the new states. The sentiments behind such views may well have been illiberal, as they were held by some people who on other questions took the strong Russian nationalist line that the country was better off without its former dependencies.

Fundamentalist Nationalist popular views tended to cluster more tightly than opinions in the liberal and pragmatic bands of the spectrum. They were particularly pronounced among older respondents who shared regret at the passing of the USSR and a desire to re-establish the Union in some form. In some contexts such sentiments translated into support for a new Great Russian state.[87] Some of the same people figured prominently among the fifth or so who thought early on that the CIS was destined to collapse, though their prognostications became somewhat less confident through the course of 1993 (the number predicting collapse declined from 20 to 25 per cent in 1992 to 11 to 18 per cent in 1993).[88]

The most widely supported view of CIS prospects, and one which grew in popularity through 1993, was that of a long and difficult haul towards agreement. Most of the third or more who saw developments running along these lines fell into the Pragmatic Nationalist grouping. In large part they also assessed CIS policy performance as middling to low, an appraisal similar to that found among political élites.[89] Along with most Russians, they did not want a restoration of the USSR, but favoured a new, looser union. Rather than this involving all the former republics, priority was to be given to the other Slav states, Ukraine and Belarus, with Kazkakhstan a poor third.[90]

The viability of any such union was seen mainly in economic terms. Popular support for closer economic relations was qualified by considerable mistrust of the new states as trading partners. Twice as many respondents, in a late 1993 survey, thought the new states dishonest as considered them trustworthy. Familiarity appeared to make Russians far more suspicious of their neigbours than their potential Western trading partners.[91] Some of these misgivings were perhaps reflected in wariness of close economic ties with Belarus, probably because of the likely economic costs for Russia. Despite the general popularity of strengthening the economic dimension of the CIS, only one in ten respondents in a June 1994 poll favoured the idea of economic unification unequivocally; a fifth were opposed to the scheme and a further third approved as long as it brought Russia no disadvantage.[92]

This mixture of wariness and qualified support for closer involvement with the other CIS states came through in attitudes to Russia's overall role in the region. On the central issue of whether the CIS should be a 'zone of special interest', opinion seemed evenly divided (in a May 1994 survey two-fifths took a Monroe Doctrine line while slightly fewer supported relations being ones between independent states).[93]

Support for a Russian Monroe Doctrine did not of course mean endorsement of the use of military force. Responses to questions on intervention in conflicts revealed a strong majority preference for diplomatic and political rather than military means. Two out of three Russians, in one mid-1993 survey, opposed the use of military force to resolve conflicts within the former Soviet area.[94] There did not appear to be significant divisions between socio-economic groups on this issue, the partial exception being enterprise managers and higher-educated respondents, who were somewhat more prone to condone forceful action, especially where

Russian minority rights were at stake. Tolerance of intervention appeared to be more widespread among political élites.[95] On this question the public seemed to be considerably more liberal. Even the older, more conservative groups, who were nostalgic for the old Union and supported the strong defence of borders and Russian minorities, did not automatically endorse intervention.[96]

The large majority of Russians opposing the use of force gave a variety of reasons for their position, ranging from liberal objections against coercive intervention to more Pragmatic Nationalist anxieties about embroiling Russian troops in Afghan-type situations. This may help to explain why, when questioned in July 1993 about Russian involvement in Tadjikistan, a plurality of respondents (two-fifths) preferred troop withdrawal, or at least mediation, rather than military reinforcement.[97] In general, half wanted troops withdrawn and a further quarter supported their continued presence only so far as this was necessary to defend local Russian minorities.[98] The strength of public dislike of forceful means, especially when used in a clumsy and brutal fashion, was brought home in late 1994 and early 1995 by the overwhelmingly critical popular response to 'inner-abroad' intervention in Chechnya. On intervention, as on so many issues bearing on Russian policy towards its neighbours, popular opinion gravitated to the central, Pragmatic Nationalist part of the spectrum.

## Links with domestic issues

Comparative studies of beliefs and attitudes would lead us to expect little correlation between views on domestic and international questions.[99] One 1995 analysis of Russian values and attitudes found relatively weak correlations between domestic and foreign dimensions.[100] On many external issues, the surveys examined suggest weak relationships between opinions held on internal and international questions. There seemed to be little association, for instance, between views on the use of force in Moscow in October 1993 and concern about conflicts in the CIS. There appeared to be no significant connection between anxiety about the loss of Great-Power prestige and positions on economic reform.

Areas in which attitudes towards economic developments did seem to be associated with external matters include economic dependence on the West[101] and assessments of the trustworthiness

TABLE 4.1. *Attitudes to economic reform and* rapprochement *with the West, April 1994 (rounded percentages)*

| Respondents' preference | Rapprochement *with the West has done Russia* | |
|---|---|---|
| | more good | more harm |
| accelerated economic reform | 66 | 12 |
| restoration of state price control | 41 | 26 |

*Source*: Data from VTsIOM (Vserossiiskiy Tsentr Izucheniya Obschestvennogo Mneniya) 94-M-4 (*n* = 2,935).

TABLE 4.2. *Attitudes to domestic reform and to relations within the former Soviet Union, February 1994 (rounded percentages)*

| Preferences on domestic reform | Preferences on relations | | |
|---|---|---|---|
| | Live and let live[a] | Co-operation[b] | Great Russian state/USSR[c,d] |
| priority to economic reform over democracy | 21 | 63 | 13 |
| priority to democracy over economic reform | 19 | 61 | 16 |
| relinquishing of reform if this helps restore Great Russian state in area of old USSR | 16 | 38 | 39 |
| hard to say | 19 | 53 | 20 |

[a] They wanted freedom and got it; let them live now as they can and we are well off without them.

[b] We should closely co-operate and integrate with them but only if this is economically advantageous.

[c] We were one country before and should do everything possible to re-establish a great state.

[d] Do everything to restore the territorial integrity of the Soviet Union by all means, including force in extreme cases.

*Source*: Data from VTsIOM ekspres 94-2 (*n* = 1,602).

of Western states as trading partners. Where attitudes towards the costs and benefits of *rapprochement* with the West are concerned, the relationship with positions on economic change is significant. Attitudes towards the economic system seemed to have more of an impact on views of relations with the West than did opinions on other domestic as well as international issues. Of the latter, stands on 'near-abroad' issues, particularly the restoration of the USSR, apparently carried greatest weight. Where domestic economic questions were concerned, the pattern was a predictable one: in one spring 1994 survey almost twice as many proponents as critics of faster economic reform evaluated *rapprochement* with the West in positive terms (see Table 4.1).

A similar pattern emerges if we turn from the 'far' to the 'near abroad' and look at how supporters and opponents of economic reform aligned in early 1994 on relations within the former Soviet Union. The overwhelming majority of those who favoured reforms opted for close co-operation or for relations between wholly independent states. Very few preferred the establishment of a strong Russian state, let alone the restoration of the USSR, choices far more popular among those opposed to domestic reform (see Table 4.2).

Opponents of domestic reform (more precisely, those who subordinated reform to the restoration of a Great Russia) were markedly more divided over their preferences for relations with the 'near abroad'. The same pattern of incongruence occurred, if in more moderate form, in the stances of supporters and opponents of accelerated economic reform on the question of *rapprochement* with the West. Those hostile to domestic reform took less congruent positions on key foreign policy issues than was the case among those who supported democracy and marketization. The February 1994 survey data already cited suggest that those who held more or less defined positions on domestic reforms and on CIS relations can be grouped roughly into the following categories. Those who expressed consistently 'liberal' views in both areas formed the largest group, somewhat over a third of all respondents. Their counterparts at the other end of the political spectrum, the consistent conservatives, who supported centralization in the CIS and anti-reform policies in Russia, amounted to just over a tenth. Something like one in five of those polled held inconsistent views in these policy areas, inclining more often to liberalism in the 'near abroad' than at home. The size of this group holding mixed or incongruent positions on domestic and external affairs was relatively small, considering the complex and volatile conditions with which the Russian public were confronted in this period. A majority of Russians apparently had fairly consistent opinons across the domestic–'near abroad' divide. And most of them gravitated towards Pragmatic Nationalist views, that is towards the centre of the policy spectrum rather than towards either the Liberal Westernizer or Fundamentalist Nationalist poles. How this configuration of popular opinion related to support for political parties is a question to which we now turn.

### Political party supporters

One would not expect opinions on international questions to have a major effect on the way in which Russians voted. Given the novelty of contested elections and the plethora of parties with confusing programmes, it is hardly surprising that in December 1993 many voters made choices inconsistent with their previous political preferences.[102] (The situation on the eve of the December 1995 elections appeared to be very similar.) Even in societies where the public has long been accustomed to competitive elections, only a third or so seem capable of making choices on the basis of foreign policy issues.[103] Like voters elsewhere, the Russian electorate are likely to have preferences about general policy directions and derive these from 'core values'.[104] Opinions on domestic economic and political issues related most strongly to party choice. Views on external matters seemed to be relatively poor predictors of party choice.[105] Even so, some of the survey data reveal interesting patterns of association between preferences on international issues and party alignment. These data give some indication of the foreign policy stances of party constituencies shortly after the December 1993 elections. As these constituencies were volatile in the period under review, any observations are very approximate and indicative of the situation in early 1994 rather than throughout the period.

The general picture that emerges from the data is one of a considerable variety of foreign affairs preferences within each of the party camps. This is particularly evident, as one would expect, on 'near-abroad' issues, where consensus across political divisions was relatively high. Supporters of the radical reformist Russia's Choice and the reformist-inclined, centrist Yabloko both displayed

a mix of Liberal Westernizer and Pragmatic Nationalist preferences on relations within the CIS (see Table 4.3). Communist voters
predictably favoured Fundamentalist Nationalist views, though
nearly two-fifths took more moderate positions. It was among supporters of the Agrarians and the Liberal Democrats (Zhirinovsky's
party), the other two members of the opposition camp, that opinions markedly failed to match party platforms. This may have
reflected the failure of the Agrarians to have any specific policies
in this area. In the case of the Liberal Democrats, the data confirm
the heterogeneity of its support. This may not have been as great
as these data suggest, since the quarter who favoured letting the new
states go their own way may have been following the Zhirinovsky
line that those former republics which did not want to return to
the fold on his terms should be simply left outside. Nearly half
of Liberal Democrat voters, however, did not seem to share their
leaders' hostility to the CIS, as they opted for close co-operation.
As a result of this incoherence there was disarray on the opposition
front, contrasting with solidarity on the side of the radical reformist and reformist centre parties. On this as on other 'near-abroad'
questions there was considerable overlap in opinion between supporters of all parties except the communists. And on some issues
relating to the CIS, such as intervention in conflicts, even the communists came broadly into line with the others.

Where issues relating to the 'far abroad' were concerned, the
groupings of reformers and opposition supporters were somewhat
more cohesive. This perhaps reflected the more clearly differentiated
stands parties took on these matters. On the general issue of the
costs and benefits of *rapprochement* with the West, for instance,
Agrarian and Communist Party supporters held almost identical
views. Liberal Democrat voters were somewhat closer to them than
to the opinions held by supporters of Russia's Choice and Yabloko
(see Table 4.4). Still, in view of Zhirinovsky's condemnation of
Western exploitation of Russia, his voters assessed *rapprochement*
in remarkably positive terms, by a ratio of two to one.

On more specific questions, such as whether economic reforms
would lead to economic dependence on the West, the overall range
of party supporters' opinion matched radical party-policy differences
somewhat better.[106] At the poles, supporters of Russia's Choice and
the Communists were further apart while the Agrarians and the
Liberal Democrats came somewhat closer together. The spectrum

TABLE 4.3. *Attitudes of party support and leadership preference groups to relations within the former Soviet Union, February 1994 (rounded percentages)*

| | Preferences on relations | | |
|---|---|---|---|
| Party voted for | Live and let live | Co-operation | Great Russian state/USSR |
| Russia's Choice | 21 | 61 | 14 |
| Yabloko | 23 | 59 | 14 |
| Liberal Democrats | 26 | 46 | 26 |
| Agrarian Party | 18 | 61 | 13 |
| Communist Party | 11 | 29 | 56 |
| Leadership preference | | | |
| Yeltsin | 18 | 64 | 16 |
| Gaidar | 22 | 69 | 8 |
| Zhirinovsky | 28 | 39 | 31 |
| Rutskoi | 4 | 53 | 34 |

*Source*: Data from VTsIOM ekspress 2-94 (1,602 urban respondents).

TABLE 4.4. *Attitudes of party support groups to* rapprochement *with the West, April 1994 (rounded percentages)*

| | *Rapprochement* with the West has done Russia | |
|---|---|---|
| Party voted for | more good | more harm |
| Russia's Choice | 64 | 8 |
| Yabloko | 57 | 16 |
| LDPR | 45 | 23 |
| Agrarian Party | 28 | 37 |
| Communist Party | 26 | 42 |

*Source*: Data from VTsIOM 94-M-4 (2,935 respondents, urban and rural).

of party supporters' opinions was wider, perhaps because the questions combined divisive domestic (economic reform) and international (dependence on the West) issues.

If we turn our attention from the alignment of political party voters to that of leadership support groups, the patterns are not very different (see Table 4.3). On some 'far-abroad' issues the 'Yeltsin effect' was perceptible. The divisions between his supporters and detractors on the question of Partnership for Peace, for instance, were sharper than those based on political party affiliations. On other issues, however, the 'Yeltsin effect' moderated opinion; support for him was identified with cautious, Pragmatic Nationalist policy preferences. This was the predominant pattern on 'near-abroad' issues, where the 'Yeltsin effect' was to narrow the range of policy differences. On the issue of intervention, for instance, there was a stronger tendency to consensus if one looks at the opinions of pro- and anti-Yeltsinites.[107] Such a configuration of views suggests that in order to maximize public support Yeltsin might have been well advised to take a cautious line on questions such as intervention and the wider issue of trying to follow a Monroe Doctrine strategy within the CIS. On this question, his strongest supporters favoured treating the former republics as fully sovereign states while his strongest critics were more inclined toward establishing a zone of special interests.[108]

On many 'near-abroad' issues, as on the prospect of economic union with Belarus, the shifts in Yeltsin's policies distanced him from supporters of democratic reform and brought him closer to the preferences of the opposition. It may be that on 'far-abroad' issues, where the split between the President's supporters and detractors was more derivative of domestic political alignment, and more marked, he had less to lose by manœuvring. On 'near-abroad' questions, which were more substantively important to the electorate and on which there was often greater consensus, there was less scope for politically low-cost change, as the Chechen crisis demonstrated.

## Parliament

Parliament contributed more directly and prominently to the policy climate than did either political parties or public opinion. Parliamentary elections brought home public views on foreign policy, as on other matters, most forcefully to decision makers. It was in the cauldron of parliamentary politics that parties defined their external policy positions. Parliamentary scrutiny and debate provided parties and lobbies with the opportunity to make an impact on foreign policy.

Establishing a foreign policy role for parliament had formed an integral part of the whole attempt to democratize the political process since the perestroika period. During the Gorbachev years, the USSR Supreme Soviet took some initial steps towards promoting scrutiny and accountability. Deputies began to vet key appointees and voice criticism of some of the most vulnerable aspects of the leadership's external policy. Debates on the INF treaty, the German settlement, and Eastern Europe saw bitter attacks on Gorbachev and Shevardnadze. Though vociferous, foreign policy critics were few in number and relatively weak in political support.

The Russian Supreme Soviet, encouraged by Yeltsin's public commitment to constitutional power-sharing with a legislature which had helped him to achieve power, aspired to go beyond its predecessor and become a fully-fledged parliament along Western, and preferably US Congressional, lines. Parliamentary practice, seeking to fulfil such aspirations, has been heavily marked by the peculiarities of 'democratization' in Russia and the other post-Soviet states. Their parliaments have proved relatively weak bodies, prone selectively to confront rather than systematically check executive power. When measured against their other CIS counterparts, the Russian parliaments appear to have played quite an effective role in scrutinizing and debating foreign policy. Only the Supreme Council in Kiev has managed effectively to air some important security issues and challenge the President on key aspects of his policy towards Russia. The Russian parliaments, over the period under review, arguably kept a more consistent and systematic watch over the executive's conduct abroad than their Ukrainian counterparts. Even so, the work of the Supreme Soviet and its successor, the Federal Assembly (State Duma and Council of the Federation) were hampered by constitutional weakness, scarcity of expertise, and confrontational relations with the executive.

Formally, the Soviet constitution gave the Supreme Soviet quite extensive powers in the area of foreign policy. It was supposed to help shape the general direction of the country's external policy. The Supreme Soviet gained the right to approve ambassadorial appointments and in early 1993 the appointment of Foreign and Defence ministers. The dispatch of armed forces abroad had to have parliamentary sanction. Most importantly, all international treaties required parliamentary ratification.

The Duma, the lower chamber of the Federal Assembly, is

considerably weaker constitutionally than the Supreme Soviet. With its ability to impeach the President or counter his vetos handicapped by two-thirds majority requirements, the Duma's key leverage lies in control over the budget. In the international sphere, it has the right to scrutinize foreign policy and ratify treaties in conjunction with the higher chamber, the Federation Council. The Council, a generally less critical body including many appointed regional executives, exercises the sole parliamentary say on the sending of armed forces abroad.[109]

The effectiveness of these formal rights has been qualified by the uncertainties surrounding all constitutional arrangements. Exact procedures, in the foreign policy area as in others, remained undefined throughout the Supreme Soviet period and far from fixed well into the life of the Federal Assembly. Fixing procedures and making them work was made more difficult by the general lack of parliamentary experience and expertise. Proceedings were often confused, particularly in the early Supreme Soviet period, and those relating to foreign policy proved no exception. Debates were frequently rushed and resolutions hurriedly put together. Legislative overload resulted in Soviet-style 'production pushes' towards the end of parliamentary sessions.[110] The enormous pressure on parliamentary time, no less intense for the Duma than for its predecessor, meant that policy issues usually received less than thorough examination. In its first session the Duma devoted an average of two days to debating and passing each bill.[111] Expertise was at a premium, especially where 'far-abroad' affairs were concerned. The few deputies with some experience and knowledge of international issues tended to dominate debate in the specialist committees and on the floor of both chambers. The standard of plenary debates was rather low, with discussion of CIS issues marred by emotion and that of matters further afield compounded by lack of information.

The emotive tenor of debate, and the whole thrust of parliamentary involvement in foreign policy as in other areas, was conditioned by a tense relationship with the executive. Supreme Soviet aspirations to Western-style parliamentary scrutiny proved ever more difficult to realize as the political partnership with the executive of 1991 and early 1992 rapidly turned into a relationship of confrontation. All parliamentary efforts to bring the government to account were seen, and often meant, as acts of outright opposition. On the international as on other fronts, the Supreme Soviet behaved in hostile fashion and tried to damage particular politicians rather than scrutinize the policies of a government the parliamentary chairman, Khasbulatov, described as a 'collective Rasputin'. Political power-struggle increasingly crowded out policy deliberation. Political relations were seen by both sides in excessively zero-sum terms for the operation of an effective and balanced system of accountability. The Foreign Minister, Kozyrev, had scant respect for parliamentary discussion of international affairs, much of which he condemned as publicity-seeking.[112] Yeltsin and his aides tended to dismiss all parliamentary criticism as hostile, to question its legitimacy, and to view the Congress of People's Deputies as 'enemy territory'.[113]

The degree of tension between the two 'territories' was often exacerbated by personal factors. The fast-shifting alignments and cross-overs between parliament and Presidency created an atmosphere of personal animosity between the two institutions. Key figures in the Supreme Soviet were incorporated into the presidential apparatus while others, notably Khasbulatov, who began as Yeltsin's allies in parliament, became bitter enemies. Such personal rivalries flowed in part from structural changes in Russian politics. In the last phase of the USSR, the Russian Supreme Soviet and Yeltsin both allied against Gorbachev, and former allies typically make the worst enemies. Institutionally, the Supreme Soviet continued to behave as if it were still part of the Presidency, trying somehow to reconcile the role of legislature monitoring the executive with that of a shadow government seeking to run its own foreign policy. Alongside such hostility there were elements of tacit co-operation between individual parliamentary leaders and the executive. Quite often Parliament served as a pool for executive recruitment, with its leaders, such as Filatov the deputy chairman, co-opted into presidential service.

A similar pattern recurred, if at a lower level of intensity, in relations between the executive and the Federal Assembly, particularly its lower chamber, the Duma. Constitutionally weaker than its predecessor, the Duma continued often to behave like a political opponent. Less politically militant than the Supreme Soviet, the Duma struck a less strident tone in criticizing government domestic policy, at least until the confrontation over Chechnya in late 1994. However, even before that crisis, Duma stands on external policy, and on the Foreign Ministry's performance, represented less of a break with Supreme Soviet tradition than many had anticipated.[114] The weakness and confusion of the executive in the foreign policy field gave parliament ample scope for criticism.

It is difficult to make a case that foreign policy was any more or less vulnerable or liable to parliamentary criticism than other areas of executive activity. Russian parliamentarians, in common with their Western colleagues, tended to see foreign policy as 'a slightly specialized branch of domestic policy'.[115] They typically made use of external issues for domestic political ends. Without arguing that foreign policy was particularly salient in parliamentary politics, the high visibility of some international issues, such as the Black Sea Fleet, the Kuriles, or the Yugoslav crisis, induced some Supreme Soviet deputies such as Rumyantsev, who were engaged mainly in domestic constitutional arenas, to make active forays into the foreign policy field. Even the politically more tempered Duma saw more extensive discussion of foreign affairs in 1994 than its limited powers might appear to have warranted.

*Patterns of activity*

The intensity and tenor of parliamentary activity on the external policy front seems to have varied more in line with overall political relations than with specific shifts in Russian foreign policy. To be sure, it is difficult to assess the relative importance of these two relationships, as the contours of domestic political change and foreign policy evolution largely coincided. Deputies' opinions certainly differed from those of the executive on 'near-' and especially 'far-abroad' issues. Yet the political climate seems to have played a larger part in shaping the conduct of Supreme Soviet deputies than the actual gap separating their foreign policy views from those of the government. This appears to be the case if we look at the overall changes in parliamentary–executive relations on international issues.

In the first half of 1992 the differences in foreign policy positions were perhaps greater than at any other time. Liberal Westernism prevailed within the executive while parliamentary critics, centrists as well as radical conservatives, called for a clearer formulation of national interests and for a *realpolitik* strategy that took these into account. Criticism, however, was rather fragmented and restrained as deputies, usually unfamiliar with the issues and lacking any coherent strategy, made disparate and largely negative points.

They charged the government with neglecting the 'near abroad' and specifically with not doing enough for Russians in Transdnestria. On policy further afield, they took the executive to task for being soft, particularly on the issue of territorial concessions to Japan. Rumours about plans to 'give away' the Kuriles gave the radical conservatives an opportunity to sway parliamentarians of more moderate political persuasion towards a critical view of the presidential and, especially, the Foreign Ministry stance. Yeltsin was berated for first assuring the Supreme Soviet that no concessions would be made and then drawing up proposals which undermined such commitments.[116] At closed Supreme Soviet hearings in July 1992, radical conservatives warned against the dangers of any territorial concessions and attacked certain Foreign Ministry officials for conspiring to strike a deal unfavourable to Russia.[117] Centrist spokesmen, notably Ambartsumov, tried to couch criticism in more moderate and less *ad hominem* terms, though they also pressed for the postponement of Yeltsin's visit and any decisions on the matter.

The policy gap narrowed markedly from late 1992 to late 1993, yet controversy over the government's international performance continued, driven mainly by the growing antagonism between parliament and executive. Even members of the centrist factions, who advocated Pragmatic Nationalist views that approximated official policies as these evolved through 1993, were drawn into parliamentary solidarity with the Fundamentalist Nationalists. Summer 1993 saw particularly heated parliamentary criticism on all fronts, and efforts were made to obstruct government policy on START-2 and complicate relations with Ukraine by provocative declarations on the Black Sea Fleet and the Crimea.[118] These reflected and helped further to intensify the tensions which culminated in the armed conflict of autumn 1993.

In the lead-up to the December 1993 elections there were widespread hopes that the new Federal Assembly would operate in a less confrontational and more professional manner. Developments in 1994 only very partially fulfilled such hopes. The constitutionally more powerful upper chamber, the Federation Council, half of whose members were appointed regional administrators, proved

politically more pliant and generally supportive on foreign policy issues. The Duma was divided roughly evenly on domestic
issues. On international questions, Fundamentalist Nationalist views
were actively expressed by a smaller number of deputies than in
the Supreme Soviet, and to less effect as far as Duma resolutions
were concerned. Criticism of the Foreign Ministry continued to be
voiced and differences aired over key 'near-abroad' issues, such
as the Baltics, Ukraine and Georgia, old questions on Yugoslavia,
and new ones on NATO. Even so, the differences were more often
ones of style, timing, and tactics rather than of fundamental strategy.
The Duma took a less determinedly hostile stance than its predecessor and proved more amenable to persuasion and negotiation.[119]
Negotiation was easier than with the Supreme Soviet not just because the general relationship was less confrontational and half
the factions had some representation in government; it was also
because Duma factions were stronger and policy bargaining between
them and with the executive more developed.[120]

Compromises and open as well as tacit co-operation, brokered
by skilled politicians such as the Duma chairman, Rybkin, became
more common. In its first session (February–July 1994) the Duma
held 60 hearings and passed the state budget and 46 pieces of legislation.[121] This record was of course far from satisfactory, and procedures remained far from systematic at the end of the Duma's first
year, but they represented a marked improvement on the Supreme
Soviet period.[122]

## Scrutiny of policy

Both parliaments were supposed to monitor government conduct
of international affairs, suggest revisions to legislation, and ratify
treaty agreements. As we have noted, while the Supreme Soviet
was armed with more constitutional powers in these areas, the
Duma took a more professional approach to exercising scrutiny.

Much of the work on external policy was carried out in the
specialized committees whose brief had an international dimension. In the Supreme Soviet these were the Committee on Inter-
Republican Relations and Regional Policy; the Committee on
Defence and Security Questions; and the Committee on International Affairs and Foreign Economic Relations. The Federation
Council had committees on International Affairs, CIS Affairs, and

Security and Defence. The corresponding Duma committees included International Affairs; Defence and Security Questions; and CIS Affairs and Ties with Compatriots.[123] A Geopolitics Committee was created to give the vociferous Liberal Democrats a foreign affairs committee of their own, in the hope that this would reduce their interference in the other committees.

The Supreme Soviet committees with which we are mainly concerned, those on Defence and on International Affairs, were predominantly Pragmatic Nationalist in outlook, their members being non-aligned or identifying with the centre parties. The Defence Committee chairman, Sergei Stepashin, was a centrist close to the government. For the first nine months he combined chairing the Committee with his job as Deputy Minister of Security; in 1994 he became head of Russian counter-intelligence. Not surprisingly, his committee enjoyed good relations with the Defence and Security Ministries.[124] Sergey Yushenkov, his successor as Committee chairman, was a radical reformer and became one of the most outspoken critics of government policy in Chechnya.[125]

The heads of the International Affairs Committee, while centrist and close to government circles, had uneasy and difficult relations with the Foreign Ministry. Both chairmen were highly critical of Kozyrev, who rightly regarded them as aspiring Foreign Ministers. Vladimir Lukin (the first chairman, had a spell as ambassador in Washington before returning to Russia to co-lead the Yabloko bloc and become head of the Duma International Affairs Committee) set the tone for relations by upbraiding the Ministry for reacting far too slowly and in too confused a fashion to international developments.[126] He kept up a steady barrage against Kozyrev, including charges of romantic and naïve Westernism, even while ambassador to the US. His successor, Evgeny Ambartsumov, continued in the same vein, accusing the Foreign Ministry of excessive pro-Americanism and lack of a coherent policy concept based on a clear notion of Russian national interests.

Throughout 1992 there was much institutional sparring, with neither side sure of how to manage the relationship. Deputies complained that the Foreign Ministry gave them neither full information nor close attention. The Ministry was understandably irritated by Committee efforts to raise its profile by asserting its rights to hold the Ministry accountable at every opportunity. The government sometimes did fail to provide adequate, consistent, and timely information in response to parliamentary probing, as over the total cost of sanctions against Iraq, Libya, and Serbia.[127] Exchanges were often sharp, with the nationalist opposition deputies setting the tone of discussion, as in sessions on Ukraine, Yugoslavia, and the Kuriles in mid-1992.

By early 1993 Committee proceedings had become less confrontational and its resolutions more moderate.[128] This moderation reflected both a settling of roles and a general shift towards consensus-building over foreign policy. Ambartsumov and the centrists became more restrained, perhaps to counter growing political polarization and to signal appreciation of foreign policy shifts towards their own position.

Vladimir Lukin, chairman of the International Affairs Committee of the Duma, in a sense continued his predecessor's efforts to curb the attempts of opposition deputies to push parliament into confrontation with the Foreign Ministry. He had a somewhat easier task, given the composition of the Committee and the Duma, although communists and Liberal Democrats (including Mitrofanov, one of the deputy chairmen of the Committee) reiterated many of the arguments made in the Supreme Soviet by the 'Red-Brown coalition'. Lukin and other reformist-minded centrists did a great deal to foster a sober and businesslike approach to the work of the Committee. They warned deputies against launching indiscriminate frontal attacks that might briefly make headlines but would annoy rather than influence government. Instead, Lukin urged realism and selective criticism which would make an impact on the executive, induce them to revise policies, and take more note of public and parliamentary opinion.[129]

A sober, critical approach was evident in the Committee's consideration in spring 1994 of the whole question of Russia's membership of Partnership for Peace. After quite careful examination of the issues involved, including many technical points, the Committee suggested terms on which Russia might agree to join. Debate in the chamber was more sharply critical, as radical conservative members made strenuous efforts to prevent Kozyrev signing any agreement. The same groups raised objections to planned joint exercises with the Americans. In an effort to mollify the conservative opposition, at a time when he was trying to persuade them to sign his Civic Accord document, Yeltsin postponed the exercises and held off preliminary signing of Partnership for Peace until the

summer.[130] Tactical concessions of this kind may well have suited
the President, as they not only aided consensus-building but also
helped to assuage critical voices within the executive. However,
they irritated the Foreign Ministry, which continued to resent what
it saw as parliamentary political interference in areas best left to
professional diplomats.[131]

Parliamentary meddling in diplomacy was a focus of Ministry
complaint which dated back to the Supreme Soviet period, when
official and especially unofficial delegations made statements in
Baghdad, or more often, Belgrade, which contradicted the Foreign
Ministry's line. Although on occasion the official delegations conveniently delivered somewhat starker messages than Moscow wished
officially to convey in public,[132] the Foreign Ministry remained
wary of such diplomatic competition. More serious competition,
which caused more international complications, came from the
tradition, set by the Supreme Soviet and continued by the Duma,
of passing statements and resolutions which diverged from official
policy and reinforced the impression abroad that Russia had more
than one foreign policy. The climate of relations with Ukraine was
made more tense by the repeated attempts of the Supreme Soviet,
and in somewhat more tempered fashion the Duma, to take a
more assertive line on Crimea.[133] Nationalist declarations from
the Russian parliament often set off megaphone diplomacy with
the Ukrainian Supreme Council that did little to help the work
of the Foreign Ministry. Such resolutions, whether on Ukraine, the
Baltic, or Yugoslavia, were largely the work of radical conservatives
whom the Foreign Minister regularly denounced as the 'party of
war'. Their attempts in mid-1994 to rally support for North Korea
provoked particularly strong language from Kozyrev (who called
them 'Red-Brown political mongrels').[134] Ironically, it was the same
conservative oppositionists whose votes in December 1994 and
January 1995 proved decisive in passing legislation in support of
government policy in Chechnya.[135]

While diplomatic visits and bold resolutions were attractive
options for conservative deputies wishing to flex their foreign policy muscles, potentially the most powerful resource at their dis-
posal was parliament's right to ratify treaties. Under the old Soviet
constitution, parliament had wide-ranging rights to ratify all international agreements and treaties. Granted at a time when all parliamentary activities had been considered pure formalities, these

ratification powers needed clarification to enable them to operate in a more genuinely parliamentary setting. The fact that the Supreme Soviet and government could not agree on legislation regulating ratification made the whole process even more confused and fraught with recrimination from both sides. The Foreign Ministry criticized deputies for abusing their ratification rights in order to score partisan political points in their struggle with the executive. Much of the opposition expressed in ratification debates did indeed fall into this category. However, some criticism, such as that voiced against START-2, reflected a combination of partisan opposition and substantive concern.[136] On their side, the deputies complained of Foreign Ministry reluctance to provide full and timely information on agreements undergoing parliamentary scrutiny. Such tensions and, more importantly, the tense general relationship between legislature and executive, resulted in several important international agreements, including that on Open Skies, going into effect without having been ratified.[137]

The new Federal Assembly inherited a large backlog of unratified treaties and some of the confusion relating to ratification which had dogged the previous parliament. While the Foreign Ministry expected the Duma rapidly to ratify over 100 treaties and agreements, it did not show the same urgency in reaching agreement on procedures to clarify and facilitate ratification. The whole of 1994 saw prolonged wrangling over legislation to regulate the ratification process. Under the 1993 constitution (Article 106), both the Federal Council and the Duma had the right to ratify and denounce international treaties and agreements (the Duma also had consultative rights on ambassadorial appointments under Article 83).[138] Efforts to agree detailed legislation revealed differences between Duma, Federation Council and the executive on a number of points. Among the most important concerned the range of agreements liable to parliamentary ratification. The President wanted to continue to select those treaties for ratification which he considered affected national legislation and were therefore the legitimate concern of parliament. The Duma pressed for more comprehensive rights.[139] Some deputies insisted that the agreement on Partnership for Peace fell within their purview, though Lukin, the chairman of the Duma International Affairs Committee, supported Kozyrev in his contention that this particular accord did not have to run the gauntlet of ratification.[140] On other ratification matters, Lukin was more critical

of the Foreign Ministry. He complained on the Committee's behalf about the Ministry's failure to consult deputies adequately on
the Russian–Georgian treaty. On this occasion the Committee was
successful in persuading the President to postpone ratification until
fuller information was made available.[141] Delays over important
CIS treaties were frequent: Russia was the last signatory of the
agreement on the CIS Economic Union to ratify the accord.[142] Given
the far-reaching implications of this agreement, as of many treaties
with CIS states, such delays were often the result of legitimate
scrutiny rather than of political obstructionism. By early 1995 it
seemed as if the increasingly regularized process of ratification
could provide an effective channel for parliamentary involvement
in the foreign policy process.

## Policy involvement: The Kuriles and Yugoslavia

### The Kuriles

The case of the Kurile Islands may serve as an example of the
nature and limits of parliamentary influence on policy climate and
outcomes. The Kuriles provided an attractive target for parliamentary criticism and policy leverage. The Russian public and political
establishment were extremely sensitive to any concessions in this
area, largely because they saw any territorial changes as trigger-
ing a flood of demands from Russia's neighbours. Vulnerability to
external criticism was increased by the uncertainty and ambival-
ence of government policy. Yeltsin spoke in early 1992 of multiple options for the Kuriles and this fed charges of incompetence
and, more particularly, increased rumours of a conspiracy to give
way to Japanese interests. Mention of a five-phase plan gave rise
to suspicions that the islands were to be returned. The governor of
Sakhalin, Valentin Fedorov, encouraged the impression that Yeltsin
was liable to give way to a pro-Japanese lobby.[143] Some nationalist opposition deputies accused the Foreign Ministry, notably
one of its leading Japanese specialists, Kunadze, of taking a pro-
Japanese line and drawing up proposals which betrayed national
interests.[144] Quite apart from the question of betrayal, such secret
plans were resented by deputies because they saw them as typical
of the Ministry's and government's tendency to try to deceive and
bypass Parliament. As was so often the case, institutional *amour*

*propre* and tensions were as important as substantive policy differences in fuelling criticism.[145] Deputies called for a postponement of the President's visit and careful analysis of the whole Kuriles problem, including a major parliamentary contribution, which would lead to a political settlement that met national interests and allayed widespread public doubts about concessions. In the event, Yeltsin did postpone his visit (not going to Tokyo until the following October) and plans for staged agreements on the Kuriles were shelved; the issue seemed to revert to its traditional non-negotiable status.

Much if not most of the explanation for this shift may be found in the hesitation within the executive and doubts about the wisdom of moving at a time of weak government in Tokyo.[146] Parliamentary action had some effect on the outer policy climate by articulating and possibly increasing public hostility to any handing over of the islands. The rehearsal of arguments supporting territorial integrity echoed and perhaps reinforced widely held feelings among all but the most Liberal Westernizer politicians. Sharp attacks on the Foreign Ministry, whether politically discounted or not, put the government and President somewhat on the defensive. More importantly, the Pragmatic Nationalist points made by many of the deputies may have underlined divisions within the executive, including those which emerged between the General Staff and the Ministry of Defence.[147] By amplifying both public and executive misgivings parliament increased the constraints on those wishing to negotiate on the Kuriles.

## Yugoslavia

There was greater parliamentary concentration on the Yugoslav conflict than on any other 'far-abroad' question. More delegations were dispatched and more resolutions passed than on any other single external policy issue. The reasons for such a focus were clear. The whole crisis was seen by many deputies as analogous to that in the former USSR and even within the Russian Federation. Some deputies, close to the political centre, saw the international dismemberment of Yugoslavia as a possible dress rehearsal for Russia.[148] Yugoslavia and the Balkans were a traditional area of Soviet/Russian influence, Serbia an historical ally. Western involvement was therefore viewed by some as a challenge to Russian national interests as well as a testing ground for the viability of Moscow's

new-found co-operative strategy. The most important reason, perhaps, for the centrality of Yugoslavia in parliament's sights was a
political one: Yugoslavia preoccupied the Foreign Ministry more
than any other 'far-abroad' issue.

In the event, the very centrality and complexity of the Yugoslav
crisis narrowed the policy gap between the two sides. Contention
was keen yet the distance between parliament and the executive
on fundamentals was narrower than on other 'far-abroad' questions.
From the outset deputies pressed the government for more effective,
and eventually more forceful, management of a strategy that they
agreed should basically be one of co-operation with the international
community. Only a small minority of deputies, on the Fundamentalist Nationalist wing, called for unilateral steps in defiance of the
UN. The tenor of debate and the spirit of Supreme Soviet resolutions
sought to push Russia to take a more assertive rather than a
wholly defiant stance.

Parliamentary efforts focused on two basic sets of issues: sanctions and military involvement. Both were seen as most important
as signals and symptoms of Russian foreign policy vitality. Sanctions figured in all Supreme Soviet attempts to influence Yugoslav
policy in 1992–3. Many deputies were concerned at the haste of
Moscow's acquiescence to Western-sponsored economic sanctions
against Belgrade in May 1992, without any consultation of parliament. They responded in June with a resolution calling for a
moratorium on sanctions. Criticism in later 1992 of the costly,
ineffective, and one-sided nature of sanctions culminated in December with a resolution which stressed the need for the extension of sanctions to all three warring parties.[149] Two months
later another resolution reinforced this line, and recommended
that Moscow press for sanctions against Croatia if Serbia went
unrelieved.[150]

Both resolutions also sought to force the government's hand on
the other major issue: military intervention. In 1992 the Supreme
Soviet concentrated much attention on the need to prevent military intervention, demanding in December that the Foreign Ministry be instructed to use its Security Council veto to achieve this
end if other means failed. Strong measures were also urged to prevent lifting of the arms embargo against Bosnia. Deputies insisted
that outside arms and forces could be used only for humanitarian peacekeeping purposes. And even here they approved rather

grudgingly of Russian involvement, echoing some of the doubts harboured by many in the military command.[151]

What effect, if any, did such calls have on policy? Early in 1993 Kozyrev spoke in tougher terms of a covert Russian veto at the UN, while stressing the ineffectiveness of an explicit one.[152] In April 1993 Russia abstained in the UN Security Council vote on tightening sanctions against Belgrade. At the same time Churkin took a tougher tone on military operations against Serbia. Ambartsumov claimed that such steps reflected parliamentary influence.[153] Foreign Ministry officials, equally predictably, denied that this more assertive stance owed anything to parliamentary and general domestic opposition pressure.[154] They explained the response in terms of a policy of balancing Russian national priorities on sanctions with Moscow's continued commitment to co-operation with the international community. And there is much to the argument that the Russian response on military intervention and sanctions formed part of a moderately more assertive stance towards what Moscow increasingly saw as overweening Western and especially US influence in the region.[155] Moscow pursued a policy of measured assertiveness: it did not give way to parliamentary insistence on the use of the veto on sanctions or the arms embargo, though in June strong hints were given of moves in this direction. Warnings to deputies against making tough statements on Yugoslavia were accompanied by a greater defensiveness from officials well aware of the domestic need for a measure of accommodation, if not appeasement, of Pragmatic Nationalism.[156] If we discount Ambartsumov's claims of successful Supreme Soviet pressure and Churkin's denials in equal measure, we may get something like a balanced picture of the significant, yet not primary, nature of the parliamentary contribution to shaping the climate in which Yugoslav policy was made.

Similar generalizations can be made about the impact of the Duma on Yugoslav policy in 1994. The policy differences dividing deputies from the executive were smaller and radical criticism more confined. Only the radical conservative opposition, often Liberal Democrats, voiced the kind of demands that had been commonplace in the Supreme Soviet. It was the Geopolitics Committee, where such extreme voices often prevailed, which called for vetoing NATO strikes and unilaterally suspending sanctions against Belgrade. It proved relatively easy for Lukin and other centrist

Pragmatic Nationalists to exercise a moderating influence.[157] Deputies were prepared to listen to arguments, from Foreign Ministry officials as well as from parliamentary colleagues, that passing radical resolutions was counter-productive unless they were credible and practicable. In April 1994 the Duma moderated its resolution on using unilateral withdrawal from sanctions as a lever against the lifting of the arms embargo on Bosnia, though in the summer it passed a resolution calling for the end of Russian participation in UN sanctions.[158] Late 1994 saw a more traditional resolution, protesting against US attempts to undermine the arms embargo on Bosnia and urging the Russian government to take countermeasures.[159] This kind of stance, demanding a more assertive policy yet one that remained broadly in line with that of the government, was typical of the Duma's position on the former Yugoslavia.

*Assessment*

Parliament played a less important role in foreign policy making over these years than its constitutional powers might indicate, and a more significant one than the overall degree of executive dominance would lead one to expect. It had an impact on foreign policy less as a body exercising formal accountability than as a forum articulating and amplifying opinions which affected the political climate in which executive decisions were made.

This generalization applies to both parliaments which operated in the period under review. The Supreme Soviet and the political groups it represented left the larger and more conspicuous imprint. Political confrontation was too brittle and mechanisms of scrutiny too flawed for the legislature to exercise consistent influence over the specific content of foreign policy. Parliament had more diffuse influence on the macro-level than on the micro-level of policy development. By sounding Fundamentalist Nationalist alarms as well as more reasoned Pragmatic ones, parliament reinforced executive trends towards greater national assertiveness. By amplifying critical opinion, the Supreme Soviet helped build the executive and Establishment consensus on foreign policy which emerged in the course of 1993.

The Duma operated for most of 1994 and early 1995 in a somewhat more settled political climate of basic consensus on the thrust of foreign policy strategy. It developed more regularized contacts with government and had some impact on the tactical dimension of international conduct. Opinion expressed in committee as well as in plenary debate encouraged a toughening of integrationist policy in the 'near abroad' and a more assertive stance on Yugoslavia and on NATO expansion. Parliamentary influence in part reflected the beginnings of policy bargaining, notably on budgetary questions. As importantly, parliamentary amplification of critical views proved more effective in a period bounded by two elections, which made the executive more sensitive to the dangers of allowing political opponents to capitalize on popular nationalist grievances.

## Conclusion

Throughout the period under review public politics remained a prominent part of the foreign policy process. External policy may have been decided in private, but it was vigorously debated and contested in public. International issues were intrinsic to the central political debate about the identity of Russia and the proper paths of its development. The Russian public, while preoccupied with domestic questions of living standards and law and order, held strong and even passionate views about Russia's standing in the world and the dangers of economic dependency on the West. Popular fears about exploitation were similar to those of the politicians; mass prescriptions for dealing with external dangers, whether in the 'far' or 'near abroad', were typically more enlightened.

Politicians, acting within parties and lobbies, treated international questions in a vigorous, unsystematic fashion. Many of the vigorous points were couched in emotive and confrontational language and shaped by instrumental partisan ends. This may be typical of the political treatment of foreign policy in most systems; it is the degree to which this occurred that distinguishes the Russian case. The extent to which parliament made foreign policy an issue of open contention with the executive complicated rather than enhanced its direct leverage and impact on policy. The legislature often strove to impose its own foreign policy, particularly as regards the 'far abroad'; the government tended to interpret policy criticism as a political challenge to its authority.

While retaining close control over decisions, government agencies

and the Kremlin were often irritated, and occasionally con-
strained or at least affected, by criticism. It was by voicing critical
opinions widespread among the political élite, and often within
executive circles, that parliament typically exercised an indirect
influence on foreign policy. There were very few instances, if any,
of the executive reversing decisions directly because of public or
parliamentary objections. There were some cases in which demands
from outside the government, especially from powerful economic
lobbies, lay behind adjustments in policy. The Kremlin's desire,
increasingly pronounced from spring 1993, to build policy consensus heightened its sensitivity to critical points made in public
debate and voiced in parliament. Conflicts still occurred, as over
Chechnya, and both sides still tried to intimidate by threat, yet
both seemed more willing in 1994–5 than in 1992–3 to negotiate
and compromise.

This climate of greater flexibility looked set to create more scope
for two dimensions of public politics to make a mark on external
policies: the climate of opinion and lobbies. The executive has
shown signs of greater susceptibility to the general prevailing mood
on international questions, shaped both by the political debate
and by popular opinion. The prevailing mood among élites and
public has gravitated increasingly to Pragmatic Nationalist preferences. In the context of the 'near abroad' this means support for
closer economic integration and for measures to ensure the security of Russian minorities throughout the region. In relation to the
wider world, support for a strategy of co-operation with the international community is mixed with growing concern about Russian economic dependency on and exploitation by the West. There
is a heightened awareness of weakness and of the need to rebuild
Russian greatness. However, such shifts do not amount to a mood
of militant nationalism that would fuel interventionist policies in
the 'near' or 'far abroad'. Some believe in uniting Russians around
a national idea. For most, nationalist feelings are concentrated on
economic issues close to home; sensitivities revolve around economic weakness and vulnerability to penetration and exploitation
by foreign investors.[160] Such national sensitivities provide fertile soil
for conservative opposition parties to reinforce their arguments for
slower domestic reform and protectionism, with appeals to nationalism and Russian ways of doing things. This was the leitmotif of
opposition leaders' election campaigns in autumn 1995. One of the

most prominent challengers to Yeltsin, General Aleksandr Lebed (already standing for the Congress of Russian Communities), underscored his commitment to the Russian cause by establishing the Honour and Motherland movement. Symptomatic of government awareness of strengthening nationalist moods were parallel efforts to clothe itself in patriotic garb, with official parties such as Our Home is Russia.

The pragmatism that lies behind such efforts to adjust to the popular mood is parallelled by increasing readiness to accommodate the preferences of well-organized parties and lobbies. Corporate lobbies may well be able to derive growing policy influence from their financial and political resources and mobilize political parties and parliament to act more effectively on their behalf. Parties and factions may well be able to use the nuisance value of parliamentary obstructionism more effectively to reach negotiated agreements on external policy issues.

The balance between professional management of foreign policy and democratic oversight, to which Andrei Kozyrev aspired and to which we referred at the start of this chapter, remains elusive. However, the trends over the first years of transformation suggest that the pattern of executive domination and sporadic political challenge could be modified by the diffuse effects of public mood and, more importantly, by the focused influence of parties and lobbies acting outside as well as through parliament.

## NOTES

[1] A. Kozyrev, *Preobrazhenie* (Moscow, 1995), ch. 14.

[2] A useful survey of parties in Russia may be found in R. Sakwa, *Russian Politics and Society* (London, 1993), ch. 4. See also B. Koval, *Partii in politicheskii bloki v Rossii* (Moscow, 1993).

[3] A useful factual pre-electoral survey of these groups is S. Markov and M. McFaul, *Russian Electoral Parties and Blocs: A Pre-Elections Summary*, report for the National Democratic Institute for International Affairs (Moscow, 1993).

[4] Apart from speeches by party leaders, we rely on party programmes, particularly those of autumn 1993, which are conveniently collected

in 'Mezhdunarodnyi blagotvoritelnyi fond politiko-pravovykh issledovanii "Interlegal"', *Politicheskie partii i bloki na vyborakh (teksty izbiratelnykh platform)* (Moscow, 1993). A particularly useful survey of 37 political parties and organizations was conducted in late 1992 by the Sociological Service of the Vostochnyi tsentr sovremennoi dokumentatsii; see I. Istoshin, 'Vneshnyaya politika Rossii: Pozitsii obshchestvennykh politicheskikh organizatsii vo vneshnei politike Rossii', *Byulleten'* 1993, no. 1, 1–19.

[5] See 'Programmnoe zayavlenie dvizheniya Demokraticheskoi Rossii' approved at the Third Congress, 19–20 Dec. 1992, sect. 10.

[6] See programme of Russia's Choice, 'Interlegal', *Politicheskie partii i bloki*, 13–14.

[7] The Economic Freedom party placed stress on the UN; see its programme in *Nezavisimaya gazeta*, 11 Jun. 1992.

[8] See Istoshin, 'Vneshnaya politika Rossii'.

[9] A. Tsipko, *Nezavisimaya gazeta*, 13 Apr. 1993.

[10] 'Interlegal', *Politicheskie partii*, 14.

[11] Speech at Tver; see ITAR-TASS, in *Foreign Broadcast Information Service: Daily Report, Central Eurasia* (hereafter *FBIS*), SOV-94-075, p. 10; and programme in ITAR-TASS, 12 Jun. 1994, in *FBIS*, SOV-94-113, p. 27.

[12] See *Obozrevatel*, 1992, no. 2 pp. 21–5.

[13] See V. Nikonov, *Nezavisimaya gazeta*, 7 Aug. 1992.

[14] See Zhirinovsky's speech in Moscow, *Pravda Zhirinovskogo*, 30 May 1995.

[15] See for instance *Den'*, 3 Oct. 1992, p. 1; and Zyuganov, *Sovetskaya Rossiya*, 19 Jan. 1993.

[16] See for instance the claims of a group of opposition deputies, as reported by Interfax, 21 Nov. 1992, in *FBIS*, SOV-92-226, p. 25.

[17] For some of his arguments on international issues, see the extensive collection of his speeches and articles, in D. A. Maiorov (ed.), *Neizvestnyi Rutskoi: Politicheskii portret* (Moscow, 1994), 258–74.

[18] Baburin, *Sovetskaya Rossiya*, 25 Apr. 1992, p. 1.

[19] *Programma Kommunisticheskoi partii Rossiiskoi Federatsii* (Moscow, 1995), 24. The 1993 programme attacked Yeltsin for trying to establish a 'dictatorship of the criminal-comprador bourgeoisie' which was out to transform Russia into a 'raw-materials colony of international capital'; see 'Interlegal', *Politicheskie partii i bloki*, 41.

[20] See Sterligov, Interfax, 3 Jul. 1992, in *FBIS*, SOV-92-131, pp. 39–40.

[21] *Programma Kommunisticheskoi partii Rossiiskoi Federatsii*, 24.

[22] Zhirinovsky and his party were particularly vocal on the need for new alliances; see *Liberal*, 1993, no. 3, p. 6.

[23] See his long and rambling articles in *Sovetskaya Rossiya*, 24 Feb. 1994, p. 3, and 26 Feb. 1994, p. 2.

²⁴ *Programma Kommunisticheskoi partii Rossiiskoi Federatsii*, 24.
²⁵ See the Liberal Democratic Party programme, 'Interlegal', *Politicheskie partii i bloki*, 47.
²⁶ See for instance Zhirinovsky's remarks about blockading Estonia in his interview in *L'Espresso*, 21 Jan. 1994, translated in *FBIS*, SOV-94-0018, p. 21.
²⁷ Sterligov, as reported by Interfax, 3 Jul. 1992, in *FBIS*, SOV-92-131, p. 41.
²⁸ See Zyuganov in *Den'*, 27 Sept.–3 Oct. 1992, p. 1. Adamishin reiterated the apartheid charge at the IFRI Conference on Russia and the World, Paris, March 1994.
²⁹ Sterligov, *Pravda*, 4 Jan. 1994, 1–2.
³⁰ See V. Zhirinovsky, *Poslednii brosok na yug* (Moscow, 1993); see also *Poslednii vagon na sever* (Moscow, 1995).
³¹ See Prokhanov, one of the leading exponents of the nationalist vision, in *Zavtra*, 1994, no. 6, p. 1.
³² This was highlighted, for instance, by the demo-patriot parliamentary Motherland group, *Nezavisimaya gazeta*, 21 Nov. 1992.
³³ Three-quarters of the sample of 400 members of major élite groups polled in January 1993 by Vox Populi wanted Russia to go its own Eurasian way and two–thirds also thought that it should enter the community of Western states; see *Mir Mnenii i Mneniya o Mire*, 1993, no. 5, p. 11.
³⁴ See 'Interlegal', *Politicheskie partii i bloki*, 27.
³⁵ See for instance the Civic Union programme's proposals in the area of economic protectionism; see D.Orlov, *Rossiiskie vesti*, 3 Dec. 1993.
³⁶ Travkin, *Rossiya*, 18–24 Nov. 1992, p. 3, in *FBIS*, SOV-92-227, p. 28; and see the party electoral programme in late 1993, 'Interlegal', *Politicheskie partii i bloki*, 34–5.
³⁷ See the survey of 115 members of the political élite conducted in summer 1993: V. Popov, 'Vneshnepoliticheskaya elita i vneshnyaya politika', *Informatsionnyi biuleten' monitoringa obshchestvennogo mneniya*, Jan. 1994, 33.
³⁸ For an early reference to this term, see the programme of the All-Russian Renewal Union, *Rabochaya Tribuna*, 16 Jun. 1992.
³⁹ V. Utekhin, *Komsomol'skaya pravda*, 21 Oct. 1992.
⁴⁰ They favoured negotiation on the Black Sea Fleet and compromise on Crimea, although here the People's Party of Free Russia took a harder line than the Democratic Party; see Istoshin, *Vneshnaya politika Rossii*, 13 (Table 10).
⁴¹ 'Interlegal', *Politicheskie partii i bloki*, 26–7.
⁴² For an informative analysis of the elections, see M. McFaul, *Understanding Russia's 1993 Parliamentary Elections*, Hoover Institution Essays in Public Policy (Stanford, Calif., 1994).

[43] See *Kommersant Daily*, 14 Mar. 1995, and *Moscow News*, 31 Mar.–6 Apr. 1995.

[44] For the party programme, see *Rossiyskaya gazeta*, 16 May 1995.

[45] It brought in an estimated 70% of foreign exchange revenues and in 1993 accounted for over a third of all budgetary receipts; see V. Vyzhutovich, *Izvestiya*, 6 Dec. 1994.

[46] See interview with Volsky, the chairman of the Russian Union of Industrialists and Entrepreneurs, in *Rossiya*, 2 Oct. 1994, who called for the establishment of a CIS Economic Union.

[47] This happened, for instance, in the case of Ukrainian gas companies affiliating to Gazprom; see *Segodnya*, 7 Jun. 1994.

[48] See A. Bekker, *Moscow News*, 14–20 Apr. 1995.

[49] See V. Razuvaev, *Segodnya*, 21 Oct. 1994.

[50] For commentary on a survey on these issues, which showed 55% favouring restrictions and 35% supporting equal competition, see Y. Glushchenko, *Delovoy Mir*, 25 Apr.–1 May 1994.

[51] For one general account of developments, see S. Viktorov, *Kommersant Daily*, 20 Nov. 1993. For the legislation, see E. Makovskaya, *Kommersant*, 7 Feb. 1995, 22.

[52] See A. Portansky, *Izvestiya*, 30 Dec. 1994, and A. Bekker, *Segodnya*, 6 Jan. 1995.

[53] See Koval, *Partii i politicheskie bloki v Rossii*, 57–63.

[54] See ITAR-TASS, 5 Apr. 1995, in *BBC Summary of World Broadcasts, Former USSR*, no. 2272.

[55] M. Berger, *Izvestiya*, 19 Nov. 1993.

[56] See L. Telen, *Moscow News*, 24–30 Mar. 1995.

[57] See *Financial Times*, 26 Apr. 1995, and V. Gurevich, *Moscow News*, 7–13 Apr. 1995.

[58] For instance, see B. B. Hughes, *The Domestic Context of American Foreign Policy*, San Francisco 1978, 90–9 and 198–220.

[59] For discussion of polling and public opinion in the late Soviet period as well as of issues for post-Soviet development, see A. Miller, W. Reisinger, and V. Hesli (eds.), *Public Opinion and Regime Change: The New Politics of Post-Soviet Societies* (Boulder, Colo., 1993); also see M. Swafford, 'Sociological Aspects of Survey Research in the Commonwealth of Independent States', *International Journal of Public Opinion Research*, 4 (1992), 346–57.

[60] Vladimir Shokarev and other members of the staff of VTsIOM (Vserossiiskiy Tsentr Izucheniya Obschestvennogo Mneniya) were extremely helpful and efficient in extracting the data required.

[61] In the estimate of a representative sample of élites, such sensitivity was combined with somewhat less care about public welfare; see N. Popov, 'Vneshnyaya politika Rossii (Analiz politikov i ekspertov)', pt. 1, *Mirovaya eknomika i mezhdunarodnye otnosheniya*, 1994, no. 3, p. 56.

[62] For an account of the closed Supreme Soviet hearings on the Kuriles, see V. Kuznechevsky, *Rossiiskaya gazeta*, 14 Aug. 1992, p. 4.

[63] Gabriel Almond made the point long ago that it is 'not the foreign or domestic character of the issue which determines the accessibility of public attention, but the intimacy of the impact'. As he puts it, 'foreign policy, save at moments of grave crisis, has to labor under a handicap; it has to shout loudly to be heard even a little.' See *The American People and Foreign Policy* (New York, 1960), 71.

[64] Data from VTsIOM, New Year survey conducted in Dec. 1992.

[65] Ibid.

[66] For instance, well over a third of respondents in a spring 1994 poll expressed no opinion on Russian membership of NATO; see Y. Korotkova, *Moskovskii Komsomolets*, 2 Jul. 1994.

[67] See VTsIOM poll 94-2.

[68] See Popov, 'Vneshnyaya politika Rossii', pt. 2, *Mirovaya ekonomika i mezhdunarodnye otnosheniya*, 1994, no. 4, p. 8. This was a survey of a total of 113 members of various élites: government bodies, Supreme Soviet factions and committees, party leaders and representatives, and journalists, conducted in Jun.–Jul. 1993.

In a poll of Muscovites in Apr. 1992, 36% thought that Russia had no enemies, 8% that the country had many; 20% thought that Russia had no friends, while in autumn 1993 a quarter considered the country to be friendless; see *Mir mnenii i mneniya o mire*, 1992, no. 6, and 1993, no. 1. By Apr. 1994, a VTsIOM poll showed showed that extreme optimists numbered 22%; see 94-Monitoring-aprel'.

[69] Only 12% of the 3,535 respondents in 30 regions of Russia surveyed in one 1994 Mnenie poll considered the US a threat (27% did think it a potential threat); see Y. Korotkova, *Moskovskii Komsomolets*, 2 Jul. 1994.

[70] 23% of Moscovites in early 1994 considered military aggression as possible before the end of the century; see report of a Mnenie poll in *Moskovskii Komsomolets*, 30 Mar. 1994, p. 3.

[71] See VTsIOM 94-4 Monitoring survey of Apr. 1994 (2,935 respondents, national sample); and Popov, 'Vneshnyaya politika Rossii', pt. 2, p. 7.

[72] Poll conducted by VTsIOM in Apr.–May 1992 (n = 2,069), reported in *Post-Soviet East European Report*, 15 Dec. 1992, pp. 3–4.

[73] VTsIOM Monitoring 94-M-4 poll, Apr. 1994.

[74] Two-thirds in a late 1992 poll; see Y. Levada, *Izvestiya*, 23 Jan. 1993, p. 4.

[75] Around three-quarters consistently rejected any concessions on the Kuriles; see polls reported in *Asahi Shimbun*, 30 Nov. 1992, and *Hokkaido Shimbun*, 8 Mar. 1993.

[76] VTsIOM polls 93-2 (Feb. 1993) and 93-3 (Mar. 1993).

[77] VTsIOM Omnibus 94-2 survey conducted in Feb. 1994; V. Sazonov, *Segodnya*, 6 Dec. 1994; and for élite opinion, Popov, 'Vneshnyaya politika Rossii', pt. 2, p. 7.

[78] See V. Sazonov, *Segodnya*, 6 Dec. 1994. For rising trends of concern, compare VTsIOM polls 92-12 (Dec. 1992) and 93-12 (Dec. 1993). The young and the highly educated were almost as concerned as their less-educated elders.

[79] V. Sazonov, *Segodnya*, 6 Dec. 1994.

[80] See VTsIOM poll 93-3 (Mar. 1993); and *Mir mnenii i mneniya o mire*, 1993, no. 2.

[81] VTsIOM ekspres poll 93-4 (Apr. 1993).

[82] VTsIOM poll 93-12 (Dec. 1993) and 95-M-1 (Jan. 1995). Around 80% disapproved of foreign ownership of large enterprises; the 7% who took a positive attitude came mainly from among the very young.

[83] See VTsIOM monitoring survey of Jan. 1995.

[84] VTsIOM polls 92-4 (Apr. 1992), 92-6 (Jun. 1992), and 93-2 (Feb. 1993).

[85] VTsIOM polls 92-12 (Dec. 1992) and 94-2 (Feb. 1994).

[86] VTsIOM poll 94-5 (May 1994).

[87] VTsIOM polls 94-2 (Feb. 1994), 92-12 (Dec. 1992), and 94-1 (Jan. 1994). Polls show almost the same level of support for the revival of the Soviet Union, at 28% and 26%.

[88] Monthly VTsIOM surveys, 1992–3.

[89] In Apr. 1992, around two-fifths gave policy performance average marks, between a third and two-fifths awarded lower ones, and only a fifth or less assigned good ones; see VTsIOM poll 92-4 (Apr. 1994). A survey of 396 members of the political élite found that a quarter gave CIS policy positive ratings while 54% gave it poor marks; see *Mir mnenii i mneniya o mire*, 1993, no. 8.

[90] See VTsIOM poll 92-12 (Dec. 1992). Under a fifth in a Dec. 1993 Mnenie poll thought that all the ex-republics should reunite; a quarter thought this impossible and two-fifths were opposed to the idea; see G. Pashkov, *Izvestiya*, 30 Dec. 1993, p. 1. A quarter polled in spring 1994 gave preference to the Slav states, only 8% to Kazakhstan; other new states hardly figured; see report of the Public Opinion Fund survey by ITAR-TASS, 21 Jun. 1994, in *FBIS*, SOV-94-119, p. 21.

[91] VTsIOM poll 93-10 (Oct. 1993).

[92] VTsIOM poll 94-6 (Jun. 1994).

[93] VTsIOM poll 94-5 (May 1994).

[94] VTsIOM poll 93-5 (May 1993).

[95] According to one late 1992 Vox Populi poll of 500 members of political élites, 29% considered intervention permissible, a further two-fifths condoned it in exceptional circumstances, and only a third ruled it out as impermissible; see *Mir mnenii i mneniya o mire*, 1992, no. 11.

[96] See N. Gorodetskaya, *Segodnya*, 14 Sept. 1993.

[97] A VTsIOM survey of late Jul. 1993 reported in *Kuranty*, 7 Aug. 1993, translated in *BBC Summary of World Broadcasts*, SU/1762, C/2.

[98] Vox Populi poll of autumn 1993 (n = 1,017) reported in N. Gorodetskaya, *Segodnya*, 14 Sept. 1993, p. 2.

[99] See P. Converse, 'The Nature of Belief Systems in Mass Publics', in D. Apter (ed.), *Ideology and Discontent* (New York, 1964), cited in Hughes, *The Domestic Context of American Foreign Policy*, 26.

[100] See S. Whitefield, 'Social Responses to Reform in Russia', in D. Lane (ed.), *Russia in Transition* (London, 1995), 91–115.

[101] VTsIOM poll 92-12 (Dec. 1992).

[102] See I. Klyamkin, *Moskovskie Novosti*, 11–18 Sept. 1994, p. 6.

[103] Hughes, *The Domestic Context of American Foreign Policy*, 95.

[104] See J. Hurwitz and M. Peffley 'How are Foreign Policy Attitudes Structured? A Hierarchical Model', *American Political Science Review*, 81 (1987), 1098–120.

[105] See Whitefield, 'Social Responses to Reform in Russia', Table 6, and Klyamkin, *Moskovskie Novosti*, 11–18 Sept. 1994, p. 6.

[106] VTsIOM poll 94-2 (Feb. 1994).

[107] VTsIOM poll 93-5 (May 1993).

[108] VTsIOM poll 94-5 (May 1994).

[109] *Nezavisimaya gazeta*, 29 Dec. 1993.

[110] G. Yavlinsky, *Obshchaya gazeta*, 29 Jul.–4 Aug. 1994, p. 1.

[111] N. Trotsky, *Obshchaya gazeta*, 29 Jul.–4 Aug. 1994, p. 7.

[112] See Kozyrev, *Preobrazhenie*, 306–7.

[113] Kostikov, quoted by R. Zaripov, *Komsomol'skaya pravda*, 12 Mar. 1993, p. 1, and Yeltsin on Russian television, 6 May 1993, *FBIS*, SOV-93-087, p. 13.

[114] For Kozyrev's disappointment see *Preobrazhenie*, 312.

[115] S. Hoffmann, *Dead Ends: American Foreign Policy in the New Cold War* (Cambridge, 1983), 101, cited in J. Dumbrell, *The Making of US Foreign Policy* (Manchester, 1990), 118.

[116] Open letter of 52 deputies, *Rabochaya Tribuna*, 14 Jul. 1992, p. 2.

[117] See the detailed account of the sessions in V. Kuznechesky, *Rossiiskaya gazeta*, 14 Aug. 1992.

[118] *Rossiiskaya gazeta*, 15 Jul. 1993.

[119] See A. Ostapchuk's interview with Andrei Loginov, the head of the Presidential Department for Interaction with Parliament, *Nezavisimaya gazeta*, 3 Aug. 1994.

[120] V. Isakov, *Sovetskaya Rossiya*, 11 Aug. 1994. Liaison work with parliament was upgraded from departmental to directorate status within the presidential apparatus; see *Kuranty*, 31 Aug. 1994, in *FBIS*, SOV-94-170, p. 11.

[121] N. Trotsky, *Obshchaya gazeta*, 29 Jul.–4 Aug. 1994. For an official

account and assessment of Duma activities in the first months by its Speaker, see I. Rybkin, *Gosudarstvennaya Duma: Pyataya popytka* (Moscow, 1994).

[122] See the rather critical appraisal by Kostikov, ITAR-TASS, 22 Sept. 1994, in *FBIS*, SOV-94-184, p. 18, and the more positive one in Rybkin's speech to the Duma, *Rossiiskaya gazeta*, 26 Jul. 1994.

[123] See *Kommersant Daily*, 18 and 19 Jan. 1994.

[124] P. Felgengauer, *Segodnya*, 18 May 1993.

[125] See, for instance, his interview in *Literaturnaya gazeta*, 21 Dec. 1994.

[126] Interview by O. Gerasimenko, *Rossiya*, 22–8 Apr. 1992, in *FBIS*, SOV-92-083, pp. 17–18, at p. 4.

[127] Kozyrev refused to agree with the figures (around $16 bn) given by the Ministry of Foreign Economic Relations; see S. Sukova and G. Bovt, *Kommersant Daily*, 16 Feb. 1993, p. 3, translated in *FBIS*, SOV-93-030, p. 36.

[128] A. Vorobyev, *Rossiiskaya gazeta*, 28 Jan. 1993; for a general account of Committee work, see A. Saltys and V. Kapanadze, *Latinskaya Amerika*, 1993, no. 1, pp. 22–5.

[129] Interviews with members and staff of the International Affairs Committee, Moscow, Jun. 1994.

[130] See S. Parkhomenko, *Segodnya*, 1 Apr. 1994, and I. Bulavinov, *Kommersant Daily*, 5 May 1994.

[131] See the critical comments on the Duma's acitivities by A. Adamishin, First Deputy Foreign Minister, interviewed by V. Kedrov, *Rossiya*, 13–19 Jul. 1994.

[132] The delegation to former Yugoslavia in Apr. 1993 made clear that Moscow would never go to war for the Serbs; see I. Nekrasov's interview with Ambartsumov, *Moskovskie Novosti*, no. 18, 1993, pp. 44–5.

[133] See, for instance, the statement issued by the Duma, reported by A. Koretskii, *Kommersant Daily*, 26 Nov. 1994.

[134] See the report by ITAR-TASS, 27 Jun. 1994, *FBIS*, SOV-94-124, p. 7.

[135] See *Kommersant Daily*, 24 Jan. 1995.

[136] A Vox Populi survey of 400 members of the élite in Apr. 1993 suggested that a majority of deputies felt that the treaty would weaken Russian security; see *Mir mnenii i mneniya o mire*, 1993, no. 1.

[137] For a good discussion of problems surrounding ratification, see V. Trofimov, *Nezavisimaya gazeta*, 29 Dec. 1993.

[138] See L. Okunkov *et al.*, *Kommentariy k Konstitutsii Rossiiskoi Federatsii* (Moscow, 1994), pp. 264 (Art. 83) and 323 (Art. 106).

[139] See S. Tsekhmistrenko, *Kommersant Daily*, 21 Oct. 1994.

[140] See P. Zhuravlev, *Segodnya*, 9 Jul. 1994.

[141] See Lukin, *Obshchaya gazeta*, 11–17 Mar. 1994.

[142] ITAR-TASS, 7 Oct. 1994, in *FBIS*, SOV-94-196, p. 43.

[143] ITAR-TASS, 5 Jul. 1992, in *FBIS*, SOV-92-129, p. 61.

[144] V. Kuznechesky, *Rossiiskaya gazeta*, 14 Aug. 1992.

[145] See the account of the International Affairs Committee session by N. Garifullina in *Sovetskaya Rossiya*, 27 Aug. 1992.

[146] Yeltsin claimed that postponement was due to the Japanese raising the issue too categorically; Radio Rossii, 11 Sept. 1992, in *FBIS*, SOV-92-177, p. 22.

[147] For one account of the decision and linked developments, see Kozyrev, *Preobrazhenie*, 294–300.

[148] *Sovetskaya Rossiya*, 26 Jan. 1993.

[149] *Rossiiskaya gazeta*, 4 Jan. and 27 Feb. 1993.

[150] *Nezavisimaya gazeta*, 19 Feb. 1993.

[151] P. Felgengauer, *Segodnya*, 18 May 1993.

[152] Russian television, 26 Jan. 1993, cited in S. Crow, *RFE/RL Research Report*, 19 Mar. 1993, p. 4; ITAR-TASS, 23 Apr. 1993, in *FBIS*, SOV-93-077, p. 5.

[153] See the interview by S. Tikhomirov, *Rossiiskaya gazeta*, 29 May 1993.

[154] Churkin, interviewed in *Unita*, 10 Feb. 1993, in *FBIS*, SOV-93-030, p. 11.

[155] From January onwards Yeltsin became generally more critical of US policy; see S. Tsekhmistrenko and A. Yedemsky, *Kommersant Daily*, 27 Jan. 1993, p. 10.

[156] For this mix, see Churkin, ITAR-TASS, 28 Apr. 1993, in *FBIS*, SOV-93-081, p. 32.

[157] Interviews with members and staff of the International Affairs Committee, Jun. 1994.

[158] For critical comment on the legal aspects, see N. Trotsky, *Obshchaya gazeta*, 29 Jul.–4 Aug. 1994.

[159] See *Rossiiskaya gazeta*, 16 Nov. 1994.

[160] For a review of some poll evidence, see V. Sazonov, *Segodnya*, 6 Dec. 1994.

# 5

# Military Factors in Foreign Policy

ROY ALLISON

This chapter focuses on the internal military factors influencing foreign policy decision-making in Russia. Foreign policy is defined to include international security policy. But the intention is not to discuss military policy in general, nor to consider external military influences on foreign policy outcomes.

The chapter is divided thematically into two parts. First, it evaluates military lobbies influencing the formation of foreign policy: the prospects for new military-political coalitions emerging (enabling the military leadership to assume a direct policy making role) and the potential influence of the increasingly independent officer corps. Secondly, it investigates the perspectives and influence of the military in specific crucial foreign policy areas.

## Sources of military influence on policy making

In post-Soviet Russia the military establishment has begun to exert a significant though unco-ordinated influence on the formation of foreign policy, especially in relation to the 'near abroad'. This reflects the conditions and specific military legacy of Russia. The CIS states share a common Soviet geopolitical heritage, which is reflected in Russian military interest in reviving some kind of 'joint military-strategic space' for as many of these states as possible. This kind of thinking, or in the case of some Russian senior officers nostalgia for the Soviet Union, has drawn Russian military leaders into foreign policy controversy over matters which they still tend to regard as domestic military business.

Certain factors have combined to raise the profile and political leverage of the post-Soviet military establishment.

First, the collapse of the Communist Party and the fragmentation of the Union left the military forces (despite a chaotic process of redeployments) as just about the only national-scale organized structure in Russia—one which indeed extended throughout the territory of the former Union. As central political control in Russia itself has weakened for periods of time and as regionalism has deteriorated into anarchy or ethnic conflict in the north Caucasus (not to mention beyond Russian borders), the agencies holding the instruments of coercive power have become more indispensable to the political authorities. The Russian Federal Security Service (FSS) has not fully recovered from the discrediting of the former KGB, while the campaign in Chechnya has confirmed the limited capacities of the Ministry of Interior forces. As a result the Russian executive has assigned the regular military forces a potent role to maintain the integrity of the Russian Federation and to stabilize conflict prone regions, which in turn provides the military command with political leverage.

Secondly, the military have gained additional political influence by default. The internecine struggle of the executive and the legislature in Moscow weakened the legitimacy of central political bodies in general and further undermined their ability to enforce decisions (or even reach consensual decisions). Consequently, the military leadership has assumed the role of actual or potential power-broker—a position which it had already experienced to some extent in the interregnum between the dissolution of the Union and the formation of the CIS in December 1991. The existence of this role has been denied by the Russian military leadership, but it undoubtedly exists in Moscow in a way that it does not, for example, in Kiev.

Thirdly, the rejection of Communist ideology, which made party control over the armed forces a hallowed principle (in Soviet military education 'Bonapartism' was anathema), removed a major psychological block to direct military intervention in politics. The military now became a potent institutional interest, which could lobby and even prescribe policy options. The Main Political Administration, which had provided an institutional framework for Party indoctrination, was swept away. The monitoring of possible military disloyalty or dissent by the former KGB passed into the hands of military intelligence subdivisions of the FSS, whose job it was in Yeltsin's words, 'to know the situation in the army'.[1]

The principle of civilian or legislative control over the military apparatus has not in itself conflicted with the new practice of military lobbying. But the extent of this control has remained very limited. Things are complicated by the fact that military officers have occupied numerous seats in the parliament and officers' assemblies have engaged in political agitation. In autumn 1994 the Chairman of the State Duma Defence Committee, Sergei Yushenkov, complained that there still existed no effective system of public control of the army in Russia, that even the President and the government had no structures capable of effectively performing these functions, and that 'the Defence Ministry stands guard on its corporate interests.'[2]

Fourthly, as a new ideology of national patriotism has replaced military loyalty to the Party or the Union, military leaders have felt justified in promoting their views of the national interest. The debate on the content of national interests among political leaders has been fluid enough to permit a military input and the high command has implied that military power is the most potent agency to enforce those interests. Restraints on the use of force internally (in the USSR) which developed in the late Gorbachev years have been swept away and apparently buried with the bloody campaign in Chechnya. For the CIS region, the defence of ethnic Russians has emerged in Moscow as a key theme coalescing military and nationalist political lobbies.

These factors of change in civil–military relations apply to the Russian military system far more than to the Ukrainian, for example. The new Ukrainian military leadership has depended on the national political leadership in its struggle with Russian and CIS officials to establish and develop independent military forces for Ukraine. Lacking the nostalgia of the Russian high command for former Soviet military power and organization, Ukraine has found it easier to confine the ambitions of its new military leaders to professional military matters.

### Prospects for military-political coalitions

The military system in Russia is politically more fragmented than the Soviet military apparatus was at any time in the postwar period. Despite this the new military organization is built on hierarchy and loyalty to the judgement of senior officers. For this reason the views of senior military leaders have been particularly influential in shaping the military ethos and world-view of the army. Their links with civilian politicians and expatriate communities may give them an input into decision-making even when they do not have access to significant formal channels of political influence.

The failed August 1991 coup attempt paralysed the top echelons of the Soviet military apparatus. The senior military command had split in several directions, between services and regional commands. Some, like the commanders of the Baltic and Moscow military districts and the Black Sea Fleet commander, actively supported the coup. Others, such as the chiefs of the Air Force and Airborne Forces, resisted the coup leaders. But the majority chose to take the path of the Leningrad and Far Eastern Military Districts and failed to align their commands in either political direction. The coup led to sweeping personnel turnover at the highest levels.[3] It also boosted the fortunes of a number of progressively minded generals who acquired advisory positions for the Russian President or state bodies.[4]

Yet such 'progressive' senior officers were exceptional among generals in the forces at large. The new top commanders typically continued to block efforts towards significant military reform, demilitarization, and the conversion of military industry. They continued to view the West as the principal if now more latent military threat. Such views extended down the ranks. Early in 1992, for example, perhaps some 80 per cent of colonels remained in broad terms conservative and only 20 per cent were reform-minded.[5]

The few reformist generals were edged aside as Russia proceeded to establish its own defence ministry, armed forces, and general staff in spring 1992 and a group of politically conservative generals were appointed to top positions. Their conservatism was not that of traditional ideological belief, but in some respects was more militant in its Russian nationalism. Among this group, Defence Minister Pavel Grachev and Generals Viktor Dubinin (who died later in 1992), Valery Mironov, Georgy Kondratev, and Boris Gromov were all linked also by shared experience as Afghan war commanders. Their beliefs were not hidden. As commander of Soviet forces in Poland Dubinin had scared Polish leaders with his bellicose statements. Mironov, the former commander of Russian troops in the Baltic states, had openly sided with local Russian officers' associations against the Baltic governments and the Russian political leadership. Gromov's political ambitions were revealed during the Russian presidential election of 1991, when he had been ex-premier Nikolai Ryzhkov's running mate. Kondratev had played a highly controversial role commanding Russian peacekeeping forces in Abkhazia.

Two other key generals based outside Moscow have played an active political role in ethnic conflicts in the 'near abroad' or in Russian 'peacekeeping' missions: Lieutenant-General Aleksandr Lebed and Colonel-General Viktor Sorokin (see below on the high command and peacekeeping). Finally, the former commander of the airborne troops and assistant to General Yazov, Colonel-General Vladislav Achalov, played a crucial political part in the confrontation between parliament and President in September–October 1993. Although Achalov had been dismissed from service for his involvement in the August 1991 coup attempt, he reappeared as military adviser to Ruslan Khasbulatov, who sought to use him to rally military support against Yeltsin.

The caucus of senior conservative generals was overshadowed from early 1992 to autumn 1993, however, by Major-General Alexandr Rutskoi, the Russian Vice-President. In this period Rutskoi emerged as the driving force behind the more politicized Russian military command and the only credible potential leader of a future military-political coalition to replace the current leadership. He came to occupy a central position in shifting alliances directed at bringing about a more conservative Russian foreign policy. His only formal external policy responsibilities were in the area of arms sales, but he developed a highly controversial role in relation to the former Union states, becoming more and more distanced from official government policy. By the end of 1991 he had also become a strong advocate for protecting the privileges of the former Soviet defence sector, thereby garnering support from the powerful military-industrial complex. A year later, with growing support from the armed forces as a whole and implicit backing from the new politicized Russian military command, Rutskoi sought to lead a popular national-patriotic opposition movement to displace Yeltsin.

Most of the new commanders in the Russian Defence Ministry appeared to support programmes embraced by nationalist politicians (some favoured Fundamentalist Nationalist positions) and this provided fertile ground for the establishing of more formal military-political ties. It was in this context that Foreign Minister Kozyrev (still in his Liberal Westernizing phase) warned of the emergence of a 'party of war'. He did not mean that a coherent military agenda had emerged on behalf of a largely unified military constituency. Rather, Kozyrev feared a specific coalition of military and civilian leaders prepared to use military force as a political weapon in conflict zones around Russia.[6]

From summer 1992 reformist Russian politicians pointed to the danger of a coalition forming around advocates of an independent Russian policy directed at preserving the industrial potential of the state and the international influence seen as befitting a great power. In one assessment the key figures in the 'party of war' were identified as Rutskoi himself, the maverick Major-General (as then) Aleksandr Lebed, Ruslan Khasbulatov (largely because of his fulminations over Georgia), Yury Skokov, Colonel-General Boris Gromov, and Arkady Volsky.[7]

The formation of such a powerful political alliance was no guarantee that the senior military command would be prepared to stake their future on open intervention in the political realm so soon after the aborted coup of August 1991. Despite the political resurgence of the Russian military leadership, Rutskoi could not claim clear support among the military high command and Yeltsin remained a master political tactician. This had been demonstrated earlier in autumn 1991 when Yeltsin assiduously and successfully courted military leaders during his political contest with Gorbachev and gained their backing before the Soviet Union was dissolved.

The position of Defence Minister Grachev was crucial in influencing the political ambitions of the top military leadership before and directly after the confrontation between executive and legislature in autumn 1993. He resisted Rutskoi by seeking to adopt a neutral stand in this political struggle and strongly criticized efforts to fracture the army along political lines through agitation among officers.[8] At a Security Council meeting on 3 March 1993, Grachev and other top commanders urged the President to adopt decisive political steps to end Russia's constitutional crisis—an implicit offer of support for Yeltsin,[9] which resulted in an open rupture between Grachev and Khasbulatov.

An evident danger in spring and summer 1993 was that Rutskoi, who aligned himself with Khasbulatov in the stand-off between parliament and the President, might attract military support as an alternative 'strong man' to challenge Yeltsin. Khasbulatov lacked standing in military circles, although in August 1993 he made a strong bid for military support by attending military and veterans' groups and calling for proper financing of the army. In parliament Grachev was assailed not only by Khasbulatov and other national patriots, but also by the so-called 'Army Reform' group of people's deputies, co-ordinated by Colonel Vitaly Urazhtsev. Urazhtsev sought to use this group to bolster Rutskoi's position, though this led to the departure from the group of prominent military supporters of Yeltsin, men such as Generals Dmitry Volkogonov and Konstantin Kobets.

As the confrontation between the President and parliament in Moscow came to a head in September, Rutskoi appealed to the military to support the parliament and swore in Colonel-General Vladislav Achalov as a new defence minister. Grachev claimed that he had the support for Yeltsin of all commanders of Russian military services, military districts, and fleets.[10] But his hesitancy in committing troops to support Yeltsin suggests uncertainty about their loyalty, as well as reluctance to enter the political fray. Indeed, it was claimed later that these commanders were more neutral. It was reported that the staffs of several military districts, as well as the Pacific Fleet, had supported the parliamentary forces.[11]

The sympathies of such officers were insufficient to prevent humiliating defeat and temporary imprisonment for Rutskoi. His efforts to develop his People's Party 'Free Russia' (PPFR) after his release from prison failed to bring much military support, and opinion polls among officers suggested that his former personal military support base had collapsed by 1994. The PPFR, which was renamed the Russian Social-Democratic People's Party (RSDPP) at its Second Congress in May 1994, sought to consolidate various social democratic forces and refrained from attempts to cultivate Russian military leaders.[12] When Rutskoi was expelled from the RSDPP in February 1995 he focused his efforts on developing his 'Derzhava' (Great Power) movement—a Pragmatic Nationalist movement more attuned to his views and presidential election ambitions.

Grachev's eventual support for Yeltsin in his hour of need transformed the Defence Minister's position after October 1993. He began to appear as more of a diplomat representing Russian interests in international forums. It was speculated that a tacit deal had been struck between Yeltsin and Grachev which provided the military command with a freer hand to influence security policy in the CIS and other issues such as the CFE Treaty and NATO eastward expansion (see later in this chapter).[13]

Potentially Grachev's role in October 1993 also offered him more domestic leverage, for example over military procurement and the size of the army. In reality, however, Grachev's personal authority in the army declined and by 1994 reports suggested his growing isolation in the Defence Ministry. At the same time Yeltsin made clear that Grachev served at the discretion of the President. The limits of military influence over the defence budget were highlighted in spring 1994 when the allocation for military expenditure was kept far below the demands of the Defence Ministry and the agrarian lobby were more successful in their bid for funds.[14]

Grachev's growing personal vulnerability and declining popularity in 1994 meant that he was in no position to organize the high command into a powerful institutional interest group on foreign or security policy even had he wished to. Instead he sought to limit the foreign policy role of potential rivals for the office of Defence Minister, fearing that such a role might bolster their claims. One of his concerns was Deputy Defence Minister Boris Gromov.

Gromov's official duties by spring 1994 included disarmament and the withdrawal of troops from abroad, and he had acted as Russia's representative in various CIS security forums.[15] He had also been connected with the popular and influential mayor of Moscow, Yury Luzhkov. Ironically, when Grachev finally cut Gromov's influence in the Defence Ministry in February 1995 after the latter's criticisms of the campaign in Chechnya, it was by shifting him to the post of 'chief military expert at large' in the Foreign Ministry. Gromov was given the rank of Deputy Foreign Minister and the task of handling relations with NATO, strategic stability in Europe, and military co-operation between CIS countries. This offered a significant input of military expertise into Kozyrev's ministry and opened up a new channel between it and the Defence Ministry. But in losing his rank of Deputy Defence Minister Gromov was prised away from military colleagues who could support his foreign policy preferences or consolidate an anti-Grachev lobby.

Grachev's other chief rival, Lieutenant-General Aleksandr Lebed, could not, as an army commander, exert formal influence on foreign policy beyond Moldova, but he gained remarkable popularity among mid-ranking Russian officers and his views on policies in the CIS region (see below) became widely known in Russia and abroad.

The downfall of Rutskoi, the weakening of Grachev's position, and the way the army was used as a political instrument against parliament in October 1993 had another result. They created a temptation for certain politicians to court senior military officers (other than Grachev), especially after the December 1993 parliamentary elections.

The support Vladimir Zhirinovsky's Liberal Democrats gained in these elections shifted the political spectrum by giving more legitimacy to Fundamentalist Nationalist views. This reduced the impact of Rutskoi's political defeat and restored the hopes of a number of extremist officers disgraced in the fighting against the President in September–October 1993, such as Colonel-General (retired) Albert Makashov and Colonel Stanislav Terekhov. Zhirinovsky could also count on the support of some die-hard 'Soviet' military opinion, associated for example with Army General Valentin Varennikov (who in September 1994 was finally acquitted of conspiracy in the August 1991 coup attempt). Other senior officers scornful of Zhirinovsky were initially impressed by the strength of the protest vote he had received. Early in 1994 unconfirmed reports suggested that Zhirinovsky was seeking to establish links with Moscow-area military commanders. His reported goal was to build a close working relationship between military leaders and his Liberal Democratic Party.[16]

Meanwhile, Zhirinovsky made clear his belief that Russian military forces had a key role to play in promoting an imperial restoration in the former Soviet region, or even further afield, and that military commanders could be viewed as the political agents for this goal. For example, he argued that Russian troops should stay in Moldova indefinitely, that the 'Dniester republic' would be included in the Russian Federation, and that the 14th Army commander, Lieutenant-General Lebed, was Russia's 'governor' of the region.[17]

However, Zhirinovsky's subsequent behaviour lowered his standing with military leaders. In the most reliable opinion-poll survey of senior officers in 1994, published in August, Zhirinovsky was viewed negatively as a successor to Yeltsin by 69 per cent of those polled (only Gorbachev attracted a more negative response among a dozen leaders proposed). He scored only about 10 per cent on a scale in this survey of 'most trusted' political or military figures, compared to 44 per cent for chairman of the Yabloko faction Yavlinsky, and 30 per cent each for Communist Party chairman Zyuganov and Rutskoi. The most trusted figures of all were generals Lebed, who scored 57 per cent, and Gromov, who scored 54 per cent.[18]

This poll indicated that senior officers did not endorse Fundamentalist Nationalist views espoused by contemporary politicians and parties, but were attracted by the idea of strong leadership, which Lebed or Gromov were seen as capable of providing. The former Commander-in-Chief of the CIS joint armed forces Yevgeny Shaposhnikov was aware of this current of feeling when he raised the possibility of some generals forming a party or public alliance (comprising 60–70 per cent of the Russian army generals), which he hoped would advance him as a presidential election candidate.[19] In fact other generals were better fitted to play this part, or to act as a military 'running mate' to a politician in a presidential election. At the end of 1994, besides Lebed and Gromov, the commander of the Border Guards, Colonel-General Andrei Nikolayev, was being recommended for this role.

By autumn 1995 a number of generals had attached themselves to political parties in the approach to the December parliamentary elections. For example, Lieutenant-General Lev Rokhlin, commander of the Volgograd corps and a prominent commander in the Chechnya campaign, was approved as a candidate for the Our Home is Russia party alongside Prime Minister Viktor Chernomyrdin. More extreme officers such as the conservative stalwart Army General Varennikov (invited to run on the ticket of the Communist Party of the Russian Federation) and Colonel Terekhov (who joined Nikolai Ryzhkov's 'Power to the People' bloc) also resurfaced as political campaigners. Rutskoi meanwhile sought to promote his new Fundamentalist Nationalist 'Power' political grouping.[20]

A military candidate for President would also be likely to attract support from the expanding state security services. In autumn 1994 Alexander Sterligov, the former KGB general and chairman of the Russian National Council Party, who campaigns for a renewed union of Russia, Ukraine, and Belarus, predicted that Yeltsin's successor would be a general.[21] A year later Sterligov was negotiating with the earlier disgraced Colonel-General Achalov on the creation of a single electoral bloc. By summer 1995 generals were at the helm of the Federal Security Service (Colonel-General Mikhail Barsukov) and the Ministry of the Interior (Colonel-General Anatoly Kulikov). Another general outside the structure of the regular armed forces, Aleksandr Korzhakov, chief of the President's Main Guard Department, openly supported the 'For the Motherland' association.

Lebed himself, who lacks higher staff-academy training, may be viewed as a political opportunist by the top Russian high command (certainly in comparison to Boris Gromov). Nevertheless, he had elicited broad support among senior and mid-ranking officers by 1995. In February that year the congress of Afghan war veterans, which was attended by a number of important Russian politicians, nominated Lebed as its candidate for the forthcoming presidential elections. Lebed entered the political fray openly when he made an alliance with Yury Skokov, leader of the Congress of Russian Communities. His foreign policy views merit attention not only because of his political ambitions but also for the echo they provide of broader military opinion.

Lebed is nostalgic about Russia's lost power and critical of Russia's failure to identify its foreign policy priorities and the scope of its vital interests. In 1992 he still hoped for a revival of Soviet power. He has also promoted the virtues of authoritarian rule for Russia (and admires the Chilean dictator Pinochet). However, he has been careful to specify that any military strongman should only be advanced through constitutional processes and he now accepts soberly that Russian greatness cannot be recaptured through force of arms in foreign countries. In this spirit Lebed refused an offer to become the minister of defence in Tajikistan, arguing 'why should I help one group of Tajiks to kill another?'[22] Similarly he has been an outspoken opponent of the Russian military campaign in Chechnya. Such views set Lebed apart from Fundamentalist Nationalists and specifically from Zhirinovsky, whom he has branded as a dangerous populist fanatic.

By autumn 1995 the scene was set for a charismatic officer-politician, such as Lebed (who had finally been provoked to resign as commander of the 14th Army), to enter the political fray with determination and the intention of building a coalition among Pragmatic Nationalists. Such a conservative coalition would have excellent links with the army but not be dependent on it for its legitimacy. It could politically outflank Fundamentalist Nationalist politicians, such as Zhirinovsky, as well as maverick, extreme officers such as Varennikov, Terekhov, Achalov, or even Rutskoi. It could advance a policy based on a sober and gradual reassertion of Russian national power, a relatively more autarkic approach to the Western powers, and a focus on functionalist reintegration in the CIS region.

### The officer corps as a political actor

The political fracturing of the post-Soviet military establishments in Russia and Ukraine after autumn 1991 was accelerated by the dissolution of the Main Political Administration of the Armed Forces (MPA), which dictated the Party line to lower ranks. Bereft of MPA guidance, senior and middle/junior officers were uncertain about the legitimacy and permissible extent of political expression and they failed to reach a consensus on key domestic and foreign policy concerns. But the new articulation of opinion through officers' assemblies during 1991–5 has turned the officer corps into a political constituency of considerable potential weight.

The collapse of the Union and the formal efforts to divide the former unified military structure into national constituents acted to politicize even the most apathetic of officers. The contest of service oaths between CIS, Russia, and Ukraine early in 1992 forced officers to identify with a specific nation-state, counter to all their 'internationalist' indoctrination.[23] This process proved to be invidious and divisive for both ethnic Russian and ethnic Ukrainian officers (and the distinction often was moot) as well as for officers of other nationality groups. A distinct 'Russian' officer stratum has only slowly emerged.

First, officers based in Ukraine who chose to affiliate with Russia were cast adrift and repatriated regardless of their will. Secondly, officers who are ethnic Ukrainians or Belarusians serving outside those states who chose to identify with their homelands could still face long periods of residence in the foreign state where they were deployed, since Ukraine and Belarus have been able to absorb the numbers of officers who wish to return only slowly. Thirdly, the position of officers who, regardless of their ethnicity,

opted to continue their service in the states in which they were
based has also been problematic. Tens of thousands of these officers have faced early retirement, despite the professionalization
of forces, as deployed formations in Russia and Ukraine have been
reduced for the new national armies. At the same time nationalists in Kiev have encouraged a campaign to reduce the number of
Russian officers serving in the new Ukrainian army (some 50 per
cent of the total). Such officers have not been fully trusted by their
new political leaders. Indeed, many of these officers took the oath
to Ukraine in the belief that the armed forces would remain joint
forces with organizational ties to Russia.

As a result of these factors, the principle that the armed forces
should be manned according to citizenship rather than nationality
has not prevented national identity from remaining a factor tend-
ing to politicize and divide the international perspectives of the
officer corps in the Slavic states.

Furthermore, during 1991–4 Russian forces outside Russian
borders in the Baltic states and Transcaucasia were beleaguered
and branded by local politicians as occupiers. Slavic officers who
were based for years in the Baltic states, and often had retired
there, actively resisted efforts to uproot them and agitated politically for their 'rights' through Baltic officer groups (see below). In
the Central Asian CIS states the overwhelmingly Slavic officer corps
has become a buttress of support for close integration between
these states and Russia. In Tajikistan no less than the Baltic states,
diaspora officers' groups appeared to vote quite heavily for Vladimir
Zhirinovsky's Liberal Democratic Party in the December 1993 elections, and provided a reliable constituency, even when repatriated,
for future Fundamentalist Nationalist political parties and factions.

*Officers' organizations*

Although Yeltsin retained the support of Grachev and some
other military commanders in spring 1993 this provided no guarantee that he could rely on key military units in a crisis with an
intransigent parliament. Indeed, Grachev's slow and reluctant commitment of military forces on behalf of Yeltsin in the crucial confrontation with parliament in September–October 1993 reflected
the ambivalent views of the officer corps at large, which had
become increasingly critical of political authority. During 1991–3

views within the Russian officer corps on reform in Russia, the CIS, and Russian national interests were often more strongly held than in Russian society at large.

The new political consciousness of the officer corps emerged in the late 1980s and was fostered by the officers who had been elected to soviets at various levels. A clear division between the senior ranks and those beneath them emerged from the voting patterns of 'officer deputies' in the Russian parliament.[24] The dividing line in rough terms was at the rank of colonel. Colonels Viktor Alksnis and Nikolai Petrushenko, leaders of the reactionary Soyuz group in the Congress of People's Deputies, clashed with proponents of radical military reform from the democratic opposition, such as Major Vladimir Lopatin. Yet many disillusioned junior officers were swayed by the nationalist rhetoric of Soyuz. Alksnis and Petrushenko sought to exploit this mood of despair and disorientation after the August 1991 coup and developed close relations with Zhirinovsky and his extremist party.

The political assertiveness within the officer corps surfaced at a huge conference of the All-Army Officers' Assembly in mid-January 1992, where some 71 per cent of 2,000 officers polled favoured the restoration of the Soviet state within its former borders. Some 76 per cent of officers at the Assembly believed that the military, rather than politicians, should have the decisive voice in questions concerning the future of the armed forces. There was strong support too, for Rutskoi as national leader—36 per cent—and Alksnis—29 per cent—compared to Yeltsin—21 per cent. Alksnis called for the creation of a Co-ordinating Council of the Officers' Assembly to represent the views of the officer corps at talks with the leadership of the post-Soviet states on military and strategic issues.[25]

The Officers' Assembly elected a Co-ordinating Council of 120–30 officers. This failed to get the specific mandate Alksnis sought. But it was not surprising that the Russian press speculated on the formation of an 'Officers' Party' united around a great-power and imperial ideology, and suggested that the fate of the army would come to be decided not in government but in the officers' assemblies.[26]

The main concern of the officers, expressed in an appeal issued by the Officers' Assembly to parliaments and heads of government of the CIS states, was during a transitional period 'to preserve the integrity of state borders, a single security system, a single strategic military territory, and a single system of command and control of the armed forces'.[27] In subsequent meetings of Russian officers in spring and summer 1992 two goals were reiterated—a unified state and a unified army.

This posed a contradiction, since officers must have been aware of the likely violent outcome of any efforts to pursue their main objective. At the January 1992 Officers' Assembly meeting some 57 per cent of officers polled believed that armed conflicts were possible in the near future between Russia and other CIS republics.[28] By June 68 per cent foresaw a high probability of armed conflict between the Russian army and armed formations of the former USSR republics in those regions where Russian units remained deployed (including in Moldova 46 per cent; Chechnya 43 per cent; Georgia 35 per cent; Azerbaijan 31 per cent; and Armenia 15 per cent).[29] While the Transdnestria enclave was clearly a flash-point, most officers were unprepared to transfer this area to Moldova, and many were reportedly ready to volunteer to go to the region if Romania were to interfere in the conflict.[30]

By May 1992 the Co-ordinating Council of the Officers' Assembly had drawn up extensive draft regulations governing its functions and activities.[31] It issued a large number of projects, decrees, and instructions in the form of so-called 'recommendations' to the commander of the CIS Joint Forces and the Russian Defence Minister on policy in the Baltics, in the Transcaucasus and in the Black Sea Fleet. However, the military command rejected these approaches and sought to disown the Co-ordinating Council.[32] By the end of 1992 Defence Minister Grachev was adamantly opposed to any political discussion by officers' assemblies, although they continued to function legally throughout the army at the regimental level and below.

Perhaps the most politicized of these assemblies have been those based outside the Russian Federation—for example the Black Sea Fleet officers' assemblies. This subgroup began to agitate more vociferously after the Dagomys agreement on the Black Sea Fleet in June 1992, which left the position of Russian naval officers more precarious. Over that summer they promoted the idea of a referendum for all Crimea and presented a series of demands to the Russian and Ukrainian leaderships.[33] Since then the focus of their efforts has been to preserve the Black Sea Fleet as a single entity for the transitional period and to keep Sevastopol as its main base.[34] The Moscow summit agreement between Yeltsin and Kravchuk in June 1993 on dividing the fleet on a 50-50 basis was promptly denounced by the officers' assembly of the fleet. Vice-President Rutskoi himself had urged the assembly to reject the agreement—a striking example of high-level agitation among discontented officers by the potential leader of a Russian military-political coalition.

The Officers' Assembly and its elected bodies preserved a certain respectability and avoided the impression of seeking overtly to intervene in inter-state matters. This was not the case with the separate, reactionary association, the Officers' Union, created in December 1991. This body appeared to have little formal connection with the All-Army Officers' Assembly. It became part of the National Salvation Front and may have harboured the ambition of developing into the Front's military wing.

Led by Colonel Stanislav Terekhov, the Officers' Union offered a cocktail of militant Russian nationalism with a strong dose of neo-communism. Terekhov railed against the 'financial-economic and political diktat of the West'. The principal goal of the Union was to restore a strong state within the borders of the former Soviet Union.[35] It sought to retain a unified, indivisible army on this territory, to stop the creation of national armies and the withdrawal of Russian troops from the former Soviet republics.[36] Terekhov opposed the right of self-determination in the area of the former Soviet Union and sought an end to the disarmament of Russia.[37]

In February 1993 Terekhov organized a meeting under the umbrella of the All-Russian Officers' Assembly (but in reality not sponsored by this body), which was attended by reactionary officers such as Colonel Alksnis, Colonel-General Albert Makashov, and the former KGB general Alexander Sterligov.[38] Terekhov repudiated the START-2 Treaty, which he interpreted as American control over Russian arms, and participants accused Defence Minister Grachev of high treason.[39] Despite the extremist tone of the meeting, at least some Russian observers claimed that it faithfully reflected real sentiments in the army and the conflict between the high command and the officer corps.[40]

A second more limited meeting was held under the same aegis in the Russian White House, in March, provoking interest in the

Union's links with parliamentary chairman Khasbulatov. In fact
the former Russian Deputy Defence Minister and Russian People's Deputy Colonel-General Vladislav Achalov, who had been
appointed chairman of Khasbulatov's 'analytical centre', attended
the officers meeting and was voted as their candidate for Defence
Minister.[41] This suggests that at least some of the senior military command may have been ready to agitate among officers on
behalf of the opposition.

A more alarming tendency still was for political parties to appeal
directly to officers and military commanders to defy the Ministry
of Defence. In November 1992 the opposition parliamentary bloc
Russian Unity sent personal messages urging the commanders of
the various arms of the Armed Forces and the Moscow Garrison
not to obey Ministry orders (on the grounds that the government
had been illegally formed).[42] This kind of agitation became more
widespread early in 1993.

The real level of support for views of Terekhov's kind among
Russian officers at large at the time is difficult to gauge. Opinion polls over summer 1992 and the data of military sociologists
that November suggested that about two-thirds of officers would
have liked to have a military-based regime introduced in Russia, and opposition nationalist forces had the support of 70 per
cent of officers. One-third of the officer corps still favoured the
re-creation of the USSR, and the same number opposed cutting
military expenditures. One Russian general regretfully concluded
that by March 1993 the officer corps had turned into a military
party 'with a clearly outlined anti-constitutional face'.[43]

Over 1992–3 Yeltsin and Grachev sought to improve the material conditions of the officer corps. Yet evidence mounted in spring
1993 that a significant part remained opposed to Grachev, and
that neither he nor Yeltsin had unreserved support even among
the Russian General Staff. Grachev had not been forgiven by many
of these officers for the fact that in August 1991 he refused to
carry out the then Defence Minister Yazov's orders and went over
to the side of the Russian leadership.

Among officers of the Moscow Military District, who are the
most politicized, the anti-presidential mood by spring 1993 was
reportedly strong. In a lecture to officers of the district a colonel
from the officers' association argued that Russia was unprotected
and defenceless, vulnerable to military intervention and extortion.[44]

Currents hostile to Yeltsin were even stronger among Russian forces in the Baltic states.[45] Reports even surfaced that an underground network of cells, commencing with troops in the Baltic States, had been formed within the armed forces, aiming at a military dictatorship and reunification of the Slavic bloc: Russia, Ukraine, and Belarus.[46]

Against this background it is not surprising that Grachev hesitated to order military action against the parliament in October 1993 and was uncertain of the reaction of officers in key units faced with the choice between supporting Yeltsin and Rutskoi-Khasbulatov (and their proclaimed 'defence minister' Achalov). In the event, open rebellion among military officers in Moscow was confined to the predictably irreconcilable Colonel Stanislav Terekhov, along with sub-units of the Union of Officers headed by Colonel-General Albert Makashov.

In addition, unco-ordinated groups of armed fighters from the 'Dniester republic', including some ex-Soviet OMON officers formerly serving in the Baltic states, and some officers from Abkhazia, joined the forces defending the Russian Supreme Soviet. In supporting Rutskoi these groups saw a chance to rebuild the Soviet Union (as one-third of officers polled a year earlier favoured). But most officers of this persuasion were not prepared to risk civil war in pursuit of such a goal. Yeltsin chose subsequently to describe those groups which came to the defence of parliament as mercenaries whose actions were unrelated to the defence of the Dniester and Abkhaz autonomous regions. Yet the incident showed that the Russian officers outside Russia or those uprooted from their foreign deployments still represented a maverick revanchist force in Russian politics.

The crushing of parliamentary resistance in autumn 1993 failed to eradicate revanchist currents in the officer corps. In April 1994 the Officers' Union, still chaired by Terekhov, held its second all-union congress, which included representatives from nine former Soviet republics, opposition political leaders, generals of the Defence Ministry, and unit commanders. Speakers at the congress stressed that the revival of 'a great union state', the restoration of Soviet power in the republics, should remain sacred to every patriot, but this goal would be striven for by political means. Vladimir Zhirinovsky urged those present to join his Liberal Democratic Party, though no formal connection was established between the

Union and this party. Instead, the officers created the Russian State Party to cater to their political interests.[47]

The congress of the Officers' Union resolved to extend its reach by building a network of military-political structures in the power ministries not only of Russia, but also in the other former republics of the USSR. These offshoots were assigned the task of helping the process of restoring Soviet power. However, this goal assumed the collusion of the officers' organizations existing in other CIS states and their readiness to accept the eventual dissolution of their national defence structures. In this respect the Ukrainian Officers' Union, for example, finds no common ground with the extremist Russian Officers' Union.

The growing emphasis on national self-assertion in official Russian foreign policy served to raise the profile of the Russian Officers' Union in 1995, despite its controversial history and its continued unofficial status. The annual meeting of what was called on this occasion the 'All-Russia Army Officers' Assembly' in February 1995 provided a platform for the disgraced Colonel-General Vladislav Achalov and retired general Valentin Varennikov. Terekhov claimed that the assembly would become a permanent body which would 'act for strengthening the defence capacity of the country and unmask anti-national forces which destroyed the USSR and are completing this process in Russia'.[48]

These views were shared not just by an extreme fringe of officers. The first extensive and rigorous survey of the opinions of senior Russian officers, in 1994, revealed a group of men deeply disenchanted with Russia's place in the world, fearful of the future and resentful of the recent past. The most popular foreign policy goal, endorsed by 55 per cent of officers in this survey, was the re-establishment of Russia as a great power enjoying respect throughout the world. The possible adverse impact of this approach on relations with the West was not a major concern since very few of the officers believed in the possibility of full co-operation with NATO.

With respect to the CIS states, the majority of the officers polled expected that Belarus and Ukraine would be reunited with Russia by the end of the decade at the latest. This was consistent with their identification of Belarus, Ukraine, and Kazakhstan as the clearest 'friends' of Russia, alongside India. In contrast, the Baltic states, together with Afghanistan, held the highest ranking among

Russia's 'enemies'.[49] This suggests that while reintegration of the Slavic core of the CIS states with Russia is a conscious expectation of senior officers, the majority now accept that the Baltic states can no longer be retrieved into the fold.

The officer corps does not represent an independent political group with united views on concrete political action. Yet the strongly held nationalist beliefs of a large proportion of senior officers (though arguably more often resembling Pragmatic Nationalism than Fundamentalist Nationalism) act as a constraint on the formation of Russian international security policies, especially in relation to the CIS. Neither Defence Minister Grachev nor his successor can afford to alienate the officer corps while political legitimacy in Moscow is so fragile. This would result in officers becoming increasingly receptive to political appeals by organizations which lie outside the normal chain of command. These in turn could emerge as powerful lobbies challenging the policies of the Russian President and his ministers.

## *The Cossack revival*

Nationalist currents in the Russian officer corps are reflected in a tendency to turn a blind eye to the controversial role assumed by revived Russian Cossack groups of defending the rights of Russians in CIS conflict zones. Cossack groups proclaim distinctly reactionary political goals. The ataman (chief) of the Union of Russian Cossacks, Aleksandr Martynov, has stated that the task of the Cossacks is to reunite the dismantled Union on a new basis. He has compared their role to that of the volunteers on the republican side in the Spanish civil war. They will take up arms and play 'an active part in settling inter-ethnic conflicts'.[50]

The Cossacks have developed a particularly strong role in the north Caucasus, where since early 1992 they have opposed the idea of a union of Caucasian states (which could include various Slavic regions in its zone of influence). But their most active commitment since the collapse of the USSR has been to the defence of the Slav enclave of Transdnestria in autumn 1991 and early 1992, which was allied politically to the Russian 14th Army. The role of the Cossacks in Moldova further strained Russian–Ukrainian relations, since Kiev was inclined to view them as Russian mercenaries acting in breach of international law.[51] The issue was particularly sensitive for Ukraine because of the interest among at least certain Cossacks in establishing an independent republic on the Don. Yet the Cossacks had powerful patrons among nationalist politicians in Moscow, initially including Rutskoi. Yeltsin has approved legislation which assigns them a formal role in protecting Russian state borders. In view of the ethnic mix of the outer borders, this traditional role is controversial and may appear provocative to other CIS states.

## The lower ranks

The political organization of the Russian officer corps overshadows that of Russian military servicemen, and the servicemen's organizations have no obvious channels to influence foreign policy decisions. But (bearing in mind the 'Afghan syndrome') the outlook of the lower ranks of the army could influence Russian state decisions on matters such as military deployments outside Russian borders and acts which threaten or cause significant military casualties, such as the campaign in Chechnya.

President Yeltsin's readiness to heed the concerns of the lower ranks was encouraged by declarations by leaders of the Shchit (Shield) Union and the Servicemen's Union in spring 1993 that the army should remain outside politics, by their support for the President, and by their condemnation of agitation by the Officers' Union.[52] In October 1993 the co-ordinating council of Shchit urged its members to support Yeltsin in his confrontation with parliament and suspended the powers of its own chairman, Vitaly Urazhtsev, for siding with parliament.[53]

The all-Russian referendum in April 1993 may have helped to politicize the lower ranks in the army, since in voting whether to place trust in President Yeltsin servicemen were also making a judgement about their military commander-in-chief. However, this danger was reduced first by the decision not to conduct the referendum among Black Sea Fleet personnel or in Russian military units stationed outside Russia (such as the Transcaucasus) and secondly by the decision that the votes of other servicemen should not be announced in military units (though they would be included in the final roll of votes).

The first decision meant that those enlisted men whose immediate concerns could have foreign policy relevance were disenfranchised. At the same time Grachev sought to placate both the lower ranks and mid-ranking officers by resolving that three-quarters of the 1993 military budget should go towards the salaries and social needs of servicemen. Ameliorating the social deprivation of servicemen has to remain a high priority on the Defence Ministry agenda to help forestall military fragmentation or anarchy at lower levels, something which would be particularly dangerous in a period of growing regionalism or secessionist impulses in the Russian Federation and on its periphery.

## *Military views and influence on foreign and security policy issues*

The preceding analysis indicates that in Russia both the military leadership and the officer corps have gained political leverage since the 1991 coup attempt and have entered the political decision-making arena. To clarify the impact of military lobbies this section analyses military perspectives and influence on specific issues for foreign and security policy.

Military influence has been expressed in three main areas. First, military leaders have shaped the formation of military doctrine, including the nature of threat perceptions, which they see as lying within their professional remit. Secondly, the Russian military command has occasionally sought direct influence over major national security or foreign policy decisions which lie beyond the scope of their professional responsibilities. Thirdly, Russian military leaders have promoted military solutions, including the use of peacekeeping forces, to restore 'stability' in the 'near abroad'.

The coherence and effectiveness of the Russian military leadership and officers' groups in political lobbying is reduced by a continued *esprit de corps* inherited from the Soviet period of a kind which tends to divide the services. This is clear with respect to plans for military reform. For example, in 1989–91 officers in the ground forces were less persuaded than those in the élite services by the need to shift from a largely conscript-based system to one emphasizing volunteer professional forces. Grachev's appointment and the Russian Ministry of Defence's adoption of the concept of Mobile Forces demonstrated the ascendancy of the Airborne Forces and Air Forces and the decline in influence of the formerly dominant ground forces command. Thus on certain issues 'military' views may reflect distinct service interests, despite the efforts of the General Staff to co-ordination these interests. These views have also reflected a certain degree of rivalry over competences between the Ministry of Defence and the General Staff.

A second complicating issue since the dissolution of the USSR has been the unrealistic attempt by CIS officials to develop common CIS-wide military reform principles or a common coalition military doctrine for at least a limited CIS subgroup of 'allies'. The decree setting up the Russian armed forces gave them the role at the outset of defending the state interests of both Russia and—within coalition forces—its allies.[54] As Commander-in-Chief of the CIS joint armed forces Marshal Yevgeny Shaposhnikov occupied an ambiguous position both in relation to the defence policy apparatus of Russia itself and that of other CIS states. The option of a limited CIS coalition receded when the joint CIS military command was dissolved in June 1993. Yet after a CIS summit in April 1994 Grachev was still calling on the member states to unite their armed forces as the first step towards a new defence union.

This outcome is hardly likely and has not been favoured by the majority of Russian officers. Already in November 1992, for example, opinion polls suggested that some 60 per cent of officers disapproved of decisions on military issues being made by the CIS heads of state.[55] Ukrainian officers have strongly resisted such a CIS role. This groundswell of discontent has helped undermine the CIS as an effective decision-making actor on military-security matters. But the discussion in CIS forums of the option of a CIS defence union or of joint CIS forces has confused the process of Russian national security decision-making. Secondly, it has further blurred the distinction for many officers, at least on the psychological level, between Russian state defence and national security policy and the defence policies pursued by other independent CIS states in the post-Soviet period. This has helped to retard Russian military disengagement from these states and made it easier for Russian military leaders (and nationalist politicians) to support the idea that Russia must adopt new security policy responsibilities for the CIS region as a whole.

## *Military doctrine and threat perceptions*

National security policy in Russia will ultimately be determined by official (if undeclared) threat perceptions and these will also underlie military doctrine. In formulating this doctrine the professional military (military officers) have played a vital role.

The General Staff's traditional role in developing the military-technical side of military doctrine was reaffirmed in the Russian Law on Defence of October 1992. The functions of the General Staff contained in this law include developing proposals relating to Russian military doctrine, and to the structure, composition, deployment, and tasks of Russian armed forces.[56] The General Staff should direct operational and strategic planning and the management of troops, while the Ministry of Defence is assigned political and administrative functions.

However, because of the political sensitivity of Russian force deployments in the CIS, these functions have overlapped in current conditions and the Ministry has played a more extensive and prominent role than suggested by the Law on Defence. This has been assisted by Defence Minister Grachev's seat in the Security Council—a privilege denied the chief of the General Staff, Colonel-General Mikhail Kolesnikov. This outcome and the growing unpopularity of Defence Minister Grachev led to discussion in autumn 1994 of the option of strengthening the General Staff, and of shifting the Ministry to a secondary role.

Whatever the balance of responsibilities between these two key military bodies, the Russian military's presence outside Russian borders, which is reinforced by its new 'peacekeeping' role, has increased its leverage on Russian international security policy overall. Its influence has also been enhanced by the fact that the military establishment has an indispensable contribution to make in tackling the most important foreign policy tasks, as they were identified, for example, in the Foreign Ministry's draft 'concept' of Russian foreign policy published at the end of 1992: (1) to curtail and regulate armed conflicts around Russia, and to prevent them from spreading to Russian territory; (2) to guarantee human and minority rights of Russians and the Russian-speaking population in the 'near abroad'.[57] The final document approved by President Yeltsin in April 1993, entitled 'Guide-lines of the Foreign Policy Concept of the Russian Federation', not only listed external threats to Russian security but identified a whole series of military-related Russian state interests.[58]

However, despite Yeltsin's 'guide-lines', the nature of military threats to Russia and the military needs of the state have been controversial and ambiguous. In the initial debate on Russian military doctrine in 1992–3 particular attention was paid to a highly controversial and in many respects regressive draft doctrine developed by the General Staff Academy (a body which for long had been directed by the highly conservative Colonel-General Igor Rodionov) and published in May 1992.[59] Unlike the Russian Foreign Ministry's draft concept of foreign policy this document did not pay much attention to the danger of conflict on Russia's periphery spilling over into Russia and undermining the integrity of the Russian Federation. It also tended to downplay the need for low-intensity operations and the means to avert them, which was implicit in the foreign policy concept. But this was not intended to downgrade the role of the armed forces. The traditional Soviet emphasis in the draft on the need to maintain massed reserve forces for the contingency of large-scale conventional war was calculated to raise the profile of the armed forces in Russian international security policy.

The most controversial section of the draft military doctrine in its foreign policy implications, however, was the declaration that 'the violations of rights of Russia's citizens and population in the former republics of the USSR who ethnically and culturally identify themselves with Russia may be a major source of conflicts.' This formally justified the role of the armed forces in supporting beleaguered Russians outside Russian borders.[60] The May draft was itself a compromise document and at least one other version was far harsher in terms of portraying Russia as a re-emerging great power and describing the need to maintain a sphere of influence in the territory of the former Soviet Union.[61]

During 1992–3 the controlling voice of the General Staff prevented military officers from promoting alternative, perhaps less conservative, versions of a Russian military doctrine or a framework for thinking about defence. The liberal Major-General Aleksandr Vladimirov was exceptional in developing an alternative draft, which he personally presented to Yeltsin in April 1992 and which he claims had some influence. This draft supported the principle of defence sufficiency and characterized the CIS as a regional subsystem of the United Nations based on UN principles.[62]

Yet all these drafts lacked legal status. The political statement on the tasks of the armed forces adopted by the December 1992 Congress of People's Deputies, or previous parliamentary resolutions and laws during summer and autumn 1992 (such as the October 1992 Law on Defence), which contained general principles underlying military doctrine, had more legal authority until the Russian military doctrine was formally approved in October 1993. However, such parliamentary resolutions were confined mainly to regulating military programmes and military spending.

Some non-military political factions acted as lobbies promoting their own principles for military policy more systematically. For example, 'national patriotic forces' represented by the Russian National Council passed a package of documents in this area at the first congress of the RNC in August 1992. A premise of these documents was that Russian military security requires the preservation and support of its military-economic and military-technical potential—a veiled reference which evokes the ambitious military goals of Soviet years.[63]

The nationalist opposition and conservative military leaders could join forces in seeking official sanction for conservative military principles and threat assessments. However, the formal arrangements for the elaboration of military doctrine suggest that the process remained under political control.

According to this procedure the Ministries of Defence and Foreign Affairs should present their views on doctrinal precepts. The parliamentary Committee on Defence and Security should in turn prepare certain parts of any draft document, which should then be discussed in the Security Council.[64] However, the key influence of the professional military was confirmed at a high-profile meeting of the Russian Security Council on 28 February 1993 when President Yeltsin asked the top Russian military leaders to play a major role in developing the *political* element of the new national military doctrine (a responsibility held by the higher bodies of the Communist Party under the old Soviet system). In so doing he effectively abdicated civilian control over this highly significant area of national security policy.

Remarkably, another item on the agenda of discussion with the military leaders at this key meeting was the concept of Russia's foreign policy. The rationale Yeltsin claimed for involving the military in this discussion was that 'until we have a properly structured concept of military doctrine and foreign policy activity we will be forced to take defensive positions'—a position, he noted, to support from his military audience, in which the armed forces had never before been placed.[65]

It is significant in this context that even the Russian Foreign Ministry's draft concept of foreign policy, referred to above, contained some of the key language of the draft Russia military doctrine: it stated that Russia would vigorously oppose all attempts to build up the political and military presence of third countries in the states adjoining Russia, and that the strengthening of the 'unified military-strategic space' was an urgent task for Russian foreign policy makers. It seems clear that in 1992–3 conservative military views were helping to shape Russian foreign policy priorities.[66]

They were also evident in the Russian military doctrine finally approved in October 1993. The participants in the meeting which clinched the terms of this doctrine included not only senior members of the government but also chiefs of the armed forces and members of the Defence Ministry collegium. The doctrine is forward-looking compared to the May 1992 draft in placing emphasis on Russian mobile and peacekeeping forces rather than on the need to maintain large-scale standing forces. But it gives the impression that Russian military forces will act as an arm of foreign policy, especially in neighbouring CIS states, and it takes a hard-headed attitude to Russian national interests.

The extent of the control exercised by the Russian high command over the development of military doctrine is highlighted by the contrary case of Ukraine. Here the draft military doctrine considered by parliament in autumn 1992 was drawn up mainly by the Ministry of Defence in Kiev, in consultation with the parliamentary Commission on Defence and State Security and the Ukrainian Defence Council. But it was revised by so many tiers of government that the distinct military input was no longer apparent.[67] Once it was presented to the Supreme Soviet by Defence Minister Morozov in November 1992 it was rejected outright anyway (largely as a result of the growing pro-nuclear current among deputies) and a revised draft in May 1993 was also shelved. The doctrine was finally approved in October of that year.

Military influence was less evident still in determining the basic foreign policy guide-lines of Ukraine. The heated debate in the Supreme Council over the draft document 'Basic Directions of

Ukrainian Foreign Policy' in July 1993 revolved essentially around whether Ukraine should exclude the nuclear weapons factor from its foreign policy—a matter of clear military interest. Yet on this matter the main division of views was clearly between parliamentary deputies and the Foreign (rather than Defence) Ministry.[68]

The Ukrainian Law on Defence assigns the Defence Ministry the formal role of defining threats to the state. Yet on issues related to the central questions of strategic nuclear weapons and defence policy *vis-a-vis* Russia, decisions appear to have originated in the presidential apparatus or the Security Council and may subsequently just have been refined in the Ministry of Defence. The military command is left to develop the military-technical side to military doctrine.

Why then has the Ukrainian military command failed to confirm for itself the central role of Russian military leaders in defining the higher *socio-political* side of national military doctrine (on the nature of threats etc.)? The root cause may be the critical division in Ukraine over the degree of threat represented by Russia—a political issue too important just for military chiefs. No clear consensus on this issue existed among senior officers. Since Ukraine became independent many have been persuaded that the main danger for Ukraine lies on its eastern and northeastern borders (from Russia). But others in the officer corps (which remains heavily Russian in composition), despite the controversy over Crimea, have been loath to abandon entirely the idea of some kind of future Ukrainian-Russian military alliance. Their belief has been that the Russian political establishment will eventually abandon any 'imperial' traits it may still harbour.[69] The military tendency to avoid defining the nature of threats was also convenient for deflecting divisions among the military rank and file of the new army, which in autumn 1993 remained only 46 per cent Ukrainian in composition.[70]

If we turn from the broad principles of military doctrine to military force structuring, weapons acquisition policy and military reform more generally, it is self-evident that the Russian military command has played a prominent role in decision-making (or in blocking decisions). However, these military matters are politically controversial and the military command has not monopolized decision-making on them. Space does not permit a detailed examination of them here.

It should be noted, nevertheless, that military leaders had an important role during 1991–3 in the push to maintain powerful diversified armed forces despite the economic burden this inflicted on the state. But this goal could only be sustained if supported by influential politicians. Vice-President Rutskoi, in particular, sought an active position in the planning process to help construct a new Russian army suitable for Russia as a great power.[71] This conservative input at a high political level encouraged unrealistic expectations within the high command that powerful Russian armed forces (or CIS joint forces) appropriate for wars on a huge scale could be reconstructed from the Soviet legacy. The General Staff lobbied to retain a reserve system to provide an enormous mobilization base of the kind maintained by the Soviet Union. This plan was a central element in the May 1992 draft military doctrine and was supported by Rutskoi.[72]

Rutskoi's disgrace in autumn 1993 removed an important sponsor of traditionalist military thinking. As a result the more reformist military officers, who were engaged in a re-evaluation of the nature of future wars, supported by civilian politicians, found it easier to gain approval in October that year for the new Russian military doctrine, which questioned previous planning assumptions by placing a new emphasis on local conflicts. Despite this, strong military influence on the content of the approved doctrine is evident from its failure even to mention the notion of military reform, let alone civilian control of the armed forces or the needs of a professional army. A decree by Yeltsin in July 1994 finally permitted Russian mobilization reserves to be run down—a clear shift from Soviet-style military planning. The shift in military planning priorities towards local conflicts has now been firmly adopted by the General Staff.

A similar dynamic between military and political inputs, mediated through the Security Council, is also likely in the case of current Russian assessments of the requirements for forward defence and the establishment of military bases in the CIS region, which has become a controversial element of Russian international security policy.

## Major foreign and security policy issues

The actual extent of military influence in foreign and international security policy decision-making in Russia may be clarified by a number of case studies of major foreign and security policy issue areas and policy outcomes. Information on the relevant decisions remains scarce, but the military input can sometimes be discerned. The cases analysed in this section are not directly related to CIS conflicts; decisions concerning such conflicts are analysed separately below.

For Russia, open military efforts to exert leverage on significant security and foreign policy decisions unrelated to CIS conflicts were most visible in the period between the August 1991 coup and the crushing of parliament in October 1993 at times when there were clear divisions in the government and when President Yeltsin himself was undecided. In other cases military leaders no doubt used back channels to relay their views on policy proposals and to exert influence in a consultative capacity. Since October 1993 there has been evidence of more direct military 'persuasion' or 'dissuasion' in major policy decisions. This experience contrasts to that of Ukraine, where there is no evidence of the military command circumventing regular consultative processes to press their views on Presidents Kravchuk or Kuchma over key security policy issues, for example over plans for the political future of Crimea. Nor has the military leadership taken its case directly to parliament in Kiev when the president has appeared undecided.

## The Kurile Islands dispute

Russian policy over the Kurile Islands is an interesting case of policy promotion by the military at the expense of the Russian Foreign Ministry line. The Foreign Ministry tended initially to favour negotiations over the disputed territories, while Russian military leaders aimed to prevent a military withdrawal by Russia from the Kuriles (let alone the abandonment of any of these territories). Russian military officers argued that the islands form a key link in the Russian Far Eastern defence system.[73]

Military involvement in this case was most obvious in the form of a General Staff document which was circulated to Russian deputies at a highly politicized Supreme Soviet meeting in July 1992 which was devoted to Yeltsin's planned visit to Japan. This document sought to provide a detailed military-strategic rationale against making any concessions to Japan over the ownership of the disputed Kurile Islands. Highly conservative in its thrust, it portrayed Japanese-American military capabilities in the region as evidence of an aggressive military buildup threatening the Russian mainland.[74] This crude lobbying certainly contributed to Yeltsin's decision to call off his controversial planned visit to Tokyo. Back-channel military lobbying could similarly have helped to persuade Yeltsin to call off his rescheduled visit in May 1993.

But there are clearly limits to the ability of the Russian military to freeze Russian–Japanese relations. Within a week of calling on the military to crush parliament in October 1993 Yeltsin finally carried out his visit to Tokyo. While he did not offer negotiations on the Kuriles he promised to withdraw the 5,000 Russian troops stationed there, which would leave only a border-guard presence.

### The conflict in the former Yugoslavia

Russian military leaders also promoted policies towards the former Yugoslavia which conflicted with the line pursued at the time by the Russian Foreign Ministry. For example, in April 1993 Defence Minister Grachev openly opposed plans to introduce additional mixed United Nations peacekeeping troop contingents on the territory of the former Yugoslavia. He also declared himself against any additional deployment of Russian troops, arguing that the policy of the Defence Ministry would be to prevent Russia from being drawn into a war which potentially could spread beyond the Balkan region.[75] He was undoubtedly thinking of the politically combustible regions on the periphery of the former USSR. In contrast, Foreign Minister Kozyrev, who had not yet abandoned a Liberal Westernizer approach, appeared at the time to favour an additional Russian military commitment if requested by the United Nations.

The Russian Foreign Ministry was criticized by military officers in Moscow for exercising a supine policy over the former Yugoslavia in the face of Western initiatives and for too readily lending support to an essentially anti-Serbian policy contrary to traditional Russian/Soviet interests. Kozyrev's subsequent sharp criticism of NATO air strikes against Serbian positions in Bosnia served to build bridges to the Russian Defence Ministry and to develop a more consistent, if critical, Russian attitude to Western involvement in this region.

### NATO membership and Eastern Europe

A similar feeling within the Russian high command that a line should be drawn in making concessions to the West in Eastern

Europe, that the Russian 'sphere of interests' should be more clearly asserted in the post-Soviet period, encouraged a harder Russian policy towards the option of extending NATO membership eastwards. This option had never been agreeable to the new Russian military leadership but was only firmly disputed after Yeltsin's reliance on the military grew in the aftermath of the storming of the Russian parliament in October 1993. In a clear reflection of opinion among Russian military planners, Yeltsin then stated that NATO should not expand eastwards but should join Moscow in guaranteeing the security of the former Warsaw Pact countries. He reversed the position he had adopted only a few weeks before, according to which Russia would not oppose Polish membership in NATO.

In this case the Russian Foreign and Defence Ministries agreed on the need to prevent Russia from becoming isolated in the face of an expanded NATO. Kozyrev, Grachev, and especially the former CIS Joint Forces commander Marshal Shaposhnikov all expressed strong views on the matter. However, Russian military leaders were the most alarmist. For example, they emphasized the risks of NATO acquiring a new role in tackling regional conflicts, perhaps as a military arm of the United Nations. In this context they denounced the idea of NATO 'peacekeeping forces' being primed for intervention in conflicts in the former Soviet Union (though this was hardly likely) as flatly unacceptable, especially given Russia's own extensive role in these conflicts.

## The Black Sea Fleet dispute

After the agreement between Yeltsin and Kravchuk in June 1993 on dividing the Black Sea Fleet 50-50, the Russian Defence Ministry publicly questioned the decisions reached at the summit level. Grachev stated openly that a joint Black Sea Fleet under a single command would be preferable to splitting the fleet and suggested that changes to the June agreement might be necessary, taking into account 'the opinion of the fleet's officers and Crimeans' needs'.[76] This was an area of international security policy where Ukrainian military leaders and the Ukrainian Ministry of Defence were likewise particularly vocal. The Russian Defence Ministry accused its Ukrainian counterpart of seeking to terminate the inter-state Yalta agreement on the division of the fleet.[77]

Russian commanders feel committed to retaining their historical

naval power in the Black Sea, while Ukrainian naval leaders have
been defiant that 'independent Ukraine will never yield the right
to have a mighty, battleworthy, and modern Navy on the Black
Sea.'[78] Economic constraints meant that the Russian aspiration
was more realistic than the Ukrainian (this was demonstrated by
the agreement reached between Presidents Yeltsin and Kuchma in
June 1995 which envisaged a division of the naval vessels of 81.7
per cent to Russia and 18.3 per cent to Ukraine). Furthermore, there
is no evidence that the Ukrainian military has sought to usurp any
real decision-making authority from political leaders in Kiev even
on this core emotive issue.

## Arms control

In the arms control and disarmament dimension of security policy,
military inputs have been more institutionalized. The Russian
General Staff (and its Soviet predecessor) has certainly been closely
involved in decisions on major arms control treaties. It can vent its
views in internal meetings and modify official negotiating positions.
Russia also inherited from the Gorbachev period a number of new
non-military bodies involved in arms control decision-making,
attached, for example, to the Foreign Ministry.

The military command supported the Conventional Forces in
Europe (CFE) and START I treaties at the ratification stage in
parliament (despite military discontent with the former). Russia
suffers under the CFE Treaty, principally because of the irrelev-
ance now of the geostrategic balance it fixes (based on conditions
when it was signed in November 1991). The main body of the
treaty has not been directly challenged by the Russian military
command. However, from the spring of 1993 Defence Minister
Grachev argued that changes would be necessary to the quota
agreements for dividing the former Soviet equipment allocations
(which were worked out between CIS states in spring 1992)—
by implication to give Russia more flexibility where to deploy its
arms.[79] More seriously, he sought to lift the CFE Treaty sublimits
for the flank regions—a reflection of the specific military priority being given by then to the North Caucasus Military District
(a flank region in the CFE Treaty to which sublimits apply) and
plans for that region as a military-base area.

This technical dispute is a litmus test of growing Russian military influence, since it was only taken up by Yeltsin as an issue

with Western states after he used the military to storm the Russian parliament in October 1993. The Russian military command viewed the CFE Treaty as an unjust treaty foisted on them by the West and 'Shevardnadze's' foreign ministry, and hoped to redress some of this injustice even at the cost of souring relations with Western CFE Treaty partners.

In contrast the START treaties did not attract direct military criticism at the higher levels, although there were latent worries about the one-sided character of Soviet concessions.[80] Officers in the strategic deterrence forces cast doubts on Yeltsin's strategic weapons reduction proposals, but these were muted.[81] Russian military officers were distracted from the START negotiation process by the simultaneous contest of will with Ukraine and Kazakhstan over CIS/Russian control of the Soviet nuclear weapons legacy.

The controversy which rapidly developed over political control of nuclear weapons, which involves the General Staff, Ministry of Defence, the President, and ground control personnel, did not clearly lead to greater political control over nuclear-release procedures. But Russian military and political leaders sought to co-operate on this issue. Actions such as the case in February 1992 when six CIS front-line strategic bombers based in Ukraine were flown by their Russian aircrew to Russian airfields were exceptional individual acts by officers rather than orchestrated provocation or defiance by the Russian Defence Ministry.

## Russian forces outside Russia and regional conflicts

Since the dissolution of the Soviet Union, military issues have played a large role in Russian policy towards the former Soviet states. This partly reflected the widespread deployment of former Soviet forces outside Russian borders at the time the Union was dissolved. Troops in the Baltic states, Transcaucasia, and Transdnestria were brought under Russian jurisdiction. The status of 'joint' forces in Central Asia was established in bilateral treaties with Russia.

Secondly, many of the unresolved questions in the CIS have been more broadly military-related. This is clearly reflected in the guide-lines of the foreign policy concept of the Russian Federation approved by Yeltsin in April 1993.[82] In itself this inflated the role of the Russian high command outside Russian borders and created new responsibilities for them. But this role expanded further, in a controversial way, with the deployment of Russian military forces as the main component of 'peacekeeping' forces in CIS zones of regional conflict.

Overall, the scale, intrusiveness, and partisan character of Russian military activity in the 'near abroad' significantly increased the role of the Russian military command in foreign policy decision-making, partly at the expense of the Foreign Ministry.

As the Russian military leadership became more of a policy maker in its own right in the CIS, this raised the danger of incompatible and non-complementary Russian foreign and security policies being promoted in the region (see Chapter 3). In 1992 Foreign Minister Kozyrev blamed military interference for the deterioration of Russian relations with several of its new neighbour-states. He argued at that time that Russian military attitudes linked to declarations by opposition nationalists in Moscow (on matters such as the future of Crimea) had sown international distrust and stimulated a nationalist backlash in certain of the successor states including Ukraine.[83] At the end of 1993 Kozyrev openly complained that 'the armed forces have a foreign policy of their own' in the 'near abroad'.[84]

In August 1992 the Council for Foreign and Defence Policy drew attention to the danger of the militarization of inter-state relations. It expressed the fear that 'the territory of the former USSR will become a zone where military power will play an essential political role.'[85] By spring 1993 Russian analysts argued that while the new Russian military command accepted that military means should be subordinated to political ends, it was increasingly convinced that the military should have a large and perhaps the decisive say in formulating the latter.[86]

In fact political leaders, including Yeltsin and even Kozyrev, avoided confrontation with such military ambitions in the period from spring 1993. Their more assertive nationalist line in the CIS harmonized to a large extent with the military's priorities. This policy shift reduced the incentive for generals in the high command to press for more explicit and independent influence over Russian policy towards other CIS states.

Despite this trend, from its inception the new Russian high command sought to define or modify Russian policy on the emotive issue of Russian force deployments outside Russia and the time-frame for troop withdrawals back to Russian territory. This stand was encouraged by rebellious demands issued by officers in the beleaguered military formations in the Baltic states, the Transcaucasus, and Moldova, and it was reflected in partisan Russian military involvement in various conflicts on the periphery of the former Soviet Union.

## The Baltic states

The Baltic states formed a kind of testing ground for autonomous Russian and Soviet military actions after the winter of 1990–1, when political leaders in Moscow failed to prevent local acts of repression or to act against conservative Russian military lobbies. As early as December 1990 an Extraordinary Congress of Representatives of the Army Community of the Baltic Region was held. It formed a Union of Baltic Servicemen dedicated to preserving the Soviet Union and taking decisive measures against separatist and nationalist activities.[87] Bodies representing the interests of these servicemen continued to exist as a powerful lobby in the Baltic states even after the latter gained their independence.

The role of officers' assemblies in the Baltic states was especially controversial. In 1991–2 they exerted consistent leverage to block any decision to withdraw Russian troops fully from the Baltic states, at least until they could be guaranteed proper accommodation in Russia. In this they had more than tacit support from the local Russian military commander, Colonel-General Mironov. After Yeltsin promised the Baltic states that local Russian forces would be fully withdrawn, the Co-ordinating Council of Officers' Assemblies of the Northwestern Group of Forces announced that they would boycott any decision to pull out. To support their case they petitioned the Russian parliament and its then chairman Ruslan Khasbulatov.[88]

The Russian military command dismissed some of the more extreme officers in the Baltic officers' assemblies from service at the end of 1992. Nevertheless, the Russian Defence Ministry unilaterally declared the suspension of troop withdrawals from the Baltic states in October 1992, despite Yeltsin's promise on withdrawals.[89] In March 1993 Defence Minister Grachev announced the suspension of force withdrawals from Latvia and Estonia. In reality Russian units continued to be withdrawn from all the Baltic states. But the high command tended to support the policy

line of the Russian parliament toward the Baltic states by seeking
to link the final withdrawal of Russian troops from Latvia and
Estonia with the repeal of legislation disenfranchising their Russian minorities.

The confusion in Russian policy may be explained by reports
that the military establishment was negotiating with the governments of the Baltic states over the withdrawal of the Northwestern Group of Forces without any political oversight. In particular
the Russian Foreign Minister was left aside during negotiations by
the Defence Ministry on the withdrawal of forces from Lithuania.
This led to strong criticism of the ensuing withdrawal accord by
Foreign Minister Kozyrev and calls by him for its revision.[90] By
early 1994 Kozyrev's new, Pragmatic Nationalist foreign policy
stance had brought him closer to Russian military opinion and led
him to suggest that a full withdrawal of troops from the region of
the Baltic states would create a security vacuum and leave ethnic
Russians undefended.[91] This posturing did not, however, prevent
the eventual withdrawal of all the regular Russian garrisons from
the Baltic states by 1995.

## The Transcaucasus

In the Transcaucasus the continued deployment of Russian troops
has been similarly influenced by military lobbies and by a growing
commitment on the part of Russian military leaders to shape the
outcome of regional conflicts. The Russian high command has
tended to view the Transcaucasian region as a single strategic
entity, and this has driven efforts to acquire military facilities in
all three CIS states.

In spring 1992 the Russian military leadership was undecided
whether to withdraw its forces fully from Transcaucasia. Vice-
President Rutskoi favoured a complete evacuation at this stage to
prevent Russian units being held hostage.[92] In their beleaguered
positions local assemblies of officers threatened to take individual
action to protect their rights if inter-state agreements failed to do
this.[93] However, most of the forces under Russian control in the
Transcaucasus were dissolved or withdrawn to Russia by late 1992.

The completion of this process was stalled by the conflict which
was taking place in the Georgian province of Abkhazia, and which
drew the Russian forces remaining in Georgia into the centre of
controversy.[94] Georgia accused them of backing Abkhazian rebels

in 1992–3 and it is likely that some Russian soldiers conscripted locally fought on the Abkhazian side. From early 1992 the Georgian president, Shevardnadze, accused Russian generals and military sub-units of constant interference in the internal affairs of Georgia through their actions in Abkhaz-held Gudauta (where a Russian division was based). This included the reported bombing of the Georgian town of Sukhumi by Russian Su-25 aircraft.[95]

Subsequently, however, a Russian policy of military engagement in the CIS region developed which reflected a growing consensus among policy making élites in Moscow (see Chapters 2 and 3). In autumn 1993 the Russian Defence Minister sought to distance Russian forces from one-sided intervention and offered to send two divisions to Abkhazia to disarm and disengage the warring parties. The Georgian government finally accepted the presence of Russian peacekeeping forces in the region in summer 1994.

Despite the signs of greater co-ordination in Russian policy, the military command was clearly pursuing its own strategic agenda in Georgia throughout this period. Grachev claimed that the Black Sea coast of the Caucasus held particular strategic and geopolitical importance for the Russian armed forces, justifying the deployment of Russian troops in the region. Leverage could be exerted on Georgia by Russian military leaders, not only by favouring Abkhaz separatists as in 1992–3, but also by providing military assistance to the Georgian government against the pro-Gamsakhurdia rebels, as was done in October 1993.[96] The agreement reached between Moscow and Tbilisi in autumn 1993, which permitted the establishment of three bases for Russian regular military forces in Georgia, should be viewed in this light.

In Armenia and Azerbaijan the opportunities for Russian military intervention in regional conflicts were limited by the disintegration and withdrawal of the former Soviet military formations, which left few deployed units in these states by spring 1993 (the 4th and 7th Armies were both disbanded). But Azerbaijan tended to blame its military failures in the Nagorny Karabakh conflict during 1992–3 partly on Russian military support for Armenia. This claim was probably unfounded in 1992, although Russian military support—perhaps in the form of intelligence—may have been a factor behind Armenian victories in summer 1993. There were also claims that Russia helped topple the Popular Front regime of Abulfaz Elchibey in Azerbaijan in this period by supplying arms to the rebel army leader. But such claims are speculative. In summer 1994 the Russian high command obtained an agreement to locate an air base in Armenia but was frustrated in attempts during 1993–4 to gain a base for its forces in neighbouring Azerbaijan.

## Transdnestria

The case of the Russian military presence in the Moldovan breakaway enclave of Transdnestria has been especially contentious. As in Abkhazia, local conscripts and perhaps even junior officers from the local Russian army (the 14th Army in Transdnestria) appear to have engaged in fighting on behalf of separatist groups—in this case in support of the 'Dnestr Republic'.[97]

This has had serious implications, since the officer corps of the 14th Army is notorious for its continued adherence to Soviet ideas and its commitment to maintaining the former Soviet border. This attitude, which is also pervasive among the Russian 'peacekeeping' contingent in the region, was encouraged by the commander of the 14th Army from 1992 to 1995, Lieutenant-General Aleksandr Lebed, who at times spoke openly in favour of restoring the USSR or a Russian empire.

Lebed vociferously expressed his political preferences in the local conflict. On different occasions he declared that his army was resolved to remain in Moldova for a long time to come; he pledged Russian military assistance to the breakaway 'Dnestr Republic'; and he endorsed the aspiration of this breakaway region to incorporate additional Moldovan territory and accede to the Russian Federation. Lebed could point to the precedent of Kaliningrad Oblast, which similarly lacks contiguity with Russia. He threatened to increase the use of force against Moldova and even defied political leaders in Moscow.[98]

In spring 1992 the Russian Foreign Minister justified the presence of the 14th Army as a 'buffer' between conflicting parties.[99] But this role held no credibility once Lebed arrived, since the 14th Army openly assisted the Transdnestrian forces and Lebed's attacks on the Moldovan leadership undermined the efforts of Russian diplomacy.[100] Only later did Lebed adopt a more critical approach to the Transdnestrian leadership.

Despite Yeltsin's discomfiture Lebed not only escaped serious censure for his role in Moldova but instead was promoted. In August 1993 he even claimed that Moscow had given him political functions in Moldova in addition to his military ones, turning him into a kind of proconsul, and he was elected to the Transdnestrian Supreme Soviet. Lebed's apparent immunity reflected the strong support he had within the Russian high command, which publicly supported his stance (although his personal relations with Grachev had badly deteriorated by 1994), and within the Russian officer corps at large. This partly stemmed from the view that Lebed's decisive use of the 14th Army in Transdnestria during 1992 had averted far greater bloodshed. But behind this were other concerns. The Russian presidential adviser Sergei Stankevich stated bluntly in February 1994 that 'every step of that Army's commander was authorized by the hierarchy of Russia's Ministry of Defence.' To have done otherwise, in his view, would have meant 'losing a valuable strategic outpost oriented toward the Balkans'.[101]

Support by the Russian leadership for the insurgents in Transdnestria also was consistent with broader Russian policy towards Moldova. For example, the recruitment of Cossacks from among Russian citizens to fight on the side of the 'Dnestr guard' against Moldova had been openly condoned earlier in 1992. Opposition nationalist circles in Moscow, especially those holding Fundamentalist Nationalist views, have tended to view Transdnestria as part of a revived Soviet Union or Greater Russia.

Yet Lebed was not simply the agent or representative of such nationalists, nor was he a mere military figure-head of the Transdnestrian Republic, though he was prepared to sit in its Supreme Soviet. This is shown by his sharp criticism of officials of the republic who sent armed fighters to Moscow to defend the Russian parliament in autumn 1993 against Yeltsin and the troops summoned by Defence Minister Grachev. By 1994, when he had acquired national stature in Russian public opinion, he had renounced any interest in an imperial revival and scorned Zhirinovsky and other extreme political figures for clinging to such ambitions.

From autumn 1994 Lebed's position became more complicated. Russian officials adopted a more conciliatory policy towards the new Moldovan government—a government which placed more emphasis on ties with Russia and which could point to the support given by Transdnestrian fighters to the disgraced Russian parliament in its confrontation with Yeltsin. The political and strategic value of Lebed's 14th Army as a bridgehead declined and the Russian Defence Ministry and political leadership considered downgrading the status of this force and reaching agreement with Moldova on its eventual withdrawal back to Russia. This, it was correctly calculated, would also result in the displacement of Lebed, whose widespread popularity among officers and independent views had by then antagonized Defence Minister Grachev.[102]

In response Lebed argued that a withdrawal of the 14th Army from the Transdnestr region should only follow the provision of appropriate political and international peace guarantees to this region; even after peace guarantees were furnished the 14th Army should remain in the region for some time to ensure the proper implementation of political decisions. It is significant that this stand, which had clear foreign policy implications, was endorsed by Yeltsin in August 1994 and only subsequently and reluctantly confirmed by Defence Minister Grachev.[103] Grachev only managed to overcome Lebed's intransigence in early summer 1995 by provoking Lebed to offer his resignation as commander of the 14th Army, which was accepted after some hesitation by Yeltsin.

These developments suggest that by 1994 Lebed's activities could no longer be viewed as an expression of Russian Defence Ministry designs in Moldova. They represent an intriguing case of powerful regional influence being wielded by a charismatic Russian military leader. While this phenomenon was exceptional in the period to 1995 it could be repeated elsewhere in the CIS or on the Russian peripheries in the future (see below on Russian plans for regional military command structures), following the precedent set by Lebed.

## Tajikistan

Finally, Russian forces have occupied an ambiguous position in the widespread civil conflict which has swept Tajikistan and spilled over into fighting on the Afghan–Tajik border. The 201st Russian Motor Rifle Division deployed in Bishkek at first tried to maintain a neutral posture, claiming that its forces were simply defending the outer border and vital installations. But since 1992 this division and other Russian units in Tajikistan have clearly been drawn into active support of the government against southern Islamic rebels. It is uncertain how far such partiality reflected from the outset the priorities held by the Russian government and how far it was a reflection of Russian military leaders promoting an independent agenda. Certainly the Russian high command has no interest in fostering the conflict in Tajikistan and is haunted by memories of its occupation of Afghanistan. But there are signs that the Russian Defence Ministry and the Russian commander of the local 'peacekeeping' forces have at times sought to block local diplomatic initiatives to negotiate with representatives of the Islamic opposition forces.[104]

### 'Peacekeeping' and forward defence in the CIS region

There is growing evidence that the assumption gained ground in the Russian high command in the early 1990s that military power should be the deciding political instrument in the 'near abroad'. This means that so-called 'peacekeeping' activities led by Russia have risked being partisan from the outset and could better be described as 'peace-enforcing'.

This use of military forces for political ends had already been actively promoted by Vice-President Rutskoi, among others, in the aftermath of the August 1991 coup as a means to stem secessionist currents. In autumn 1991 Rutskoi adopted a hard line towards secessionist demands in (as it was then) Checheno-Ingushetia. He also advocated that Crimea should be reclaimed for Russia from Ukraine. Beyond the Russian Federation, he took part in 1992 in organizing the peacekeeping process in South Ossetia and Transdnestria, while making statements to Moldovan and Georgian leaders which bordered on declarations of war.

Rutskoi's declarations were made in his capacity as Vice-President rather than as a senior military figure. But his attitudes towards the 'near abroad' helped stimulate the formation of a caucus in the Russian high command which began openly to engage in military-political actions in CIS states under the guise of 'peacekeeping'.

Until the upheavals which resulted from the Russian campaign in Chechnya, this group of commanders included Defence Minister Pavel Grachev, Deputy Defence Ministers Boris Gromov and Georgy Kondratyev (the latter of whom was made responsible for Russian peacekeeping in the CIS until his dismissal early in 1995), Lieutenant-General Aleksandr Lebed, and Colonel-General Viktor Sorokin (who headed the task force of Russian troops in Abkhazia during the period November 1992–March 1993).[105] This powerful military clique pressed for an activist military role in the CIS to support Russian minorities or to settle ethnic conflicts on terms favourable to Russia. The military doctrine for Russia approved in November 1993 confirmed that one role of the armed forces would be to protect Russian citizens wherever they might be found.

The Russian Foreign Ministry adopted a softer line on the correct use of peacekeeping forces, at least until autumn 1993, arguing that their deployment should comply with international law. In this period Russian diplomats tended to view peacekeeping mainly as a means of raising the prestige of Russia, both in the 'near abroad' and internationally. The Foreign Ministry also encouraged the idea of Western participation and Western assistance in setting up peacekeeping forces and conducting peacekeeping operations.

By contrast, the Russian Ministry of Defence has consistently viewed peacekeeping more as a means to promote Russian security interests and protect ethnic Russians, as well as to legitimize the Russian troop presence in certain of the former Soviet states. It has tended to oppose Western involvement in CIS or Russian peacekeeping operations. Moreover, the evidence suggests that the Russian Defence Ministry has managed to exert strong operational control over the three peacekeeping operations within former Soviet borders which were under way by summer 1993 (in South Ossetia and Moldova since mid-1992 and in Tajikistan since December 1992).[106] The same applies to the operation in Abkhazia, which was set up over summer 1994.

These differences prompted efforts by the two key ministries (Defence and Foreign Affairs) from spring 1992 to develop a unified approach to the participation of Russian troops in peacekeeping operations.[107] The dangers of a contradictory Russian policy in the Tajik crisis persuaded Yeltsin in July of that year to give Foreign Minister Kozyrev the task of co-ordinating the work of the Russian Ministries of Security, Defence, and Foreign Affairs in coping with the crisis.

A year later, with the conflict still unresolved, Kozyrev was made Yeltsin's special representative to handle the matter, co-ordinating the efforts and organizing the interactions of the agencies involved (see Chapter 3). But since the conflict remained highly militarized and threatened inter-state clashes with Afghanistan, Grachev was given responsibility for general operational command over Russian efforts in Tajikistan. He became responsible for interactions on the ground between the forces and resources of various ministries.[108] This represented a possible model for large-scale Russian military-security operations elsewhere on the former Soviet periphery.

The views of the high command on peacekeeping and the need to introduce Russian forces into parts of the former USSR (with or without the consent of the countries concerned) were supported after summer 1992 by the Russian Supreme Soviet and influential political figures within it such as Yevgeny Ambartsumov. For example, the parliament applied pressure on the Russian government to send airborne troops to Moldova before the agreement on peacekeeping forces for the conflict in that state was reached in summer 1992.

Yeltsin himself finally underwrote military interventionism in a guarded way in February 1993, when he called for Russia to be granted powers by international institutions, including the United Nations, as a guarantor of peace and stability in the region of the former Soviet Union. He appears to have bowed to pressures from Russian military chiefs among others. Chief of the General Staff Kolesnikov had argued in summer 1992 that the intensification of military conflicts between former Soviet states could lead to direct intervention by NATO forces.[109] This unlikely scenario was raised again by Marshal Shaposhnikov at the end of the year. In fact the military command were seeking to legitimize their arrogation of responsibility for stability throughout the territory of the former USSR in the hope that this region would be accepted as a Russian sphere of influence.

Grachev made this clear a few days before Yeltsin's February 1993 appeal when he stated openly that Russia had strategic interests on the Black Sea coast of the Caucasus, where its troops were stationed, and that every measure would be taken to ensure that Russian troops would remain there, 'otherwise we will lose the Black Sea.'[110] By autumn that year a close Russian-Georgian military relationship had been codified in inter-state agreements after Russia had manipulated its local military preponderance and its capacity to manage the conflict in Abkhazia to compel Georgian acquiescence. The Russian Defence Ministry now plans to maintain a grouping of 23,000 servicemen overall in the Transcaucasus.

It is alarming for other former Soviet states to consider which other areas of the post-Soviet 'strategic space' could be defined as vital for Russia by the increasingly assertive military leadership in Moscow. Such resurgent strategic ambitions are supported by plans in the Russian military command to construct a new mobile force structure with a rapid-reaction core, which may develop the capacity to put into practice the new doctrine of military-political intervention. Secondly, they are expressed in plans to reconstruct military bases and facilities in many of the CIS states. In April 1994 Yeltsin issued a directive, which confirmed a proposal of the Russian Defence Ministry, to establish twenty-eight Russian military bases outside Russia on the territory of former Soviet states.[111] This fleshed out a provision in the new Russian military doctrine which envisaged the basing of Russian troops outside Russian borders.

Thirdly, military ambitions for a 'forward defence' in the CIS region were upheld by a Russian Security Council decision in autumn 1993 not to seek to construct border defences on Russian borders but to maintain large parts of the old Soviet borders, which had become the outer CIS borders, especially in Central Asia and perhaps the Transcaucasus.[112] This decision is consistent with Yeltsin's description of the Tajik–Afghan border as 'in essence the border of Russia'. Such plans could only fuel military hopes for some kind of reconstituted union and reintegrated joint CIS military structure, despite the dissolution of the CIS joint military command in June 1993. The deployment of 'CIS border guards' in Central Asia was confirmed at a CIS summit in April 1994, and Yeltsin referred to the possibility of similar arrangements with Ukraine, Belarus, Armenia, and Georgia, which could put Russian troops back on the borders of Turkey, Poland, Slovakia, and Romania under CIS auspices.[113]

By autumn 1994 the Russian military push to create a 'common military-strategic space' in the CIS region had succeeded in embracing to a lesser or greater degree the Central Asian states, Georgia, and Belarus. However, by this time the commitment to a forward security zone in the CIS region was no longer a goal associated principally with a caucus of generals in the Russian high command. It appeared to be shared by most of the Russian political leadership, including the Foreign Ministry. Kozyrev's position on the functions of peacekeeping had shifted significantly. By autumn 1993 he began to argue that military bases in conflict zones used for the conduct of peacekeeping operations could be a means for Russia to avoid fully withdrawing from its 'zones of traditional influence'.[114] This functional, *realpolitik* view of peace-keeping and the purposes of military engagement in other CIS countries fused with broader nationalist rhetoric during 1993–4. Despite this growing consensus, and the 'forward' strategic ambitions of the Russian military command, this body of officers has not been an advocate of military adventurism in other CIS states, let alone further afield, of the kind promoted by the Liberal Democrat leader Zhirinovsky and other more extreme political groups.

This is reflected in the equivocal commitment of senior Russian officers to maintaining a strong military presence in Tajikistan, since the duration and long-term outcome of this presence has not been clarified and the financial support for such operations has been jeopardized by declining Russian defence budgets.[115] Furthermore, many officers have felt that military involvement in such internal political struggles or civil wars further politicizes the army in a way contrary to their professional military instincts. Finally, military commanders have been far better aware than nationalist politicians of the real underlying weaknesses in Russian military capabilities, despite the growing rhetoric about Russia as a great power, of the limited progress in military reform and restructuring since 1991, and of continuing serious failures in military recruitment, morale, and training.

## The impact of the conflict in Chechnya

These uncertainties in the Russian military command about combat commitments surfaced abruptly towards the end of 1994, when the decision by Yeltsin and the Russian Security Council chiefs to send a large military force into Chechnya was sharply criticized by most of the caucus of military leaders who had become associated over the previous few years with assertive peacekeeping operations. Early in 1995 Deputy Defence Minister Kondratev (responsible for peacekeeping in the CIS) and Colonel-General Mironov lost their commands; Deputy Defence Minister Boris Gromov was transferred from the Ministry of Defence to the Foreign Ministry. Lieutenant-General Aleksandr Lebed survived unscathed only because of his political popularity, although the Chechnya crisis may have been an additional pressure leading to his eventual resignation as commander of the 14th Army. The authority of Defence Minister

Grachev himself was gravely weakened by the initial failures of the Chechen campaign.

A particular concern of these military leaders was the effect of the large-scale use of military force in an 'inner-abroad' region, within the Russian Federation, in conditions where Russian civilian casualties were inevitable. But the outbreak of very public divisions in the higher echelons of the military command over Chechnya, including open opposition to the Defence Minister, is a precedent which has made it less certain that significant political decisions on security policy outside Russia in the CIS region, which require the use of armed forces, will necessarily be supported and implemented by military commanders, let alone junior officers. This is especially the case when 'political generals', such as Lebed, can voice their criticisms with impunity.

Consequently it has become more difficult to view the engagement of Russian military forces in the conflicts besetting the CIS region as driven by the ambitions or lack of foresight of military commanders. Secondly, these divisions in the high command make the attempt to identify possible future top-level military-political coalitions even more problematic.

Thirdly, these developments raise the possibility later in the 1990s of local military commanders siding with local regional authorities, in defiance of central directives from Moscow on matters with foreign policy implications. For example, the commanders of the Far East or Transbaykal military districts (or of planned joint commands for these regions) could support a more belligerent policy towards China than that sanctioned by the political and military leaderships in Moscow. Various scenarios of Russian military coalition-building with local political forces in CIS states are also conceivable in addition to the example provided by Lebed in the Transdnestria region. This introduces new uncertainties over the influence of regional deployments of Russian forces on Russian foreign policy outcomes.

The one certainty is that Russian leaders will continue to rely on the military instrument to impose order in Russia and keep disorder as far as possible from Russian borders, possibly through further developing a strategy of forward defence and the assumption of security tasks in the CIS region. This will ensure continued political influence for those in control of the army.

In a document passed to parliament in February 1995 Yeltsin said that he foresaw more Chechnya-type situations in the future. He believed Moscow would encounter 'special danger from armed conflicts breaking out in Russia and on its borders, on the territory of the former Soviet Union, because of aggressive nationalism and religious extremism'. The document stated that the country's security interests may require 'the presence of Russian troops in other CIS states to prevent destabilizing developments'.[116] Given the conflicting views of Russian military officers concerning this role and the unclear links between them and future political leaders, it would be mistaken to interpret such deployments either simply as having such a stabilizing effect or alternatively as forming the cutting edge of Russian nationalist ambitions abroad.

## Conclusion

It is evident that the salience of military influences in Russian foreign policy decision-making during 1991–5 has reflected failures in the broader political process and the development of democratic political norms in Russia more than a self-conscious effort by military commanders to extend their remit. Whether in response to political deadlock in Moscow or confrontation between the centre and regional leaders, the military has projected itself as the only institution capable of averting anarchy or civil war—at least until the intervention in Chechnya exposed the limits of the possible. This role has grown in regions of direct conflict in other CIS states, where military diplomacy and coercion have become natural instruments in the attempt to restore stability or to underpin an expansive interpretation of Russian national interests.

In these circumstances it is not surprising that politicians have vied for the support, tacit or explicit, of military commanders, especially at times of serious political discord, and that this has increased the possibility of military-political coalitions of one hue or another arising. If political power comes to be mediated in this way then it is clear that Russian foreign policy within and beyond the CIS region will become less accountable and more nationalist at root, though not necessarily driven by an effort to restore past positions of strength. The rise of Pragmatic Nationalist political currents has also raised the significance of the officer corps as a lobby which has been receptive to and a reservoir for such views.

Officer lobbies can exercise more direct influence when the military leadership is divided.

The Chechnya war has shown that the Russian military command is no more cohesive than the political leadership. Personal divisions and professional rivalries in the high command have reduced its influence even with respect to the crucial question of the defence budget and have limited its leverage on Russian international security policy overall. Such influence has largely been confined to issues where military considerations are essential, such as the content of military doctrine, CFE Treaty revision, or NATO expansion.

It is true that the southern CIS states have become an arena of inordinate Russian military involvement. But the military institution could become a hostage to fortune in the unpredictable conflicts plaguing these states and find itself driven by the unrealistic ambitions of extreme political groupings in Moscow. Peacekeeping and the urge to maintain a forward defence may provide military leaders with opportunities to claim an indispensable role in securing Russian national interests. But the performance of this role and, therefore, the position of senior officers is vulnerable to set-backs and failures. Most likely the military aspect of Russian foreign policy will remain highly significant, but as suggested by the experience of 1991–5 it will only partly be shaped by the military élite itself.

## NOTES

[1] Speech to leadership of the FSK, 26 May 1994, in *Rossiiskaya gazeta*, 28 May 1994.

[2] P. Anokhin, in *Rossiiskiie vesti*, 17 Sept. 1994.

[3] See S. Foye, 'Personnel Changes in the High Command', *RFE/RL Research Report*, 27 Sept. 1991, 1–6. By February 1992 seven deputy defence ministers, ten military district and fleet commanders, and eight commanders of central directorates had been relieved of their posts owing to their actions during the coup, according to Marshal Shaposhnikov, in *BBC Summary of World Broadcasts: Former Soviet Union*, SU/1308, i.

[4] These included Army-Gen. K. Kobets (RSFSR State Defence Adviser

and Chairman of the Committee for Military Reform); Col-Gen. D. Volkogonov (State Adviser for Defence to the Russian President and Chairman of the USSR Defence Ministry Commission for the Abolition of Political Bodies); Maj-Gen. Tsalko (Deputy Chairman of the Russian State Defence Committee); Maj-Gen. N. Stolyarov (Chairman of the USSR MOD Committee for Work with Personnel); Maj-Gen. A. Vladimirov (who some projected early in 1992 as Minister of Defence of a shadow government).

[5] Estimate by Col. Urazhtsev, head of the unofficial 'Shield' military trade union, in personal interview, Moscow, 14 Feb. 1992.

[6] It is ironic that the consolidation of such a coalition (even if military leaders were junior partners within it) occurred later in 1993–4 when the Russian political leadership, including Kozyrev, co-opted much of the agenda of the national patriots.

[7] V. Lipitsky, 'Mira dobilas' "partiya voiny"', *Nezavisimaya gazeta*, 12 Aug. 1992.

[8] In his speech to the Russian Congress of People's Deputies in Dec. 1992 he appealed for deputies not to try to play the 'army card' in political struggle; see *Krasnaya zvezda*, 8 Dec. 1992.

[9] *Izvestiya*, 4 Mar. 1993.

[10] ITAR-TASS World Service, Moscow, 23 Sept. 1993, in *BBC Summary of World Broadcasts*, SU/1902, C/6; *BBC Summary of World Broadcasts*, SU/1803, C/4.

[11] Article by Y. Voronin, *Pravda*, 15 Feb. 1994; *Washington Post*, 5 Oct. 1993; S. Foye, 'Confrontation in Moscow: The Army backs Yeltsin, for now', *RFE/RL Report*, 22 Oct. 1993, 13–14.

[12] 'Party of Rutskoi: Positioned for Power?', *Moscow News*, 7–13 Oct. 1994, 6.

[13] This is argued by M. Desch, 'Why the Soviet Military Supported Gorbachev and Why the Russian Military might only Support Yeltsin for a Price', *The Journal of Strategic Studies*, 16 (1993), 472–3.

[14] See P. Felgengauer, in *Segodnya*, 17 May 1994.

[15] *Moskovskii komsomolets*, 25 Mar. 1994.

[16] See report in *Moskovskii komsomolets*, 27 Jan. 1994.

[17] Interview on 18 Jan. 1994, in *RFE/RL Research Report*, 4 Feb. 1994, 11.

[18] *Militäreliten in Russland 1994*, Friedrich Ebert Stiftung (Munich/Moscow, 1994), 19, 21. The poll was carried out for the Friedrich Ebert Stiftung—the German social-democratic think-tank—by the Munich-based Sinus polling group in co-operation with sociologists at a Russian military academy.

[19] Interview on Russia TV, 14 Jun. 1994, in *BBC Summary of World Broadcasts*, SU/2024, S1/2.

[20] T. Yakhlakova, 'Military enters the election race', *Moscow News*, 1995, no. 33.

[21] Interview in *Argumenty i fakty*, 1994, no. 37, p. 3.

[22] *Financial Times*, 6 Sept. 1994. Article by Lebed in *Nezavisimaya gazeta*, 16 Nov. 1994.

[23] As an example of the views of officers on these issues, expressed just before the All-Union Conference of Officers' Assemblies (on which see later in this chapter), see interviews with Col. V. Baranets in *Pravda*, 17 Jan. 1992, and those recorded by A. Orlov in *Sovetskaya Rossiya*, 17 Jan. 1992.

[24] In the Russian parliament their voting pattern showed that the great majority of junior and middle-ranking officers tended to affiliate politically with the reformist Democratic Russia. This set them against the majority of senior military deputies, who voted with the Communist Party. See 'Narod i nomenklatura—ediny', *Argumenty i fakty*, 1990, no. 29, 1990, p. 2.

[25] A. Putko, 'Nastroeniya v armii bespokoyat i samikh voennykh', *Nezavisimaya gazeta*, 5 Feb. 1992; Alksnis on Moscow television, 17 Jan. 1992, in *BBC Summary of World Broadcasts*, SU/1282, C1/8; and see S. Parkhomenko, 'Parlament v pogonakh', *Nezavisimaya gazeta*, 18 Jan. 1992.

[26] A. Kravtsov in *Moskovskii komsomolets*, 29 Jan. 1992; cited in *Joint Publication Research Service Report: Central Eurasia, Military Affairs* (henceforth *JPRS-UMA*)-92-005, 12 Feb. 1992, 23–4. See also P. Felgengauer, in *Nezavisimaya gazeta*, 14 Jan. 1992.

[27] Appeal in *Krasnaya zvezda*, 21 Jan. 1992.

[28] *Nezavisimaya gazeta*, 5 Feb. 1992.

[29] Opinion poll conducted by the All-Russian Centre for the Study of Social Opinion in mid-June 1992 among participants of an expanded session of the Co-ordinating Council of Officers' Assemblies, 'Chto segodnya trevozhit ofitserov', *Armiya*, 1992, no. 15, pp. 12–13.

[30] According to Aleksandr Mochaikin, chairman of the Co-ordinating Council of Officers' Assemblies, in ITAR-TASS World Service, 20 May 1992, in *BBC Summary of World Broadcasts*, SU/1387, C2/2.

[31] 'Ustav Ofitserskogo sobraniya OVS SNG', *Krasnaya zvezda*, 7 May 1992.

[32] See *Nezavisimaya gazeta*, 26 May 1992.

[33] See 'Ultimatumy voennykh', *Russkii vestnik*, 1992, no. 26; 'Ostanovit' raspad Chernomorskogo flota', *Rossiiskaya gazeta*, 9 Jul. 1992; 'Obrashchenie koordinatsionnogo soveta', *Flag rodiny*, 5 Sept. 1992; 'Resolyutsiya ofitserskogo sobraniya SVVMIY', *Flag rodiny*, 9 Sept. 1992.

[34] Meeting of Black Sea Fleet officers' assemblies on 21 Jan. 1993, reported on Mayak Radio, 21 Jan. 1993, in *BBC Summary of World Broadcasts*, SU/1598, C1/1.

[35] See 'Tovarishchi ofitsery ob'edinyaites!', *Glasnost* , 20–6 Aug. 1992; 'Soyuz ofitserov', *Kommersant*, 24 Oct. 1992; 'Obrashchenie', *Narodnaya pravda*, 1992, no. 41.

[36] I. Shkamikova, 'Soyuz ofitserov voz'metsya za Yeltsina i Gracheva', *Nezavisimaya gazeta*, 14 Jan. 1993.

[37] For the geostrategic views of Officer's Union members in general see *Pravda*, 1 Apr. 1993.

[38] For Sterligov's views see his polemical booklet *Opal'nyi general svidetel'stvuet* (Moscow, 1992).

[39] I. Dunaeva, 'Fars, no opasnyi po kolichestvu mundirov', *Nezavisimaya gazeta*, 23 Feb. 1993; Russia TV, 20 Feb. 1992, in *BBC Summary of World Broadcasts*, SU/1620, C2/6–7; 'Uroki porazhenii—preddverie pobed', *Pravda*, 23 Feb. 1993. For the political appeal issued to create a government of national salvation, see 'Pobeda budet za nami!', *Den'*, 21–7 Feb. 1993. For the full resolution adopted see *Rossiya*, 1993, no. 4.

[40] A. Zhilin, 'Gospoda ofitsery', *Moskovskie novosti*, 28 Feb. 1993.

[41] 'Generala zapasa Achalova v armii ne zhdut', *Ivestiya*, 26 Mar. 1993. For Achalov's views on policies in the CIS and the role of Russia as a great power, see 'U patrioticheskoi Rossii—patrioticheskaya armiya', *Den'*, 12 Sept. 1993.

[42] See the article by M. Aleksandrov in *Kommersant*, 27 Nov. 1992.

[43] Maj-Gen. V. Dudnik in *Novoye vremya*, 13 Mar. 1993, 16–17. See the opinion poll data in this and his article 'Voennye ekzamenuyut politikov', *Moskovskie novosti*, 14 Feb. 1993.

[44] Lecture by Col. Ye. Morosov, in *Der Spiegel*, 29 Mar. 1993, 168; cited in *JPRS-UMA-93-016*, 19 May 1993, 5–6.

[45] See I. Chernyak, 'Za kem poidet chelovek s ruzh'em?', *Komsomolskaya pravda*, 30 Mar. 1993.

[46] A. Zhilin, 'Podpol'nyi komitet deistvuet?', *Moskovskie novosti*, 14 Mar. 1993.

[47] See report in *Sovetskaya Rossiya*, 19 Apr. 1994; A. Zhilin, 'Union of Officers Changes its Tactics', *Moscow News*, 1994, no. 16.

[48] Cited in *OMRI Daily Digest*, 20 Feb. 1995.

[49] *Militäreliten in Russland 1994*, 31, 34, 36–7. The sample was of 615 senior officers in 7 military regions, including 60 generals.

[50] Interview on TASS World Service, 9 Jan. 1992, in *BBC Summary of World Broadcasts*, SU/1275, B/2. See also interview in *Izvestiya*, 10 Mar. 1992.

[51] Ukrainian Radio, 14 Mar. 1992, in *BBC Summary of World Broadcasts*, SU/1332, B/9.

[52] ITAR-TASS Agency World Service Report, 25 Mar. 1993, in *BBC Summary of World Broadcasts*, SU/1649, C2/2.

[53] RIA Agency Report, Moscow, 4 Oct. 1993, in *BBC Summary of World Broadcasts*, SU/1812, C/13.

[54] Decree of 7 May 1992, in *Rossiiskaya gazeta*, 9 May 1992.

[55] Cited in V. Dudnik, 'Voennye ekzamenuyut politikov', *Moskovskie novosti*, 14 Feb. 1993.

[56] Article 16; see 'Zakon Rossiyskoi Federatsii ob oborone', *Krasnaya zvezda*, 10 Oct. 1992.

[57] 'Konseptsiya vneshnei politiki Rossiiskoi Federatsii', *Diplomaticheskii vestnik*, special issue Jan. 1993, p. 3. For a fuller discussion of the preparation and content of the 'concept', see Chapter 2.

[58] *Moscow News*, 1992, no. 30. Such interests included: (1) setting up an effective system of collective security; (2) ensuring the status of the Russian Federation as the only nuclear power on the territory of the ex-USSR; (3) strengthening the external borders of the CIS; (4) settling the status of Russian troops and military bases on the territory of former Soviet republics; (5) preserving the military infrastructure, which constitutes an integrated system to ensure the military security of Russia and other former Soviet republics; (6) preventing the escalation of armed conflicts in the ex-USSR republics; (7) the participation of Russia in the further development of a peacekeeping mechanism; (8) the implementation of this mechanism also for the rejection of foreign military contingents and military bases in the ex-Soviet republics.

[59] The draft is contained in 'Osnovy voennoi doktriny Rossii',*Voennaya mysl'*, special issue, May 1992. The details of the draft doctrine may have been written by the Centre for Operational-Strategic Research of the General Staff. But the principles of military doctrine were extensively discussed and new doctrinal proposals were forwarded at the General Staff Academy conference under the auspices of the Ministry of Defence on 27–30 May 1992. These discussions are reported in *Voennaya mysl'*, special issue, Jul. 1992. Rodionov has sought to turn the General Staff Academy into the 'Academy of National Security and Defence of the Russian Federation'; see interviews with him in *Krasnaya zvezda*, 28 Jan. and 13 May 1992.

[60] 'Osnovy voennoi doktriny Rossii', 4, 7.

[61] According to Stephen Foye in *Baltic Security Conference*, RFE/RL Research Institute (Munich, n.d.), 25–6.

[62] See Gen. Vladimirov, 'Eta sistema mogucha i dostatochno zla', *Rossiyskaya gazeta*, 22 Sept. 1992.

[63] S. Modestov, 'Voennaya politika russkogo natsional'nogo sobora', *Nezavisimaya gazeta*, 27 Aug. 1992.

[64] This process was confirmed by Viktor Stepashin, Chairman of the Supreme Soviet Committee on Defence and Security, in a round-table discussion in London on 28 Jan. 1993.

[65] See reports by V. Kononenko and V. Litovkin in *Izvestiya*, 4 Mar. 1993; V. Kuznetsova, 'Sovet bezopasnosti', *Nezavisimaya gazeta*, 4 Mar. 1993.

[66] See J. Lough, 'The Place of the "Near Abroad" in Russian Foreign Policy', *RFE/RL Research Report*, 12 Mar. 1993, 27–8.

[67] For the elaborate process of developing this doctrine, see Defence Minster Morozov in *Uryadovyy kuryer*, Kiev, 4 Dec. 1992, cited in *BBC Summary of World Broadcasts*, SU/1565, C3/8.

[68] See report of debate on 2 Jul. 1993, *Izvestiya*, 7 Jul. 1993.

[69] For contrasting views see Col. V. Petenko and Col. S. Chetverov in *Za vilnu Ukrayinu*, 20 Feb. 1991; cited in *JPRS*-UMA-92-011, 1 Apr. 1992, 46, 49.

[70] As reported in parliament by Defence Minister Col-Gen. V. Radetskyy; Radio Ukraine World Service, 8 Oct. 1993, in *BBC Summary of World Broadcasts*, SU/1817, D/1.

[71] His views are fully presented in 'My dolzhny postroit' armiyu, dostoinuyu velikoi Rossii', *Krasnaya zvezda*, 22 May 1992.

[72] See A. Rutskoi, 'Voennaya politika Rossii: Soderzhanie i napravlennost'', *Voennaya mysl'*, 1993, no. 1, p. 7, where he talks of the need to take account of the mobilization needs of the armed forces and the state as a whole of up to 15 per cent of the Russian population.

[73] See S. Foye, 'The Struggle over Russia's Kuril Islands Policy', *RFE/RL Research Report*, 11 Sept. 1992, pp. 37–9.

[74] 'Genshtab: Ostanovit' sokrashchenie voisk na yuzhnykh kurilakh', *Nezavisimaya gazeta*, 30 Jul. 1992. For an alternative view on this issue at the time see I. Kots, 'Ostrova v pogonakh', *Komsomolskaya pravda*, 28 Jul. 1992.

[75] Statement by Defence Minister Grachev, ITAR-TASS Agency World Service, 1 Apr. 1993, in *BBC Summary of World Broadcasts*, SU/1659, A1/2.

[76] Statement by Grachev reported by ITAR-TASS, 2 Jul. 1993, in *BBC Summary of World Broadcasts*, SU/1735, C2/1.

[77] See statement by Russian Ministry of Defence in *Krasnaya zvezda*, 8 Apr. 1993.

[78] Rear-Adm. Oleksiy Ryzhenko, Chief of Staff and First Deputy Commander-in-Chief of the Ukrainian Navy, in *Narodnaya armiya*, 4 Jun. 1994.

[79] Interfax, Moscow, 2 Mar. 1993, in *BBC Summary of World Broadcasts*, SU/1628, C1/2.

[80] See the assessment by V. Solov'ev, 'SNV-2: Vzglyad iz ministerstva oborony Rossii', *Nezavisimaya gazeta*, 16 Mar. 1993.

[81] For example, views of officers on Radio Russia, 7 Feb. 1992, in *BBC Summary of World Broadcasts*, SU/1300, C4/1.

[82] See the principles of this document, which was dated 23 Apr. 1993, in *Moscow News*, 1993, no. 31.

[83] See, for example, his views in *Izvestiya*, 1 Jul. 1992; *Krasnaya zvezda*, 26 Nov. 1992.

[84] As cited in *International Herald Tribune*, 1 Dec. 1993.

[85] Joint statement in *Nezavisimaya gazeta*, 19 Aug. 1992. For more information about the Council on Foreign and Defence Policy, see Ch. 2.

[86] See M. Shevelev, 'Generaly delayut politiku?', *Moskovskie novosti*, 7 Mar. 1993.

[87] *Sovetskaya Latviya*, 22 Dec. 1990; cited in *JPRS*-UMA-91-006, 4 Mar. 1991, 6–7.

[88] A. Sidyachko, 'Baltiiskie ofitsery ob'yavili boikot ministerstvu', *Megapolis express*, 21 Oct. 1992. See also 'Ofitserskie sobraniya protestuyut protiv prikaza', *Kommersant*, 23 Dec. 1992.

[89] See statement by the Russian Defence Ministry in *Krasnaya zvezda*, 21 Oct. 1992. For a general discussion see D. Bungs, 'Soviet Troops in Latvia', and S. Girnius, 'Progress in Withdrawal of Troops from Lithuania?', both in *RFE/RL Research Report*, 28 Aug. 1992, pp. 18–28 and 29–33, respectively.

[90] See J. Lough, 'The Place of the "Near Abroad" in Russian Foreign Policy', *RFE/RL Research Report*, 12 Mar. 1993, 24.

[91] ITAR-TASS Agency Report, 18 Jan. 1994, in *RFE/RL News Briefs*, 10–21 Jan. 1994.

[92] See his interview on Russian TV on 11 Mar. 1992, in *BBC Summary of World Broadcasts*, SU/1328, B/2.

[93] For example, the appeal on 14 Jul. 1992 to the Russian political and military leadership from the officers' assemblies of the 7th Army in Armenia, 'Obrashchenie ofitserov shtaba 7 gv, armii', *Russkii vestnik*, 1992, no. 30–1.

[94] N. Broladze, 'Spory o statuse rossiiskikh voisk', *Nezavisimaya gazeta*, 22 Dec. 1992.

[95] For the Russian military involvement in these attacks see *Izvestiya*, 19 and 20 Mar. 1993; C. Dale, 'Turmoil in Abkhazia: Russian Responses', *RFE/RL Research Report*, 27 Aug. 1993.

[96] See 'Rossiiskie voennye otritsayut svoe uchastie v konflikte', *Kommersant*, 23 Oct. 1993.

[97] See 'Russian Army Helps Rebels in Moldova', *The Guardian*, 23 Jun. 1992.

[98] See 'General Lebed' stavit ultimatum prezidentu Rossii', *Izvestiya*, 8 Jul. 1992. His most controversial statement is published in full in A. Lebed, 'Tragediya na Dnestre', *Sovetskaya Rossiya*, 7 Jul. 1992.

[99] Yu. Leonov, 'Ispol'zovanie armii v pridnestrov'e opravdanno', *Nezavisimaya gazeta*, 15 Apr. 1992.

[100] For analyses of the role of Lebed and the 14th Army see 'Komandarm 14-I', *Krasnaya zvezda*, 22 Jul. 1992; '14-ya', *Krasnaya zvezda*, 26 Jun. 1992; V. Socor, 'Russian Forces in Moldova', *RFE/RL Research Report*, 28 Aug. 1992. When the first agreements were signed between the Russian and Moldovan defence ministries on the withdrawal of Russian troops

from Moldova, Lebed stated again defiantly that Russia would continue to support Transdnestria; see *Izvestiya*, 1 Sept. 1992.

[101] *Rossiskiie vesti*, 2 Feb. 1994. See also Y. Selivanov, *Segodnya*, 24 Mar. 1994.

[102] Officers of the 14th Army issued a statement to the MOD in support of their commander S. Gamova, in *Izvestiya*, 10 Aug. 1994.

[103] For Yeltsin's view see V. Litovkin, in *Izvestiya*, 16 Aug. 1994; for the statement by Defence Minister Grachev see *Krasnaya zvezda*, 27 Aug. 1994.

[104] See S. Shermatova, 'Suppression or Conciliation?', *Moscow News*, 1993, no. 12, p. 4.

[105] For short biographies of these generals see *Moscow News*, 1993, no. 14. For a profile of Sorokin see *Krasnaya zvezda*, 20 Mar. 1993.

[106] See J. Green, 'The Peacekeeping Doctrines of the CIS', *Jane's Intelligence Review*, 5 (1993), 158–9.

[107] See article by V. Savvin, *Kommersant*, 7 May 1993.

[108] Report of sitting of Russian Security Council on 26 Jul. 1993, in *BBC Summary of World Broadcasts*, SU/1753, C3/1. Other aspects of this presidential decision are discussed in Chapter 3.

[109] He claimed that this could be under the pretext of guaranteeing 'international control' over the nuclear potential of the former USSR. See *Nezavisimaya gazeta*, 1 Aug. 1992. Kolesnikov was First Deputy Chief of the Russian General Staff at the time he made this statement.

[110] Grachev on Russia TV, 22 Feb. 1993, in *BBC Summary of World Broadcasts*, SU/1622, C1/5; and see 'Gruziya mozhet prevratit'sya v novyi Afganistan', *Nezavisimaya gazeta*, 25 Feb. 1993.

[111] Directive of 5 Apr. 1994, in *Rossiiskie vesti*, 7 Apr. 1994. For controversy about this directive see *Segodnya*, 8 and 9 Apr. 1994.

[112] Reported by P. Felgengauer in 'Starye granitsy i "novye" bazy', *Segodnya*, 16 Sept. 1993.

[113] *The Guardian*, 19 Apr. 1994.

[114] Interview in *Nezavisimaya gazeta*, 24 Nov. 1993.

[115] For criticism of the Russian military mission in Tajikistan by Boris Gromov, former commander of Soviet forces in Afghanistan, on the grounds that Russia is repeating its 'bitter Afghan experience', see I. Rotar, *Nezavisimaya gazeta*, 20 Nov. 1993; interview of Gromov, *Krasnaya zvezda*, 27 Nov. 1993.

[116] Document passed to parliament before Yeltsin's 16 Feb. address to that body, as reported in *OMRI Daily Digest*, pt. 1, 17 Feb. 1995.

# 6

# Conclusion

## ALEX PRAVDA AND NEIL MALCOLM

This study has examined major aspects of the domestic politics of Russian foreign policy. These concluding observations seek to draw together some of the main strands of the analysis and highlight some of the defining features of the domestic political interactions that bear on foreign policy making in Russia. They also consider the patterns of change identified in the main chapters and assess their wider analytical significance.

Russia provides rich if challenging material for considering the vexed question of the relationship between domestic and foreign policy. The period 1992–5 saw a remarkable confluence of internal and external developments. The very profusion of cross-currents between the domestic and foreign policy streams makes Russia a peculiarly complex and important case study. It has a large number of specific features. The revolutionary flux of the period under review makes it difficult to be anything except very tentative when generalizing about overall patterns of interaction between the domestic and foreign, let alone about the wider analytical significance of such patterns. Transformation on such a scale, embracing the social, economic, and political as well as the international, restricts the range of analogues and perhaps limits direct comparison. Some of the transformations are analogous to those in other post-Soviet states but their size and ex-colonial status make contrasts perhaps more telling than similarities.

The very scale and flux of change that makes generalization challenging also offers the analyst a particularly revealing view of the politics of foreign policy. Interaction between the internal and external was intense as well as extensive. Policy makers faced inward and outward simultaneously on a wide range of issues. The intense and fundamental nature of reassessment on all fronts means that one can see through to underlying structural shifts in the politics of beliefs and power struggle, changes that are soon overlaid by day-to-day politics in more stable states. Russia in this period sheds a good deal of light on the ways in which structural domestic changes impinge on realignments in foreign policy in conditions of complex instability. The very complexity of the overlap between the domestic and foreign, the differentiation of the 'intermestic' sphere, opens up possibilities for comparisons between the role of internal factors in the two and arguably three concentric circles of external policy. To the categories of 'near abroad' and 'far abroad' used through-out this study, one can add that of the 'inner abroad', involving relations with regions and republics within the Russian Federation, which came to the fore with the intervention in Chechnya in late 1994. The degree of 'domestic shading' decreases as one moves outward. For obvious reasons internal factors figure most prominently within the 'inner-abroad' and 'near-abroad' policy circles. Less obviously, domestic factors operate in a more complex fashion here than in external issue areas further afield. It is on such questions, as well as on the dynamics of domestic influence in conditions of structural transformation, that recent developments in Russia throw particularly interesting light.

The preceding chapters have been concerned with examining the intertwining of the domestic and the foreign in the areas of élite debate, policy and decision-making, public politics, and military affairs. Our concern has not been to assign any precise weighting to domestic factors. Rather, it has been to try to map and explore when and how domestic political factors matter, how they bear on foreign policy. In order to underline some of the findings arising from the main body of this study, it may be useful to focus on the following clusters of issues. The first concerns the relationship between values and preferences on domestic and international fronts. Here the predominant pattern appears to be one of neo-Soviet congruence. More visibly than in the old Soviet system, liberalism on domestic questions seems to be associated with support for accommodationist external policies. The nature of the coupling varies, though, with circles of foreign policy—those relating to the 'inner', 'near', and 'far abroad'.

The second cluster embraces the ways in which domestic constituencies and policy networks shape foreign policy. Here in the post-Soviet period greater vulnerability of fragmented executive hierarchies to outside pressures has modified rather than seriously curtailed their policy power. Executive fragmentation has made the course of Russian foreign policy a more tortuous one. The fitful incursions of other political forces into foreign policy have accentuated its meanderings more than they have altered its overall direction.

The final cluster of questions has to do with patterns and dynamics of change. At the level of opinion and debate the shift has been from polarization between Liberal Westernism and Fundamentalist Nationalist stress on Eurasian priorities to greater consensus based on Pragmatic Nationalist views of Russian interests. This has broadly parallelled moves in foreign policy from passive co-operation with the West to greater national assertiveness. Over the same period, the Russian political system has moved from a confused pluralism towards a state with elements of authoritarianism and nascent corporatism. At first sight it appears that pluralism and elements of democracy are therefore linked structurally, rather than merely chronologically, with co-operation, while authoritarianism goes hand in hand with assertiveness. In the first phase of Russian foreign policy, Westernism was, to be sure, an important element of the political mood which coloured both domestic and international preferences. On closer examination, institutional dislocation and perceived restrictions on the scope for international manœuvre may be as important in explaining Moscow's policy of passive co-operation. In accounting for the changes in Russian foreign policy over this period, the uncertainty of a nervous and authoritarian executive about the international and domestic viability of existing policy may be particularly important. Our analysis of recent developments in Russia suggests that executive fragmentation and fragility appear to be particularly salient features of the domestic environment as far as foreign policy is concerned.

The light this study can shed on the interaction between these changes in domestic and foreign policy in Russia may contribute some insights to the academic debates about the bearing political regimes have on foreign policies. Enough work has been done to show that there are no simple correlations and that much depends on circumstances, both domestic and international.[1] To associate the development of political democracy, for instance, with peaceful international behaviour is simplistic. The way in which change takes place, and especially the stability of the process, seems to be just as or more important than the direction of development.[2]

## *Values and preferences*

Discussion of foreign policy during this period took place within a cauldron of emotions, values, and ideas which fused the external and internal. The vigour and critical tenor of the debate on foreign policy priorities gave external issues a high level of salience in terms of the attention and, especially, the controversy they attracted.[3] The energetic participation of diplomats and politicians as well as specialists embedded discussion of foreign policy deeply into domestic disputes. The debate, detailed in Chapter 2, brought foreign policy issues into domestic political discussions at several levels. At the level of political polemic, critics of the government attacked its foreign policy and ministers occasionally replied. Such exchanges almost invariably involved wider dispute about the strategic line the new Russia should pursue. Central to this strategic level of the debate was the question of defining Russian national interests. However much the notion of national interest was counterposed to traditional Russian leanings towards ideology in foreign policy, discussion of interest was often enmeshed with quasi-philosophical reflection and controversy about interest and identity. Dispute on such fundamental issues was all the more intense because it became part of the search by the intelligentsia, the main participants in the debate, for their own identity and role in the new Russia.

The fact that Russia was formed as an empire, and continues in many ways to be an empire-state, made the search for identity a process of defining relations with the outside world. Defining which kind of Russians fall within the ambit and protection of the Russian state was central to any definition of policy towards the 'near abroad'. Extending boundaries in this way meant expanding the reach of the 'intermestic' sphere, where domestic and international issues coalesce.

Further linking the two sets of issues was a preoccupation in the debate with defining a set of values which would inject the new foreign policy with a new mission. Debate over the strategic line of Russian foreign policy often amounted to contention over strategic ideology.[4] All participants in the debate, as Margot Light notes, seemed to accept the need for a Russian mission even if they differed over its contents. In the wake of the Soviet collapse Kozyrev championed a pragmatic approach to foreign policy which left behind both Marxism-Leninism and the universalistic notions favoured by 'New Thinking'. The Foreign Minister argued that Moscow needed no new doctrine. In the event, the government put together a foreign policy concept, partly in response to Fundamentalist and Pragmatic Nationalist demands for a defined new line. Acceptance of the need for a new concept, implicitly of the need for a new doctrine, even by self-declared pragmatists like Kozyrev, meant in practice going along with an emotionally charged approach to foreign policy which favoured the nationalist wing and further enmeshed foreign policy with domestic issues.

### Varieties of congruence

To expect to find neatly delineated and stable connections between stances on internal and external issues would be unrealistic given the heated, changing, and complex political climate. Part of the complexity lay in the multiple and shifting attachments of the participants to their positions. Individuals and groups often had a mixture of attachments: value-based, functional, and politically instrumental. Many views on foreign policy issues were projections of principled, often temperamental and emotional, stands on domestic questions. This helps to explain the lack of focus of much of the discussion on specific foreign policy issues. The broad ideological nature of many stances produced uninformed and incoherent arguments. In other cases, particularly where professional or sectoral groups were concerned, a more functional logic prevailed and positions were more precisely defined. The linkage was partial and issue-specific, embracing particular segments of foreign policy. Military-industrial groups, for instance, promoted an arms export policy untrammelled either by moralistic constraint or by concern for the sensitivities of Western competitors.

Most widespread was the instrumental use of foreign policy for domestic political ends. Two factors made this an unusually strong and extensive linkage between domestic and foreign policy spheres. External policy, first, presented critics of the government with a particularly rewarding target area. The more politically central questions of economic reform exposed the government to more frequent attacks. But economic problems were more intractable and none of the opposition groups could offer credible alternatives. Criticism of government foreign policy resonated quite widely with the population and political élites. Points were easy to score and nationalist broadsides difficult to counter effectively. Foreign policy provided a convenient platform for a wide range of opposition groups which disagreed on key aspects of domestic policies. The political utility of foreign policy criticism was further enhanced by government officials who made a practice of highlighting their own vulnerability. Kozyrev repeatedly, often in dramatic fashion, pointed to the ways in which nationalist opposition made political capital out of official foreign policy moves. Designed to help soften Western responses, this ploy made the government's foreign policy all the more vulnerable to opposition forces encouraged by the prominence ministers accorded them on the international stage.

Political tactics therefore strengthened the alignment between positions on domestic and foreign policy. One of the major patterns that emerges from this study is that preferences and stances on external issues broadly correspond to those on internal affairs. In specialist discussions, as in the political debate, we found a significant congruence between the two areas of policy, stronger perhaps than that which commonly occurs among élites.[5]

A certain amount of caution is required in this area: the evidence available on élite views and political stances must be treated with care. In the volatile, hothouse climate of Russian politics individuals frequently put forward incoherent and inconsistent views which changed in tune with political circumstances rather than international conditions. There was a good deal of self-labelling by the proponents of all major foreign policy approaches (see Chapter 2). Positions were commonly taken either at the most general, ideological level or on the basis of support for specific moves; the area in between, that of strategy, was relatively neglected. It is still possible, however, to map patterns of domestic-foreign issue congruence among the three main positions, distinguishable within the spectrum of foreign policy views, which we have defined as Liberal Westernizer, Pragmatic Nationalist, and Fundamentalist Nationalist. The overall nature of congruence varied between these major positions as well as between different issue areas.

The Liberal Westernizer position exhibited the strongest positive linkages, tying together domestic and foreign policy preferences at the level of values, function, and power politics. Central to this web of preferences was support for development in the direction of Western democratic and market reform, which allowed and required economic and political openness to the West. At the other, Fundamentalist Nationalist, end of the spectrum, the coupling between domestic and foreign was as strong, though more negative in linkage. Policy positions were often defined in terms of what was opposed rather than supported. Antipathy to following Western models spanned internal and external policies. There was a thread of nostalgia for Russian 'greatness' and traditions, if variously of the communist or pre-Soviet kind. Most favoured a powerful state, steering slow-paced economic reform at home and assertive Russia-first policies abroad. These included protection against Western economic domination and determined measures against damage to Russian interests and prestige in the 'near abroad' as well as selectively further afield.

It was in the Pragmatic Nationalist band of the spectrum that coupling became looser, hence the label 'demopatriot' which was often attached to those favouring this approach. The location of this centre band varied according to issue area. On domestic issues, the pragmatists came closer to the liberals than to the fundamentalists, with most advocating marketizing change and democratic safeguards. On the overall international orientation of Russia, many Pragmatic Nationalists took 'moderate Eurasianist' stands which resonated more with the Fundamentalist Nationalists than with the Westernizers. However, they were less negative, expressing critical rather than rejectionist views of Western aims. On particular government policies in the 'near' or 'far abroad', scoring critical political points sometimes prevailed over values, and Pragmatic Nationalists differed in tone and degree rather than kind from the Fundamentalist Nationalist opposition. Such differential positions made coupling between domestic and foreign stances less tight, with the strongest strand being economic. Here preferences for more moderate economic reform at home went logically with scepticism about a completely open-door policy and with advocacy of acceptance of aid and investment only on conditions advantageous to Russia.

Interesting variations in patterns of views emerge when one considers them through the prism of different circles of foreign policy. In the outer circle—'far-abroad' policy issues—the lines of demarcation between the main positions were relatively clear. Values and utility reinforced one another in varying proportions. For Liberal Westernizers the practical issue of foreign aid strengthened principled attachment to Western models. For their critics and opponents the political vulnerability of 'immoderate Atlanticism' to charges of national betrayal loomed larger than matters of principle, even if they were concerned about the small scale and intrusive conditionality of aid offered by the West. As far as developments in the former Yugoslavia were concerned, scoring points by attacking Kozyrev for kowtowing to NATO seemed more important to Nationalists than supporting the Serb cause.

On 'near-abroad' questions the major groupings were less at odds politically than one might expect, given the differences in their basic stances. In principle, Liberal Westernizers favoured treating the former republics as equal sovereign states. Fundamentalists, both Reds and Browns, regarded the new states as subordinate to Russia, the communists envisaging a resurrected Union and the non-communists the establishment of Russian dominance. Pragmatic Nationalists wanted firm policies to ensure Russian interests, especially those of the diaspora. All were agreed, however, that Moscow had to take responsibility for the rights of Russians living in the new states. They differed mainly over the means by which these rights should be defended. Liberals prescribed legal and political measures; the Fundamentalists argued for a full panoply, including force, while the Pragmatists favoured a flexible mix of the legal and the economically and politically coercive. Where problems arose over Russian minority rights, as in Estonia and Latvia, the widely shared feeling that Moscow had to protect compatriots tended to temper criticism of government policy.

Similarly, the universal wish to minimize conflict in the south of the CIS reduced the political expression of differences over the means of Russian intervention. Compression of the range of stances on interventionism was due largely to the movement of Liberal Westernizers in a nationalist direction. In adopting tougher policies on the 'near abroad', proponents of general Westernizing strategies paid little attention to the logical, if rarely explicitly expressed, link with domestic policies. Radical reformers, however, showed some concern about the domestic economic implications of CIS integration plans.

Concern about the domestic political consequences of an interventionist security policy did not really surface until the Chechen crisis of late 1994. What increased awareness of the linkage was political proximity and political process. As Chechnya formed part of the 'inner' rather than 'near abroad', Russian action there clearly had even more direct implications for all aspects of domestic policy. The ruthless way in which the executive pushed through the intervention regardless of due process forced the statist linkage to the fore. The pressure fully exposed divisions within the Liberal Westernizer camp around the statist axis, between those like Yegor Gaidar, who followed liberal principle and opposed the action, and authoritarian economic liberals like Boris Fedorov, who seemed more concerned with a strong state than with government observance of democratic procedure and human rights. For many political groups, especially on the nationalist wing, Chechnya presented an opportunity to criticize clumsy executive action while voicing rhetorical moral objections. For instrumental reasons, communists found themselves alongside liberal political bedfellows, opposing action to reinforce the kind of central control which they had long advocated.

The Chechen crisis provided an extreme instance of a wider tendency: the closer that external policy came to home, the more considerations of political utility overlay the lines of established principled positions. Under less extreme political conditions, 'near-abroad' questions also blurred divisions and congruence between views on domestic and foreign policy, though with different political results. In most 'near-abroad' cases, such as intervention in Tajikistan, the blurring produced general support for government action. It was on controversies further afield, whether over Yugoslavia, the Kurile Islands, or the export of technology, that established positions were most directly carried into political action, precisely because views on the 'far abroad' were more instrumental in the first place. In general, then, distance seems to have improved the definition of congruence; proximity blurred rather than erased it. In all circles of external policy, there was a telling congruence between values and preferences relating to domestic issues and foreign policy questions.

## Constituencies and policy networks

The number of carriers of foreign policy preferences expanded rapidly but they remained poorly organized and weakly enfranchised. Few if any of these carriers, whether interest groups or even political parties, produced anything like coherent foreign policy platforms. They produced far more critical noise than policy signal. The channels available for the transmission of such signals allowed for only limited policy access, let alone influence. The politicization of external policy was not accompanied by a commensurate democratization of foreign policy making. Democratization took place in as much as external issues and official policy were freely discussed in parliament and the media. At the same time, executive dominance over the foreign policy process remained strong, albeit uneven (see Chapter 3). The actual making of foreign policy decisions, while far from regularized and efficient, remained jealously guarded by the President and his coterie. In that sense Kozyrev was right in claiming that foreign policy in Russia was presidential.[6] In other ways the control of the top executive over the policy process was far from certain. At the formulation and implementation stages of the process, inter-agency competition and the lack of clear organizational jurisdiction and co-ordination created opportunities for outside influence. Outsiders included political parties and sectoral groups acting through parliamentary as well as less formal channels.

*Political parties and parliament*

Parties were insufficiently developed as organizations to have any major impact on foreign policy. Clubs of activists constantly forming and reforming in a kaleidoscopic political universe, parties rarely managed to generate anything resembling alternative foreign policies. They were too preoccupied with formulating domestic agendas designed to keep together their fissiparous constituent parts. The major parties did take general positions which reflected and helped to coalesce the main approaches taken in the foreign policy debate. By voicing criticism of government foreign policy from Westernizer as well as Nationalist stand-points, party leaders helped to sharpen rather than shape public opinion on external policy questions. Given the loose nature of Russian voter party affiliation, the impact on opinion was very limited, particularly on 'near-abroad' issues (see Chapter 4). On questions of Russia's Great-Power status and economic dependence on the West, nationalist party leaders of Pragmatic and especially Fundamentalist hue catalysed public disquiet. By linking international humiliation and dependence with domestic economic and social crisis, the extreme opposition parties increased

their electoral support and impressed on government the domestic advantages of a more assertive foreign policy.

It was through parliament that political parties, organized in factions of deputies, notionally had the greatest opportunity directly to affect foreign policy. On paper, constitutional powers, particularly in 1991–3 in the case of the Supreme Soviet, gave parliament the potential to play a key role in shaping foreign policy, through committee scrutiny of performance and plenary ratification of international treaties. In practice, both operated fitfully and like most constitutional checks had relatively little real impact on the executive. Having to account for foreign policy moves and submit agreements for ratification had little more than nuisance value. Committee objections were discounted as politically prejudiced and failure to ratify was often ignored. Even the Federal Assembly, where procedures became more regularized, failed in its first year to exercise the kind of constraining and pre-emptive influence over foreign policy enjoyed by the US Congress, to which Russian parliamentarians aspired. Such Western parliamentary influence was vitiated by the dominance of the executive and its confrontational relationship with the legislature. This was the case particularly in the lifetime of the Supreme Soviet, which tried to undermine rather than revise government policy and sought to advance its own independent, more nationalist line. Abroad, parliamentary initiatives, in Moldova, Serbia, or Iraq, further complicated already fragmented Russian diplomatic activity. At home, parliamentary attacks on 'passive Westernism' helped catalyse assertive foreign policy moods among political élites outside and within the executive. The degree of discord between executive and legislature depended less on the distance separating deputies' foreign policy preferences from those of the government than on the overall political tensions between President and parliament. From late 1992 to autumn 1993, for instance, disagreements on foreign policy moderated, yet growing hostility between executive and legislature induced most deputies to pass disruptive opposition resolutions on 'near-abroad' as well as 'far-abroad' issues. A similar political logic underlay the overwhelming votes in the Duma against government policy in Chechnya. Generally, though, the constitutionally weak Duma and the somewhat more empowered if politically tame Federation Council had relatively civilized relations with the executive. Better-organized and more willing to bargain, both chambers of the Federal

Assembly in their first year arguably exercised more influence than had the Supreme Soviet on a government interested less in confrontation than coalition-building. Even so, direct parliamentary influence in 1994–5 amounted to affecting the tone and tactics rather than the strategic direction of a dominantly executive foreign policy.

## Economic groups

The power of a sprawling neo-Soviet executive over external policy decisions created a favourable environment for the exercise of influence by sectoral groups and lobbies. Given the large intersection between external economic strategies and domestic development, one would have expected major producer groups to have made foreign policy an early priority target. It took some time for established and initially disoriented sectoral interests to adjust to rapidly changing circumstances. Their lobbying activities became marked from 1993. Such lobbying operated through a combination of neo-Soviet channels, often using ministerial networks scarcely altered since the days of Communist Party rule, and newer personalized material and political links particularly suited to the court politics of the Yeltsin era. The impact of economic lobbies on the overall shape of foreign policy was limited by the diversity and particularism of group interests and the fragmentation and confusion of the policy agencies and processes targeted. Economic constituencies, as is often the case, tended to be segmented along lines of market position and competitiveness.

In certain issue areas, especially relating to the 'near abroad', lobbying signals were clearer and sectoral demands more effectively advanced. The powerful energy sector, and especially the gas industry, had specific interests in maintaining its dominant position throughout the area of the former Soviet Union. The gas lobby and most of the oil corporations therefore favoured a strategy of economic integration of the CIS, a preference which tallied with their support for slower and more moderate Russian economic reform (proponents of radical reform opposed CIS economic integration in large part because of its incompatibility with rapid economic progress in Russia). It is difficult to attribute the ascendancy of the economic reintegration strategy specifically to the influence of the energy lobby. Most of the established producer groups also favoured strengthening existing ties which secured existing inputs

and outlets. Important groups within the government and presidential administration supported partial reintegration for security as well as economic reasons. However, the interests of the gas
lobby in this as in other areas certainly informed Prime Minister
Chernomyrdin's priorities.

If one looks at more defined issues relating to economic relations with the 'near abroad', more differences appear to emerge
between the preferences of major sectors and government. The
line taken by the Foreign Ministry on the national distribution of
rights to oil reserves on the Caspian shelf might be interpreted as
further evidence of the precedence given by Moscow to strategic
over economic priorities. The concessions made to Washington
over the sale of cryogenic missile technology to India may be seen
as a clearer instance of the same pattern operating in the 'far
abroad' (see Chapter 3). However, in both instances, and particularly in that of the Caspian, it is less a case of economic and political priorities being in conflict than being entangled in a mixture
of bureaucratic confusion and infighting. In the controversies surrounding missile technology transfer to India, the Foreign Ministry
enjoyed the support of some space-agency groups (interested in
lucrative contracts with the US). The late intrusion of the Foreign Ministry into the Caspian oil agreement may be attributed to
rivalry with the Ministry of Energy and Lukoil, and to institutional assertiveness as well as an ill-co-ordinated effort to exercise
more political leverage over Azerbaijan on pipeline routes and wider
strategic issues.

The precedence of political over economic priorities in major
foreign policy issues depended on the balance of stakes as well as
on the relative strengths of the lobbies making the case. In 1995
the size of the contract to deliver nuclear reactors to Iran, and
growing irritation with US protectionism, gave added policy weight
to those arguing the economic case. This, and the coincidence of
economic and regional strategic gains in going ahead with Iran,
probably helped induce the Foreign Ministry to defend the agreement against US objections in spring 1995 and persuade the
President to concede less to Washington than had been granted over
the Indian deal nearly two years earlier. It is important to recall
that over the same period the wider Russian policy environment
had shifted in the direction of greater assertiveness abroad and a
greater political role for economic corporate interests at home. Late

1994 and early 1995 saw an increasingly overt corporatization of politics, as key established parties and new blocs, like Our Home is Russia, became closely identified with major business interests.

## *The military*

By far the most prominent and influential of the corporate groups active in the area of foreign policy was the military. Sidelined by civilian advisers under Gorbachev, military leaders worked their way back to centre stage in security and foreign policy under Yeltsin. While the officer corps were divided on many issues, organizationally they seemed relatively cohesive in a policy landscape of agency fragmentation. Pivotal in the balance of political forces in the country, military leaders had excellent access to the President and a key voice on security matters. That voice had a selective and often indirect impact on policy in the 'far abroad'. Views of Russia as a Great Power or even a Superpower were more prevalent within the General Staff and the officer corps than among other élites; they informed the new military doctrine as well as some of the political elements of the foreign policy concept. Military commanders were particularly resistant to making any territorial concessions, and reinforced doubts within the top executive about taking forward negotiations over the Kuriles in autumn 1992 and spring 1993 (see Chapter 5). Political leaders responded to military sensitivities, especially after autumn 1993, in adopting a more robust position on issues like the CFE Treaty and NATO expansion.

If on 'far-abroad' questions military influence hinged on politicians making allowance for commanders' preferences, in many aspects of 'near-abroad' policy it was the military which made the running. They successfully advanced priorities through a combination of resources in Moscow and in the field. Moves made by local commanders, in Transdnestria or in Abkhazia, were in part independent initiatives; key decisions were often taken, however, with the tacit and sometimes explicit agreement of military authorities in Moscow (see Chapter 5). Such action on the ground in conflict zones narrowed options available to the Kremlin and so steered policy in a direction favoured by the military. The Ministry of Defence conducted what often amounted in 1992–3 to its own 'near-abroad' policy, much to the annoyance of the Foreign Ministry, whose efforts the military sometimes appeared to sabotage.

The activity of local commanders in sensitive regions and the corresponding promotion by central military authorities of security priorities certainly helped to militarize Moscow's general approach to problems in the 'near abroad'. This does not mean that the military necessarily favoured an active general strategy of forceful interventionism. Some polls suggested that officers were more strongly opposed than politicians to the use of force to resolve conflicts in the 'near' or 'inner abroad'.[7] It was hardly surprising that top military commanders, most of whom had served in Afghanistan, showed little enthusiasm for major involvement in Tajikistan and even less for the intervention in Chechnya. Nevertheless, the military leadership favoured policy moves to assert a security *droit de regard* over the former Soviet area and contributed to the official adoption of a Monroe Doctrine line towards the 'near abroad' in early 1993. As Roy Allison notes in Chapter 5, the military converted the political leadership to a doctrine of forward defence and successfully promoted the priority of establishing a network of bases in the south of the CIS.

The more pronounced military edge to plans for CIS integration in 1994–5 and wariness of external involvement in peacekeeping in part reflected the increasing policy prominence of the military establishment in Moscow. The greater account taken of military sensitivities on critical security and foreign policy questions, after the domestic clashes of autumn 1993, reflected the efforts of the President to foster support in a group so decisive for the political balance of forces. Such efforts were all the more important given the unpopularity of the Minister of Defence, Grachev, and the divisions among senior officers. These divisions, highlighted by the Chechen crisis, may have impaired the corporate policy power of the military. Had the military been more united behind a forceful popular commander they might have exercised a predominant influence over security policy. Even with their organizational strength impaired, they were a formidable policy force with which political leaders had to reckon, particularly on 'near-abroad' issues. The prominence of military candidates in the December 1993 elections further raised the political profile of the armed forces. The weight of the military, as indeed that of the economic corporate groups, in shaping external policy strategy grew as Yeltsin moved from mid-1993 towards consensus and coalition-building. And it is to the patterns of shifts in the domestic and foreign policy landscapes that we now turn as we consider the final cluster of issues with which this volume is concerned.

## Patterns and dynamics of change

As the period under review is one of pervasive flux, marked in 1994–5 by elements of post-revolutionary consolidation, it sheds especially interesting light on linkages between changes on the domestic politics and foreign policy fronts. The phases through which Russian external policy passed broadly corresponded to stages in internal political development. In the first half of 1992 a policy of unqualified Westernism was deployed by a new government committed to radical economic and political reform along Western lines. For the following year or so, foreign policy went through an uneasy transition towards the kind of more assertive stance advocated by centrists. A parallel move occurred on the domestic front where, partly in response to centrist criticism, the government advanced Westernizing economic and political reform in a slower and more cautious fashion. From spring 1993, foreign policy took on a more determinedly assertive hue which became more pronounced as it became grounded in firmer élite consensus in the course of 1994. Domestic strategy, particularly on the economic front, appeared to be more uneven, with commitment to continuing marketization mixed with pledges to a more strongly social market. Politics were more volatile, with a weak government trying to foster defensive solidarity among power élites and fashion a stronger state.

The linkages between these parallel phases of policy may be mapped in terms of a triangular relationship between changes in foreign policy, élite views, and the domestic political system. In mapping these linkages we are dealing with associations and can therefore venture generalizations about patterns of correlation rather than causation.

Phases in the development of élite preferences on external issues were closely related to those in foreign policy. Early 1992 saw the staking out of positions, with both the Liberal Westernizer and the Fundamentalist wings taking up diametrically opposed stances on all major questions. The months from mid-1992 to spring 1993, the second phase, witnessed the rise of the centrist Pragmatic Nationalist approach which, as the year and the third phase proceeded, began to erode the Liberal Westernizer wing. By early 1994 this élite movement from radical reformism to centrist pragmatism, on domestic as well as international affairs, was also evident in government policy. One can picture the spectrum of élite preferences as a train with three coaches, each representing one of the major approaches or groupings. Over the period there was a sizeable movement from the lead Liberal Westernizer coach into the middle Pragmatic Nationalist one, while the whole train inched backward in the direction of the conservative and fundamentalist rearguard. (The shifts in preferences and the domestic-foreign policy linkages involved are summarized in Figure 1.1.) The overall movement of the train reflected a rising tide of nationalist sentiment. This was evident, to some extent, in the growing concern of the population as a whole about international humiliation and the need for Russia to act as a Great Power. There was heightened anxiety about the dangers of economic dependence. Among the élites, such concerns were accompanied by stronger support for national assertiveness, particularly in the 'far abroad'. In part this was a response to the development in relations between Russia and the West. That response was itself also coloured by the growth of nationalist sentiment integral to the search for Russian identity and national purpose.

Given the polarization of the political struggle in 1992–3, one might have expected a similar movement in élite policy stances, with the middle coach of the preference train emptying out into the other two. In political alignment terms this happened, particularly in the months leading up to the showdown of autumn 1993. In policy terms, however, the middle was expanded by erstwhile radical reformers disillusioned with the results of the linked projects of rapid marketization and a strongly Westernist foreign policy. At the same time, the executive deliberately moved, even before autumn 1993, to try to take some of the policy ground of its opponents, in an attempt to broaden the scope for the coalition-building efforts which became increasingly central to Yeltsin's strategy through 1994–5. This strengthened the emergence in 1994 of a consensus on slower economic reform steered by a stronger state. Support for statism went hand in hand with a groundswell in patriotism. The Chechnya crisis initially seemed to weaken this growing consensus, aligning nearly all political groupings against a wilful executive. However, as the immediate crisis receded in spring 1995, so the dominant pragmatic centre seemed to swing back behind the government agenda of slow domestic reform and an assertive Russia-first foreign policy in the 'near' and 'far abroad'. These patterns suggest a close linkage between movements in élite foreign policy preferences and shifts in the configuration of domestic politics.

If we consider the relationship between élite stances on external issues and government foreign policy, the evidence points to some tentative generalizations. One is that élite preferences shaped climates, or more precisely moods, of thinking about external issues, which had some effect on government policy. Clearly, the more pronounced the preferences, the more widely echoed in the population and the more strongly voiced by the élites, the more responsive the executive. But responsiveness was more evident in foreign policy rhetoric than action. This was the case with the question of Russian minorities in the 'near abroad' and with that of Russian involvement in the former Yugoslavia. When it came to action rather than words, the top executive was generally impervious to outside criticism. Only rarely was there any apparent association between critical views and changes in executive conduct, as in the case of the postponement of Yeltsin's visits to Japan in autumn 1992 and spring 1993. On most 'far-abroad' questions, loud public contention resulted in policy whispers. On the 'near abroad', less radically critical voices seemed to have a greater impact on policy.

The greater the distance separating critical élite views from those of the executive, the more their policy impact tended to hinge on the overall balance of the costs and benefits involved for the executive. These plainly included international as well as domestic considerations. In the case of the Kuriles, for instance, the uncertainty of the financial gains flowing from major concessions and the fragile position of the Japanese government reduced the advantages of an early deal. Weighed against such uncertain benefits, the domestic costs of a settlement appeared to be considerable, given the strength of public as well as élite feelings against any concessions. Calculation of the final balance was affected by the domestic political environment: on the one hand, sharp conflict with the opposition, which used the Kuriles issue as a cutting edge of attack; on the other, divisions within the executive. Outside objections fostered a mood hostile to concession, which was probably used by those members of decision-making groups out to stiffen the Russian negotiating

304 Alex Pravda and Neil Malcolm

strategy, as much for partisan domestic reasons as for ones of policy substance.[8] Differences within the executive, as well as political relations between the executive and legislature, mediated and shaped the power of outside criticism. The nature of the regime, in other words, conditioned the degree and method of domestic influence on foreign policy.

## Regime types

The relationship between political regimes and foreign policies has attracted lively academic debate. It was Kant who first formulated the hypothesis that democratic states are less likely to go to war. More recently, the case for 'democratic peace' has been refined to the argument that democratic states, or more precisely liberal democracies, do not go to war with each other.[9] It has been argued that institutionalized democratic processes and the liberal culture of consent and compromise create a predisposition to peaceful resolution of conflicts and an inhibition against adventurist interventionism. The empirical evidence for the more peaceable nature of democratic states is not, however, very persuasive; democracies do not seem necessarily less prone to interventionist foreign policies. In any case, defining democratic states is far from straightforward; parsimony is often achieved by overstretching the concept of democracy. What is really meant is a particular form of developed and stable liberal democracy.

Applying the yardstick of democracy to the post-Soviet Russian regime is problematic. It is difficult to show that the regime was more or less democratic at various times in the period under review, let alone relate its democratic qualities to the different stages of foreign policy. The period of flux with which we are dealing involves less any clear movement towards or away from democracy than the emergence of a mixed regime. The most one can hazard, very tentatively, is that this regime appeared in 1995 to combine weak elements of representative democracy with stronger ones of corporatism and authoritarianism.

For purposes of analysing linkages between regime and foreign policy, it is most useful to focus on features of the process of transformation rather than on the definition of its product. Degree of liberalization could provide a serviceable yardstick by which to gauge developments in the political regime and relate these to external policy. Since liberalization is linked in Russia with concepts of Westernization, its fortunes coincide with the promotion of more open and accommodating external policies. Many of the entrepreneurial groups which prosper under more liberal domestic policies have a strong vested interest in maintaining access to world markets and Western aid. It is tempting to argue that less liberal, authoritarian regimes enfranchise corporate groups which promote more closed, protectionist strategies. Such generalizations are broad-brush and questionable, however, unless refined by taking into account the frequent differentiation of group preferences which we have noted.

Finer-grained patterns may be discerned by using yardsticks based on two characteristics of regimes, identified by Hagan, that seem particularly relevant to the elaboration and conduct of state policy: vulnerability and fragmentation. Vulnerability denotes the strength of a regime in relation to the wider political environment. Fragmentation refers to divisions within the political leadership and executive.[10] For our purposes, vulnerability may be applied to relations between the executive on the one hand and parties, lobbies, and parliament on the other. We may fruitfully also consider the different strategies used by the political leadership to cope with problems of vulnerability.

If we look at our three phases of foreign policy in terms of vulnerability and executive strategies, interesting patterns emerge. Levels of vulnerability were relatively low in the initial phase (first half of 1992), rose in the second (summer 1992–spring 1993), and declined, with some fluctuation, from six months or so into the third (since autumn 1993). There is no simple, linear relationship between levels of vulnerability and shifts towards greater assertiveness in foreign policy. The rise in vulnerability which coincided with the second phase might have had some bearing on the appearance of greater assertiveness in the 'near' and 'far abroad'. At the same time, the second phase saw a strategy of domestic political confrontation which tended to limit policy responsiveness. Tense confrontation appeared to continue until the autumn of 1993, half a year into the third foreign policy phase, yet responsiveness and policy adjustment seemed to increase from the spring. This may be explained in part by the fact that the executive began trying to build a consensus on foreign policy (as on domestic) from early 1993, seeking to isolate the extreme opposition in parliament. After the armed showdown of October 1993, and especially after the December elections, the Kremlin and the government deployed a more sustained consensus- and coalition-building strategy. This was associated with a more pronounced assertiveness in foreign policy, the product in part of an effort to enlist the support of as wide a spectrum of domestic political forces as possible. Such efforts to satisfy a range of domestic constituencies sometimes diluted policy coherence. Vacillation and procrastination over Partnership for Peace in spring 1994 coincided with the efforts by Yeltsin to persuade opposition parties to sign up to the Civic Accord.

All this suggests that executive strategies in domestic politics may have been more significant for foreign policy than levels of vulnerability in Hagan's sense. Such a conclusion is reinforced by the fact that throughout the period, levels of vulnerability (by comparison with Western regimes) remained relatively low. This is explained in part by the strong statist tradition of Russia, and neo-Soviet continuities in the structure and, especially, the culture of politics.[11] The lack of cohesion within the parliamentary opposition and within major lobbies helped ensure that even a fragmented executive retained close control over foreign policy and a divided leadership was able to dominate decision-making (see Chapter 3). It is of course important to distinguish between the 'vulnerability' of the executive *vis-à-vis* other political institutions, and opposition forces, which is what we have been considering here, and the wider 'vulnerability' and weakness of political leaderships in unstable democratizing regimes. The effect of the latter kind of vulnerability on foreign policy we shall return to below.

Fragmentation of the political leadership and the executive structure, particularly the power ministries, was high throughout the period and especially evident in the second foreign policy phase (summer 1992 to spring 1993). It was in these months that the conflicts between the Foreign and Defence Ministries were most acute and the absence of any co-ordinating agency most palpable (see Chapter 3). The same period saw a high degree of policy ambiguity and even outright confusion and contradiction. Even in the consensus-building third phase persistent rivalry, albeit at a lower level, plus lack of inter-agency co-ordination, resulted in policy discord. Divisions between and within power bureaucracies, as well as within the political leadership, helped lend a spasmodic assertiveness to external policy. This was particularly evident in response to problems in the CIS and, even more so, in the 'inner abroad', as exemplified by the manner of intervention in Chechnya.

Having stressed the qualified and complex nature of domestic influences on foreign policy, where does this leave us on the simple question posed at the outset: when and how do domestic political factors matter? Throughout the volume we have been concerned with how domestic factors impinge on foreign policy. Clearly it would be possible to construct a convincing explanation of the course of Russian foreign policy since 1991 that would rest on shifts in, and changes in Russian perceptions of, the international environment, making little reference to domestic factors. In relation to the West, it would emphasize disappointed expectations of economic assistance and of co-operation (even incorporation) in the political and security fields. In relation to the 'near abroad', it would emphasize, say, geopolitical shifts, the effects of nationalist assertiveness in Kiev and elsewhere, civil wars and transborder conflicts, and perhaps especially the unforeseen economic costs of fragmentation of the former Soviet space. However, we have assumed a complementary relationship between domestic and international factors in shaping external policy and have therefore not attempted to weigh one against the other in order to try to establish primacy.[12] We see international factors as a necessary but far from sufficient explanation for Russian foreign policy in this period.

Several types of domestic factors, as we have argued, mattered in various ways and in various circles of policy. Élite, and to some extent public, views on international issues were associated to a significant extent with preferences on domestic questions. This was particularly the case where the 'far abroad' was concerned. Domestic views helped colour perceptions of foreign policy priorities and, by creating a mood within the attentive public and political establishment, affected the thinking of decision makers. The heavily executive structure and culture of Russian politics limited the role of legislatures to indirect influence on policy decisions. Weakness and lack of unity at the top meant, on the other hand, that economic lobbies, towards the end of the period, were gaining policy access and leverage and having an important, if inconsistent, impact on certain areas of policy. Military influence, too, fed on agency and political leadership fragmentation, which was one of the most telling domestic correlates of foreign policy development. The military came to enjoy very considerable prerogatives on a wide range of security questions and shaped policy alternatives, as well as implementation, on many security aspects of 'near-abroad' policy.

It is important to keep in mind the wider context of political instability generated by the stresses and strains of democratization. Whatever the truth about the pacific or belligerent inclinations of authoritarian regimes on the one hand and mature democracies on the other, the upheavals of democratization seem frequently to have been associated with unpredictability and recklessness in foreign policy.[13] Political leaders in Moscow have faced the task of forging domestic alliances and accumulating public support at a time when new groups are on the rise, longer-established ones are threatened, and consensus is difficult to find. In such a situation, adopting nationalist rhetoric and launching military adventures represent ways for a beleaguered leadership and its opponents to bid for backing from all sections of a deeply divided society. In the years under review in this volume it was the internal factors associated with the stability and instability of change, rather than with its political direction, which impinged most on external policy, leaving their mark more on the precise course rather than on the overall evolution of Russian international behaviour.

# NOTES

[1] See, for instance, J. D. Hagan, 'Regimes, Political Oppositions, and the Comparative Analysis of Foreign Policy', in C. Hermann, C. W. Kegley, Jr., and J. Rosenau (eds.), *New Directions in the Study of Foreign Policy* (London, 1987), 339–65.

[2] For a recent assessment, see E. Mansfield and J. Snyder, 'Democratization and War', *Foreign Affairs*, 74 (1995), 79–97.

[3] For a useful discussion of salience, see K. Goldmann, *Change and Stability in Foreign Policy: The Problems and Possibilities of Detente* (New York, 1988), 52–4.

[4] For this term see J. Snyder, *Myths of Empire: Domestic Politics and International Ambition* (London, 1991), 31.

[5] On congruence, see H. Müller and T. Risse-Kappen, 'From the Outside In and From the Inside Out', in D. Skidmore and V. Hudson (eds.), *The Limits of State Autonomy: Societal Groups and Foreign Policy Formulation* (Boulder, Colo., 1993), 39–40.

[6] A. Kozyrev, *Preobrazhenie* (Moscow, 1995), 293.

[7] For élite poll evidence suggesting greater reluctance to sanction the use of force, see the poll of 500 members of a cross-section of élites in Moscow taken in Nov. 1992, in relation to the CIS, in *Mir mnenii i mneniya o mire*, no. 2 (January) 1993, p. 1 and that conducted in Mar. 1993 with reference to the Russian Federation, *Mir mnenii i mneniya o mire*, no. 2 (March) 1993, p. 1.

[8] For one version of developments surrounding policy on the Kuriles, see Kozyrev, *Preobrazhenie*, 295–300.

[9] See B. Russett, *Grasping the Democratic Peace* (Princeton, NJ, 1993); M. Doyle, 'Liberalism and World Politics', *American Political Science Review*, 80 (1986), 1151–69; J. Owen, 'How Liberalism Produces Democratic Peace', *International Security*, 19 (1994), 87–125. For critiques see C. Layne, 'Kant or Cant: The Myth of Democratic Peace', *International Security*, 19 (1994), 5–49; D. Spiro, 'The Insignificance of the Liberal Peace', *International Security*, 19 (1994), 50–86; R. Cohen, 'Pacific Unions: A Reappraisal of the Theory that "Democracies do not go to War with each other"', *Review of International Studies*, 20 (1994), 207–23.

[10] For a discussion of these terms, see Hagan, 'Regimes', 344–50.

[11] For a discussion of state traditions and foreign economic policy, see P. Katzenstein, 'International Relations and Domestic Structures: Foreign Economic Policies of Advanced Industrial States', *World Politics*, 31 (1976), esp. 14–19.

[12] See Müller and Risse-Kappen, 'From the Outside In', 25–6.

[13] On the importance of stability, see Mansfield and Snyder, 'Democratization and War'.

# CHRONOLOGY OF EVENTS IN RUSSIAN POLITICS AND INTERNATIONAL AFFAIRS, DECEMBER 1991 TO SEPTEMBER 1995*

*Entries in italics refer to events in Russian domestic politics*

## 1991

**8 December 1991**

*Presidents of the RSFSR, the Belorussian, and the Ukrainian Republics sign an agreement establishing the Commonwealth of Independent States*

**15 December 1991**

President Yeltsin requests diplomatic recognition of Russia by the United States

**25 December 1991**

*Gorbachev resigns as President of the USSR; the RSFSR is renamed the Russian Federation*

**30 December 1991**

Representatives of eleven member states of the CIS (excludes Georgia and the three Baltic states), meeting in Minsk, agree that nuclear weapons will be placed under a single CIS strategic command, and undertake to observe international agreements signed by the USSR

**31 December 1991**

*Final dissolution of the USSR*

---

* More detailed chronologies are available in K. Dawisha and B. Parrott, *Russia and the New States of Eurasia: The Politics of Upheaval* (Cambridge, 1994), 298–310; *Problèmes politiques et sociaux*, nos. 675–6, 683, 687, 694, 700, 706, 711, 718, 724, 730, 735, 742, and 747 (1992–5); R. Sakwa, *Russian Politics and Society* (London, 1993), 419–21. These publications, and the *BBC Summary of World Broadcasts* (1992–5), have been used in compiling the list of events which follows.

## 1992

**2 January 1992**

*Prices of most goods and services are freed in Russia*

**3 January 1992**

Ukrainian government declares that all armed forces deployed on its territory (apart from strategic weapons but including the Black Sea Fleet) are subordinate to the Ukrainian President and Ministry of Defence

**19 January 1992**

South Ossetia votes by referendum to secede from Georgia and join the Russian Federation

**23 January 1992**

Russian Supreme Soviet passes a resolution demanding a review of the constitutionality of the 1954 decision to transfer Crimea to Ukrainian rule

**30 January 1992**

Yeltsin visits London

**31 January 1992**

Yeltsin visits the United States, addresses the United Nations Security Council, and signs a joint declaration with the President of the United States describing relations between their countries as ones of friendship, partnership, and mutual trust

**5 February 1992**

Yeltsin visits Paris

**14 February 1992**

CIS summit meeting in Minsk; Russian Marshal Shaposhnikov is named Commander-in-Chief of the unified CIS forces

**23 February 1992**

*Nationalist/communist demonstration in Moscow on Armed Forces Day*

**3 March 1992**

*Yegor Gaidar is appointed First Deputy Prime Minister of Russia*

**10 March 1992**

Eduard Shevardnadze is elected head of the Georgian State Council

**16 March 1992**

*Russian Ministry of Defence is established, with Yeltsin as Acting Minister*

**16–22 March 1992**

Russian Foreign Minister Andrei Kozyrev visits China, South Korea, and Japan

**21 March 1992**

*Population of Tatarstan votes for the republic to assume the status of a subject in international law, establishing relations with the Russian Federation on the basis of treaties*

**31 March 1992**

*Eighteen constitutent republics of the Russian Federation (all except Tatarstan and Chechen-Ingushetia) sign the Federal Treaty*

**3 April 1992**

Yeltsin announces his intention to place the Black Sea Fleet under Russian command

**3–5 April 1992**

Visit by Vice-President Aleksandr Rutskoi and State Councillor Sergei Stankevich to Crimea and Moldova; Rutskoi and Stankevich express doubt about the legality of the transfer of Crimea to Ukraine and defend the continued existence of the separatist Transdnestrian Republic

**6 April 1992**

Ukrainian President Kravchuk declares that all conventional forces in Ukraine, except for part of the Black Sea Fleet, are under the control of the Ukrainian Ministry of Defence

*Opening of Sixth Congress of People's Deputies of the Russian Federation: deputies return the draft of a new constitution for further discussion and criticize the government's implementation of economic reforms*

**5 May 1992**

*Russian Security Council is established*

**6 May 1992**

Last of Ukrainian tactical nuclear weapons are transferred to Russian territory for dismantling

**7 May 1992**

*Armed forces of the Russian Federation are established by presidential decree*

Addressing the Council of Europe, Andrei Kozyrev requests that Russia be admitted as a full member

**15 May 1992**

CIS summit in Tashkent: collective security treaty is signed by Russia, Armenia, Kazakhstan, Kyrgyzstan, Tajikistan, and Uzbekistan

**18 May 1992**

*Pavel Grachev is appointed as Russian Minister of Defence*

**21 May 1992**

Russian Federation Supreme Soviet passes a resolution declaring the transfer of Crimea to Ukraine in 1954 illegal

**23 May 1992**

Belarus, Kazakhstan, Ukraine, Russia, and the United States sign Lisbon Agreement: the first three will adhere to the Nuclear Non-Proliferation Treaty, recognizing Russia as the only nuclear-weapons state in the CIS

**30 May 1992**

*Viktor Chernomyrdin is appointed as Deputy Prime Minister with responsibility for the energy industry, and Vladimir Shumeiko (2 June) as First Deputy Prime Minister responsible for industrial administration*

**1 June 1992**

Russia joins International Monetary Fund

**11 June 1992**

*Russian Supreme Soviet adopts privatization plan for state and municipal enterprises*

**15 June 1992**

*Yegor Gaidar is appointed as Acting Prime Minister*

**15 June 1992**

Yeltsin flies to United States, holds talks with President Bush and addresses the Congress; both leaders declare their support for the territorial integrity of the CIS member states, adopt an understanding on strategic arms reductions, and sign an agreement on co-operation in space

**21 June 1992**

*Centrist alliance set up under the title 'Civic Union', bringing together industrialists' organizations, the Democratic Party of Russia, and the People's Party of Free Russia*

**23 June 1992**

Yeltsin and Ukrainian President Kravchuk meet at Dagomys, declaring their intention to maintain friendly relations

**24 June 1992**

At meeting with Georgian President Shevardnadze, Yeltsin agrees a common approach to the conflict in South Ossetia

**28 June 1992**

Aleksandr Lebed is named as commander of Russian 14th Army in Moldova

**30 June 1992**

*Kozyrev protests about influence of 'party of war' on Russian CIS policy*

**3 July 1992**

Yeltsin invited to Munich Group of Seven meeting, on 'Seven Plus One' basis

**6 July 1992**

CIS leaders, at Moscow Summit, agree to set up a joint CIS peacekeeping force

**21 July 1992**

Yeltsin, Moldovan President Mircea Snegur, and Transdnestrian leaders sign a joint statement acknowledging both Moldova's sovereignty and Transdnestria's right to autonomy, and to independence should Moldova decide to become part of Romania

**29 July 1992**

*At a meeting of the Constitutional Commission, Yeltsin calls for a strengthening of state institutions*

**3 August 1992**

Yeltsin and Kravchuk, in Yalta, sign an agreement on temporary joint Russian-Ukrainian command of the Black Sea Fleet

**10 August 1992**

Yeltsin decrees establishment of Russian embassies in all former Soviet states

**11 August 1992**

Russian Supreme Soviet delegation visits Belgrade, and criticizes the Russian Foreign Ministry for supporting UN sanctions against Serbia

**19 August 1992**

Russia and Kazakhstan sign military co-operation agreement

*Council on Defence and Foreign Policy publishes its 'Strategy for Russia'*

**10 September 1992**

Yeltsin's planned visit to Japan is postponed

**1 October 1992**

*Start of distribution of privatization vouchers to Russian population*

**6 October 1992**

Speaking to the Supreme Soviet, Yeltsin declares that the 'near abroad' is Russia's main foreign policy priority

**9 October 1992**

Bishkek CIS summit: support given to Russian military presence in Tajikistan; Ukraine obstructs an agreement on the transfer of all strategic arms to Russian control

**27 October 1992**

*In an address to a meeting of its Collegium, Yeltsin criticizes the work of the Ministry of Foreign Affairs*

**30 October 1992**

Yeltsin suspends withdrawal of Russian forces from the Baltic states

**5 November 1992**

*Decree transforming state-owned gas concern Gazprom into a shareholding company*

**10 November 1992**

Yeltsin, on visit to Budapest, apologizes to the Hungarian parliament for the actions of Soviet troops in 1956

**23 November 1992**

*Addressing the Collegium of the Ministry of Defence, Yeltsin emphasizes the need to build strong Russian armed forces*

**1 December 1992**

*Convocation of Seventh Congress of People's Deputies: after disputes with the executive an agreement is reached for a referendum on a new constitution to be held in April 1993*

**14 December 1992**

*Viktor Chernomyrdin is appointed as Prime Minister, displacing Yegor Gaidar*

**15 December 1992**

At CSCE meeting in Stockholm, Kozyrev spells out a possible alternative, more assertive Russian foreign policy line

**16 December 1992**

Visit of Yeltsin to Beijing

*Decree on establishment of Inter-Agency Foreign Policy Commission of the Russian Security Council*

## 1993

**1 January 1993**

Russia announces it will charge world prices for all its oil and gas exports, except where bilateral agreements exist

**3 January 1993**

START-2 strategic arms reduction treaty signed by Presidents Yeltsin and Bush in Moscow

**7 January 1993**

*Sergei Filatov replaces Yury Petrov as Head of the President's Administration*

**18 February 1993**

Resolution of the Russian Supreme Soviet calls on the UN Security Council to reduce sanctions against Belgrade and to introduce sanctions against Bosnia

**28 February 1993**

Addressing a gathering of the Civic Union, Yeltsin calls on international institutions to grant Russia special powers as guarantor of peace and stability in the former Soviet Union

**10 March 1993**

*Opening of Eighth Congress of People's Deputies in Moscow: agreement to hold a constitutional referendum in April disavowed; deputies deprive Yeltsin of a number of his powers*

**16 March 1993**

Shevardnadze accuses Russia of supporting separatist forces in Abkhazia

**20 March 1993**

*In television address, Yeltsin announces he has decided to sign a decree instituting a period of special rule, and to hold a national vote of confidence in himself and a constitutional referendum on 25 April*

**23 March 1993**

*Constitutional Court declares certain of Yeltsin's recent decisions illegal*

**26 March 1993**

*Opening of Ninth Congress of People's Deputies in Moscow: Yeltsin and deputies compromise, agreeing on questions for a referendum on 25 April on confidence in the President and on the need for new presidential and parliamentary elections; Yeltsin survives impeachment vote, but loses many of remaining prerogatives*

**3 April 1993**

Yeltsin and United States President Bill Clinton meet in Vancouver, agree on lifting of trade restrictions on Russia, including those in COCOM framework; Clinton expresses support for Yeltsin in forthcoming referendum

**15 April 1993**

Kozyrev arrives in Tokyo to attend meeting of foreign and finance ministers of Group of Seven and to have talks with Japanese leaders

**16 April 1993**

*Vice-President Rutskoi, addressing Supreme Soviet, declares that he will not resign, and accuses leading reformist politicians of corruption*

**25 April 1993**

*In referendum, voters give support to Yeltsin and his policies, but insufficient numbers back parliamentary elections to clear the high threshold fixed by the Congress of People's Deputies*

**29 April 1993**

Publication of summary version of the Russian foreign policy concept agreed in Security Council

**30 April 1993**

*Presidential draft constitution published*

**1 May 1993**

*Violent clashes in Moscow between police and National Salvation Front opposition supporters*

**6 May 1993**

*Oleg Soskovets is named as First Deputy Prime Minister*

**11 May 1993**

*Yury Skokov is dismissed as Secretary of Russian Security Council*

**14 May 1993**

Estonia and Lithuania are admitted to Council of Europe, despite Russian objections

Shevardnadze and Yeltsin sign agreement on cease-fire in Abkhazia

**5 June 1993**

*Opening of Constitutional Conference in Moscow*

**11 June 1993**

*Yevgeny Shaposhnikov is named as Secretary of Russian Security Council; parliament refuses to confirm the appointment*

**15 June 1993**

CIS joint military command is dissolved

**21 June 1993**

Estonian parliament passes law classifying as 'foreigners' those inhabitants whose parents settled in the country after 1941

Russia suspends oil and gas deliveries to Estonia

**7 July 1993**

Yeltsin attends part of Group of Seven summit meeting in Tokyo

**9 July 1993**

Supreme Soviet declares Sebastopol a Russian city; Yeltsin dissociates Russian government from the declaration

**10 July 1993**

Prime Ministers of Russia, Ukraine, and Belarus declare their intention of setting up an economic union

**15 July 1993**

Agreement is reached with the United States on supply of Russian rocket engines to India, and on Russian-American co-operation in space

*Publication of draft of new constitution, agreed by Constitutional Conference*

**27 July 1993**

*Viktor Barannikov is dismissed as Minister of Security, and replaced by Nikolai Golushko*

**3 August 1993**

Yeltsin and Kravchuk, meeting at Massandra, discuss the transfer of Ukrainian nuclear warheads and most of the Black Sea Fleet to Russia in return for uranium supplies and the cancellation of energy debts

**24 August 1993**

On visit to Poland, Yeltsin declares that Russia does not oppose Polish entry to NATO; this position subsequently disavowed by Russian Foreign Ministry

**17 September 1993**

Last Russian troops leave Poland

**18 September 1993**

*Yegor Gaidar is named First Deputy Prime Minister; Oleg Lobov is named Secretary of the Security Council, in place of Yevgeny Shaposhnikov*

**20 September 1993**

Azerbaijan agrees to become an active member of the CIS

**21 September 1993**

*Parliament is dissolved by presidential decree: new elections are to be held on 11 and 12 December, simultaneously with a constitutional referendum; Constitutional Court rules decree illegal; parliament resists, appointing Rutskoi as President*

**23 September 1993**

*Yeltsin offers to stand for re-election on 12 June 1994*

**29 September 1993**

At CIS summit in Moscow, a framework agreement for an economic union is signed by nine states (Azerbaijan, Armenia, Belarus, Kazakhstan, Kyrgyzstan, Russia, Uzbekistan, and Ukraine and Turkmenistan as associate members); Georgia agrees to join CIS as associate member

**4 October 1993**

*Parliament buildings stormed by troops after armed clashes in Moscow; leaders of parliamentary resistance arrested; some opposition parties and newspapers banned*

**12 October 1993**

Yeltsin visits Tokyo, agreeing to a reduction in the Russian forces stationed on the Kurile Islands

**23 October 1993**

Russia and Azerbaijan sign agreement allocating 10 per cent share in Baku oil contract to Russian firm Lukoil

**6 November 1993**

*Yeltsin announces that he will stay in office until the end of his full term as President, in June 1996*

**9 November 1993**

*Yeltsin presents draft text of new constitution to be submitted to referendum on 12 December*

**18 November 1993**

*Publication of outline of new Russian military doctrine*

**19 November 1993**

Ukrainian Supreme Soviet ratifies the START-1 treaty and the Lisbon agreement on nuclear weapons

**3 December 1993**

NATO offers membership in 'Partnership for Peace' to states of Central and Eastern Europe and of the former Soviet Union

**9 December 1993**

Yeltsin visits NATO and EU in Brussels, calling for the setting-up of a new pan-European security system, and signing a joint declaration endorsing the conclusion of a Partnership and Co-operation Agreement between Russia and the EU

**12 December 1993**

*Constitution approved in referendum; in several of the national republics the constitution is voted down, or gains insufficient support, and Chechnya refuses to participate; opposition nationalist and neo-communist parties (LDPR, CPRF, Agrarians) make gains in elections to the federal Duma*

**13 December 1993**

Kazakhstan parliament ratifies Nuclear Non-Proliferation Treaty

**21 December 1993**

*Ministry of Security replaced by Federal Counter-Intelligence Service*

**28 December 1993**

*Anatoly Chubais, head of the State Property Commission, announces that two-thirds of small firms and large industrial enterprises have been privatized*

## *1994*

**10 January 1994**
*First session of newly elected Russian Duma*

**14 January 1994**
Signing of trilateral treaty in Moscow between the United States, Russia, and Ukraine, agreeing denuclearization of Ukrainian armed forces over a seven-year period

**17 January 1994**
*Yegor Gaidar resigns as First Deputy Prime Minister*

**18 January 1994**
Kozyrev declares the CIS states and the Baltic states a zone of Russia's vital interests

**21 January 1994**
Duma votes to request the ending of UN economic sanctions against Serbia

**30 January 1994**
Presidential election in Crimea is won by Yury Meshkov, on platform of closer ties with Russia

**8 February 1994**
Ukraine accedes to NATO Partnership for Peace

**15 February 1994**
*Russia and Tatarstan sign a treaty defining relations, and agreeing the division of powers between Moscow and Kazan*

**17 February 1994**
Bosnian Serbs agree to withdraw their forces from immediate environs of Sarajevo in return for a contingent of Russian troops being deployed in the area as part of UNPROFOR

**19 February 1994**
Kozyrev sets off on visits to Prague, Budapest, and Warsaw; in Warsaw he calls for a European security partnership based on the CSCE, rather than expansion of NATO to include Central and East European states

**23 February 1994**
*Duma declares an amnesty for all those connected with the attempted coup of August 1991 and with the events of September–October 1993*

**24 February 1994**
Yeltsin states Russia's opposition to any enlargement of NATO from which it would be excluded

**10 March 1994**
*Yeltsin proposes to political and social organizations to sign an Agreement on Civil Accord, renouncing violent methods in the settlement of disputes*

**16 March 1994**
Moldova joins NATO Partnership for Peace

**18 March 1994**
In talks in Moscow with United States Defense Secretary William Perry, Chernomyrdin indicates that Russia is ready to participate in the Partnership for Peace without any special conditions

**23 March 1994**
Georgia joins NATO Partnership for Peace

**6 April 1994**
Yeltsin's office issues directive concerning establishing of Russian military bases in the republics of the CIS and Latvia; reference to Latvia is subsequently referred to as a mistake

**8 April 1994**
Yeltsin declares that Russia envisages achieving a special relationship with NATO rather than joining the Partnership for Peace on an equal footing with other former communist states

**11 April 1994**
Yeltsin protests about the failure by the Western powers to consult Russia before NATO air strikes against Serb positions near Gorazde in Bosnia

**12 April 1994**
Prime Ministers of Russia and Belarus sign agreement in principle on unifying currencies

**18 April 1994**
CIS summit in Moscow: general agreement to maintain peacekeeping forces in Tajikistan; agreement between Yeltsin and Kravchuk in principle on division of Black Sea Fleet

**28 April 1994**
*Signing of Agreement on Civil Accord by most Russian social and political organizations, except Yabloko moderate opposition party and Communist Party of Russian Federation*

**30 April 1994**

Russian-Latvian agreement on withdrawal of Russian troops by 31 August, and on maintenance of Russian radar station at Skrunda for five years

**4 May 1994**

Azerbaijan joins NATO Partnership for Peace

**9 May 1994**

WEU offers 'associate partner' status to Central and South-Eastern European states and to Baltic states

**10 May 1994**

Turkmenistan joins NATO Partnership for Peace

**16 May 1994**

Cease-fire agreement in Nagorny Karabakh reached, after Russian Ministry of Defence mediation

**21 May 1994**

Crimean parliament votes to re-establish provisions of 1992 constitution affirming its sovereignty and right to regulate relations with Kiev by means of treaties; parliament in Kiev subsequently suspends Crimean constitution

**23–4 May 1994**

*Speakers of the upper and lower house of parliament Vladimir Shumeiko and Ivan Rybkin are named as full members of Security Council*

**25 May 1994**

*Yeltsin visits Federal Counter-Intelligence Service; address by Director, Sergei Stepashin, refers to desires in West to obstruct recovery of Russian power*

**27 May 1994**

Kazakhstan joins NATO Partnership for Peace

**1 June 1994**

Kyrgyzstan joins NATO Partnership for Peace

**14 June 1994**

Ukraine signs Partnership and Co-operation Agreement with EU

*Presidential decree announcing a programme of drastic measures in the fight against crime*

**21 June 1994**

Visit by Chernomyrdin to the United States, where he signs documents concerning the lifting of trade restrictions on Russia, and US-Russian co-operation in space

*Speaker of the Council of the Federation, Vladimir Shumeiko, proposes postponing the parliamentary elections due in December 1995*

**22 June 1994**

Russia adheres to NATO Partnership for Peace, on the understand-ing that a direct relationship between NATO and Moscow will also be formalized

**23 June 1994**

Aleksandr Lukashenko elected as President of Belarus on platform of seeking closer ties with Russia

**24 June 1994**

Yeltsin signs Partnership and Co-operation Agreement between Russia and the EU, and proposes eventual Russian membership

**29 June 1994**

Addressing graduates from military academies, Yeltsin declares that a CIS-wide security system must be established, and that no one can remove Russia's moral and political responsibility for territories which have been part of Russia for centuries

**8 July 1994**

Russia participates in political discussions at Group of Seven meeting in Naples and signs joint final statement

**10 July 1994**

Leonid Kuchma wins second round of Ukrainian presidential election after campaigning for the restoration of economic ties with Russia

**26 July 1994**

Agreement reached between Russia and Estonia on withdrawal of Rus-sian troops and on status of retired Russian military personnel

**30 July 1994**

*'Provisional Council of Chechnya' declares President Dudaev divested of his powers, and announces its intention of normalizing relations with Moscow*

**10 August 1994**

Russian and Moldovan military delegations agree on a three-year time-table for withdrawal of Russian troops

**28 August 1994**

Kozyrev, visiting Belgrade, calls for a softening of UN policy towards Serbia

**31 August 1994**

Last Russian forces leave Estonia and Latvia

Yeltsin and Kohl attend ceremony to mark the departure of the last Russian forces from Berlin

**17 September 1994**

*Presidential decree on arrangements for the sale of shares in Gazprom*

**20 September 1994**

Signature of Baku oil contract by consortium of Western firms and Russian oil corporation Lukoil

**22 September 1994**

Publication of report by Russian Foreign Intelligence Service about integration in the CIS

**24 September 1994**

Visit by Yeltsin to United Kingdom

**26 September 1994**

Visit by Yeltsin to United States, to address the United Nations General Assembly and for talks with President Clinton

**11 October 1994**

*Rouble falls by over 20 per cent against the dollar; Yeltsin sets up commission of inquiry*

**17 October 1994**

Visit by Queen Elizabeth II and British Foreign Minister Douglas Hurd to Russia

**18 October 1994**

*Russian journalist investigating allegations of corruption in the Russian army is assassinated*

**21 October 1994**

Summit meeting of CIS in Moscow establishes a supranational 'Inter-State Economic Committee'

**24 October 1994**

*Presidential decree fixing establishment of Russian military forces at 1.7 million (reduction of 40 per cent from 1992)*

**9 November 1994**

Visit by Kozyrev to Iraq, following agreement by Saddam Hussein to recognize the statehood and frontiers of Kuwait; Kozyrev calls for easing of sanctions on Baghdad

**23 November 1994**

United States and Kazakhstan agree on the sale to the former of 600 kg of enriched uranium

**1 December 1994**

Kozyrev refuses to sign documents implementing Russia's participation in the NATO Partnership for Peace, in protest against plans for prompt NATO expansion in Central and Eastern Europe

**5 December 1994**

Meeting in Budapest of OSCE heads of state: Yeltsin criticizes NATO expansion plans and warns of the danger of a 'cold peace'; Ukraine, Belarus, and Kazakhstan sign Nuclear Non-Proliferation Treaty

**7 December 1994**

*Security Council instructs Nikolai Yegorov, a new Deputy Prime Minister, to take all necessary measures to restore constitutional order in Chechnya*

**11 December 1994**

*Russian troops launch large-scale armed intervention in Chechnya*

**23 December 1994**

*Duma votes for a cessation of hostilities in Chechnya in order for negotiations to take place*

**31 December 1994**

*Russian military assault on Grozny is repulsed with heavy losses*

## 1995

**6 January 1995**

*Centre of Grozny bombarded by Russian heavy artillery, as attempt to take city bogs down*

**10 January 1995**

Council of Europe announces freeze on Russian accession process because of civil rights violations in Chechnya; Russia gives permission for an OSCE mission to visit war zone

*Yeltsin statement emphasizes non-voting status of 'power ministers' in Security Council: five full members are President, Prime Minister, two speakers of parliament, and Secretary of Security Council*

**11 January 1995**

*Yeltsin announces that the Chiefs of Staff will in future report directly to him, and not to the Minister of Defence*

**20 January 1995**

Agreement signed between Presidents of Russia and Kazakhstan on the creation of a joint military command for planning and training, and another for border patrols, as part of a long-term plan to unite the two states' armed forces

**23 January 1995**

European Union foreign ministers condemn 'serious violations of human rights' in Chechnya, but refrain from imposing economic sanctions on Russia

**24 January 1995**

*Vladimir Polevanov, head of Russian State Privatization Committee, is sacked after excluding foreign advisers from his agency and talking of need for extensive renationalizations*

**5 February 1995**

Opening of Wehrkunde conference in Munich, not attended by Pavel Grachev after German Defence Minister Volker Ruhe made clear he would not be welcome because of his behaviour towards critics of the Chechnya operation; chairman of the Russian Duma Defence Committee Yushenkov denounces the Chechen war, but advises against expanding NATO in Eastern Europe

**16 February 1995**

Addressing parliament, Yeltsin defends his government's actions in Chechnya and opposes NATO expansion plans: 'This continent has already generated two global military catastrophes, and we do not want Europe and the world to return to old or new division lines'

**6 March 1995**

European Union foreign ministers agree to delay ratifying an interim trade pact intended to pave the way for full implementation of its Partnership and Co-operation Agreement with Russia until progress has been made in resolving the situation in Chechnya; Kozyrev affirms Russia's readiness to accept a long-term OSCE mission in Chechnya

**10 March 1995**

IMF agrees in principle terms with Moscow for $6.4 billion stand-by loan

**11 March 1995**

*Gaidar's Russia's Choice party announces that it will not support Yeltsin in any future presidential election campaign*

**15 March 1995**

*Russian parliament passes government's stabilization programme budget for 1995*

**19 March 1995**

European Union foreign ministers propose that NATO sign a non-aggression accord with Russia

**20 March 1995**

Ukraine signs agreement on rescheduling its debts to Russia, brokered by IMF, which is itself negotiating large stand-by loans to the two governments

**23 March 1995**

After a meeting with the United States Secretary of State, Kozyrev declares that 'the honeymoon is over' in relations between their countries

**30 March 1995**

*Russian government approves a further phase in its privatization plans, intended to raise £1.3 billion from sales of shares in over a hundred companies*

**3 April 1995**

In talks with the United States Defense Secretary, Chernomyrdin rejects his plea to reconsider the sale of nuclear reactors to Iran, while Grachev protests about plans for NATO expansion and threatens to abandon the CFE agreement if its clauses on the amount of troops and equipment permitted in Russia's northern and southern flank areas are not revised

**14 April 1995**

Russian human rights campaigners appeal to President Clinton and other Western leaders to protest about Russian army attack on civilians in Samashki, Chechnya

**18 April 1995**

Kozyrev states that Russia is prepared to use military force 'to protect our compatriots abroad' in the CIS

**25 April 1995**

*Chernomyrdin announces that he is setting up a centrist political grouping to fight the December 1995 parliamentary elections*

**10 May 1995**

Clinton–Yeltsin summit meeting in Moscow. It is announced that Russia's participation in NATO's Partnership for Peace will restart, and also efforts to build a special Russia–NATO relationship; Clinton also agrees on the need to revise CFE treaty limits

**26 May 1995**

Yeltsin complains about NATO decision to carry out air strikes on Bosnian Serb positions without consulting Russia, and offers Russia's services as a mediator in Yugoslavia

**31 May 1995**

*General Lebed tenders his resignation from the Russian armed forces in protest at Ministry of Defence plans to run down the 14th Army in Transdnestria*

**14 June 1995**

At a session of the Sino-Russian Economic Commission in Moscow the Russian Foreign Trade Minister declares his hopes of a sharp growth in bilateral trade on a market basis

*Russian Parliament approves legal framework for Western investment in the oil and gas sector*

**18 June 1995**

*Chernomyrdin begins negotiations on release of hostages from Chechen imprisonment in Budyonnovsk and launch of peace talks*

**1 July 1995**

*After dismissal of Yerin as Minister of Interior and Stepashin as head of FSS, Duma fails to pass second motion of no confidence in government; Chernomyrdin declares it will maintain its tough monetary and fiscal policy*

**17 July 1995**

Interim agreement signed by Russia and EU on bringing into force trade provisions of Partnership and Co-operation Agreement

**31 July 1995**

*Russian and Chechen sides sign a peace agreement envisaging a cease-fire, release of prisoners, and demilitarization*

**5 August 1995**

Russian Foreign Ministry denounces Croatian government after its military advances in Krajina region, and criticizes Western foot-dragging in negotiations on a settlement in Bosnia

**6 September 1995**

Opening of EU–Russian summit meeting; head of Commission and chairman of Council of Ministers of EU promise support for Russia's admission to Council of Europe

**8 September 1995**

Yeltsin demands a halt to NATO air strikes against Bosnian Serbs and warns that expansion of the alliance into Eastern Europe raises the risk of dividing the continent into opposing military blocs

*Yeltsin declares that he is dissatisfied with the work of the Russian Foreign Ministry, and hints at personnel changes in it*

**9 September 1995**

Duma votes to suspend trade sanctions against Serbia unilaterally, and requests Yeltsin to suspend co-operation with NATO

**11 September 1995**

Grachev warns US Secretary of Defense that NATO actions in Bosnia are putting at risk Russia's participation in Partnership for Peace, and its adherence to a string of East–West arms control agreements

**12 September 1995**

Foreign Ministry protests that a UN–NATO agreement on the use of force in Bosnia was reached on 10 August without Russia being consulted

**14 September 1995**

US Deputy Secretary of State Talbott, in Moscow, proposes Russian troops participate in policing a peace settlement in Bosnia agreed after an international conference

**21 September 1995**

Kozyrev welcomes Western proposals to relax CFE flank limits for Russia, but warns that Moscow will not accept any deals in exchange for NATO expansion

**25 September 1995**

*Russian government announces start of second phase of privatization: banks will manage state stake in companies, in exchange for loans to the government*

**26 September 1995**

Addressing the United Nations Security Council, Kozyrev warns against relying on military blocs and about the danger of provoking a new Cold War; NATO proposes to Moscow developing a special political and military relationship

Council of Europe announces reactivation of accession process for Russia, frozen after outbreak of war in Chechnya

**28 September 1995**

NATO study on enlargement in Central and Eastern Europe published, stressing that special relationship with Russia should develop in parallel with enlargement; NATO officials hint that enlargement will come about only with EU expansion in the region

**29 September 1995**

*International Foundation of Electoral Systems opinion poll results issued in Moscow show 14 per cent support in a future presidential election for General Lebed, 12 per cent for Grigory Yavlinsky, 10 per cent for Chernomyrdin, 7 per cent for Yeltsin; three-quarters are deeply dissatisfied with the current situation in Russia and over 50 per cent support reintroduction of state control of economy*

# BIBLIOGRAPHY

ADOMEIT, H., 'The Atlantic Alliance in Soviet and Russian Perspectives', in Malcolm, N. (ed.), *Russia and Europe: An End to Confrontation?* (London, 1993), 31–58.

—— 'Great to be Russia? Russia as a "Great Power" in World Affairs: Images and Reality', *International Affairs*, 71 (1995), 35–68.

ALLISON, G., 'Conceptual Models and the Cuban Missile Crisis', *American Political Science Review*, 63 (1969), 689–718.

—— *Essence of Decision: Explaining the Cuban Missile Crisis* (Boston, 1971).

—— and HALPERIN, M., 'Bureaucratic Politics: A Paradigm and some Policy Implications', in Tanter, R., and Ullman, R. (eds.), *Theory and Policy in International Relations* (Princeton, NJ, 1972), 40–79.

ALLISON, R., *Military Forces in the Soviet Successor States* (Adelphi Paper 280; London, 1993).

—— *Peacekeeping in the Soviet Successor States* (Chaillot Papers 18; Paris, 1994).

ALMOND, G., *The American People and Foreign Policy* (New York, 1960).

ARBATOV, A., 'Imperiya ili velikaya derzhava', *Novoe vremya*, 1992, no. 50, pp. 20–3.

—— 'Russia's Foreign Policy Alternatives', *International Security*, 18 (1993), 5–43.

—— 'Rossiya: Natsional'naya bezopasnost' v 90-e gody', *Mirovaya ekonomika i mezhdunarodnye otnosheniya*, 1994, no. 7, pp. 5–15.

—— 'Russian National Interests', in Blackwill, R., and Karaganov, S. (eds.), *Damage Limitation or Crisis? Russia and the Outside World* (Washington, DC, 1994), 55–76.

ASPATURIAN, V., *Process and Power in Soviet Foreign Policy* (Boston, 1971).

—— 'The Soviet Military-Industrial Complex: Does it Exist?', *Journal of International Affairs*, 26 (1972), 1–28.

BIRYUKOV, V., 'MID i ekonomicheskie preobrazovaniya Rossii', *Diplomaticheskii vestnik*, 1992, no. 19–20, pp. 36–40.

BLACKWILL, R., and KARAGANOV, S. (eds.), *Damage Limitation or Crisis? Russia and the Outside World* (Washington, DC, 1994).

BLAGOVOLIN, S., 'O vneshnei i voennoi politike Rossii', *Svobodnaya mysl'*, 1992, no. 18, pp. 8–9.

BOGATUROV, A., KOZHOKIN, M., and PLESHAKOV, K., 'Vneshnyaya politika

Rossii', *SShA: ekonomika, politika, ideologiya*, 1992, no. 10, pp. 27–41.

BRECHER, M., *The Foreign Policy System of Israel: Setting, Images, Process* (London, 1972).

BREMNER, I., and TARAS, R. (eds.), *Nations and Politics in the Soviet Successor States* (Cambridge, 1993).

BRESLAUER, G., *Khrushchev and Brezhnev as Leaders* (London, 1982).

BROWN, A., 'The Foreign Policy Making Process', in Keeble, C. (ed.), *The Soviet State: The Domestic Roots of Foreign Policy* (Aldershot, 1985), 191–216.

BURNELL, P., *Economic Nationalism in the Third World* (Brighton, 1986).

CALLAGHY, T., 'Toward State Capability and Embedded Liberalism in the Third World: Lessons for Adjustment', in Nelson, J. (ed.), *Fragile Coalitions: The Politics of Economic Adjustment* (Oxford, 1989), 116–37.

CHECKEL, J., 'Russian Foreign Policy: Back to the Future?', *RFE/RL Research Report*, 16 Oct. 1992, 15–29.

CHERBYAKOV, V., 'Rasshirenie NATO i izmenenie balansa sil v Yevrope', *Svobodnaya mysl'*, 1994, no. 6, pp. 27–47.

CHERESHNYA, A., 'Big Brother as an Equal', *New Times*, 1993, no. 17, pp. 12–13.

CHERNYAEV, A., *Shest' let s Gorbachevym* (Moscow, 1994).

CHICHKIN, A., 'Islamskii vopros', *Molodaya gvardiya*, 1992, no. 3–4, pp. 99–107.

CHUGROV, S., 'Rossiya mezhdu Vostokom i Zapadom?', *Mirovaya ekonomika i mezhdunarodnye otnosheniya*, 1992, no. 7, pp. 76–85.

—— 'NATO Expansion and the Chechen Link', *European Brief*, vol. ii, no. vi (Mar.–Apr. 1995), 5–6.

—— *Russia between East and West* (New York, forthcoming).

COHEN, B., *The Public's Impact on Foreign Policy* (New York, 1973).

COOPER, J., *The Soviet Defence Industry: Conversion and Reform* (London, 1991).

—— *The Conversion of the Former Soviet Defence Industry* (London, 1993).

CROW, S., 'Personnel Changes in the Russian Foreign Ministry', *RFE/RL Research Report*, 17 Apr. 1992, 18–22.

—— 'Competing Blueprints for Russian Foreign Policy', *RFE/RL Research Report*, 18 Dec. 1992, 45–50.

—— 'Russia Seeks Leadership in Regional Peacekeeping', *RFE/RL Research Report*, 9 Apr. 1993, 28–32.

—— 'Ambartsumov's Influence on Russian Foreign Policy', *RFE/RL Research Report*, 17 May 1993, 36–41.

—— *The Making of Foreign Policy in Russia under Yeltsin* (Munich, 1993).

—— 'Why has Russian Foreign Policy Changed?', *RFE/RL Research Report*, 6 May 1994, 1–6.

DALLIN, A., 'The Domestic Sources of Soviet Foreign Policy', in Bialer, S. (ed.), *The Domestic Context of Soviet Foreign Policy* (Boulder, Colo., 1981), 335–408.

DAWISHA, K., *Soviet Foreign Policy Towards Egypt* (London, 1979).

—— 'The Limitations of the Bureaucratic Politics Model: Observations on the Soviet Case', *Studies in Comparative Communism*, 13 (1980), 300–26.

—— and PARROTT, B., *Russia and the New States of Eurasia: The Politics of Upheaval* (Cambridge, 1994).

DE NEVERS, R., *Russia's Strategic Renovation* (Adelphi Paper 289; London, 1994).

DESCH, M., 'Why the Soviet Military Supported Gorbachev and Why the Russian Military might only Support Yeltsin for a Price', *The Journal of Strategic Studies*, 16 (1993), 455–89.

DEUDNEY, D., and IKENBERRY, J., 'The International Sources of Soviet Change', *International Security*, vol. XVI, no, iii (Winter 1991–2), 74–118.

DOBRYNIN, A., 'Za bez'yadernyi mir, navstrechu XXI veku', *Kommunist*, 1986, no. 9, pp. 18–31.

DUMBRELL, J., *The Making of US Foreign Policy* (Manchester, 1990).

'Fondu vneshnei politiki Rossii—rovno god', *Diplomaticheskii vestnik*, 1993, no. 5–6, pp. 57–9.

FOYE, S., 'Personnel Changes in the High Command', *RFE/RL Research Report*, 27 Sept. 1991, 1–6.

—— 'The Struggle over Russia's Kuril Islands Policy', *RFE/RL Research Report*, 11 Sept. 1992, 34–40.

—— 'Confrontation in Moscow: The Army backs Yeltsin, for now', *RFE/RL Research Report*, 22 Oct. 1993, 10–15.

FRASER, P., 'Russia, the CIS and the European Community', in Malcolm, N. (ed.), *Russia and Europe: An End to Confrontation?* (London, 1994), 199–223.

FYODOROV, Yu., 'Foreign Policy Making in the RF and Local Conflicts in the CIS', in Ehrhart, H.-G., Kreikemeyer, A., and Zagorski, A. (eds.), *Crisis Management in the CIS: Whither Russia?* (Baden-Baden, 1995), 115–27.

—— *The Role of Economic Interest Groups and Lobbies in Russian Foreign Policy Decision Making* (RIIA Post-Soviet Business Forum Briefing Paper 5; London, 1995).

GAIDAR, Ye., *Gosudarstvo i evolutsiya* (Moscow, 1995).

GELMAN, H., *The Brezhnev Politburo and the Decline of Detente* (London, 1983).

GILL, S., and LAW, D., *The Global Political Economy* (Baltimore, 1988).

GOLDMANN, K., *Change and Stability in Foreign Policy: The Problems and Possibilities of Detente* (New York, 1988).

GRAHAM, L., 'Democracy and the Bureaucratic State in Latin America', in Wiarda, H. (ed.), *The Continuing Struggle for Democracy in Latin America* (Boulder, Colo., 1980), 255–71.

GREEN, J., 'The Peacekeeping Doctrines of the CIS', *Jane's Intelligence Review*, 5 (1993), 158–9.

GRIFFITHS, F., 'A Tendency Analysis of Soviet Policy Making', in Skilling, H., and Griffiths, F., *Interest Groups in Soviet Politics* (Princeton, NJ, 1971).

—— *Images, Politics and Learning in Soviet Behavior towards the United States* (Ph.D. dissertation, Columbia University, 1972).

GUSTAFSON, T., *Reform in Soviet Politics: Lessons of Recent Policies on Land and Water* (Cambridge, 1981).

HERMANN, C., KEGLEY, C. W., JR. and ROSENAU, J. (eds.), *New Directions in the Study of Foreign Policy* (London, 1987).

HILL, C., 'Introduction', in Wallace, W., and Paterson, W. (eds.), *Foreign Policy Making in Western Europe* (Farnborough, 1978).

HINCKLEY, R., *People, Polls and Policymakers* (Lexington, Va., 1992).

HOLSTI, K., *International Politics: A Framework for Analysis*, 6th edn. (London, 1992).

HOLZMAN, F., and LEGVOLD, R., 'The Economics and Politics of East-West Relations', in Hoffmann, E., and Fleron, F. (eds.), *The Conduct of Soviet Foreign Policy* (New York, 1980), 428–78.

HOUGH, J., *Soviet Leadership in Transition* (Washington, DC, 1980).

—— 'Soviet Policymaking towards Foreign Communists', *Studies in Comparative Communism*, 15 (1982), 166–83.

HUGHES, B., *The Domestic Context of American Foreign Policy* (San Francisco, 1978).

HUNTINGTON, S., *Political Order in Changing Societies* (New Haven, Conn., 1968).

HURWITZ, J., and PEFFLEY, M., 'How are Foreign Policy Attitudes Structured? A Hierarchical Model,' *American Political Science Review*, 81 (1987), 1098–120.

'Ideologiya mirovogo pravitel'stva', *Elementy*, 1992, no. 2, pp. 1–2.

'Interesy Rossii v SNG', *Mezhdunarodnaya zhizn'*, 1994, no. 9, pp. 13–35.

'INTERLEGAL' (Mezhdunarodnyi blagotvoritel'nyi fond politiko-pravovykh issledovanii 'Interlegal'), *Politicheskie partii i bloki na vyborakh (teksty izbiratelnykh platform)* (Moscow, 1993).

ISTOSHIN, I., 'Vneshnyaya politika Rossii: Pozitsii obshchestvennykh politicheskikh organizatsii vo vneshnei politike Rossii', *Byulleten'*, 1993, no. 1, pp. 1–19.

JACKSON, R., *Quasi-States: Sovereignty, International Relations and the Third World* (Cambridge, 1990).

JONES, E., and BRUSSTAR, J., 'Moscow's Emerging Security Decisionmaking System: The Role of the Security Council', *Journal of Slavic Military Studies*, 6 (1993), 345–74.

KARAGANOV, S., 'Problemy zashchity interesov rossiisko–orientirovannogo naseleniya v "blizhnem" zarubezhye', *Diplomaticheskii vestnik*, 1992, no. 21–2, pp. 44–5.

—— 'Russia's Élites', in Blackwill, R., and Karaganov, S. (eds.), *Damage Limitation or Crisis? Russia and the Outside World* (Washington, DC, 1994).

'Key Officials in the Russian Federation: Executive Branch', *RFE/RL Research Report*, 4 Mar. 1994, 8–17.

'Key Officials in the Russian Federation: Legislative Branch', *RFE/RL Research Report*, 4 Mar. 1994, 18–20.

KHRUSTALEV, M., 'Evolyutsiya SNG i vneshnepoliticheskaya strategiya Rossii', *Diplomaticheskii vestnik*, 1992, no. 21–2, pp. 39–40.

KISSINGER, H., 'Domestic Structure and Foreign Policy', *Daedalus*, vol. xcv, no. ii of the Proceedings of the American Academy of Arts and Sciences (Spring 1966), 503–29.

KITRINOS, R., 'The CPSU Central Committee's International Department', *Problems of Communism*, 33 (1984), 47–65.

KLUCHEVSKY, V., *A History of Russia*, tr. C. J. Hogarth, 5 vols. (London, 1931; 1st pub. 1904–21).

KOMACHI, K., 'Concept-Building in Russian Diplomacy: The struggle for Identity: From "Economization" to "Eurasianization"', paper presented at the Center for International Affairs, Harvard University, 1994.

'Kontseptsiya vneshnei politiki Rossiiskoi Federatsii', *Diplomaticheskii vestnik* (special issue), Jan. 1993.

KORTUNOV, A., 'Konfliktnyi potentsial "blizhnego" zarubezh'ya i adekvatnaya strategiya Rossii', *Diplomaticheskii vestnik*, 1992, no. 21–2, pp. 41–3.

—— 'The Soviet Legacy and Current Foreign Policy Discussions in Russia', paper presented to the Russian Littoral Project Conference, Washington, DC, 1993.

KOSOLAPOV, N., 'Natsional'naya bezopasnost'' v menyayushchemsya mire', *Mirovaya ekonomika i mezhdunarodnye otnosheniya*, 1992, no. 10, pp. 5–19.

—— 'Mezhdunarodnaya bezopasnost'' i global'nyi politicheskii protsess', *Mirovaya ekonomika i mezhdunarodnye otnosheniya*, 1992, no. 11, pp. 5–18.

KOSOLAPOV, N., 'Vneshnyaya politika Rossii: Problemy stanovleniya i politikoformiruyushchie faktory', *Mirovaya ekonomika i mezhdunarodnye otnosheniya*, 1993, no. 2, pp. 5–20.

KOSOLAPOV, N., 'Sila, nasiliye, bezopasnost': Sovremennaya dialektika vzaimosvyazei', *Mirovaya ekonomika i mezhdunarodnye otnosheniya*, 1993, no. 11, pp. 45–58.

—— 'Novaya Rossiya i strategiya zapada: Stat'ya vtoraya', *Mirovaya ekonomika i mezhdunarodnye otnosheniya*, 1994, no. 2, pp. 5–15.

KOVAL, B., *Partii i politicheskie bloki v Rossii* (Moscow, 1993).

KOZYREV, A., *Preobrazhenie* (Moscow, 1995).

KRAMER, M., 'The Role of the CPSU International Department in Soviet Foreign Relations and National Security Policy', *Soviet Studies*, 42 (1990), 429–46.

LAGUNINA, I., 'Pochemu ne ustraivaet partnerstvo?', *Novoe vremya*, 1994, no. 14, pp. 28–9.

LENCZOWSKI, J., *Soviet Perceptions of US Foreign Policy* (London, 1982).

LEPINGWELL, J., 'The Russian Military and Security Policy in the Near Abroad', *Survival*, vol. XXXVI, no. iii (1994), 70–92.

LIGHT, M., 'Approaches to the Study of Soviet Foreign Policy', *Review of International Studies*, 7 (1981), 127–43.

—— *The Soviet Theory of International Relations* (Brighton, 1988).

—— 'Soviet Policy in the Third World', *International Affairs*, 67 (1991), 263–80.

—— 'Economic and Technical Assistance to the Former Soviet Union', in Taylor, T. (ed.), *The Collapse of the Soviet Empire: Managing the Regional Fallout* (London, 1992), 58–75.

LINDEN, C., *Khrushchev and the Soviet Leadership* (Baltimore, 1990).

LOBANOV, M., 'Komy ugrozhaet novaya Rossiya?', *Molodaya gvardiya*, 1994, no. 4, pp. 79–87.

LOUGH, J., 'Defining Russia's Relations with Neighbouring States', *RFE/ RL Research Report*, 14 May 1993, 53–60.

—— 'The Place of the "Near Abroad" in Russian Foreign Policy', *RFE/ RL Research Report*, 12 Mar. 1993, 21–9.

LUKIN, V., 'Our Security Predicament', *Foreign Policy*, no. 88 (Fall 1992), 57–75.

LYNCH, A., 'After Empire: Russia and its Western Neighbours', *RFE/RL Research Report*, 25 Mar. 1994, 10–17.

McFAUL, M., *Understanding Russia's 1993 Parliamentary Elections* (Stanford, Calif., 1994).

MACKINTOSH, M., 'The Military Role in Soviet Decision-Making', in Keeble, C. (ed.), *The Soviet State: The Domestic Roots of Soviet Foreign Policy* (Aldershot, 1985), 173–90.

MAIOROV, D. (ed.), *Neizvestnyi Rutskoi: politicheskii portret* (Moscow, 1994).

MAKSUDOV, S., and TAUBMAN, W., 'Russian-Soviet Nationality Policy and Foreign Policy: A Historical Overview of the Linkage Between them', in Mandelbaum, M. (ed.), *The Rise of Nations in the Soviet Union: American Foreign Policy and the Disintegration of the USSR* (New York, 1991), 15–43.

MALCOLM, N., *Soviet Political Scientists and American Politics* (London, 1984).

—— (ed.), *Russia and Europe: An End to Confrontation?* (London, 1993).

—— 'The New Russian Foreign Policy', *The World Today*, 50 (1994), 28–32.

MANSFIELD, E., and SNYDER, J., 'Democratization and War', *Foreign Affairs*, 74 (1995), 79–97.

MARKOV, S., and McFAUL, M., *Russian Electoral Parties and Blocs: A Pre-Elections Summary*, report for the National Democratic Institute for International Affairs (Moscow, 1993).

MELVIN, N., *Forging the New Russian Nation* (RIIA Discussion Paper 50; London, 1994).

MIALL, H. (ed.), *Redefining Europe* (London, 1994).

*Militäreliten in Russland 1994*, Friedrich Ebert Stiftung (Munich/Moscow, 1994).

MILLER, A., REISINGER, W., and HESLI, V. (eds.), *Public Opinion and Regime Change: The New Politics of Post-Soviet Societies* (Boulder, Colo., 1993).

MORAVCSIK, A., 'Introduction: Integrating International and Domestic Theories of International Bargaining', in Evans, P., Jacobson, H., and Putnam, R. (eds.), *Double-Edged Diplomacy: International Bargaining and Domestic Politics* (Berkeley, Calif., 1993), 3–42.

MORGENTHAU, H., *Politics among Nations: The Struggle for Power and Peace* (New York, 1963).

MORSE, E., 'The Transformation of Foreign Policies: Modernization, Interdependence and Externalization', *World Politics*, 22 (1970), 371–92.

MOSCOW STATE INSTITUTE OF INTERNATIONAL RELATIONS (Centre for International Research), *Sodruzhestvo nezavisimykh gosudarstv: protsessy i perspektivy* (Moscow, 1992).

MÜLLER, H., and RISSE-KAPPEN, T., 'From the Outside In and From the Inside Out', in Skidmore, D., and Hudson, V. (eds.), *The Limits of State Autonomy: Societal Groups and Foreign Policy Formulation* (Boulder, Colo., 1993), 25–48.

NAROCHNITSKAYA, N., 'Russia's National Interest', *International Affairs* (Moscow), 1992, no. 4–5, pp. 105–13.

NINCIC, M., *Democracy and Foreign Policy: The Fallacy of Political Realism* (New York, 1992).

ODOM, W., 'A Dissenting View on the Group Approach to Soviet Politics', *World Politics*, 28 (1976), 542–67.

PARROTT, B., *Politics and Technology in the Soviet Union* (London, 1985).

PAVLOV, S., 'Rossiya i evropeiskaya bezopasnost'', *Novoye vremya*, 1994, no. 10, pp. 24–5.

PAVLOVA-SIL'VANSKAYA, M., 'Vverkh-vniz', *Novoye vremya*, 1994, no. 17, pp. 4–6.

PETROV, V., 'Pravda ob Amerike', *Nash sovremennik*, 1992, no. 2, pp. 171–3.

PETROVSKY, V., 'Sovetskaya kontseptsiya vseobshchei bezopasnosti', *Mirovaya ekonomika i mezhdunarodnye otnosheniya*, 1986, no. 6, pp. 3–13.

POPOV, N., 'Vneshnyaya politika Rossii (Analiz politikov i ekspertov)', *Mirovaya ekonomika i mezhdunarodnye otnosheniya*, 1994, no. 3, pp. 52–9; no. 4, pp. 5–15.

POZDNYAKOV, E., 'We Must Rebuild what We have Destroyed with our Own Hands', *International Affairs* (Moscow), 1992, no. 4–5, pp. 129–36.

PRAVDA, A., 'Introduction: Linkages between Soviet Domestic and Foreign Policy under Gorbachev', in Hasegawa, Ts., and Pravda, A. (eds.), *Perestroika: Soviet Domestic and Foreign Policies* (London, 1990), 1–24.

—— 'The Politics of Foreign Policy', in White, S., Pravda, A., and Gitelman, Z. (eds.), *Developments in Soviet and Post-Soviet Politics* (London, 1992), 208–33.

—— 'Relations with Central- and South-Eastern Europe', in Malcolm, N. (ed.), *Russia and Europe: An End to Confrontation?* (London, 1993), 123–50.

PUSHKOV, A., 'Letter from Eurasia: Russia and America: The Honeymoon's Over', *Foreign Policy*, no. 93 (1993–4), 76–90.

PUTNAM, R., 'Diplomacy and Domestic Politics: The Logic of Two-Level Games', *International Organization*, 42 (1988), 427–60; also in Evans, P., Jacobson, H., and Putnam, R. (eds.), *Double-Edged Diplomacy: International Bargaining and Domestic Politics* (Berkeley, Calif., 1993), 431–68.

RAHR, A., ' "Atlanticists" versus "Eurasians" in Russian Foreign Policy', *RFE/RL Research Report*, 29 May 1992, 17–22.

—— 'Yeltsin's New Team', *RFE/RL Research Report*, 28 May 1993, 18–21.

—— 'Yeltsin and New Elections', *RFE/RL Research Report*, 22 Aug. 1993, 1–6.

RANZIO-PLATH, C., 'Business Partners', *European Brief*, vol. I, no. vi, 41–2.

RAZUVAEV, V., 'Budushchee Evropy svyazano c Rossiei', *Mezhdunarodnaya zhizn'*, 1991, no. 11, pp. 39–47.

ROSENAU, J., *Scientific Study of Foreign Policy* (New York, 1971).

'Rossiya i yug v mirovom soobshchestve', *Mirovaya ekonomika i mezhdunarodnye otnosheniya*, 1994, no. 5, pp. 69–89.

'Russia's Foreign Policy: Agenda for 1993', *International Affairs* (Moscow), 1993, no. 3, pp. 15–32.

'Russia's Foreign Policy Concept', *International Affairs* (Moscow), 1993, no. 1, pp. 14–16.

'Russia's National Interests', *International Affairs* (Moscow), 1992, no. 8, pp. 134–43.

RUTLAND, P., *Business Elites and Russian Economic Policy* (London, 1993).

—— 'The Economic Foundations of Foreign Policy in the States of the Former Soviet Union' (mimeo, 1993).

—— 'A Twisted Path toward a Market Economy', *Transition*, 15 Feb. 1995, 12–20.

RYBKIN, I., *Gosudarstvennaya Duma: pyataya popytka* (Moscow, 1994).

SAKWA, R., *Russian Politics and Society* (London, 1993).

—— 'The Russian Elections of December 1993', *Europe-Asia Studies*, 47 (1994), 195–227.

SAVEL'EV, V., 'Parlamentskaya diplomatiya', *Diplomaticheskii vestnik*, 1993, no. 9–10, pp. 53–5.

SCHAPIRO, L., 'The International Department of the CPSU: Key to Soviet Policy', *The International Journal*, 32 (1976–7), 41–55.

SEGAL, G. (ed.), *Openness and Reform in Communist States* (London, 1993).

SHASHENKOV, M., 'Russian Peacekeeping in the Near Abroad', *Survival*, vol. XXXVI, no. iii (1994), 46–69.

SIMES, D., *Detente and Conflict: Soviet Foreign Policy 1972–1977* (London, 1977).

—— 'The Politics of Defence in the Soviet Union: Brezhnev's Era', in Valenta, J., and Potter, W. (eds.), *Soviet Decisionmaking for National Security* (London, 1984), 74–84.

SKIDMORE, D., and HUDSON, V. (eds.), *The Limits of State Autonomy: Societal Groups and Foreign Policy Formulation* (Boulder, Colo., 1993).

SNYDER, J., 'The Gorbachev Revolution: A Waning of Soviet Expansionism?', *International Security*, vol. XII, no. iii (1987–8), 93–131.

—— *Myths of Empire: Domestic Politics and International Ambition* (London, 1991).

SNYDER, J., 'East–West Bargaining over Germany: The Search for Synergy in a Two-Level Game', in Evans, P., Jacobson, H., and Putnam, R., *Double-Edged Diplomacy: International Bargaining and Domestic Politics* (Berkeley, Calif., 1993), 104–27.

SORENSEN, G., 'Brazil', in Carlsson, J., and Shaw, T. (eds.), *Newly-Industrializing Countries and the Political Economy of South–South Relations* (London, 1980), 101–20.

STAVRAKIS, P., 'Government Bureaucracies: Transition or Disintegration?', *RFE/RL Research Report*, 14 May 1993, 26–33.

STERLIGOV, A., *Opal'nyi general svidetel'stvuet* (Moscow, 1992).

'Strategiya dlya Rossii', *Nezavisimaya gazeta*, 19 Aug. 1992.

'Strategiya dlya Rossii (2): tezisy Soveta po vneshnei i oboronnoi politike', *Nezavisimaya gazeta*, 27 May 1994.

SWAFFORD, M., 'Sociological Aspects of Survey Research in the Commonwealth of Independent States', *International Journal of Public Opinion Research*, 4 (1992), 346–57.

TIMOFEEV, T., 'O vozmozhnykh variantakh dal'neishego razvitiya SNG', *Polis*, 1993, no. 1, pp. 37–43.

TOLZ, V., 'Russia: Westernizers Continue to Challenge National Patriots', *RFE/RL Research Report*, 11 Dec. 1992, 1–9.

—— 'The Burden of the Imperial Legacy', *RFE/RL Research Report*, 14 May 1993, 41–6.

TORBAKOV, I., 'The "Statists" and the Ideology of Russian Imperial Nationalism', *RFE/RL Report*, 11 Dec. 1992, 10–16.

'A Transformed Russia in a New World', *International Affairs* (Moscow), 1992, no. 4–5, pp. 85–104.

'TsK VKPB o strategicheskom partnerstve mezhdu SSha, NATO i Rossiei', *Bol'shevik*, 1994, no. 14, pp. 2–3.

ULAM, A., 'Anatomy of Policymaking', *The Washington Quarterly*, 6 (1983), 71–82.

VALENTA, J., 'The Bureaucratic Politics Paradigm and the Soviet Invasion of Czechoslovakia', *Political Science Quarterly*, 94 (1979), 55–76.

—— *Soviet Intervention in Czechoslovakia, 1968: Anatomy of a Decision* (London, 1979).

WALLACE, W., *Foreign Policy and the Political Process* (Oxford, 1971).

WALTZ, K., *Theory of International Politics* (Reading, Mass., 1979).

'What Foreign Policy Russia should Pursue: A Forum', *International Affairs* (Moscow), 1993, no. 2, pp. 8–21.

WHITE, S., *After Gorbachev* (Cambridge, 1993).

—— PRAVDA, A., and GITELMAN, Z. (eds.), *Developments in Russian and Post-Soviet Politics* (London, 1994).

WHITEFIELD, S., 'Social Responses to Reform in Russia', in Lane, D. (ed.), *Russia in Transition* (London, 1995), 91–115.

X, 'The Sources of Soviet Conduct', *Foreign Affairs*, 25 (1947), 566–82.

YARYGINA, T., and MARCHENKO, G., 'Regional'nye protsessy v byvshem SSSR i novoi Rossii', *Svobodnaya mysl'*, 1992, no. 14, pp. 17–28.

YASMANN, V., 'The Role of the Security Services in the October Uprising', *RFE/RL Research Report*, 5 Nov. 1993, 12–18.

—— 'Security Services Reorganized', *RFE/RL Research Report*, 11 Feb. 1994, 7–14.

ZAGORSKY, A., 'Russia and Europe', *International Affairs* (Moscow), 1993, no. 1, pp. 43–51.

—— 'The Commonwealth', *International Affairs* (Moscow), 1993, no. 2, pp. 45–53.

—— ZLOBIN, A., SOLODOVNIK, S., and KHRUSTALEV, M., *Posle Raspada SSSR: Rossiya v novom mire* (Centre of International Research, Moscow State Institute of International Relations, Moscow, 1992).

ZHIRINOVSKY, V., *Poslednii brosok na yug* (Moscow, 1993).

—— *Poslednii vagon na sever* (Moscow, 1995).

ZIMMERMANN, W., 'Markets, Democracy and Russian Foreign Policy', *Post-Soviet Affairs*, 10, 1994, 103–25.

# INDEX

# 346 *Index*

Caucasus 136, 190, 192, 231, 249
centrists 170, 171–2, 188, 208, 211
  and Pragmatic Nationalism 179–82
  support for 182–3
CFE, *see* Conventional Forces in
  Europe
change:
  dynamics of 288, 301–8
  external and domestic causes 81–8
Chechnya crisis 23–5, 231, 232, 244,
  287
  Defence Ministry 150
  effect on international organizations
  3, 85
  effect on political élite 81–2,
  302–3
  implications for domestic policy
  293–4
  and Kozyrev 174
  and Lebed 240, 275
  and parliament 206, 212, 220
  public opinion on 189, 197, 203
  Russian military influences 275–7,
  278, 300
  Yeltsin on 146, 147
Chernomyrdin, Viktor 22, 142
  economic groups 144, 185, 298
  Our Home is Russia 183, 239
  as Prime Minister 23, 127–8, 135
China 10, 65, 66, 177, 276
Chinese model:
  economics 26
Christian Democratic Movement 175
Churkin, Vitaly 139, 217
CIS, *see* Commonwealth of
  Independent States
Civic Accord agreement 211, 306
Civic Union 83, 180, 182, 187
civil rights, *see* rights
COCOM 142, 144
Committee for the Defence Sector
  142
Committee on Defence and Security
  255
committees: foreign policy 209–10
Commonwealth of Independent States
  (CIS) 44
  Council for Foreign and Defence
  Policy on 64
  defence 50, 145, 248–9, 252
  economic policies 86, 126–7, 185,
  297–8
  establishment 6–10

  in foreign policy debate 56–61,
  71–2
  peacekeeping in 11, 54–5, 63, 86,
  145, 271–5
  public opinion on 194–7
  and radical conservatives 178
  ratification of treaties 214
  Russian forces in 263–71, 278
  Russian role in 23, 26, 46, 47–8,
  74–5
  Western attitudes to 126
  *see also* Soviet states, former
Commonwealth of Independent States
  Affairs, Department of 119–20,
  121
Communist Party of the Russian
  Federation 201, 202, 211, 239
  election success 5, 83
  and Fundamentalist Nationalism
  50, 175, 176, 178
Communist Party, Soviet 13, 107
  control of military 124
  decline of 14–16, 231
  legacy of 101–5
  policy concepts 39
Conference on Security and Co-
  operation in Europe (CSCE) 3,
  59, 68, 81, 85
  Russia as peacekeeper 11, 60, 76
conflicts:
  former Soviet states 86, 190, 192,
  196–7, 263–71
  inter-agency 102–5, 116–17,
  131–8, 306–7
  Russian management of 59–61,
  75–7
  *see also* specific places
Congress of People's Deputies 106–7,
  255
Congress of Russian Communities
  240
conservatives, radical 171–2, 188,
  208, 217
  and Fundamentalist Nationalism
  175–9
Conventional Forces in Europe (CFE)
  73, 85
  Treaty 237, 262–3, 278, 299
corruption 187
Cossacks 178, 249–50, 269
Council for Foreign and Defence
  Policy 117, 264
  'Strategy for Russia' 61–7, 137–8

military influences on policy
259–60, 299
parliamentary influence on policy
214–15
political use of 176, 182, 189, 208,
294, 303
Kyrgyzstan 57

language:
Russian 63, 75
Latin America 47, 66
Latvia 10, 149, 192, 265–6, 293
withdrawal of Russian troops 22
Law on Defence (1992) 253, 255
leadership:
military 299; influence of 299–300;
military–political coalition
232–41; as power broker 231
political 14–16, 308; former Soviet
states 5, 9; strategies 19–21;
support groups 202–3
League for the Support of the
Defence Industry 184
Lebed, Aleksandr 221, 234, 235, 239
Chechnya crisis 275
on CIS policies 237–8, 271–2, 276
politics 240–1
Transdnestria 268–70
Liberal Democratic Party 175, 211,
243, 247–8
Geopolitics Committee 210, 217
policies 176, 178
success of 5, 182–3
support for 138, 201, 202, 238,
242
Liberal Westernism 24, 135, 288
on Chechen crisis 294
on ethnic Russians 60
in foreign policy 21–2, 26, 207,
301–2
and foreign policy concept 61–2
in foreign policy debate 83–8,
129–30; first stage 44–6, 87–8;
second stage 51–3, 54–5, 56–7;
third stage 34–5, 71–2, 77–8
on former Soviet states 58–9, 293
on national security 191
on NATO expansion 80
on Partnership for Peace 78
in political parties 172–4, 200–1
in public opinion 193, 195
Libya 130, 211
Lithuania 10, 125, 266

lobbies:
economic 17–19, 183–8, 220, 221,
297–9, 307
political 169–83, 219, 221
Lobov, Oleg 111, 117, 136, 146–7,
150
Lopatin, Vladimir 243
Lukin, Vladimir 138–9, 181
criticism of Foreign Ministry 210,
213–14
International Affairs Committee 211
Yugoslavia 217–18
Lukoil 143, 298
Luzhkov, Yury 237

Mackinder, Halford 49
Main Political Administration (MPA)
231, 241
Makashov, Albert 238, 245, 247
Manilov, Valery 111, 113–14, 116
market economy 67
disillusionment with 84–5
views on 34
Western models 37–8
Martynov, Aleksandr 249
Middle East 48, 66, 177, 193
military:
in CIS 9–10
doctrine 72–3, 251, 253–8
influence on foreign policy 21,
251–2, 258–71, 277–8, 299–300,
307–8
influence on politics 230–2
involvement in political issues 59,
125, 133
military–political coalitions 232–41,
277
political role of officers 241–50,
277–8
political role of servicemen 250–1
reform 251–2, 258
relations with Yeltsin 138, 140
threat perceptions 253–8
*see also* conflicts; peacekeeping
minority rights, *see* rights
Mironov, Valery 233–4, 265, 275
Missile Technology Control Regime
141
Mitrofanov, Aleksei 211
Mobile Forces 252
Moldova 10, 238, 244, 296
in CIS 7
Cossacks in 249–50

Lightning Source UK Ltd.
Milton Keynes UK
17 September 2009

143816UK00003B/2/A